D0583916

April 2007

For Consuelo & Tomas —

My friends, my teachers,

my sister and brother . . .

Your lives and teaching

JAMES HILLMAN UNIFORM EDITION

2

has touched my soul

and my spirit. I

share this with

love and respect.

Michael

THE UNIFORM EDITION OF THE WRITINGS OF
JAMES HILLMAN

JAMES HILLMAN

CITY

&

SOUL

Edited by
Robert J. Leaver

With a preface by
Gail Thomas

SPRING PUBLICATIONS, INC.
PUTNAM, CONNECTICUT

Uniform Edition of the Writings of James Hillman
Volume 2

Published by Spring Publications, Inc.
Putnam, Conn.
www.springpublications.com

Inquiries should be addressed to:
PO Box 230212
New York, N.Y. 10023
editor@springpublications.com

Distributed by The Continuum International Publishing Group
80 Maiden Lane, Suite 704
New York, N.Y. 10038
Tel: 212 953 5858
Fax: 212 953 5944
www.continuumbooks.com

First edition 2006

Printed in Canada

Designed by white.room productions, New York

Cover illustration:
James Lee Byars, *Untitled*, ca. 1960. Black ink on Japanese paper.
Estate of James Lee Byars, courtesy Michael Werner Gallery, New York

Library of Congress Cataloging-in-Publication Data

Hillman, James.
  City & soul / James Hillman ; edited by Robert J. Leaver ; with a preface by Gail
Thomas.
    p. cm. — (Uniform edition of the writings of James Hillman ; v. 2)
  ISBN-13: 978-0-88214-577-8 (hardcover : alk. paper)
  ISBN-10: 0-88214-577-0 (hardcover : alk. paper)
  1. Cities and towns. 2. Cities and towns — Psychological aspects. 3. Soul. 4. Social
psychology. 5. Sociology, Urban. I. Leaver, Robert J. II. Title. III. Title: City and soul.

HT151.H484 2006
307.76 — dc22

                                    2006029515

∞The paper used in this publication meets the minimum requirements of the
American National Standard for Information Sciences — Permanence of Paper
for Printed Library Materials, ANSI Z39.48-1992.

Contents

Part Two

Politics of Beauty

Part Three

Places of Practice

Part Four

Responsive Environmentalism

The Uniform Edition of the Writings of James Hillman
is published in conjunction with

Dallas Institute Publications, Joanne H. Stroud, Director

**The Dallas Institute of Humanities and Culture
Dallas, Texas**

as integral part of its publications program concerned with
the imaginative, mythic, and symbolic sources of culture.

Additional support for this publication has been provided by

The Fertel Foundation, New Orleans, Louisiana

Pacifica Graduate Institute, and
Joseph Campbell Archives and Library,
Carpinteria, California

Editor's Preface

When I asked James Hillman some years ago to edit these papers, I wanted to make his work more visible and accessible to a wider range of thinkers and planners who are shaping our cities: urbanist architects, developers and planners, community psychologists, activists, and artists serving the public realm. Since cities are, perhaps, the major container in which the soul of the world comes alive, these papers have a lot to say to each profession as they do their work in making places.

The following chapters span thirty-two years, from 1973 to 2005. The style of thinking and writing shows several phases. The earlier papers rely more on myth for observations and insight, while the second period, addressed directly to an engaged public, places the observer in the thick of it all, cajoling citizens to attend more acutely to the world around them. Later work reflects on summary themes, blends observer with activist, and hints at future possibilities.

The original format of these papers includes delivered lectures on formal occasions, journal articles, transcription of audio tapes, pieces from magazines, and letters to editors. In each case the form defines the voice, and I have left each voice as I have found it. Because basic ideas — the importance of mythical and archetypal foundations, *anima mundi* and animating the soul of the world, the politics of beauty and ugliness, city as nature, community and the common — are central to Hillman's thought, these themes repeat throughout the book, a repetition that is necessary to the integrity of its inspiration.

Robert J. Leaver

Introduction

This is a book for city planners, for developers, and for the heads of departments of city services. It is also a book for psychologists of all persuasions because the city is the metaphor for the collective psyche. The city *is* the soul, given physical form, animated, and speaking.

In this book of his collected talks and papers on the city, James Hillman asks, "What are our cities for?" Hillman has always asked the difficult question. And, I have learned, he asks the question he most desires to answer himself. The city is an appropriate topic because it is big enough and complex enough to challenge his probing imagination.

What are cities for? Ultimately, Hillman will claim that cities offer a way of recovering our soul life. He sees no disconnect between cities and our individual soul work.

> It's our inside that counts, says the psychologist. And the very interest in the exterior of projects — the arts district, the malls — reflects the exteriorization of our interior concerns. Human beings adapt to their surroundings, and we shall have human beings designed like our interiors, human beings of gold and silver and glass, with hollow atriums, uniformly illuminated by shadowless light, without upper orientation, and with only the crassest, simplest right-angled norms and straight rules for connecting the principles of the heavens with the ways of the earth. These shall be the inhabitants if these be our inhabitants.

His keen intelligence teases us to drop our preconceived notions of how things are and to consider the invisible forces from which our notions emanate. It is, of course, these invisible forces that are seldom considered by the makers of cities. And it is these considerations that make this book so important.

Joanne Stroud, Robert Sardello, and I invited Hillman to Dallas in 1978. Though he would be ending thirty-five years of expatriate experiences in Europe, he came because he was psychologically intrigued with an aggressive modern city like Dallas. He identified Dallas as "the city of Aphrodite" because of its allure, and possibly, because he felt Dallas to be psychologically fascinating with its focus on ornament and display while aspiring toward power and control. He wanted to know what made it work.

A group of educators working together at the University of Dallas was concerned about the ever-increasing shallowness of our culture and the compartmentalizing of our education. We were seeking a deeper understanding of the needs of the human soul, observing how phenomena actualize in the physical world when basic soul needs are denied. Hillman became an active part of this group, which met frequently and exchanged challenging ideas to develop a vision for education, culture, and the future of the city. This exchange of ideas led to the formation of the Dallas Institute of Humanities and Culture, of which he was one of the six founders. Hillman became an active participant in city affairs, speaking to the Dallas City Council at City Hall, and to other civic organizations. He came to Dallas, as he said, "to move the furniture around." And he did.

James Hillman is uniquely gifted in rearranging the furniture. He calls it "seeing through," and his vision penetrates every aspect of our taken-for-granted everyday life. Imagination is the whole thing. No matter if he is considering transportation issues or beauty, the police, or violence in sports, how ceilings determine our relationship with the cosmos or the artist as civic leader, Hillman gives a complete set of tools with which to work. First one must realize the idea, then allow the image to form, then proceed with the practical application. When we read Hillman, we recognize what we are all missing, whether we are city planners, or administrators, or educators: We are missing the image, and we are missing imagination. If we get the image right, *it* (the image) actually moves the project.

Much has changed in the twenty-five years since James Hillman first began speaking of the soul of the city. The wave of New Urbanism in city planning has caught the attention of city builders and has stimulated a concern for attention to the character of towns and cities. We in the twenty-first century are now aware that we must use a different perspective in the making of cities. It has been a slow change during the decades of the 1960s, 1970s, and 1980s. Now the change is escalating at a rapid pace. In major cities today, every new project seems to display a "Green" perspective. Whether the developer has become more sensitive to human needs for walkable and livable places, or this shift is an effort to attract financial backing from environmentally conscious funding resources, or it is to receive tax benefits from the city is not known. We do know, however, that city planners, architects, park departments, water utilities departments, and river authorities are all using different words than they were uttering twenty years ago. There seems to be more concern for forces at work other than just efficiency and productivity.

These forces comprise the spirit of place. And, the most powerful of these forces is Love. "The city is for lovers," Hillman says. He asks us to love the city. He claims we have an erotic connection with a city, and if cities are to survive, we must become re-enchanted with them. And Hillman enchants us as we read, not only with words but with powerful, provocative images . . . images that beckon and captivate. James Hillman's words and images reflect his love of poetry, art, architecture, history, politics, and governmental affairs. Consider these enticing allures:

An erotic imagination pervades great cities.

The city belongs to the saxophone. And to the Imagist poets. In "A Station of the Metro," Ezra Pound witnesses, "Like a skein of loose silk blown against a wall / She walks by railing of a path in Kensington Gardens . . . "

It is luxury per se to be the seat of all seven sins. It is pure appetite, a mammoth magnet, a Rabelaisian consumer of hopeful innocents.

The most repressed of all phenomena in today's world is beauty. And this repression helps explain much of the boredom, monotony, and blatant ugliness in the cities of today.

I do believe that were the public to awaken to its hunger for beauty, there would be rebellion in the streets. Was it not aesthetics that took down the Berlin Wall and opened China? Not market consumerism and Western gadgets, as we are told, but music, color, fashion, shoes, fabrics, films, dance, lyrics, and the shapes of cars.

Boredom and monotony are such soul-destroying experiences because they are the very devil. In administration we find the Devil in the in-basket — office memos, official-ese, routines, and meetings that dull the mind, dull language, dulled hours, copied and recopied, screaming for coffee.

More than 50% of the world population are now living in cities. We are no longer able to tolerate the soul destroying experiences we encounter in towns and cities that have lost their character and their calling. The making of good cities has become the highest noble enterprise. And, the makers of cities have been waiting a long tome for this book.

— Gail Thomas
Dallas, 2006

Part One

Patient as Citizen

1

City

The City is the greatest of all human works of art, said Lewis Mumford, thereby placing the city in the realm of imagination. What amazing fantasies are these phenomena arising from fields and forests, besides rivers and oceans — these incredible symphonic blasts un-needed except to give physical grandeur and tumultuous extrapolations to human imagination. Beehives, anthills, rodent burrows are necessities to their constructors; but ours? What really are our cities for? We imagine them into existence and afterwards we explain them with our ideas.

So, there are many, many ideas of the city — their origins, their importance, their functions, ideas proposing to account for the preposterous cluster of disjuncted habitations, ceremonial avenues, engineered facilities, and the sophistications of styles, speech, and manners, the plagues and invasions, the downfalls and dispersions. In dreams we find ourselves in cities we have never visited, cities that do not exist on earth, dream cities like Oz's Emerald City, conjured by their names alone, cities of redemption like Jerusalem, of fear and mystery like Calcutta, of whitened memory like Athens. Where are they now, the magnificent cities of empires and holiness, and where are the grand ideas of cities that encompass their magnificence?

Instead, Megapolis, Metroplex: a vast *res extensa* of throw-away suburbs, exurbs, divisions and subdivisions; beltways, strips, squatters, squalor, slums, and smog; choked traffic on clogged arteries; cities as way-stops for transients, commuters, tourists, shelters for the homeless;

Preface to an Italian book of paintings by Pierluigi Isola and poems by Gabriella Pace entitled *Ars Memorativa* (Florence: Galleria Falteri, 2003). It has not previously been published in English.

buried shopping malls and high-rise car-parks amid faceless offices of restless despair. Cities become look-alike "centers." "You can resume your flight whenever you like," writes Italo Calvino, "but you will come to another Trude, absolutely the same, detail by detail. The world is covered by a sole Trude which does not begin and does not end — only the name of the airport changes."

Ideas of cities have compacted into the "problems" of cities. Abstractions in computer files marked: Congestion. Security. Emergency. Evacuation. Crime. Taxable Assessment. Rent Control. Waste Disposal. Demographics. Commuter Transportation. Parks and Recreation. Centers. Zones. Codes. Departments. The imagination of city dissected into a corpse for committees of particularized specialists who elaborate its life-support systems.

That flowing imagination which founded the city in the first place can be re-found. It is planted in our midst always ready to flower — if we begin, not with the "problem" of what needs to be changed, or moved, or built, or demolished, but begin with what already is here, still stands and sings of its soul, still holds the sparks of the mind that initiated it — whether in a Roman wall, or a clapboard New York hot-dog stand, whether an Osaka street of vertical neon, or an overgrown yard behind a Glasgow row-house. The chaotic jumble of any bright downtown or decayed neighborhood can discriminate into its particular images in words, paint or photographic prints, revealing the intimacy of the impulse that continues to make cities. The *poiesis* of cities. Cities not like Trude that are planned to solve problems, but cities formed by desire into works of art, shoulder to shoulder anachronisms, purposeless cacophonies, utterly miraculous that they can function at all, that they can rise at dawn, their millions of feet striding into each new day.

The city asks for discovery, for fresh perception, not for new planning; the secret city, the momentary eternal city that springs from imagination and surprises the heart. We may catch it in a glance through a doorway, reflected in a puddle, heard in the closing of a heavy door. The city belongs to the saxophone. And to the Imagist poets. "In a Station of the Metro," Ezra Pound witnesses "The apparition of these faces in a crowd; / Petals on a wet, black bough." Again:

"Like a skein of loose silk blown against a wall / She walks by the railing of a path in Kensington Gardens . . ."

An erotic imagination pervades great cities. We love them because they hold us in their bodies, excite us, exhaust us, don't let us leave. Or, we quit them as from a lover because we can't take it anymore. The eros emanating from a stranger, at a bar, in the waiting room of a city office. Possibilities of seduction on a cross-town bus: not the frames and builds of agrarians but city bodies wrapped in allure. Falling in love by the Seine, the Neva. Bridges, quais, thin canals in winter, even the paving stones are in love. And where love, there is revolution: the cities as cores of *polis* and the hot blood of politics.

Like failing in love and like revolution, the city is the ultimate luxury not because of its polished offerings, but because it is luxury *per se*, the seat of all seven sins as zealots since the Bible have declared. It is pure appetite, a mammoth magnet, a Rabelesian consumer of hopeful innocents. Luxurious, yet nonetheless needed, if not by its inhabitants or for its functions, cities are necessary to Mnemosyne and her daughters, the Muses. They own the apartments and meet in the cafés. Smaller towns have smaller memories — perhaps a battle, a singular product, the birthplace of a native star — while the countryside has no memory: it moves in seasonal waves and tides. The great city is a record, a document, a memorial. Not the spirits of nature, but the ghosts of civilization inhabit the city ground. It is constructed of deeds, deeds that arise in private minds, often in the quiet desperation required by the Muses who are the true ghosts of civilization.

These ghosts nourish the intimacy, the extraordinary privacy found only in great cities. Despite all the pastoral romance of musing by a brook, the arts and sciences constellate in the minds of crowded cities — dense, complex, elegant. Cities are novels, poems, dances, theories. They are packed with ideas that tell of the transactions of the Muses. Their mother, Memory, needs cities for the sake of her daughters, that they may flourish, wildly, that they may be honored with libraries and concert halls and theatres, remembered in museums, and permitted private intercourse with poets and painters in the intimacy of conversations.

2

City and Soul

It seems presumptuous for a psychologist — a depth psychologist who works with soul — to address the subject of city and in such expert company. Psychology's work, soul work, is notoriously so shut away, closeted in a consulting room, two persons in armchairs far above the street, not even the telephone interrupts. Yet what walks into the consulting room is the street: the welfare mother in the confusion of urban blight, the depressed suburban matron, the delinquent, the runaway, the addict, and the success-driven office-and-airport man hell-bent on suicide. Our work is with city people and the city is in the soul of our clients, so, of course, you find us depth psychologists in the big cities. You won't find many of us in Cheyenne or Bismarck. The founders of our field had their schools named after their cities: Paris, Nancy, Vienna, Zurich, as if to confirm that soul work belongs to city culture.

Because psychology belongs in cities, there have been arguments which blame psychic illness on city life. In the eighteenth century, it was gin mills and poverty or chocolate and luxury. In the nineteenth century, the fast locomotion of train travel, bad air and crowding, parasols and too much reading; in short what British psychiatry in 1867 called "the feverish activity of life" caused psychic distress. A French psychiatrist, in 1819, said: "Cities of four to five hundred thousand persons are deviations from nature." The soul ails from urban stress. One of humankind's favorite fantasies is that the soul is best off in nature and needs to slow down to nature's pace, for in cities the psyche

A talk first delivered at the seminar "Planning the City," held in the Council Chambers of the new Dallas City Hall on April 22, 1978 and sponsored by the Center for Civic Leadership of the University of Dallas.

becomes sophisticated and corrupted. The Yellow Emperor of China in 2600 B.C. was already bemoaning the intemperate and disorderly behaviors of his civilization compared with those of a more ancient era. Wrong habits of food, sleep, sex, and drink — already then, 4500 years ago at the dawn of history. Clearly, some part of the human soul continually imagines a better, truer life "back in nature," away from the city. There is a statistical third in each of us that just wants out, a driving urge with no rational ground. If we must blame the ruin of downtown, the death at the heart of the city, upon someone, then let it be blamed on Jean-Jacques Rousseau who evoked the feelings for the return to nature and took our heart out of the city.

I do not at all accept this anti-city view and warn you from being lured by its sentimental charm. It places city and soul in opposing camps, resulting in soulless cities and city-less souls, uncivilized souls, simple, romanticized animals, barbarians who abandon civilization for a hermit's cell or a hippie's dig in the wildwood. An ecology that restores the soul does not take place in the High Sierras only, out and away from it all; we restore the soul when we restore the city in our individual hearts, the courage, the imagination and love we bring to civilization.

Let's recall that the word "soul" itself returned into our popular vocabulary from the streets of the big and hurting cities, its soul music, its soul food and soul brothers.

I have understood my job today as one of reaffirming the soul-city connection. This I would like to do by showing in a few broad lines how and where soul exists in city. To do this we must rely on a few traditional ideas and images of soul.

The first one is the idea of reflection. The soul has always been associated with a reflective part in us or the reflective function. This is built into our cities as pools, ponds, malls, shades, shadows, where reflections occur. Glass and mirrors especially make reflection possible. But mirrors have always had another association in traditional symbolism, not only of reflection, but also of Vanitas and Narcissus. There is a danger of empty vanity and superficiality in the use of mirror glass surfaces, that is, they only reflect themselves or they only reflect each other. The glass would have to be used for soul; it would have to deepen and make more complex the sense of our city, by reflecting some recessed dimension and not only dazzle, if it is to touch the soul.

Secondly, the soul ever since the early Greeks was associated with the idea of depth. It's very hard for this Texan city, I understand, to go concretely deep: the shale resists and the ground temperature changes are extreme. So we would have to imagine the creation of depth by means of levels, which can be experienced in different ways, such as levels of light, shadings of light which give the impressions of leveling and depth. Qualities of contrasting texture and materials also afford varieties of depth. Through narrowing as intensifying, going further into something gives one a sense of deepening. The city alley, as the place of depth at the city's heart, is the dark part of the city, the mystery of the city. I'm sure no one speaks in favor of alleys nowadays. I'm sure they all have to be lighted and opened; but the alleyway and the narrow way, bending and twisting, provide modes of intensifying and adding a depth dimension.

Then, too, there is interiorizing: emphasizing the interiority of what is in front of you or where you are. The deeper meanings, the deeper complexities of something, so that each time you look at it or enter it, it takes on another level of significance. When one looks at a painting, at first it is only a flat surface; and yet there is depth within it. Each time one engages with it, it becomes deeper and you become deeper. There's always a danger to soul if one goes upward only, that is, if one emphasizes skylines, towers, and does not keep the heights relative to depths.

A third traditional idea of soul has to do with emotional memory. Emotional experiences: things that mattered to you in your own life; things that mattered to the community, the history of it. We have emotional memories in our cities through memorial parks, memorial statues, the war memorials, and the lore of the founders. Old cities were built originally on the tumulus or burial mound of the founder of the family or the founder of the clan or the city. So we find the memories of local heroes in place-naming that pay tribute to emotions which happened in the past and on which the city is founded. The city, then, is a story that tells us of itself as we go through it. It signifies something, it echoes with depth from the past. There is a presence of history in the city. There is much less presence of history in the countryside except a particular fork in the lane, a particular piece of woods, the name of a field, or this creek which changes its course.

We are further reminded of soul by the emotional experience of tragedy. The city as a *memento mori* with places that remind us of death. Remembrances of particular dark episodes remind of the mortality of life. So cities have cemeteries in them. They have altars, clinics, shrines, asylums, prisons — even sites where fateful assassinations have occurred. This dark side of human life reminds us of soul, so that the city that speaks to soul and of soul keeps nothing out. It isn't only that Thanksgiving Square would have to be open as was just suggested in Dallas, but the fact that nothing be shut out, that the city embraces all aspects of the human soul — its red light areas and sad cafés. Then we are reminded, as when you were a child, of those places in us each that we now call disabled or challenged but once were called crippled, insane, blind, or deaf and dumb — much more vivid and soul-searing words. Tragedy belongs with soul life. *Memento mori.*

Fourth, the soul tends to animate, to imagine by means of images and symbols. The words *Bild* (image) and *Bildung* (culture or moral education) in German are closely related as are the words *cult* and *culture;* and our word *animate* derives directly from the Latin word for soul, *anima.* A city that would have culture does need to be animated by images. We would have to begin by taking stock of just what images have already become cult objects in our city for they are an inherent part of its culture.

Without images, we tend to lose our way. This happens, for example, on freeways. Rectangular signs, uniform in size and all painted green (or all painted brown at the airport) with numbers and letters, are not images, but magnified verbal concepts. We don't know where we are except by means of an abstract process of reading and thinking, remembering and translating. All eyeballs and head. Lost is the bodily sense of orientation. We might even consume less gasoline — all those wrong turns — if our way through the city were landmarked by images like those of the old crossroads, the hangman's tree, the sign of the red ox, the fountain.

The soul wants its images, and when it doesn't find them, it makes substitutes: billboards and graffiti, for instance. Even in countries where ads are not allowed, slogans still are written large on walls and placards posted. Spontaneously, the human hand makes its mark, insisting on personalized messages, as human nature everywhere immediately chalks its initials on monuments.

These marks made in public places, called the defacing of monuments, actually put a face on an impersonal wall or oversized statue. The human hand seems to want to touch and leave its touch, even if by only obscene smears and ugly scrawls. So, let us make sure that the hand has its place in the city, not only by means of shops for artisans and displaying crafts, but also by animating and bringing culture to the walls and stones and spaces left bleakly untouched by the human hand. Surely, a city as a masterpiece of engineering form and architectural inspiration would not be despoiled by the presence of images that reflect soul through the hand.

The last of these ideas of soul reflected in a city is the notion of human relations. That is probably what comes first to your mind when you think of soul — the relations between human beings, at eye level in particular. When we think of the cities, our contact with them (with New York, for instance) is craning the neck upwards. The rube tourist goes to New York sightseeing its wonders and ends his vacation with a stiff neck.

The eye-level relation between human beings is a fundamental part of soul cities. The faces of things — their surfaces, their facings — is how we read what meets us at eye level. How we see into each other, look at each others' faces, read each other — that is how soul contact takes place. So a city would need places for these eye-level human contacts. Places for meeting. A meeting is not only a public meeting; it is meeting in public, people meeting each other. Pausing where it is possible to have a moment of eye-level touching. If the city doesn't have places for pausing, how is it possible to meet? Strolling, eating, talking, gossiping. Terribly important in city life are those places where gossip can take place. People stand by the water cooler and tell about what's happening and that gossip is the very life of the city. We speak differently from behind a desk than we do in the coffee alcove.

Who saw whom where, what, what's new, what's happening — here is some of the psychological life of the city. That grapevine of gossip.

We also need body places. Places where bodies see each other, meet each other, are in touch with each other, like the people who leave their offices in Paris and swim in the Seine river or have a lunch break in Zurich and swim in the lake, or skate. This emphasizes the relationship of body to the daily life of the city, bringing one's physical body into the town. In other words, I am emphasizing the value of intimacy within a city, for intimacy is crucial to the soul. When we think of soul and soul connections, we think of intimacy, and this has nothing to do with the size of the city or the height of its buildings. There is always the possibility for corners, for pauses, for being together in broken-up interiors where intimacy is possible.

Let's use, as an image of this aspect of soul in city, one of the main streets of Dallas: Lovers Lane. If you imagine a city as a place for lovers, then you may understand the idea I'm trying to express. I don't believe love interferes with business or efficiency or the tax base or retail sales or any of the rest — at all. I think a city is built on human relations, of people coming together, and it would increase, if anything, the very things that are desirable in a city. So, it is not a matter of splitting again into two things, that is, work and pleasure, city and soul, public daytime and private nighttime, because that cuts soul off from city. There have always been places built within the city where there is a break with the seeming purpose of the city. It is only recently, of course, that we think the purpose of cities is economical or political. The purpose of the city from the beginning was something instinctual in human beings wanting to build them: to want to be together, to imagine, talk, make, and exchange. One needs those so-called market places, places where the break can take place: the coffee break, or the pub, the café, beer hall, the morning coffee or the sandwich shop, or the locker-room, the skating rink, or just the bench in the sun where it is possible to have a break within our daily duties and strivings.

My job today has been to speak for the psyche. So I must sound one caution in its behalf. A city of the magnificent spirit is not enough. Not enough, palaces and monuments, museums, cathedrals, and halls that tend toward heaven. A city that neglects the soul's welfare makes the soul search for its welfare in a degrading and concrete way, in the shadow of those same gleaming towers. Welfare, mainly an inner city phenomenon, is not only an economic and social problem, it is predominantly a psychological problem. The soul that is uncared for — whether in personal or in community life — turns into an angry child. It assaults the city which has depersonalized it with a depersonalized rage, a violence against the very objects — store fronts, park monuments, public buildings — which stand for uniform soullessness. What city-dwellers in their rage have in recent years chosen to attack (stores and banks and cars), and chosen to defend (trees and old houses and neighborhoods) is significant.

Once the barbarians who attacked civilization came from outside the walls. Today they spring from our own laps, raised in our own homes. The barbarian is that part of us to whom the city does not speak, that soul in us who has not found a home in its surroundings. The frustration of this soul in face of the uniformity and impersonality of great walls and towers destroys like a barbarian what it cannot comprehend: structures which represent the achievement of mind, the power of will, and the magnificence of spirit, but do not reflect the needs of soul, For our psychic health and the well-being of our city, let us continue to find ways to make place for soul.

3

Anima Mundi:
Return of the Soul to the World

Maior autem animae pars extra corpus est.
(The greater part of the soul is outside the body.)
— Sendivogius

To speak, to ask to have audience today in the world, requires that we speak to the world, for the world is in the audience; it, too, is listening to what we say. So these words are addressed to the world, its problems, its suffering in soul. For I speak as a psychologist, a son of soul, speaking to psyche.

To say "son of soul" is to speak in a Renaissance, Florentine mode, following Marsilio Ficino who was the first to place the soul in the center of his vision, a vision which excludes nothing of the world's affairs because the psyche includes the world — all things offer soul. Each and every thing of our constructed urban life has psychological import.

The renaissance of a psychology that returns psychic reality to the world will find its starting point in psychopathology, in the actualities of the psyche's own suffering where depth psychology always arises, rather than in any psychological concepts about that reality. The discrepancy between actual psychic reality and psychology's conceptions

First delivered as a lecture in Italian in the translation by Bianca Garufi at Palazzo Vecchio, Florence, Italy, October 1981. First published in *Spring: An Annual of Archetypal Psychology and Jungian Thought* (1982), and subsequently as the second half of *The Thought of the Heart and the Soul of the World*. (Previous formulations are footnoted on page 71 of the 1982 edition.)

shows nowhere better than in *psychology* itself which today is more exhausted than the patients who turn to it. Depth psychology seeks its own renaissance. It has become self-enclosed, pretentious, commercial, permeated with the *mauvaise foi* of disguised power, not reflecting Ficino's sense of soul, but insidiously adapting to a world that has increasingly ignored that soul. Yet psychology reflects the world it works in; this implies that the return of soul to psychology, the renaissance of its depth, calls for a return of psychic depths to the world.

I find today that patients are more sensitive than the worlds they live in. Rather than patients not being able to perceive and adapt "realistically," it is the reality of the world's phenomena that seems unable to adapt to the sensitivity of the patients. I am astounded by the life and beauty in the patients vis-à-vis the dead and ugly world they inhabit. The heightened awareness of subjective realities, that soul sophistication resulting from one hundred years of psychoanalysis, has become incommensurable with the retarded state of external reality, which moved during the same one hundred years toward brutal uniformity and degradation of quality.

When I say that the patients' complaints are real, I mean realistic, corresponding with the external world. I mean that the distortions of communication, the sense of harassment and alienation, the deprivation of intimacy with the immediate environment, the feelings of false values and inner worthlessness experienced relentlessly in the world of our common habitation are genuine realistic appraisals and not merely apperceptions of our intra-subjective selves. My practice tells me I can no longer distinguish clearly between neurosis of self and neurosis of world, psychopathology of self and psychopathology of world. Moreover, it tells me that to place neurosis and psychopathology solely in personal reality is a delusional repression of what is actually, realistically, being experienced. This further implies that my theories of neurosis and categories of psychopathology must be radically extended if they are not to foster the very pathologies which my job is to ameliorate.

Not so long ago the patient's complaint was inside the patient. A psychological problem was considered to be intra-subjective; therapy consisted in readjusting inner psychodynamics. Complexes, functions, structures, memories, emotions of the interior person needed realigning, releasing, developing. Then, more recently, owing to group and family therapies, the patient's complaint was located in the patient's social relations. A psychological problem was considered to be inter-subjective; therapy consisted of readjusting interpersonal psychodynamics within relationships, between partners, among members of families. In both modes, intra-psychic and inter-psychic, reality was confined to the subjective. In both modes the world remained external, material, and dead, merely a backdrop in and around which subjectivity appeared. The world was therefore not the province of therapeutic focus. Therapists who did focus there were of a lower, more superficial order: social workers, counselors, advisors. The deep work was inside the person's subjectivity.

Of course social psychiatry, whether behaviorist, Marxist, or more broadly conceived, strongly emphasizes external realities and locates the origins of psychopathology in objective determinants. The "out there" largely determines the "in here," according to this view. This was especially the American dream, an immigrant's dream: change the world and you change the subject. However, these societal determinants remain external conditions, economic, cultural, or social; they are not themselves psychic or subjective. The external may cause suffering, but it does not itself suffer. For all its concern with the outer world, social psychiatry, too, works within the idea of the external world passed to us by Aquinas, Descartes, Locke, and Kant.

Precisely this external, non-subjective view of the world now needs to be reworked.

Before we can proceed with it, we have first to recollect the idea of reality which generally operates throughout depth psychology. Psychological dictionaries and schools of all orientations agree that reality is of two kinds. First, the word means the totality of existing material objects or the sum of conditions of the external world. Reality is public, objective, social, and usually physical. Second, there is a psychic reality, not extended in space, the realm of private experience that is interior, wishful, imaginational. Having divided psychic reality from hard or external reality, psychology elaborates various theories to connect the two orders together, since the division is worrisome indeed, it means that psychic reality is conceived to be neither public, objective, nor physical, while external reality, the sum of existing material objects and conditions, is conceived to be utterly devoid of soul. As the soul is without world, so the world is without soul.

Therefore, when something goes wrong in a life, depth psychology still looks to intra- and intersubjectivity for the cause and the therapy. The public, objective, physical world of things — buildings and bureaucratic forms, mattresses and road-signs, milk packages and busses — is by definition excluded from psychological etiology and therapy. Things lie outside the soul.

Psychotherapy has been working successfully within its province of psychic reality conceived as subjectivity, but it has not revisioned the notion of subjectivity itself. And now, even its success comes into question as the patients' complaints bespeak problems that are no longer merely subjective in the former sense. For all the while that psychotherapy has succeeded in raising the consciousness of human subjectivity, the world in which all subjectivities are set has fallen apart. Breakdown is in a new place — Vietnam and Watergate, bank scandals with government collusion, pollution and street crime, the loss of literacy and the growth of junk, deceit, and show. We now encounter pathology in the psyche of politics and medicine, in language and design, in the food we eat. Sickness is now "out there."

The contemporary use of the word "breakdown" shows what I mean. Nuclear power plants like Three Mile Island and Chernobyl provide vivid examples of possibly incurable, chronic breakdowns. The traffic system, the school systems, the courts and criminal justice system, giant industries, municipal governments, finance and banking — all undergo crises, suffer breakdowns, or must be shored up against the threat of collapse. The terms "collapse," "functional disorder," "stagnation," "lowered productivity," "depression," and "breakdown" are equally valid for human persons and for objective public systems and the things within the systems. Breakdown extends to every component of civic life because civic life is now a constructed life: we no longer live in a biological world where decay, fermentation, metamorphosis, catabolism are equivalents for the dysfunction of constructed things.

My colleague and friend in Dallas, Robert Sardello, writes,

> The individual presented himself in the therapy room
> of the nineteenth century, and during the twentieth
> the patient suffering breakdown is the world itself.
> The new symptoms are fragmentation, specialization,
> expertise, depression, inflation, loss of energy, jargoneze,
> and violence. Our buildings are anorexic, our business
> paranoid. Our technology manic.

Wherever the language of psychopathology occurs (crisis, breakdown, collapse), the psyche is speaking of itself in pathologized terms,
attesting to itself as subject of the *pathos*. As breakdown appears in
all these symptoms on Sardello's list, so then does psyche or psychic
reality. The world, because of its breakdown, is entering a new moment of consciousness: by drawing attention to itself by means of
its symptoms, it is becoming aware of itself as a psychic reality. The
world is now the subject of immense suffering, exhibiting acute and
crass symptoms by means of which it defends itself against collapse.
So it becomes the task of psychotherapy and its practitioners to take
up that line initiated first by Freud: the examination of culture with a
pathological eye. At the conclusion to his *Civilization and Its Discontents*,
Freud wrote,

> There is one question which I can hardly evade. If the
> development of civilization has such . . . similarity to
> the development of the individual . . . may we not be
> justified in reaching the diagnosis that . . . some epochs
> of civilizations — possibly the whole of mankind — have
> become neurotic? An analytic dissection of such neuroses
> might lead to therapeutic recommendations which could
> lay claim to great practical interest.

Let us carry Freud's notion of neurosis and the therapeutic analysis of it,
beyond the community of individuals, to the communal environment.

This examination, as well as the therapeutic eros that draws the
practitioner into the world as patient, has been vitiated at the very

start by tracing dysfunction in the world back to individual subjectivity. Depth psychology has argued that architecture cannot change, or politics or medicine, until architects, politicians, and doctors go into analysis. Depth psychology has insisted that the pathology of the world out there results simply from the pathology of the world in here. The world's disorders are man-made enactments and projections of human subjectivity.

Is this view not depth psychology's denial of things as they are so as to maintain its view of the world? Is psychology itself unconscious of its own ego-defenses? If depth psychology is wrong on this count, then another of its defenses, its idea of projection, also needs reversing. Not only my pathology is projected onto the world; the world is inundating me with its unalleviated suffering. After one hundred years of the solitude of psychoanalysis, I am more conscious of what I project outward than what is projected onto me by the unconsciousness of the world.

Working with a patient two or even five hours a week, and extending this work into therapy of milieu, family, and office team, cannot prevent the spread of epidemic psychic infection. We cannot inoculate the individual soul nor isolate it against the illness in the soul of the world. A decaying marriage can be analyzed to its intra- and intersubjective roots, but until we have also considered the materials and design of the rooms in which the marriage is set, the language in which it is spoken, the clothing in which it is presented, the food and money that are shared, the drugs and cosmetics used, the sounds and smells and tastes that daily enter the heart of that marriage — until psychology admits the world into the sphere of psychic reality — there can be no amelioration, and, in fact, we are conspiring in the destruction of that marriage by loading onto the human relationship and the subjective sphere the repressed unconsciousness projecting from the world of things.

The inclusion of these matters into the therapy hour can have immediate practical effect. The married partners no longer focus only on themselves and their relationship. Together they turn their eyes to the indignities imposed on them by the world. Personal rage with each other turns to outrage, and even compassion, as they awaken from their anesthetized slumber of subjectivism. They emerge from the cave with a new sensitivity in the possibility of fellowship, comrades in arms; into the smog-filled sunlight which psychoanalysis had taught them was a place of mere shadows, only the scenery and machinery against which backdrop they played their inter- and intra-subjective drama. Now they can analyze social forces, environmental conditions, and the impact of the design of things on them with the same acuity they hitherto reserved only for themselves. Those who were in couple therapy become the therapeutic couple whose patient is their world.

In place of the familiar notion of psychic reality based on a system of private experiencing subjects and dead public objects, I want to advance a view prevalent in many cultures (called primitive and animistic by Western cultural anthropologists), which also returned for a short while in ours at its glory through Florence and Marsilio Ficino. I am referring to the world soul of Platonism which means nothing less than the world ensouled.

Let us imagine the *anima mundi* neither above the world encircling it as a divine and remote emanation of spirit, a world of powers, archetypes, and principals transcendent to things, nor within the material world as its unifying pan-psychic life principle. Rather, let us imagine the *anima mundi* as that particular soul-spark, that seminal image, which offers itself through each thing in its visible form. Then *anima mundi* indicates the animated possibilities presented by each event as it is, its sensuous presentation as a face bespeaking its interior image — in short, its availability to imagination, its presence as a *psychic* reality. Not only animals and plants ensouled as in the Romantic vision, but soul is given with each thing, God-given things of nature and man-made things of the street.

The world comes with shapes, colors, atmospheres, textures — a display of self-presenting forms. All things show faces, the world not only a coded signature to be read for meaning, but a physiognomy to be faced. As expressive forms, things speak; they show the shape they are in. They announce themselves, bear witness to their presence: "Look, here we are!" They regard us beyond how we may regard them, our perspectives, what we intend with them, and how we dispose of them. This imaginative claim on attention bespeaks a world ensouled.

More — our imaginative recognition, the childlike act of imagining the world, animates the world and returns it to soul.

Then we realize that what psychology has had to call "projection" is simply animation; as this thing or that spontaneously comes alive, our attention is drawn to it. This sudden illumination of the thing does not, however, depend on its formal, aesthetic proportion which makes it "beautiful"; it depends rather upon the movements of the *anima mundi* animating her images and affecting our imagination. The soul of the thing corresponds or coalesces with ours. This insight that psychic reality *appears* in the expressive form or physiognomic quality of images allows psychology to escape from its entrapment in "experience." Ficino releases psychology from the self-enclosures of Augustine, Descartes, and Kant, and their successors, often Freud and sometimes Jung. For centuries we have identified interiority with reflexive experience. Of course, things are dead, said the old psychology, because they do not 'experience' (feelings, memories, intentions). They may be animated by our projections, but to imagine their projecting upon us and each other their ideas and demands, to regard them as storing memories or presenting their feeling characters in their sensate qualities — this is magical thinking. Because things do not experience, they have no subjectivity, no interiority, no depth. Depth psychology could go only to the intra- and interpersonal in search of the interiority of soul.

Not only does this view kill things by viewing them as dead; it imprisons us in that tight little cell of ego. When psychic reality is equated with experience, then ego becomes necessary to psychological logic. We have to invent an interior witness, an experiencer at the center of subjectivity — and we cannot imagine otherwise.

With things returned again to soul, their psychic reality given with the *anima mundi*, then their interiority and depth — and depth psychology too — depend not on their experiencing themselves or on their self-motivation, but upon self-witness of another sort. An object bears witness to itself in the image it offers, and its depth lies in the complexities of this image. Its intentionality is substantive, given with its psychic reality, claiming but not requiring our witness. Each particular event, including individual humans with our invisible thoughts, feelings, and intentions, reveals a soul in its imaginative display. Our human subjectivity, too, appears in our display. Subjectivity here is freed from literalization in reflexive experience and its fictive subject, the ego. Instead, each object a subject, and its self-reflection is its self-display, its radiance. Interiority, subjectivity, psychic depth — all out there, and so, too, psychopathology.

Hence, to call a business "paranoid" means to examine the way it presents itself in defensive postures, in systematizations and arcane codes, its delusional relations between its product and the speaking about its product, often necessitating gross distortions of the meanings of such words as good, honest, true, healthy, etc. To call a building "catatonic" or "anorexic" means to examine the way it presents itself, its behavioral display in its skinny, tall, rigid, bare-boned structure, trimmed of fat, its glassy front and desexualized coldness and suppressed explosive rage, its hollow atrium interior sectioned by vertical shafts. To call consumption "manic" refers to instantaneity of satisfaction, rapid disposal, intolerance for interruption (flow-through consumption), the euphoria of buying without paying (credit cards), and the flight of ideas made visible and concrete in magazine and television advertising. To call agriculture "addictive" refers to its obsession with ever-higher yields, necessitating ever more chemical energizers (fertilizers) and mass killers (pesticides, herbicides) at the expense of other life forms and to the exhaustion of agriculture's earthen body.

This new sense of psychic reality requires a new nose. More than the psychoanalytic nose that searches for depth of meaning and hidden connections, we need the nose of common animal sense, an aesthetic response to the world. This response ties the individual soul immediately with the world soul; I am animated by its anima, like an animal. I re-enter the Platonic cosmos, which always recognizes that the soul of the individual can never advance beyond the soul of the world because they are inseparable, the one always implicating the other. Any alteration in the human psyche resonates with a change in the psyche of the world.

We have tried, hitherto in depth psychology, to regain the psyche of the world by subjectivist interpretations. The stalled car and blocked driveway became my energy problems; the gaping red construction

site became the new *operatio* going on in my Adamic body or an opening to the female. We could give subjectivity to the world of objects
only by taking them into our interior subject, as if they were expressing our complaint. But that stalled car, whether in my dream or in my
driveway, is still a thing unable to fulfill its intention; it remains there,
stuck, disordered, and claiming attention for itself. The great wound
in the red earth, whether in my dream or in my neighborhood, is still
a site of wrenching upheaval, appealing for an aesthetic as much as a
hermeneutic response. To interpret the world's things as if they were
our dreams deprives the world of its dream, its complaint. Although
this move may have been a step toward recognizing the interiority of
things, it finally fails because of the identification of interiority with
only human subjective experience.

Does this mean that psychotherapists will now analyze their couches? Will they now point out to their office ventilating machines that
these on-and-off blowhard persons interrupt conversations with an
inconsiderately timed and passive-aggressive cold monotone? Do we
now analyze the car and deposit the drivers in a day-care lot? Not
quite. But let me suggest what we can do with this extended view of
psychic reality.

Aisthesis

We can respond from the heart, reawaken the heart. In the ancient
world the organ of perception was the heart. The heart was immediately connected to things via the senses. The word for perception or
sensation in Greek was *aisthesis*, which means at root a breathing in or
taking in of the world, the gasp, "aha," the "uh" of the breath in wonder, shock, amazement, an aesthetic response to the image *(eidolon)*
presented. In ancient Greek physiology and in biblical psychology
the heart was the organ of sensation: it was also the place of imagination. The common sense *(sensus communis)* was lodged in and around the
heart, and its role was to apprehend images. For Marsilio Ficino, too,
the spirit in the heart received and transmitted the impression of the
senses. The heart's function was aesthetic.

Sensing the world and imagining the world are not divided in the
aesthetic response of the heart as in our later psychologies deriving

from Scholastics, Cartesians, and British empiricists. Their notions abetted the murder of the world's soul by cutting apart the heart's natural activity into sensing facts on one side and intuiting fantasies on the other, leaving us images without bodies and bodies without images, an immaterial subjective imagination severed from an extended world of dead objective facts. But the heart's way of perceiving is both a sensing and an imagining. To sense penetratingly we must imagine, and to imagine accurately we must sense.

By "heart" I do not mean the sentimental subjectivism that came as a Romantic consequent of the loss of *aisthesis*. I am not talking of body-feelings in a simplistic psychology — whatever I feel is good; deep down inside my heart, I'm okay; what comes from the heart is good per se. Let us keep to one side these more familiar meanings of heart: the pump-and-muscle idea, the Augustinian-confession idea, the religious-conversion idea, the Valentine-Love idea. Each has its history and its reason. Let us stay with the aesthetic heart of our ancient and Florentine tradition.

It is this heart I am trying to awaken in an aesthetic response to the world. The *anima mundi* is simply not perceived if the organ of this perception remains unconscious by being conceived only as a physical pump or a personal chamber of feelings.

Awakening the imagining, sensing heart would move psychology itself from mental reflection toward cordial reflex. Psychology may then become again Florentine; for the move "southward" that I have been urging these last twenty years — from the clinics of Zurich and Vienna, from the white laboratories and black forests of Germany, from the positivist and empiricist dissections of Britain and America, to say nothing of the gymnastics of the tongue in France — cannot be accomplished without moving as well the seat of the soul from brain to heart and the method of psychology from cognitive understanding to aesthetic sensitivity. With the heart we move at once into imagination. For when the brain is considered to be the seat of consciousness we search for literal locations, whereas we cannot take the heart with the same physiological literalism. The move to the heart is already a move of *poiesis*: metaphorical, psychological.

Another organ and another method move psychology to another altar, Venus. In addition to Saturn, systems, and fathers, in addition to ego-development and heroics of Mother and Child, or Apollonic elucidation and medical detachment, or Minerva and grey-eyed practical counseling, or Dionysian participation in communal soul, or Hermes's transactions and mediating communication — there is also Aphrodite who was called the world soul in Ficino's translation of Plotinus and to whom Ficino awards the sensate world. To grasp the Greek account of perception, psychology must already, as did Psyche in Apuleius's tale, stand in the temple of Aphrodite, recognizing that each thing smiles, has allure, and calls forth *aisthesis*. "Calling forth" provoking, *kaleo*: this was Ficino's derivation of Aphrodite's main characteristic, *kallos*, beauty.

If we could re-originate psychology at its Western source in Florence, a way might open again toward a meta-psychology that is a cosmology, a poetic vision of the cosmos, which fulfills the soul's need for placing itself in the vast scheme of things. This has been impossible so long as psychology had its home in the alien "north" where cosmology was absorbed by ontology and metaphysics, conceptual systems without aesthetic images, without myths and faces of the Gods, without pathologized images — an alienation that distorted the soul's care into an alienist's cure.

To come back to our own heart, its stirrings as it comes to consciousness, may be a crucial contributing factor in contemporary heart and circulatory disorders. Puzzling symptoms have often ushered in new eras of psychological awareness: hysteria and Freud, schizophrenia and Jung. If we live in a world whose soul is sick, then the organ which daily encounters this sick world-soul first and directly through *aisthesis* will also suffer as will the circulatory channels which transmit perceptions to the heart. Psychotherapy needs to affirm the sufferings of the heart, its disease in the world of things, that they are ugly, empty, wrong, bereft of a sense-making cosmos, and by this affirmation that, yes, we are heart-sick because we are thing-sick, psychotherapy will lift the anesthetized stupor from our reactions, lift the repression in the ugliness of things themselves, so that psychotherapy can move again, as it always must do, in the direction that the symptoms are leading it, now toward an appreciation of the world ensouled.

The so-called "number-one killers" cannot be restricted to heart disease and cancer. Death lurks in things: asbestos and food additives, acid rain and tampons, insecticides and pharmaceuticals, car exhausts and sweeteners, televisions and ions. Matter is more demonized than ever it was in the plague. We read labels of warning, feel invisible evils descend through the air, infiltrate the water, and permeate our vegetable sustenance. The material world is inhabited again; the repressed returns from the matter declared dead by Aquinas and Descartes, now as Death itself and because of this resurrecting ghost in matter we are aware at last again of the *anima mundi*. Psychology always advances its consciousness by means of pathologized revelations, through the Underworld of anxiety. Our ecological fears announce that *things* are where the soul now claims psychological attention.

Things are composed of poisonous and flammable substances, stamped out of uniform molds, internally fastened cheaply, quickly with the least care, untouched by the human hand. They cannot weather or age. Their existence is hurried by the push of obsolescence as one generation succeeds the next within a few months. Sold by barkers on the slave-blocks of the market, competing by price only and not by pride or inherent beauty, their suffering is written on their faces. The postures of their strange-shaped bodies, like figures in Hell, show them cursed by the materialism in whose image they have been made, with no *epistrophé* possible, no way back to the Gods.

To move with the heart toward the world shifts psychotherapy from conceiving itself as a science to imagining itself more like an aesthetic activity. If unconsciousness can be redefined as insensitivity and the unconscious as the anesthetic, then training for psychotherapy requires sophistication of perception. Training will be based in the imagining, sensing heart: call it forth and educate it. Psychotherapy will study in its training programs the embodiments of the *anima mundi*, whether in language, in arts, or rituals, attempting to train the eye and ear, nose and hand to sense truly, to make right moves, right reflexive acts, to craft well. The invisible work of making soul will find its analogies in the visibility of well-made things.

The cognitive task will shift from the understanding of meaning to a sensitization to particulars, the appreciation of the inherent intelligibility given in the qualitative patterns of events. We will recognize health of soul by its aesthetic response in which judgment always inheres, rather than separating out the judgments into moral (good and bad), medical (ill and well, progress and regress), or logical (true and false) assessments. Humanistic education as conceived in Florence becomes a necessity again: differentiated language, fine arts, handworks, biography, criticism, history, cultural anthropology, manners and customs, life among things of the world. And our questions will be addressed to what things are, and where, and *who*, and in *which* precise way they are as they are, rather than *why, how come*, and *what for.*

Please, let me insist: by aesthetic response I do not mean beautifying. I do not mean planting sidewalk trees and going to the galleries. I do not mean gentility, soft background music, clipped hedges — that sanitized, deodorized use of the word "aesthetic" that has deprived it of its teeth and tongue and fingers. Beauty, ugliness, and art are neither the full content nor true base of aesthetics. In the Neoplatonic understanding, beauty is simply manifestation, the display of phenomena, the appearance of the *anima mundi;* were there no beauty, the Gods, virtues, and forms could not be revealed. Beauty is an epistemological necessity; *aisthesis* is how we know the world. And Aphrodite is the lure, the nudity of things as they show themselves to the sensuous imagination.

Thus, what I do mean by aesthetic response is closer to an animal sense of the world — a nose for the displayed intelligibility of things, their sound, smell, shape, speaking to and through our heart's reactions, responding to the looks and language, tones and gestures of the things we move among.

Thing-consciousness could extend the notion of self-consciousness from the constrictions of subjectivism. An analyst sitting in his chair all day long is more aware of the faintest flickers of arousal in the seat of his sexuality than of the massive discomfort in the same seat brought by the chair: its wrongly built back, its heat-retaining fabric, its resistant upholstery and formaldehyde glue. His animal sense has been trained to notice only one set of proprioceptions to the exclusion of the psychic reality of the chair. A cat knows better.

Some Positive Effects

Cultivation of the aesthetic response will affect issues of civilization that most concern us today and which have remained largely
intractable to psychological resolution. First, an aesthetic response
to particulars would radically slow us down. To notice each event
would limit our appetite for events, and this very slowing down of
consumption would affect inflation, hyper-growth, the manic defenses and expansionism of the civilization. Perhaps events speed up
in proportion to their not being appreciated; perhaps events grow
to cataclysmic size and intensity in proportion to their not being
noticed. Perhaps, as the senses become refined, there is a scaling down
of gigantism and titanism, those mythically perennial enemies —
giants and titans — of culture.

Attention to the qualities of things resurrects the old idea of *notitia*
as a primary activity of the soul. *Notitia* refers to that capacity to form
true notions of things from attentive noticing. It is the full acquain-
tance on which knowledge depends. In depth psychology *notitia* has
been limited by our subjective view of psychic reality so that attention is refined mainly in regard to subjective states. This shows in our
usual language of descriptions. When for instance I am asked, "How
was the bus ride?" I respond, "Miserable, terrible, desperate." But these
words describe *me*, my feelings, my experience, not the bus ride which
was bumpy, crowded, steamy, cramped, noxious, with long waits. Even
had I noticed the bus and the trip, my language transferred this attention to notions about myself. The "I" has swallowed the bus, and my
knowledge of the external world has become a subjective report of
my feelings.

An aesthetic response does require these feelings but it cannot remain in them; it needs to move back to the image. And the way back
to the bus ride necessitates words which notice its qualities.

Since the Enlightenment our adjectives have moved from qualify-
ing the world to describing the self — fascinating, interesting, boring,
exciting, depressing. These words neglect the things that evoke the
subjective states, and even the states have lost the precision of image and depth of metaphor and simile. A restoration of soul to world

means knowing things in that further sense of *notitia:* intimate inter-course, carnal knowledge. The appreciation of the *anima mundi* requires adverbs and adjectives that precisely imagine the particular events of the world in particular images, much as the ancient Gods were known through their adverbial and adjectival epithets — grey-eyed Athene, red-faced Mars, swift-footed, chaste Artemis. To perceive the value of things and the virtues in them requires a language of values and virtues, a return of the secondary qualities to things — colors, textures, tastes.

This "adjectival revolution" would overthrow the canon of good writing, the ascetic Puritanism — "plainness, simplicity, orderliness, sincerity" — of Strunk and White and of Fowler (in English), that contemporary form of Protestant iconoclasm which bans the adorn-ment of adjectives and adverbs in favor of bare nouns and verbs mak-ing definite assertions in the active voice — a grammatical world of heroic subjects doing things to objects, without ambiguity, passivity, or reflexiveness.

These rules of style, so innocently straightforward and un-meta-physical, actually deface the world's physiognomic characters and keep our consciousness within the dead-world view, where all quali-ties, according to the main line of Western philosophy, refer only to changes in the subject. The world only *seems* to lie about us, so beauti-ful, so various, so new; for as Hume writes, "All the sensible qualities of objects, such as hard, soft, hot, cold, white, black, etc., are merely secondary, and exist not in the objects themselves, but are perceptions of the mind, without any external archetype or model, which they represent." And Kant continues, "The taste of a wine does not belong to the . . . wine . . . but to the special constitution of sense in the sub-ject that tastes it. Colors are not properties of the bodies . . . but only modifications of the sense of sight."

The improvement of the quality of life depends on a restoration of a language which notices the properties of bodies, the qualities of life.

Our way back to the bus thus leads back to the Renaissance insis-tence on rhetoric, incorporating along the way the poetic methods of Imagism, Concretism, Objectivism, Projective Verse — modes of language that do not dwell in "experience" and that instead enliven things, giving them back their animated faces.

Second, that unspoken religious fervor in psychotherapy would shift its focus from saving the soul in the personal patient to saving the soul of the world, the restoration of the world rather than the resurrection of man, the celebration of creation before the adoration of creativity in the individual. Here I refer again to Ficino, who writes that "Creation is a more excellent act than illumination," so that the task of "raising consciousness" (as redemption of the soul is now disguised in modern therapy) becomes a raising of consciousness of created things, a therapy of the physical world's psychic reality.

This new focus would affect the ecology movement and such 'mundane matters' as energy policy, nourishment, hospital care, the design of interiors. No longer would these be external — that is, political or professional — activities only, but a focus of psychotherapy, because no longer would we be able to divorce consciousness-raising of the patient from the creation itself, while illumination of the patient would be contingent upon therapy of the creation. This larger sense of therapy begins in the smaller acts of noticing.

A third positive effect would return value from the subject to the thing, where it has been preempted by price. The most universal of all modern religions, economics, has appropriated into its literalism the sense of value, removing psychic reality from credit, trust, interest, inflation, and the like. We buy in order to save, as saving has been reduced utterly to an economic term. Appreciation, too, the very key to *aisthesis,* more commonly refers to a higher price. As value capitulates to price, the symbolic numbers of psychic import, the threes, sevens, tens, twelves are sold out to ninety-five, ninety-eight, or ninety-nine in a fractional debasement of whole digits like the chips and filings off true coins.

If soul value can be found only in the safe of psychotherapy, its price will rise, while the things with which we live — underwear, auto tires, place mats, pillowcases — get cheaper. Recognition that the soul is also in the world may awaken us from the psychotherapeutic trance in which we pay a hundred dollars for an hour of subjectivism and no more than $19.95 for a beach chair in whose cold metallic arms and plastic lap reflection actually takes place, day after day. What use becoming conscious in analysis and remaining anesthetized to the chair?

Were the chair a better value, were it cooperating in soul-making, would analysis still be so valuable, so dear?

Fourth, we might be relieved of the desperation for intimacy the transference clutch, the narrow personalization of love, the fear of loneliness. This because, as William James saw, intimacy occurs when we live in a world of particular, concrete events, noticeable for what he called their "eachness." Each thing bears "importance" in Whitehead's sense. Or in Ortega's sense, only personified, individualized things can be loved. The aesthetic response is never a fuzzy pantheism, a generalized adoration of nature or even of the city. Rather it is that joyful scrutiny of detail, that intimacy of each with each such as lovers knows. Here, individuation itself moves from the individualized realization of self to the individuation of matter.

A world without soul offers no intimacy. Things are left out in the cold, each object by definition cast away even before it is manufactured, lifeless litter and junk, taking its value wholly from my consumptive desire to have and to hold, wholly dependent on the subject to breathe it into life with personal desire. When particulars have no essential virtue, then my own virtue as a particular depends wholly and only on my subjectivity or on your desire for me, or fear of me: I must be desirable, attractive, a sex object, or win importance and power. Without these investments in my particular person, coming either from your subjectivity or my own, I, too, am but a dead thing among dead things, potentially forever lonely.

If particulars — whether images, things, or the events of the day — are to afford significance, the burden has been on the subject to maintain libidinal cathexes, "to relate," so that depersonalization and derealization do not occur. It has been up to us to keep the world aglow. Yet these syndromes, depersonalization and derealization, are latent in the theory of the external world as soulless. Of course I am lonely, unrelated, and my existence throwaway. Of course therapy must focus on relations rather than on contents, substantialities, things that matter, because connection becomes the main work of therapy when the world is dead. Ego psychology is inevitable, for the patient must find ways to connect the psyche of dream and feeling to the dead world so as to reanimate it. What stress, what effort it takes to live in a cemetery; what terrible need for willpower. So of course we fall prey to ideologies and cults that relieve the burden of this subjectivity. Of course I am in desperate narcissistic need, not because I have been neglected or still neglect my inmost subjectivity, but because the world without soul can never offer intimacy, never return my glance, never look at me with appeal, with gratitude, nor relieve the essential isolation of my subjectivity.

But at that moment when each thing, each event presents itself again as a psychic reality — which does not require the magic of synchronicity, religious fetishism, or any special symbolic act — then I am held in an enduring intimate conversation with matter. Then grammar breaks its hold: subject and object, personal and impersonal, I and thou, masculine and feminine find new modes of intermingling; plural verbs may disagree with their singular nouns as the imagination in things speaks its language to the heart. Then Eros descends from being a universal principle, an abstraction of desire, into the actual erotics of sensuous qualities in things, materials, shapes, motions, rhythms.

A fifth despair of our civilization would also be radically affected by this turn toward the world soul. This issue, technology, would no longer be contrasted romantically with nature, technology bad and nature good, cities bad and country good, soul in trees but not in the saws that cut them. Rather, all things, whether constructed or natural, by presenting their virtues carry soul.

When I look to history for a model for this soul in manufactured things, I make a classical, Renaissance move: turn back to ancient Egypt. There, *l'objet parlant* was common at hand. Each thing spoke of the Gods which were inherent in all actualities from a cosmetic box, a beaker, or a jar, to the river and the desert. Even where things were made in innumerable multiples, thousands cast from the same molds, they were each a speaking object. It is not numerical singularity that guarantees uniqueness; rather, eachness derives from the imaginal potential, the God, in the thing.

Technology is not necessarily the enemy of the heart; technology is not inherently soulless. We are less endangered by the brute facts of nuclear, genetic, computer, and chemical technology as such, than we are by the brute anesthetized conception of these technical inventions as soulless mechanisms. Because they are conceived in the Cartesian-Christian fantasy, they become objective, brute, and mute. Technical inventions have become the great repressed slaves, obedient to mechanical laws, disallowed breakdown, and so we fear them. We want the most from them at the least cost. The paradigm of our mind-set allows soul only to subjective persons; therefore, technology is not considered part of what Whitehead calls "nature alive," a realm of speaking objects with faces and is instead a fearful Frankenstein monster. Technology becomes psychopathological when, like any phenomenon, it is deprived of soul, as it has been by the very theoretical assumptions that gave birth to it in the first place. It was monstrously conceived, but now cheeky, perky R2D2 has replaced Boris Karloff. The Monster subsides along with Newtonian mechanism. Technology can be reconsidered, each thing imagined anew in terms of *anima mundi*.

Concluding Affirmations

Catastrophe fantasies haunt us; they announce the end of the world. As with suicide fantasies we must ask them precisely what world is coming to its end. An answer comes hard because we take the fantasies so literally that we can barely sit with them for more than a moment. Anesthesia: Robert J. Lifton calls it "psychic numbing." And we are drugged not only by the industry of distillers, dope-runners, pharmaceutical firms, and pill-prescribing physicians. We are anesthetized as well by the subjectivism of psychotherapy, as if the end-of-the-world were an "inner problem."

The very literalism of the catastrophe fantasies hint at what world is coming to an end. They fulfill the Christian apocalyptic vision, and they fulfill all too literally the doctrine of a world already declared dead by the Western tradition, a world over whose autopsy the Western, Northern mind has been presiding since Newton and Descartes. Can we now see what Blake always knew: the apocalypse that kills the soul of the world is not at the end of time, not coming, but apocalypse now and Newton and Locke, Descartes and Kant are its Horsemen.

The fantasies of the literal end of the world, however, announce the end of this literalist world, the dead, objective world. As such, the catastrophe fantasies also reflect an iconoclastic process of the psyche which would smash the soulless mechanical idol of the world that we have worshiped ever since Christ said his Kingdom is not of this world and left it to the legions of Caesar. Thereby, the aesthetic, imaginative, polytheistic animation of the material world was cursed into demonism and heresy, while psychology allowed psyche only to self-reflective confessional egos, inflating them to titanic monstrosity.

That vast insensate edifice — the doctrine of a soulless world — now streaked with acid rain and stained by graffiti has, in our fantasies, already exploded into dust. Yet that cataclysm, that pathologized image of the world destroyed, is awakening again recognition of the soul in the world. The *anima mundi* stirs our hearts to respond: we are at last, *in extremis*, concerned about the world, love for it arising, sensate things again lovable. For where there is pathology there is psyche, and where psyche, eros. The things of the world again become precious, desirable, and even pitiable in their millennial suffering from Western humanity's hubristic insult to material things.

Ecology movements, futurism, feminism, urbanism, protest and disarmament, personal individuation cannot alone save the world from the catastrophe inherent in our very idea of the world. They require a cosmological vision that saves the phenomenon, "world" itself, a move in soul that goes beyond measures of expediency to the archetypal source of our world's continuing peril: the fateful neglect, the repression, of the *anima mundi*.

Repressed, yet there nonetheless; for an idea of the soul of the world runs through all Western thought, to say nothing of archaic, primitive, and oriental cultures. What I have been asking you to entertain is neither altogether radical nor new. It is affirmed in differing ways in Plato, the Stoics, Plotinus, and in Jewish and Christian mystics; it appears splendidly in the Renaissance psychology of Marsilio Ficino, in Swedenborg; it is revered in Mariology, Sophianic devotion, in the Shekinah. We find notions of it in German and British Romantics and American Transcendentalists; in philosophers of various sorts of panpsychism from Leibniz through Peirce, Schiller, Whitehead, and Hartshorne. The world soul returns also in the pluralistic position of William James through his interest in Fechner and his concern for "the particular, the personal, and the unwholesome," or the "eachness" of events rather than abstracted wholes. *Anima mundi* reappears in further guises as "the collective unconscious" in Jung, as physiognomic character in the Gestalt psychology of Koffka and Köhler, in the phenomenology of Merleau-Ponty, of van den Berg, in the poetics of matter and space in Bachelard, and even in Roland Barthes, and of course, ever and again in the great poets, specifically of this century in Yeats and Rilke, Williams and Stevens. What I have been proposing has a noble inheritance, and I cite these names not only to show the pedigree of the idea, but to suggest that it is the *anima mundi* that gives these names their nobility.

For all this, the psychic reality of the world of things seems a strange idea in psychotherapy, because *anima mundi* does not occur in the tradition from which psychotherapy believes it stems: eighteenth-century enlightenment and nineteenth-century science. And their offspring, therapy's cousins: positivism, materialism, secularism, nominalism, reductionism, personalism, behaviorism.

Hence to rework our notion of psychic reality implicates each of us in reworking our background, the tradition which continues to feed our theory-forming and our idea of reality. I urge that the tradition to which we must turn in face of the fantasies of cataclysm lies not in the Himalayas, not on Mt. Athos or Patmos, or the far planets of space, nor does it lie in nihilistic terror that foreshadows the cataclysm. It dwells in the imagining heart of the Renaissance city, in its streets, its language, its things, in the city of the heart of the world.

We will not be able to move in this direction until we have made radical shifts of orientation so that we can value soul before mind, image before feeling, each before all, *aisthesis* and imagining before *logos* and conceiving, thing before meaning, noticing before knowing, rhetoric before truth, animal before human, anima before ego, what and where and who before why. We would have to let fall such games as subject-object, left-right, inner-outer, masculine-feminine, immanence-transcendence, mind-body — the game of oppositions altogether. A great deal of what we now hold dear would break down so that the emotion held by these cherished relics could break those vessels and flow back into the world.

Breaking the vessels is the return, the turn again to the world, giving back what we have taken from it by storing inside ourselves its soul. By this return we regard the world anew, having regard for it as it shows its regard for us and to us in its face. We pay respect to it simply by looking again, re-specting, that second look with the eye of the heart.

This respect demands reconstitution of our language so that it speaks again of qualities — naming what is there rather than what we feel about what is there and abstraction away from what is there. Language with referents that are not mere objective correlatives of our emotions or mere objective descriptions. Instead, the emptied sense of our words would be refilled by concrete images, our talk, an animal talk, echoing the world.

Finally, we would have to consider that the entire intrasubjective model with which psychotherapy works — psychodynamics, psychopathology, the unconscious, even personality itself — might also apply to the world and its things. For if the world is ensouled, then the language psychoanalysis has developed for psyche is also appropriate to the world and its objects. To pursue this revision of psychic reality implies that we shall have to let our present sustaining paradigm break down, a catastrophe of the mind rather than of the world, allowing to emerge a renaissance of soul in the midst of the world and with it, from the depths of its breakdown and ours, a renaissance of psychology.

4

"Man Is by Nature a Political Animal": Patient as Citizen

There is nothing for it but to summon help from the Witch — the Witch metapsychology, Without metapsychological speculation and theorizing — I had almost said "phantasy," we shall not get a step further.
— Sigmund Freud (1937)

The theory of the instincts is, as it were, our mythology. The instincts are mythical beings, superb in their indefiniteness.
— Sigmund Freud (1933)

For many years I have been engaged in the selection, teaching, analyzing, and judging of candidates in training for the profession of analytical psychotherapy. That term "analytical psychotherapy" is meant here to be neutral, covering psychoanalysts of the Freudian persuasion, individual psychologists of the Adlerian, analytical psychologists of the Jungian and others who follow Reich, Honey, Winnicott, Balint, Kohut, Lacan, Klein, et al.

In the intense examination of these candidates from their first application and interviews through supervision sessions and case reports, an outstanding omission occurs, an omission in our methods of inquisitional scrutiny that I came to recognize only in the last years when my own metapsychological speculations bewitched me toward the world.

Invited talk, auspices of the Freud Museum, London, October 1990. First published in *Speculations after Freud: Psychoananlysis, Philosophy, and Culture*, eds. S. Shamdasani, M. Münchow (London: by Routledge & Kegan Paul, 1994).

Sunflower Seed
Oatmeal
Sugar
Powdered Milk
Lentils
Rice Mixed

Multi Vitamin
Kirkland

Multi Vit (2)
Bread (2)
2% Milk

9

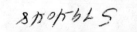

S 7474048

BOTANIC CHOICE®
Natural Health Care Since 1910

Give Your Supplements
Time To Work!

Dr. Gary Gendron B.S., D.C., C.C.S.P.

"When taking nutritional supplements, I tell my patients to be patient.

"Vitamins and supplements take time – usually one to three months for maximum results. The important thing is to **take your proper dose, consistently, every day.**

"Certain vitamins, like Vitamin C, are water-soluble, so they're washed out of your system and need to be restored daily. Others, like Vitamins A, D and E are fat-soluble, and must be taken with food in order to be broken down and absorbed by your body. No absorption, no health benefits.

"Unfortunately, you can't flood your body with vitamins and minerals over night. Supplements work constantly over a few months to replace your body's depleted nutrients. Take comfort knowing that you're working towards good health, *naturally*. The time you invest will be well worth it."

Risk-Free 100% Money-Back Guarantee
A guarantee of effectiveness, quality, purity and potency

You must be 100% totally satisfied with your purchase. If you're unhappy in any way, for any reason, just return the unused portion for a full, prompt 100% refund – no questions asked.

The omission? We never inquired into the political life, history, opinions, and activities of the candidates, nor was the political life of the patient whose case was being supervised and reported in great detail ever brought into discussion.

Religion, yes. Economic level, of course; earning power is certainly not neglected. Family history, work, ethnic roots, emotion, ideals, of course; dreams, memories, and sexual frissons with great finesse; even films, literature, gardening, automobiles, theater, art, pop music — but no politics. To what party did the patient belong, if any; what political engagement in the community; what leanings in regard to the daily issues — left, right? What causes and concerns is the patient now engaged with; how do politics play a role in family fights? What was the political history of the family: labor, anarchistic, Marxist, socialist, landed conservative, red-white-and-blue (i.e., redneck, white skin, and blue collar), knee-jerk liberal, shopkeeper individualist, parlor pink, black-shirt fascist, protester? In other words, how and in what manner, to what extent was the patient a citizen?

If we concede that a major aspect of our lives is not only social, that is, not only enmeshed in the web of a class and a style, an economic strata and a favored language, and if we concede that the social context affects attitudes, moods, reflections, or what we call psychological consciousness, is all this not true as well for the political? How and why had it been omitted?

Omission, whatever its reason, is a lacuna in consciousness, indicating — I suppose we here in a Freudian context all agree — a repression. Or, to put it more vigorously, this lacuna indicates the presence of denial, a defense mechanism against the political, keeping analytical psychotherapy immune from infection by the body politic, *au-dessus de la mêlée.*

Though my thrust is to condemn this absence, else I would not have felt it enough to have written a paper about it, I shall try to back off and neutrally inquire: what is its necessity? Let's take the defense as a symptom, as essential and necessary to the *Sache.* And let us ask what does the absence of the political serve? What is the presence in the absence?

I suggest we read the defense as an immunological defense, a shield to keep analytical psychotherapy from invasion by the passions of the passing parade, inviolate, so that the psycho-patho-phenomena of the individual may bud, bloom, and flourish in dream and mood, fantasy and feeling, projection, symbolization, association, and transference within the confines of the consulting room, its *temenos*, its hermetic vessel. As the work must be kept immune from too much metapsychological reading, too much gossip, social encounters, family members, the easy commerce of usual life — so it must be kept safe from politics.

The political, in other words, is only one of the infections and invasions against which therapy sets up its immunological defense. We do not see, professionally, members of our own or of the same family. We do not see the lovers of our patients or their husbands, wives, children. We do not work with our friends; we do not attend seminars, performances or exhibitions of our patients, nor do they come to ours. This is the new discipline of immunity called professional ethics, unimagined by Freud. We do not engage in the patient's lives in any way; only their psyches. The lines are defined, strictly disciplined, and nowadays, policed. The thickness of these barriers attest to the importance given to the fantasy of a complete separation of life and reflection, of exterior and interior, of person as patient and person as citizen.

Clearly here the metapsychological Witch is at work, for these barriers, separations, and defenses, this system of immunization conceals anthropological and ontological assumptions about the nature of human being and the nature of being itself:

1. that human being and being itself can be sectioned;
2. that the conscious will can maintain these divisions without seepage;
3. that segmentation favours psychological awareness;
4. that the psychological and the political can be conceived as two distinct discourses;
5. or, to put it as an extreme contradiction so as to be most clear: the political is not psychological and the psychological is not political.

Most probably analytical therapy wants to remain within the confines of its territory as prudent mystics of the interior. That could be our discipline and our job; the inquisitional pursuit in reflective quiet of individual dream, fantasy, mood, image. The investigation and understanding of the individual person. Yes, this is an endeavour, but is it therapy of soul? Does it make the unconscious conscious, as Freud set our task? For that we must go where the soul is sick and where the unconscious most darkly and thickly reigns: the *polis*. For the unconscious does not stand still. That's what the word implies, Where is this unconscious today; certainly not in childhood, family, sexuality, symptomatic anomalies, feelings, relationships, arcane symbols — that stuff is on every talk show, in every self-help manual. What was once the "unconscious" appearing as a slip of the tongue is now on the tip of the tongue. Where we are least able, however, most suffer from, and anesthetize against, i.e., repress, with ear plugs, door bolts and alcohol, with electronics, hi-fi, coffee and shopping, is the world out there, the polis. We remove psyche from it and we are unconscious in regard to it — the polis is the unconscious. We have become superconscious patients and analysts, very aware and very subtle interiorized individuals, and very unconscious citizens.

Individualism as Disease

The patient cannot, definitely not, by definition not, become citizen so long as the model of the psyche which therapeutic analysis serves remains fixed where it is. This model locates psyche either as intrapersonal (within the human subject) or interpersonal (between subjects in relationships, transference, group dynamics, and family systems). Soul is not in the world of things like trees, rocks, cars, and ashtrays, nor is it in the world of systems like education, finance, party politics, language and technology. Even if today more and more physical and institutional phenomena are spoken of as "sick," we still locate psychopathology in the human individual.

Of course culture critics, like Szasz or Illich or Foucault, can show the absurdities of this isolating location and the relativity of the word "sick" depending altogether on a cultural definition. Yet they do not go further out on the limb to conclude that if the definition of psychopathology resides in the culture, then psyche itself may be defined to reside there as well.

No, we have not drawn that conclusion and remain dedicated to individualism. We still restrict psychopathology to the human person and therefore psyche, too, belongs ontologically to the human subject. Analytical psychotherapy continues to argue that if nature or culture show sickness, this is because of human actions; we are its cause. So, cure the human first, everyone in analysis — architects, politicians, teachers, businessmen — and then the world will get better.

This hasn't worked, won't work, because the model is faulty. It leaves soul out of the world — things are soulless and the individual human must carry with the should of his shoulder the substantiating burden of soul, reanimating by his and her personal projective breath what the theory declares by definition dead.

The death of the world soul was articulated by the French, Jesuit-educated, bachelor-soldier-gentleman Descartes, who called it *res extensa*. Out there, as well as everything in this room including our bodies, is just dead matter. Descartes, if not the 1500 years of Christianity before him, killed off the world, turning it into a soulless mass, a littered field. Descartes and the Christians invented litter and pollution, and shopping, too. Of course, M. Descartes was confirmed by a European consortium including Mr. Newton and Herr Kant — this despite Plato and Plotinus and Ficino, and the Romantics for whom the great God Pan was never dead, and especially Spinoza whose God and world were one substance, that is, whose world was utterly and completely ensouled, spirited, divinized — or in our measly secular language, libidinally cathected. Let us remember this bit of philosophical history usually called Descartes-bashing. Let it remind us that analytical psychotherapists are indeed French Freudians, that is, Cartesians. So long as we regard the world external to therapy and the individual as the only possible place of consciousness, we may be practicing with the tools of Freud, but what we practice is the theory of Descartes. And the soul can't get out of analysis until it can get out of Cartesianism and, allow me to add, Christianism.

Now Freud does try to get out. (I venture to say that his insistence upon his Jewishness was part of his attempt to free himself from the Cartesian-Christian *Weltbild*. But that is just an aside.) Freud tries to escape from individualism by appealing to the universality of the Oedipal theory; by grounding the libido in a biological substrate; by widening eros to a cosmic principle beyond the erogenous zones of the skin; by descending to archaic depths like the primal horde, the primordial id, *thanatos*, nirvana, entropy. These metaphysical bewitchments imagine collective forces beyond the individual.

Yet, if we look closely at his 1922 paper, "The Libido Theory," we see he blocks his own escape. Immediately following the paragraph on narcissism, he refutes Jung's broader collective view of libido and then refutes Trotter's herd instinct which "impels individuals to come together into larger communities." "Psychoanalysis," says Freud, "finds itself in contradiction to this view. Even if the social instinct is innate, it may . . . be traced back to . . . the childhood of the individual . . ."[1] Or, as he says in 1921 on the herd instinct: "Let us venture, then, to correct Trotter's pronouncement that man is a herd animal and assert that he is rather a horde animal, an individual creature in a horde led by a chief."[2]

I think his escape route can be found in that same 1922 encyclopedia article where he describes "object libido." This, as you all recall, is the libido that flows out to objects and absorbs libido back from objects. You also know well the corollary idea that "the pathogenic process as witnessed in dementia praecox is the withdrawal of the libido from objects."[3] The ego itself becomes an object of the libido, that narcissistic state in which one is in love with oneself.

If mourning is that feeling which recognizes the death of the object, that psychic condition which bespeaks an object libido no longer cathected to the world, then are we not in mourning all of the time? And is not the ideology of consumerism — which runs the economy of the West and broke through the Berlin Wall — as manifested in shopping, our major leisure-time activity? Is shopping a symptomatic compromise that compulsively mourns object loss by concretely attempting to recathect? Because the Wicked Witch of western metapsychology has declared the world dead, only I, *res cogitans*, am. Of course I live concurrently both omnipotence and mourning. Of course I am depressed, the major syndrome presenting itself in Western medical practices, and of course I feel *Weltschmerz*, and of course the world soul, Sophia, as the Gnostics and alchemists said, laments. Congenital chronic depression and the manic defense against it, including that manic idealization called hope for salvation and redemption, are the price we continue to pay for the death of Pan and the pagan world soul.

Some recent American social and ecological psychology — of course without mention of pagan gods or an *anima mundi* — has been subverting psychotherapy by revealing its foundations in nineteenth-century, liberal, humanistic individualism. I am referring to works by Sandel, Bellah, Cahoone, Wicker, and especially Sampson, whom I shall be quoting. (As you can begin to feel, there is already a social and ecological psychology in my move: I am replying to France from America, and privileging my own viewpoint, not deconstructing, but arguing, positing, just like an old-fashioned modernist.)

I quote now Edward Sampson: "There are no subjects who can be defined apart from the world; persons are constituted in and through their attachments, connections, and relationships."[4] A Cartesian *res cogitans*, detached, unencumbered, free to choose, self-owning and self-defining (making up one's "own mind"), prior to community and its government and for whom community and its government exist, presents the modernist fantasy of individualism that is by definition anomie, long before anomie was discovered by Durkheim as a sociological phenomenon. This is the strong individual with a strong ego, able to cope and manage and handle problems as an independent entity endowed with freedoms to speak, think, worship, assemble, travel, print, own land and will it to descendants; whose communal life is not inherent but derives from social contract freely entered into else life would be brutish and short, and whose reason is independent of any context. This individual whom analytical psychotherapy attempts to shore up with its notions of self-determining ego development is simply an anachronism. It is a view of human nature reaching its apogee in the Western nineteenth century, the political context of Freud's time and place. In fact, the theory of the person that continues to dominate analytical psychotherapy is itself a sociological or ecological reflection of a particular psychological climate which also saw the apogee of colonialism, industrialism, capitalism, etc.

From this ecological, or political if you prefer, point of view our theories of the person who is the patient and the practice of understanding the person apart from political context in which "I," the person, is embedded and by which "I," the person, is constituted can only further the delusion of a transcendental subject — a subject transcendent to community, requiring a guarantor for my isolated subjectivity, i.e., a transcendent original self or God. This ultimately unknowable and non-phenomenal guarantor is either a neurotic fiction or an omnipotence fantasy which urges each therapeutic analysis towards an unreachable and utopist goal. Moreover, this elaborate fantasy of individualism repeats not merely the splendid isolation of the colonial administrator, the captain of industry and the continental academic in his ivory tower, it also reconstructs in the consulting room the theological God of monotheism — anomic, transcendent, omniscient, omnipotent. Because we do not practice politics, we practice religion. Freud and Jung had to tackle religion again and again, and Lacan had to state that if religion wins, psychoanalysis is doomed. Religion, by which I mean our Western monotheistic God-apart-from-world, will always threaten analytical psychotherapy since the *anthropos*, the patient, is created precisely in the image of that God. The endeavor of psychotherapy to understand the individual, and then, using that model, apply what is revealed by analytical investigation to the body politic — in the manner of the Freudian left and Norman O. Brown — is delusional because there is no longer that individual. The paradigm has shifted, so that Sampson can say: "Quite simply, understanding the individual as individual is no longer relevant to understanding human life."[5] Chaos, anarchy, decentralization, networking, ecology, deconstruction — dehumanizing existential protagorean man as measure of all things — will force the latent citizen from his hiding place as patient to make a run for it, driven by object libido toward a new refuge among the community of soul in the world.

Let us go back for a moment to Aristotle's sentence: "Man is by nature a political animal" (*anthropos phusei politikon zoon*). Let us expand upon the four terms. 1. *Anthropos*: not merely man, but mankind, human being, and the completely realized human being, since form and *telos* imply each other. The formal cause provides the image toward which, for the sake of which, for the actualization of which, humankind is. We not only are political animals by nature; we are most complete and actualized as political animals. 2. *Phusei:* the basic stuff and structure, the original substance, the essence, the nature, the reality of human kind, is political. 3. *Politikon:* from *polis,* the city; and citadel. The word polis means in its etymological roots and cognates: throng, crowd, runny, connected for instance with *palude* (swamp), pour, flow, fill, fill up, flood, overflow, swim, an innately plural meaning, e.g., poly, many, as in the Latin cognate *pleo-plere, plenus, plerus, plebs, plus, plural.* The "political," therefore, suggests Jung's collective unconscious and Trotter's herd instinct — the communal urges in life — the Greek *demos* (Dionysos is said to have been the favorite divinity of the *demos*). 4. *Zoon:* the animal force of life, an organic vitality, an *élan vital,* any individual person. *Zoe* was one of the main words associated with Dionysos.

Patient as Citizen

What would it be like were we to imagine the patient as citizen? What then would be the nature of therapeutic discourse? Can we imagine a therapy session, an interview with a new candidate, a case supervision within the polis of Athene, rather than under the tutelage of Oedipus and his *heuriskein* or figuring out, his blind drive to "know thyself," *gnothi seauton.*

I am suggesting that we can imagine a post-analytic therapy, a post-self-centered therapy that dissolves those identities which recent deconstructionism has shown to be problem-ridden if not invalid; identities such as gender, family role, historical continuity of the person, even the subjectivity of ego. If identity can be dissolved, with it goes those isolating individualisms of therapeutic language such as unity, centeredness, wholeness, integration, and especially that intensely reflective substantive mythologem or bewitching Godterm, Self.

For this term, Self, is the last redoubt of all substantialism and all identity. It has yet to experience its own identity crisis. Wherever it appears and sometimes in disguise of person and personality, individual and individuality, it assumes itself as carrier of reflexive consciousness — which is of course its primary meaning. In that word is the mirror. And its earliest compound meanings in English (late medieval) as selfsame and self-willed point directly to the term as carrier of identity. In other words, the attack on subjective identity needs a further displacement of the basic supporting idea of all analytical psychotherapy, the idea of Self.

Suppose we were no longer to imagine Self as a homeostatic interior dynamics of a biological organism, or as the moral spark of an unknowable transcendent, or as the simply given, reflexive activity of consciousness, or as the *auton,* or autonomy (self-willed and selfsame) of any distinctly defined system. Suppose we were to recognize, see through, bracket out and then discard these favorite notions of Self. One reason for the discard being that none of these favorite notions require external relations; no necessity for an outer, an other, even an echo, They can be imagined wholly for themselves, and so one can know oneself wholly by and with oneself, in the gaze of self-reflective *inspectio,* as Descartes called it. As fundamentally self-reflectively self-satisfied, they require the outer and other only for narcissistic supplies, as transitional objects, as flat glassy mirrors, in order to "have experiences" like going through fusion and separation, envy, authority problems, castration feelings, and so on.

Instead let us imagine another definition, neither biological, theological, psychological nor ontological — instead political — Self as the interiorization of community. Then to ask in a therapeutic session about the political is to ask about Self. Then to pursue self-development requires community pursuits. Then one turns for confirmation of one's self-steering course — am I on track or off, am I repressing, am I centered? — to the actual community of one's actual life. Then the pursuit of insight necessitates an objective correlative, the place where insight arises, the community, rather than the transference.

I don't want to literalize community as the actual politics of neighborhood, or any of the myriad political levels of engagement. Rather, I am intending toward Alfred Adler's *Gemeinschaftsgefühl,* a social feeling that fictionalizes many goals, many literal political activities, as retorts for the feeling, where object libido can be intensified, differentiated, manifested. Throughout, one *imagines* oneself as citizen where discourse about Self and the reading of this Self and its actions is conceived always within a context of *Gemeinschaftsgefühl.*

If Self and its draw toward reflective interiority refers not to an immanent soul-spark of a transcendent God, or to a germ, seed, truth, center, or core of will power, but rather is constituted of communal contingencies, then the draw toward interiority must at the same time be a draw toward exteriority, toward the contingencies of the actual ecological field — where I am placed, with whom I am, what is happening with my animals, my food, my furniture and what the toaster, the newspaper, and the refrigerator's purr do in the field I am in. To find myself I must turn to them, visibles and invisibles. Then to work on the unconscious, to foster my growth, my self-understanding and to cure my illness, I will no longer drift into dream, walk solitary in nature, shut myself off to meditate, to analyze or recall my childhood, expecting something inside my skull or skin to reveal itself and guide me. Instead I turn to what is simply there, my rooms and their trash, my acquaintances and their reactions, my neighbors and their concerns, for this presents my Self, for it is of them I am constituted. Interiorization of community means taking in, noticing, attending to what actually engages me and enrages me. The environment is now the mirror and insight is now outrage.

Emotions remain dominant, but no longer are they conceived to be literally interior, only within my physiology, in the deep id, older brain, neurovegetative recesses, hormonal secretions. Instead, an emotion may be imagined as a "divine influx" as William Blake said, "afforded" by the world in J. J. Gibson's sense, as "affecting presences" as Robert Armstrong called them, revealing "importance" in Whitehead's sense, carried by objects, scenes, and situations as their "physiognomic character" in the manner of classic Gestalt psychology. An emotion now becomes a field of signification and value, affecting me to move out, *ex movere*, of self-enclosure.

As mourning would no longer be interiorized as depression and treated as an inner state independent of the object losses in the world soul, so rage will not be regarded as a private condition of aggression or hostility inside my individualized self-responsible personality.

Instead, rage presents a primal outrage over an actual situation. I am affected by the presence of the enraging. In Wallace Steven's words: "The lion roars at the enraging desert / Reddens the sand with his red-colored noise."[6] So, too, shame will not be interiorized as guilt and attached to an imaginary structure called ego or self and owned by it, but shame will reflect specific "falls", i.e., sins of omission and commission that the I, as human, carry as I walk through the world. Nor will fear — that supreme emotion for acknowledging the power of the object — be converted to objectless anxiety and considered wholly intrapsychically. Nor, finally, will desire that reaches as far as the heart can fathom and lifts repression from the world's face disclosing its desirability — desire as the response to the radiance of the world — , nor will this be stuffed into the closet of personal needs.

For patient to become citizen, analytical psychotherapy can hardly do more at first than return to the world the emotions which call the patient to the world. By following the innate extraversion of emotion, its fascination with the object and its libidinously sticky attachment to the other, the patient's involvement changes from self to object. Yet all the while an interiorizing is going on, making more subtle and sophisticated the emotional field, attending to the world's need for soul and the soul's need for a world beyond itself. For the world calls to the libido from the face of every object. It lures and screams and terrifies, to which we remain deaf, defended by our doctrinal immune system that declares these calls to be projections because emotions have been locked up inside.

Therapy as Symptom

In these last pages let us focus again upon the practice of analysis. "Clinical practice" as the professionals like to call it.

In the circle of my hermeneutic colleagues, more and more I hear three sorts of complaints: the first, "I believe I have a slight narcolepsy; I fall asleep, doze off in the middle of the hour." The second, "I wish I really could cut down. I'm doing twenty-five, thirty-five or forty-five hours a week and it's too much." The third — this complaint is not spoken directly — refers to sexual compulsions, indiscretions between analyst and patient, ethics committees, testimony, investigations, denunciations for what is called "acting out in the sexual sphere."

What is the psyche doing in these three afflictions that occur in therapy, to therapy, perhaps because of therapy? One thing is clear in all three symptoms: some force wants to put an end to analysis. Let us take the third one first, the sexual compulsion.

Quite clearly the consciousness and the conscience of the analyst knows that breaking the rule of erotic restraint not only ends analysis as such, but also may well end the analyst's career as analyst. None the less, the acting out, as it is called, occurs in more cases than are officially reported or admitted. There are many interpretations of this symptom. Let me attempt a reading of the sexualized compulsion in terms of the "object libido."

The other person in the room — patient or analyst — embodies the only human possibility within an analysis to whom object libido can flow. The person on the couch or in the other chair represents cure of the analytic narcissism simply by being there as an other. Moreover, the patient for the analyst and the analyst for the patient become such compelling objects because they have also been tabooed by the analytical rules as libidinal possibilities. Analyst and patient may not act their desire for each other. The narcissism of the situation — that libido is turned to the ego and not to the world (except world as other person in the other chair) — makes them absolutely necessary to each other, while the taboo sets them absolutely outside of each other. The outside object, however, is also inside analysis. So patient for analyst and analyst for patient become the symbolic mode of ending analysis by means of falling in love.

Of course, the persons are often torn by the love dilemma of the narcissistic patient: "cure by love" in preference to "cure by analysis."[7] We must ask, however, whether this neurotic choice, as Freud calls it, arises from the narcissism of the patient and of the analyst or whether it arises from the narcissism of the analytical situation. After all, the fantasy of an opposition between love and analysis occurs within the prior fantasy of cure which has brought the persons together in the first place. The erotic compulsion besetting both persons is a symptom not of their ethical fallibility or of their vulnerability to personal repressions. Rather it is a symptom of therapy.

It is therapy generating its own symptom to which neither patient nor analyst are immune because therapy's isolated narcissistic individualism cannot confine the instinctual drive of object libido which appears in the guise of the disease, erotic obsession, a disease which seeks to cure the persons of the more fundamental disease, therapy itself.

The first of our three conditions, narcolepsy or falling asleep, like falling in love, also puts closure to analysis as a prolonged hovering over the case exposed, closure to consciousness itself as it is defined by "attention," "wakefulness," "cortical activation," "apperceptive alertness," "continuity of awareness." The psyche absents itself from the analytical activity. In fact, it enters the state of the dream, the primary condition requiring analysis. Falling asleep, like falling in love, is the fall from self-control; the subject utterly displaced back into the Zuider Zee. Curiously, like falling in love, the overpowering drowsiness occurs only in the analytical session, not at home, not watching the telly, not driving the car, not during other conversations, lectures, committee meetings. The narcolepsy is a "therapeugenic" symptom, as if therapy in the person of the analyst was not merely deconstructing itself, but was hell-bent on destruction of analytical consciousness.

The language of the second complaint — "I wish I could cut down, do less, get away more, rearrange my schedule, but I haven't been able to" takes us into the realms of addiction. The addiction to my schedule; that is to the regular hours for seeing patients each week, each month, even years in advance, literalizes and substantiates time into exact blocks in an appointment book. To mislay or lose the agenda is utterly disorienting: one has become agenda-dependent, even looking forward to September or January each year for the newly-bound, blank schedule book.

Although I have set this schedule myself, I am not its master. I have become the slave of analytical time. Schedule as Robot, Golem, Till Eulenspiegel, Dr. Frankenstein. Desire attempts to break free. Desire imagines libidinal objects other than analytical hours, but the sched-

ule does not allow it, "I must check my schedule." I have become dependent upon the autonomy of substantiated time. Schedule as other
overrides my will. I see little difference between substance dependency like alcohol and drugs and substantiation dependency like time-
slots and schedules. Both declare the defeat of independent individualism. I am bound over to an objectification, which is what the object
libido desires. But the obscure objects of desire that bind me to the
world and make me co-dependent with its desirability — we so desperately need each other — remain unfulfilled and the object libido compromised when the objects are not the things of an animated world,
but are its substitute: alcohol, drugs, tobacco, love object, shopping
for bargains, schedule.

None the less, we know from Freud that every symptom has its *telos*.
As compromise, a symptom intends to cure the condition in which the
symptom originates. The symptoms I have just sketched threaten individualism right into its citadel, the double-door closed keep of the
analytical chamber. These three symptoms — erotic compulsion, narcolepsy, and schedule addiction—attest to a breakdown in the model of
analytical psychotherapy, that model which supposes itself immune to
movements, not only of the world, but movements of the object libido
reaching for the world, movements too often theoretically distorted by
and therefore clinically disguised as "projection" and "acting out."

As I have done in the past, I am reading the pathologizing (this time
the pathologizing going on in therapy itself) as a necessary falling
apart (this time a breakdown of its immune system), a disclosing of its
liberal humanist notion of self-determination, a crack in its Christian-
ized personalized skin-bounded soul, and a return of the object libido
from the inherently agoraphobic, apolitical, self-enclosed individualism of therapy to the animation of the world soul, the *anima mundi*,
whose claim on the patient as political animal is prior to the claim
of therapy.

When analysis can recognize that citizen takes priority over patient, then analysis can revert its differentiated subtle attention to that
ground against which Jung and Freud limned individuality: the collective, the herd instinct, the primal horde, that throng and flood of the

polls and the call of the agora. Then, no longer would our motto be Apollonic and Oedipal, "know thyself"; no longer, *cogito ergo sum* but *convivo ergo sum* — freely translated: "I party, am of a party, and therefore am."

1. Sigmund Freud (1922), "The Libido Theory," *Collected Papers* V (London: Hogarth Press, 1950), p. 134.

2. Sigmund Freud (1922), *Group Psychology and the Analysis of the Ego*, trans. J. Strachey (London: Hogarth Press, 1948), p. 89.

3. Freud, "The Libido Theory," p. 133.

4. Edward E. Sampson, "The Challenge of Social Change for Psychology: Globalization and Psychology's Theory of the Person," *American Psychologist* 44/6 (June 1989), p. 918.

5. Ibid., p. 916. See also Edward E. Sampson, "The Decentralization of Identity: Toward a Revised Concept of Personal and Social Order," *American Psychologist* 40/11 (November 1985) and "The Debate on Individualism: Indigenous Psychologies of the Individual and their Role in Personal and Societal Functioning," *American Psychologist* 43/1 (January 1988).

6. Wallace Stevens, "Notes Toward a Supreme Fiction," in *The Collected Poems of Wallace Stevens* (New York: Knopf, 1978), p. 384.

7. Sigmund Freud, "On Narcissism: An Introduction," *Collected Papers* IV, p. 59.

5

From Mirror to Window:
Curing Psychoanalysis of its Narcissism

The apparently individual conflict of the patient is revealed as a universal conflict of his environment and epoch. Neurosis is thus nothing less than an individual attempt, however unsuccessful, to solve a universal problem.
— C.G. Jung (1912)

Narcissism is now the rage, the universal diagnosis. In Freud's world, the new attention was on conversion hysteria; in Bleuler's, *dementia praecox*. Earlier we find all ills attributed to the English malady, to spleen, to hypochondriasis, to melancholia, to chlorosis; in Paris, a myriad of *phobies* and *délires*. Different times and places, different syndromes.

Narcissism has its theoreticians — Kohut, Kernberg, Lacan — and modern Jungians are following the rage. The collective consciousness of psychology makes us collectively unconscious, much as Jung said when writing about the collective ideas in his day. Being "with it" also means being in it. The epidemic diagnosis Narcissism states that the condition is already endemic to the psychology that makes the diagnosis. It sees narcissism because it sees narcissistically. So let us not take this diagnosis so literally, but place it within the historical parade of Western diagnoses.

Talk given in Rome, October 1988, and consequently published as "Dal narcisismo alla finestra . . ." in *Itinerari del pensiero junghiano*, eds. Paolo Aite, Aldo Carotenuto, trans. Maria Carbone. Milano: Cortina. First English publication in *Spring* 49 (1989).

Eminent culture critics — Karl Krauss, Thomas Szasz, Philip Rieff, Christopher Lasch, Paul Zweig, and the notorious Dr. Jeffrey Masson — have each seen that psychoanalysis breeds a narcissistic subjectivism inflicting on the culture an iatrogenic disorder, that is, a disease brought by the methods of the doctors who would cure it.

I shall continue their line of thought, but I shall use a method that Wolfgang Giegerich has so brilliantly exposed in many of his papers. If depth psychology itself suffers from a narcissistic disorder, then what we analysts need first to probe is the unconscious narcissism in analysis itself. Our first patient is neither the patient nor ourselves, but the phenomenon called "analysis" that has brought us both to the consulting room.

The term "Narcissism" is probably British. Havelock Ellis is credited with its invention, though Freud gave us its psychoanalytic meaning. What did Freud say? As I go through some of his descriptions, let us hear them narcissistically, as self-referents, descriptive of psychology and of ourselves in psychology.

1917: "We employ the term narcissism in relation to little children and it is to excessive narcissism of primitive man that we ascribe his belief in the omnipotence of his thoughts and consequent attempts to influence the course of events in the outer world by magical practices."[1] Does not analysis have this primitive omnipotence fantasy of influencing events in the outer world by its magical practices? The omnipotence of subjective reflection is attested to by many classic Jungians like Harding, Bernhard, Meier, von Franz, Baumann, etc. As Jung himself says, we are each "the makeweight that tips the scales"[2] that determine the outcome of world history." The rituals of self-engagement remove projections from the world so that, supposedly, the world itself is transformed by psychoanalysis.

1922: ". . . narcissistic disorders are characterized by a withdrawal of the libido from objects."[3] *The withdrawal of the libido from objects* — I ask you to remember this statement. We shall come back to it.

1925: Freud describes three historic blows to humankind's narcissism. These, he says, are the cosmological blow of Copernicus, the blow of Darwinian evolution theory, and the psychoanalytic blow (of Freud) which wounded the omnipotence fantasy, or narcissism, of the ego as sole self-willed ruler. Here, psychoanalysis becomes itself a giant omnipotence fantasy, a creation myth of our culture equivalent with astronomy and biology, promulgating itself with narcissistic grandeur.

This pronouncement appears in Freud's discussion on resistance to psychoanalysis.[4] By means of this idea, resistance, analysis brilliantly maintains its invulnerability to criticism. Questioning the validity of analysis is impugned as resistance to it. Even more: the very attacks demonstrate resistance and therefore help to validate analytical theory. As Freud says, "The triumph of narcissism, the ego's victorious assertion of its own invulnerability. It refuses to be hurt by the arrows of reality. . . It insists that it is impervious to wounds dealt by the outside world."[5]

Later, Freud considered narcissism not to be rooted in love at all, i.e., as self-love, but to be rather a defense against aggressive impulses. Let us consider for a moment the value of "aggressive impulses;" at least and at best they take the object, the world out there, into account: I feel enraged about societal injustice, nuclear danger, media crap, industrial callousness, the corporate mind, political ideologues, hideous architecture, etc. But, owing to my narcissistic defenses against the involving call of aggression, I go to the spa, work out, meditate, jog, diet, reduce stress, relax my body armor, improve my orgasms, get a new hairstyle, and take a vacation. And see my therapist: very expensive, very good for me, because he or she devotes complete attention to my problems, especially our transferential frame. Instead of the world and my outrage, I work on my analysis, myself, the Self. This Self, too, fits a narcissistic definition: "the incorporation of grandiose object images as defense against anxiety and guilt"[6] or, as Fenichel puts it, one feels oneself in "reunion with an omnipotent force,"[7] be that force an archetype, a God or Goddess, the *unus mundus*, or the numinosity of analysis itself.

Freud's paper "On Narcissism" states that both introspection and conscience or "being watched" derive from and serve narcissism. Yet, psychotherapy practices self-scrutiny as the principal method in its treatment and "being watched" or supervision as the principal component of its training. A candidate goes to hour after hour of institutionalized narcissism of watching and being watched.

The institutionalization of narcissism in our profession — the idea of resistance, the idealization of the Self, the practices of introspection and supervision, the omnipotence fantasies about its own importance in world history, its technique of referring all events back to itself as the vessel, the mirror, the *temenos*, the frame — bears immediately upon that central obsession of analysis today, transference.

By transference, here, I mean that self-gratifying analytical habit which refers the emotions of life to the analysis. Transference habitually deflects object libido, that is, love for anything outside analysis, into a narcissistic reflection upon analysis. We feed analysis with life. The mirror that walks down the road of life (Flaubert) replaces the actual road, and the mirror no longer reflects the world, only the walking companions. They may as well have stayed indoors, less distracted by the trees and the traffic.

The principal content of analytical reflection as transference is the child we once were, a fact which accords with Freud's observation that the object choice of the narcissist is "someone he once was." This helps account for the faddish popularity of Alice Miller's writings. Her idealized children exhibit what Freud said: the narcissist is "not willing to forego his narcissistic perfection in his childhood" and "seeks to recover the early perfection."[8] The focus on childhood traps the libido only further into subjectivity, and therefore we must recognize that erotic compulsions in analysis are produced primarily by the analysis, rather than by the persons. Analysis acts itself out through them quite impersonally so that they often feel betrayed and ashamed by the impersonality of the emotions they undergo and are unable to recognize that what they are suffering is the object libido trying to find a way out of analysis. Instead, the narcissistic viciousness of our theory says that transference emotions are compelling the persons to go deeper into analysis.

Let us recognize that the other person — patient or analyst — embodies the only possibility within an analysis to whom object libido can flow. The person in the other chair represents cure of analytical narcissism simply by being there as an Other. Moreover, the patient for the analyst and the analyst for the patient become such numinous objects because they have also been tabooed as libidinal possibilities. Analyst and patient may not act their desire for each other. The narcissism of the *situation* makes them absolutely necessary to each other, while the taboo sets them absolutely outside of each other. This outside object, however, is also inside the analysis. So, patient for doctor and doctor for patient become the symbolic mode of ending analysis by means of love.

Of course, the persons are often torn by what Freud calls the love dilemma of the narcissistic patient: "the cure by love, which he generally refers to cure by analysis."[9] We must ask whether this neurotic choice, as Freud calls it, arises from the narcissism of the patient or from the narcissism of the analytical system in which the patient is situated. After all, the fantasy of an opposition between love and analysis occurs within the prior fantasy of cure which has brought the persons together in the first place.

By elaborating ethical codes, malpractice insurance, investigations, and expulsions that blame the participants, analysis protects itself from wounding insights about its own narcissism. The vulnerability of analysis — that its effectiveness is always in question, that it is neither science nor medicine, that it is aging into professional mediocrity and may have lost its soul to power years ago despite its idealized language of growth and creativity (a language by the way, never used by its founders) — this vulnerability is overcome by idealizing the transference.

As well as transference love, there is also hatred. Perhaps the client's hatred of the analyst and the hatred of the analyst for the client are also not personal. Perhaps, these intense oppressive feelings against each other arise in both to present both with the fact that they are in a hateful situation: the object libido hates the attachment of transference. Analysis hates itself in order to break the narcissistic vessel imprisoning the libido that would go out into the soul in the world.

The horned dilemmas of transference, including the analyst's stare into the mirror of his own counter-transference, the feelings of love and hatred, this agony and ecstasy and romantic torture convince the participants that what is going on is of intense importance: first, because these phenomena are expected by the theory and provide proof of it, and second, because these phenomena re-enact what analysis once was in its own childhood in Vienna and Zurich, analysis in primary fusion with its origins in Breuer and Freud and Jung, in Dora and Anna and Sabina. The feelings are cast in therapeutic guise because this is the healing fiction of the analytic situation. In other words, transference is less necessary to the doctor and the patient than it is to analysis by means of which it intensifies its narcissistic idealization, staying in love with itself. We therapists do not sit in our chambers so many hours a day only for the money, or the power, but because we are addicted to analytical narcissism. Our individual narcissism is both obscured and reinforced by the approved narcissism of the analytical profession.

When one partner imagines a tryst or the other imagines resisting a seduction, or when either imagines that love is a solution to misery, then they are framed in the romantic conflicts of *Madame Bovary*, *Wuthering Heights*, and *Anna Karenina*, reconstituting the Romanticism of the nineteenth century and the origins of psychoanalysis, not in your or my personal childhoods, but in its own cultural childhood. This means we have to locate the narcissism of contemporary analysis within a much wider narcissism: the Romantic movement.

Literary tradition differentiates at least four principal traits of this genre. We have already spoken of one, "idealization of the love object." And indeed analysis idealizes the patient as an "interesting case," "difficult patient," "good patient," "borderline personality." Or consider all the literary fabulations that have made patients into eternal literary figures — Dora, Ellen West, Babette, Miss Miller, Wolfman, Ratman, Little Hans, all the way to Freud and Jung themselves in the novels *The White Hotel* and *The House of Glass*. Think of the Romanticism in our theoretical constructs: Love and Death, Empathy, Transformation, Growth, The Child, The Great Mother, The Mirror, Desire and *Jouissance*, and the Transitional Object. In the patient there takes place such idealized events as a *hieros gamos*, a quest for self-discovery and a journey into wholeness. Synchronicities outside of causal laws, transcendent functions, integration of the shadow and the realization of the Self on whom the future of civilization depends. We record our idealization of the love object, i.e., analysis, in taped and filmed analytic sessions, paying meticulous and expensive attention to trivial conversations and gestures. Analysis is in love with its idealized image.

A second essential trait of Romanticism is said to be the opposition between bourgeois society and the inner self which, with its dreams, desires and inspirations, tends to oppose, even contradict, the outer world of usual things. Psychoanalysis from its beginnings imagines itself fundamentally opposed to the civilization and its institutions of religion, family, medicine, and the political community disdained as "the collective." Freud's emphasis on himself as Jew and hence marginal, as well as Jung's favorite position as heretical old hermit (despite the bourgeois lives they led and values they held) still shapes the imagination of the profession and distorts its relation to the ordinary world.

Third, imprisonment another basic theme in Romanticism, especially French and Russian. In Dostoevsky's *The Possessed*, Maria's song says: "This tiny cell suffices me, there I will dwell my soul to save." The consulting room provides the confining physical place for the psychic imprisonment of analysis as such its devotion to the secret nooks and crannies of the private world, decorating with reconstructive rococo (i.e., psycho-dynamic intricacies) the narcissistic cell of personality.

Fourth, the Romantic genre has been defined as one that simultaneously seeks and postpones a particular end. This fits therapy. Its entire procedure seeks to restore the person to the world, yet postpones this return indefinitely. (Meanwhile, do not make major changes in your actual life. Don't act out. The cure of analysis becomes more analysis—another analyst, another school — and the improvement of training becomes ever more hours.) The simultaneity of seeking and postponing an end occurs in the basic conundrum of every analysis, its contradictory two commandments: encourage the desires of the unconscious (Thou Shall Not Repress) and forbid gratification (Thou Shall Not Act Out). Our work is with the libidinous and our method is by way of abstention. The end is unforeseeable; there is no completion. Analysis interminable, as Freud said. This is the Romanticism of eternal longing.

There is no way out of Romanticism's consulting room and the subjectivism of its eros, unless we turn to what is beyond its purview, turn to what narcissism and romanticism leave out: the objects, the unidealized, immediately given, actual world of dull and urban things. By turning psychological attention from the mirror of self-reflection to the world through the window, we release "object libido" to seek its goal beyond narcissistic confinement in analysis. For "object libido" is but a psychoanalytic name for the drive which loves the world, the erotic desire for *anima mundi*, for soul in the world.

Perhaps it becomes clearer why I have been emphasizing John Keats's remarkable phrase; "Call the world . . . The vale of Soul-making. Then you will find out the use of the world. . ." Also, you will understand why I have held myself back from that side of Jung which expounds upon meaning, Self, individuation, *unus mundus*, wholeness, mandalas, etc. These large and introverted ideas envelop me and usually my patients with a grandiose, invulnerable aura. As well, I keep a distance from the current Kohut craze and Lacanian mystique. Although recognizing narcissism as the syndrome of the times (even if the groundwork for this was prepared long ago in the metaphysical catastrophe of Augustinian and Cartesian subjectivism), yet Kohut attempts its cure by the same means of narcissistic obsession: an ever more detailed observation of subjectivity. And a subjectivity within the oppressive confines of a negatively reconstructed childhood. The child archetype dominates contemporary therapy, keeping patients (and analysts) safe from the world. For this archetype feels always endangered by the actual world, lives not in the present but in futurity, and is addicted to its own powerless infantilism. By so focusing on the child, analysis disenfranchises itself from the wider realm of soul-making in the adult community of *polis*.

Nevertheless I must confess to a serious longstanding error on my part regarding Keats's phrase. I always considered the world out there to be useful for making one's own soul. Narcissism again. My soul, your soul — not *its* soul. For the Romantics, however, ensouling *the world* was a crucial part of their program. They recognized the traps of narcissistic subjectivity in their vision. Hence, they sought the spirit in physical nature, the brotherhood of all mankind or *Gemeinschaftsgefühl*, political revolution, and a return to the classic Gods and Goddesses, attempting to revivify the soul of the world with pantheism.

We must therefore read Keats as saying we go through the world for the sake of *its* soul-making, thereby our own. This reading suggests a true object libido, beyond narcissism, in keeping with Otto Fenichel's definition of love. Love can only be called such when "one's own satisfaction is impossible without satisfying the object too."[10] If the world is not satisfied by our going through it, no matter how much beauty and pleasure our souls may receive from it, then we live in its vale without love.

There is a way out, or I wouldn't be standing here. For my specific style of narcissism, my pose before the mirror, today is heroic. My style insists on resolution of the issues raised. The method I shall be using here follows the method which I usually employ for resolving issues. First, we look back into the history of psychoanalysis for a model; second, we turn to some peculiar bit of pathologizing for a clue; and third, we resolve problems by dissolving them into images and metaphors.

So, let us turn back to the first psychoanalytic case, Anna O., and her doctor, Josef Breuer, who, with Freud, wrote *Studies in Hysteria*. As you recall, after a year of almost daily sessions often of several hours, he suddenly terminated. You recall also the intensity of her transference, that she developed a hysterical pregnancy and childbirth, after Breuer tried to end the treatment. He, according to Jones, after a final visit to her "fled the house in a cold sweat. The next day he and his wife left for Venice to spend a second honeymoon which resulted in the conception of a daughter."[11] Whether fact or not, and Ellenberger says not, the fantasy shows a founding patron of our work escaping both cure by analysis and cure by love for the beauty of Venice and the conception of a daughter. His object libido returns from the oppressive narcissism of psychoanalysis to the Romanticism of the wider world.

This wide world remains merely that, merely a place of escape or acting out, so long as the world "out the window" is imagined only in the Cartesian model as sheer *res extensa*, only dead matter. To show more vividly how that world is, as Keats said, a place of soul, let us go straight through the window into the world. Let us take a walk in a Japanese garden, in particular the strolling garden, the one with water, hills, trees, and stones. While we walk, let us imagine the garden as an emblem for the peripatetic teacher or the therapeutic guide (psycho-pompos), *the world itself as psychoanalyst showing us soul*, showing us how to be in it soulfully.

I turn to the garden and to Japan because of insights given while in Kyoto gardens several years ago, and also because the garden as metaphor expresses some of the deepest longings — from Hesperides, to Eden's paradise, and Maria's *hortus inclusus* — for the world as home of the soul. So by entering into the Japanese garden now we shall be stepping through the window into the *anima mundi*.

First we notice that the garden has no central place to stand and view it all. We can but scrutinize a part at a time. Instead of overview and wholeness, there is perspective and eachness. The world changes as we move. Here a clump of iris, there a mossy rock. Instead of a center (with its etymological roots in the Greek *kentron*, "goad" or "prick," and being compelled toward a goal by means of abstract geometric distancing), there are shifts of focus relative to the body's location and attitude.

Second: as one strolls, each vista is seen again from a different perspective. The maple branching down to the pond edge, the floating leaves appear less melancholic after the path bends. These shifts of seeing again are precisely what the word "respect" means. To look again is to "re-spect." Each time we look at the same thing again, we gain respect for it and add respect to it, curiously discovering the innate relation of "looks" — of regarding and being regarded, words in English that refer to dignity.

Third: when the garden, rather than the dream or the symptom or the unconscious, becomes the *via regia* of psyche, then we are forced to think anew about the word "in." "In" is the dominant preposition of all psychoanalysis — not *with*, not *from*, not *for*, but "in." We look in our souls, we look in a mirror. "In" has been taken utterly literally, as an invisible, spaceless psychic stuff inside our skins, or the meanings inside our dreams and symptoms, or the memories locked in the past. Interiority of the garden, however, is wholly present and wholly displayed. "In" holds the meanings of included, engaged, involved, embraced. Or, as Jung said, the psyche is not in us; we are in the psyche. This feeling of being in the psyche becomes most palpable when inside the ruins of a Greek temple, in an Egyptian tomb of a king, in a dance or a ritual, and in a Japanese garden. Jung's phrase *"esse in anima"* takes on concreteness then, as it does in a clear-cut forest, a bombed city, a cancer ward, a cemetery. Ecology, architecture, interior design are other modes of feeling the *anima mundi*. In fact, the relation or body and psyche reverses. Instead of the usual notion of psyche in body, the body strolling through the garden is in the psyche. The world itself is a psychic body; and our bodies as we move, stand, look, pause, turn, and sit are performing an activity of psychic reflection, an activity we formerly considered only mentally possible in the mirror of introspection. To know oneself in the garden of the world then requires being physically in the world. Where you are reveals how you are.

Fourth: the idea of individuality also changes, for in the Japanese garden trees are trimmed at the top and encouraged to grow sideways. Rather than an individuality of the lone tree, towering (and Jung said the single tree is a major symbol of the individuating Self),[12] these trees stretch their branches toward others. Individuality is within community and, takes its definition from community. Furthermore, each tuft in the soft branches of the pine trees is plucked by gardeners. They pull out needles, allowing emptiness to individualize the shape of each twig. It is as if nothing can be individualized unless it is surrounded by emptiness and yet also very, very close to what it is most like. Individuality is therefore more visible within the estranged separateness and close similarity, for instance, of family than in trying to be "different" from family.

Fifth: not only are aged trees supported with crutches and encouraged to flower — blossoming belonging therefore not only to youth — but also the garden includes dead trees. What more wounds our narcissism than these images of old age, these crutched, dependent, twisted and dead trees?

Sixth: the Karesansui gardens, or Zen-inspired gardens, present mainly white sand and found stones, rarely trees. In this bare place the mind watches itself making interpretations. The nine rocks in the raked sand are a tiger family swimming through the sea; the nine rocks are mountain tops peaking through white mist and clouds; the nine rocks are simply rocks, aesthetically placed with genius. One legend after another, one philosophy, theory of literary criticism, or psychological interpretation rises to the mind and falls back into the white sand. The garden becomes wholly metaphor, both what it is and what it is not, presence and absence at once. The concrete koan of the rock garden transforms the mind itself into metaphor, its thought transient while image endures, so that the mind cannot identify with its own subjectivism — narcissism overcome.

Finally, I shall insist that the garden is not natural; nor is psyche natural. The garden was designed and is tended to maintain an artificiality that imitates nature. In Fort Worth, Texas, a large and marvelous Japanese garden was constructed years ago. But since adequate funds were not set aside for gardeners from Japan, nature slowly destroys that garden. Without the pruners' perverted twist to each inch of nature, the garden declines into merely another part of the forest. A garden's elaborated display of soul-in-the-world is an *opus contra naturam*, like alchemy. Like alchemy, the garden is a work of intense culture. Unlike alchemy, its matter, its body, is out there, rather than inside the glass vessel.

Because the garden is artificial, as the alchemist was called *artifex*, all conceptions of soul must be plucked of naturalistic fallacies. The soul as *opus contra naturam* will not be served adequately by fallacious comparisons with organic growth, cyclical process, and myths of nature Goddesses. Nor does the garden shelter the child from which grows the creative person as psychotherapy is fond to believe. By insisting upon the artificiality of our work with soul, I am trying to keep us from the Romantic error of confusing the ideal (Eden and the Elysian fields; Horaiko, in Japanese) with the natural. The garden as metaphor offers a romantic vision that saves us from Naturalistic Romanticism by twisting and sophisticating nature through art.

This twist to nature that wounds idealizations of garden is presented in our culture, as in Roman culture, by our ancient God of gardens
and gardeners, Priapus. Priapus is neither young nor beautiful. Unlike lovely Narcissus, unlike the semi-divine figures of Adam and Eve,
Priapus is mature, bald and paunchy, and so distorted that his mother,
Venus, deserted him at birth. His very presence repels romantic idealizations and the gaze into the mirror of Venusian vanity as well as Narcissus's rapt reflection. Priapic reflection starts the other way around;
his preposterous swollen condition reflects the vitality of the world.
The same force displays in him as in the buds and germinating pods.
By means of distortion which deceptively seems "only natural," Priapus invites the grotesque pathologized disproportions of imagination
— and imagination, says Bachelard, works by deformation.

So, when I invoke Priapus, I am not speaking of priapismus; I am
not speaking of machismo; and I am not anti-feminine. Let me be quite
clear. I am speaking of the generative artificiality that is the essence of the
garden and of the psyche. Each dream, each fantasy, and each symptomatic complication of natural health and normative humanity bears
witness to the psyche's libidinal pleasure in exaggeration, its fertile
genius for imaginative distortion. If this God of gardens is also a God
of psychoanalysis — and from Charcot through Lacan the priapic has
been invoked — he brings to its work an archaic reflex beyond the
romantic or baroque, a rousing urgency forward and outward. (Priapus
was not permitted indoors in Hestia's closed rooms where his presence
becomes only violent and obscene.)

Moreover, this God needs no mirror to know himself, for his self
is wholly displayed. His nature cannot be concealed within, so he is
quite free of hidden meanings and subtle innuendos that keep psychoanalysis hopefully addicted to one more revelation, one more transformation, interminable. Priapus knows no metamorphosis, no transfigu-
rations. Priapus is without ambiguity; metaphor is forbidden to him;
he displays all, reveals nothing. Like the garden, all there. The rocks
are the rocks.

1. Sigmund Freud, "One of the Difficulties of Psycho-Analysis," *Collected Papers* 4 (London: Hogarth Press, 1950), p. 350.

2. C.G. Jung, *Collected Works (CW)* 10, trans. R.F.C. Hull, Bollingen Series (Princeton: Princeton University Press; and London: Routledge, Kegan Paul, 1953-), p. 586.

3. Sigmund Freud, "Two Encyclopedia Articles: (A) Psycho-Analysis," *Collected Papers* 4, p. 124.

4. Sigmund Freud, "One of the Difficulties of Psycho-Analysis," *Collected Papers* 4, pp. 350–52.

5. Sigmund Freud, "Humour," *Collected Papers*, 5:217.

6. Christopher Lasch, *La Cultura del narcissismo* (Milan: Bompiani, 1981), p. 49.

7. Otto Fenichel, *The Psychoanalytic Theory of Neurosis* (New York: Norton, 1945), p. 40.

8. Sigmund Freud, "On Narcissism: An Introduction," *Collected Papers* 4, 51.

9. Ibid., p. 59

10. Otto Fenichel, op. cit., p. 468.

11. Ernest Jones, *Sigmund Freud: Life and Work*, vol. 1 (London: Hogarth Press, 1953), p. 247.

12. C.G. Jung, *CW*, 13, pp. 350, 458f., 482.

13. Maurice Olender, "Priape, le mal taillé," in *Corps Dieux* (Paris: Gallimard, 1986).

6

The Right to Remain Silent

Let me note at the beginning my two key assumptions. First, I assume that you most likely do therapeutic work with children or younger people, where the term "therapeutic" is used to cover the wide field of the helping professions. Second, by children and younger people I do not mean only those whom we meet in schools, offices, and consulting rooms. I refer as well to the inner child, the child and teenager within, that unreconstructed, uninitiated, sometimes a bit retarded or left back, sometimes hyper-fantastic and over-achieving younger person we each carry around wherever we go and who gives us each so much trouble that he or she has to use counterphobic shibboleths like "Hey, no problem," and "I'm okay."

This figure is the part to whom we refer when we say of ourselves, or someone says of us, that we are immature, childish, undeveloped, infantile, autoerotic, narcissistic, or just a big baby. And this big baby, who appears in our moods and demands and walks around in our dreams in the guises of children we knew from early school years, keeps us in therapy with ourselves. We are in the helping profession partly because we are working in behalf of the needy and disturbed behavior of children out there and also partly because we are working in behalf of the needy and disturbed childish behavior in here, in ourselves.[1] We are all therapists and all cases in that we are all working on ourselves much of the time.

Adaptation of Keynote Address, Symposium on the Creative Arts and Human Rights in Counseling, AACD Convention, New Orleans, April 24, 1987. First appeared in print in *The Journal of Humanistic Education and Development* 26/4 (1988).

So I am as much speaking about something as I am addressing something in you from something in me. This style of proceeding is what I mean by *psychological talk:* the subjective element is never too far out of sight. We can never get out of the psyche. Whatever we say about something says something about us.

The basic metaphor for the therapeutic work to be explored here is taken from the law; "You have the right to remain silent. Anything you say can and will be used against you." A fuller statement of this warning is shorthanded and called "Miranda" from a Supreme Court decision.

I use this tough statement deliberately to cut through the naive optimism that pervades, if not perverts, much of the work done with children. From Jean-Jacques Rousseau's romantic naturalism through Spencer Tracy's fatherly goodness in "Boystown" and Alice Miller's innocent, sexless children, there is an idealized child image. This idealized child influences us to be empathetic educators and sentimental do-gooders. *In loco parentis* has come to mean not just in place of parents but *better* than parents.

I am not trying to cut through the idealization of the child — which, by the way, I think is absolutely necessary to our work: we must idealize youth and let their ideals inspire us. I am out to get the sentimental obfuscation of our own awareness, that narcissistic idealization of ourselves as good, helpful, saving people, which leads to a dimming of our sharpness. When helping younger people "to grow" we tend to become sentimental, and sentimentality softens the edge.

"You have the right to remain silent," Hah! What a laugh! If only they would remain silent and sit still. Zooming around the room like propelled missiles or helicopters. Lying, popping off, hyper, incessant. Or they abuse the right by closing off, monosyllabic and sullen.

A woman whose art therapy I supervised for a while calmed the bedlam and focused attention of some fifteen children, aged 4 to 7, by telling them a story. They were drawn in. At the end of the tale she asked them each to draw the story. Mostly they did a figure from it, the duck, the house, the little girl under the tree. Then she asked them to make another drawing of the story. This second one usually turned out to be less an illustration of a figure directly linked with the story and more a descent into mood and theme that freed fantasy to go further.

Two or three useful things emerge from this example. First, her telling a story draws children into silence. This kind of silence produces a quality of attention different from disciplinary silence, which is repressive. Hence, that squirming at the edge of giggling and rebellion, or the vacuity of not listening. Second, the example shows that imagination deepens in silence. The drawings went from illustrations still attached to the outer referent, the story with duck, house, and little girl under the tree, to what is not spoken, not here. In contemporary terms, the imagination moved from presence to absence: imagination tends to go to what is not there. That is why some call making visible what is not there *creative expression*.

Notice in my account the curious play on the word "draw." The children were drawn into silence by the story and, as the story was drawing out its details, the children made drawings of it and from it. The imagination "draws." It drags attention along with it, and it draws, sketches, or configurates images. To put it another way, imagination shapes itself by means of images; these images draw and hold attention. They concentrate thoughts and feelings, suspending action.[2] Whether it requires silence for this drawing to take place or whether silence results from this drawn-into-itself or withdrawn concentration of the psyche in the midst of images, there is some important, necessary, and curious relation between silence and the drawing power of imagining.

I tend to feel silence as an animal silence, like a watching cat, a pointing dog, a still lizard on the wall. There seems to be a phylogenetic level of the soul, an animal being that connects with actual animals in silence, and especially gets on well with the childish piece of the psyche. I tend to think that this animal being, which is very old and not at all stupid, is that invisible to which therapy must appeal and with which it must connect for therapy to take place. And this connection requires the silence of an animal noticing. The notions of therapeutic trust, empathy, security, and support seem to refer to and rest upon a more basic animal silence. The question then becomes how do we speak without using what we say against the silence?

Interpreting Against Imagination

The phrase "whatever you say can and will be used against you," here, refers to interpretations. We tend to use what people say to us against them or someone else — an abusing parent, a probation office, an anonymous bureaucrat. The idealization of youth and growth often evokes a countertendency. We want to be *realistic*, to grind down and rub a nose in the dirt. We may not do this down-putting directly. We may do it indirectly with reductive explanations, especially sexual. What's *really* going on in this case is the result of sexual abuse, sexual fantasy, psychosexual maturation, sexual inferiority, obsession, seduction, jealousy, or a lack of sexual identity, and so on. Sexual interpretations of problems are no more real than any other interpretations. They seem more realistic only because they provide an earthy, maybe dirty, polar counterpart to idealizations.

Similarly, sentimental idealizations of an innocent, asexual childhood provide a polar counterpart to sexuality and deny the child his or her own authentic early sexuality. Moreover, sexual interpretations tend to make us counselors feel wiser and more experienced than our young clients, thereby weakening their power to imagine their own experiences.

There are other effective interpretations that result in using interpretations against the client. For instance, "You must hate your father; I suppose you want to hit him" or "You're jealous of your mother having lovers when you can't get it on with any boy at all." Interpretations against the client's family are a particular favorite. Other reductive explanations sound like this: "You think no one cares; you feel useless and failed; you think you shouldn't feel what you feel." Again these examples point out negative structures. They explain by saying what is wrong. They shoot down the stars.

But there is an even greater poison hidden in the interpretations we give our clients. Our accounts tend to be rational, causal, and conceptual. They are on a different wavelength, which creates a jamming static that breaks into silence and interrupts imagining. Imagining is a process of significant elaboration; it goes on and on elaborating its own material, as the children elaborate the duck, the house, and the girl under the tree into a frog pond with an empty car near and a rain cloud coming with lightning in it; like a boy who does not want his father to come home while imagining himself on a motorbike with a girl on the back and going to Mexico with the guys.

This activity of significant elaboration channels emotions into images, or by means of images. Imagining is not headlong and heedless. It proceeds in definite patterns that are almost stereotypes or clichés. So again and again, the whole world over, there are basic significances: falling and flying and crossing a stream; building up and tearing down; opposing forces and reconciliations; climates and altitudes; fire and water: body parts and body stuffs; waste areas, dugout shelters, dark forests and seas. There are machines and tools and colors and numbers, animals and stars, personages of power, of kindness and teaching, of protection of persecution and cruelty. These figures and these themes or mythemes appear in folk and fairy tales, in stories, in theme parks and television, in religious rites and neighborhood games, and in dreams of and drawings by patients. They give patterns of significance to our lives. They are the universals of the imagination, the archetypal. Because we can never get out of the psyche, we can never be but in one or another of these patterns.

Our lives are already significant before we understand them, before we explain them. Or, better said, our lives become significant the moment we recognize a pattern of imagination going on in the midst of a mess. Each mess is an elaboration of imagining. A mess is indeed "all in the mind."

So, interpretations, explanations, arid accounts of what you are doing and why — all the "because" answers to the question "why?" — mainly translate images into concepts. Huddled under the doorway becomes "sheltering"; blood dripping from a pierced finger becomes "wounding"; tree with mottled brown bark and wide roots translates into the concept "growth." We begin to think about growth and as we use the word growth, we lose the tree. It has levels and branches and trunk and wide roots, all of which are growing and decaying. The tree, vital with its own beauty and richly elaborating itself, vanishes. We have exchanged that tree for "growth" as we exchanged the image for the concept. The black snake in the dream from which you try to run becomes your "mother problem," your "sexual problem," or your "death anxiety." The snake, which is a snake, becomes a "problem." A snake, which had to be watched carefully and responded to, becomes an "anxiety." Now it is a dead snake, stuffed with psychological concepts. It has been interpreted: whatever we say has been used against it. To keep the imagining going on with its life of significant elaboration, these conceptual interpretations need to be silenced.[3] We need to respect the doorway huddle, the dripping blood, the mottled tree trunk, and the black snake as such. They are silent as paintings are silent, as dance is, and as music is, too.

In short, the image is primary; the concept, secondary. The image is poetic; the interpretation, prosaic. The image is emotionally significant as such; interpretation recollects the emotion in rationality. The image is intensely vivid. It moves with its own life. It is chilling, fascinating, loathsome, gorgeous, painful, and desirable, with particularized energy, intensely individual, that is, your image alone arriving silently out of the blue. You alone beheld it. Images arise in individuals freely and spontaneously. They have an individualizing effect, almost anarchic because of their unpredictability. This autonomy or anarchy of the image is the source of personal expression, making each painting, song, and story different. Also, this anarchy is the source of the struggle we have when trying to give understandable expression to our private images.

The good interpretation speaks to the image in its own language.[4] The good interpretation does not use big, flabby concepts like growth, sexuality, creativity, aggression, and anxiety, but responds with compact images like the black snake wants to get closer to you, to touch you. Does it want more body warmth? Huddled under the doorway, what are you wearing? Whose doorway is it? What sort of building? Is there anybody else around? Could you make a little fire there, or is it too windy, or what? These remarks do not ask for answers. They do not explain anything; instead they lead into further silent imagining. The imagination is prompted to go back into itself, to watch and hear and feel, and to think further. Again, this sensing, feeling, and thinking is intensely individualized, an individuality that drowns in the bog of collective words like aggression, anxiety, sexuality, and so forth.

Furthermore, these responses appeal to the image itself to be present in the response. We answer from the doorway or in the presence of the snake. When talking with the child we are by the duck pond. We are *in the image* and not detached observers.

Let us return to our motto: "whatever you say can and will be used against you.' There are two "yous" in the sentence: the "you" who is imagining and the "you" who is asking questions and explaining. These two "yous" may be enacted by two persons in counseling, and they may be enacted also by each of us alone in our silent dialogues back and forth with ourselves when exploring our private dreams and fantasies. Because the "you" who interprets often explains away the power of its images, the dream asks for silence so as to be kept vital and intact.

This analysis poses a dilemma between two wrongs, between saying nothing on the one hand — just a Rogerian reflective "yes," which often is a repetitive nonintervention — versus conceptualized snake-killing explanations on the other. So, to avoid this dilemma, I do not propose literal silence as if all speech were destructive to imagination. Silence does not have to mean literal silence.

The question is not whether to speak or not to speak. The question is: *how* to speak, *what* to say, *when* to utter? The "when" of intervention, the "what" theoretical framework you use in interpreting, and the "how" of technique to assure, coax, limit, or confront are well-known to counselors. In your training you have lots about timing, theories, and technique. So, let me instead press my point about *whom*.

This "who" who speaks must originate in the same place and speak in the same style as the material spoken to. This inherent correspondence is more than empathy. It is more than a feeling skill. Rather, it is the animal response that gives a human voice to the silence of imagination. It is the voice of a freely imagining agent at home both in the dream and in the arts.

Human Rights

Having linked silence with imagining and wrong speech with injuring imagination, I now want to show both that imagining is important for human rights and that the basis of these rights lies in silence.

Silence presupposes an interior life. When activity is stilled, stimuli are shut down and dulled, and the pressures of relatedness are relaxed, imagination germinates freely — in freedom. Thus, silence has political implications.

Before the right to free speech, free press, free worship, and free elections is the right to remain silent, because this right assumes the free person within, who speaks, who prints, who worships, and who votes — that individualized "who" who shall not be abused, invaded, or constrained. Rights, according to our political notions, are inalienable: they are lodged in the individualized soul; and freedom, according to these same political notions, is exercised by this agent who has something to say or print, who votes personal choices and considers personal gods. All other rights require, first of all, an imagining someone who can consider alternatives, improvise actions, express values, and fantasize outcomes.

Silence assumes the primacy of a psychic person. Inalienable rights are the powers of this inalienable person whose imagining mind has not been alienated. This notion derives from a view of soul which holds that it comes natively endowed. There is individuality from the beginning, and silence is a condition for its flourishing.

The fear of silence, therefore, is not so much a fear of emptiness, the fear that should we be still we would fall into that void of nothing to say or show or tell. Quite the contrary, the fear is of fullness, of the incredible, unpredictable and freewheeling fantasies that are native to the mind and show themselves so readily in dreams. The fear is of our inwardness, which threatens to be an Aladdin's cave or a primeval forest teeming with wildlife.

If silence invites the imagining agent on whom political freedoms depend, then weakening the imagining agent weakens the roots of freedom without attacking the freedoms directly. There is no need to repress freedom of speech or assembly or the right to worship if there is no one "at home" with something to say or with the need to pray. Freedom implies someone who can imagine things otherwise.

Totalitarian states submit imagination to doctrine. The individual imagination is harnessed and censored. Under these conditions of duress, silence stands out as a most precious right; it is clung to fanatically and literalizes into a paranoid secrecy that resists even torture. The human right to remain silent becomes a sacred obligation, a last-ditch defense of the soul. How else can we understand the incredible witness of silence unto death from Salem to Siberia, from Christian martyrs to underground radicals? And how else can we understand the reluctance to tell afterward of the horror endured under torture by its victims: "unspeakable," they often say.

We can also begin to understand the repression in totalitarian states of the other freedoms (e.g., speech, assembly, worship). Sheer freedom, without a responsive imagining agent, runs riot and perverts into chaotic libertinage in a vicious circle of control or chaos. Freedom imagined as total release remains totalitarian. This idea of freedom is merely the imagination of a captive or a slave indicating that the imagination is still captive, still slave to total solutions. The first step out of this totalitarian circle of control or chaos is not the restoration of political freedoms, but the restoration of imagination itself so that it can adequately imagine freedom as located in the inward silence of a concentrated and responsive imagining agent on whom the free exercise of human rights depends.

In short, the sort of democracy envisioned by our founding documents and ensured, one hopes, by the Supreme Court derives from a populace of keenly and lively imagining persons. This democracy is not the numerical democracy so often misrepresented as the egalitarian, quantitative measurement of opinions, which reduces to a democracy of the lowest common denominator; nor is it a democracy of free enterprise, which is actually the misrepresentation of individuality of imagination as individualistic exploitation.

Neither the excessively egalitarian nor the excessively individualistic view is manifested in the founding documents. Rather, they emphasize individualities as the ultimate seat of power, widely differing individualities and an almost anarchic condition of gun-bearing citizens, each of whom is in pursuit of differing happiness and defends private domains. The differing individual imaginations manifesting themselves as differing religious concerns, geographical loyalties, philosophical commitments, and economic goals must be fundamentally affirmed, not dissolved in the ogre's cauldron called America, the

Melting Pot. The founding documents assume these inalienable differences of imagination in the citizenry and so the Constitution had to provide means for negotiating differences — elective, judicial, legislative — as well as be amended by a Bill of Rights.

The Arts in American Education

The relationship between silence, imagination, and human rights in the American democracy raises familiar questions. Do the arts belong in public schools? Why should there be courses in music appreciation? Why learn an instrument at public expense? Why take trips to museums, or offer clay and painting studio classes? Why memorize poems or play theater? What have these activities — usually classed as extracurricular emphasizing their extraneous nature — to do with the earthly ethics of social and economic democracy? Do they in any way make a more informed citizenry and build a better public opinion base regarding the issues of the day? What indeed is the value of the arts for social studies, for society?

The old answers to these questions said the arts were useful for learning history. Or, creative expression fostered personal growth, made a person happier, and thus enriched society. Or, these soft or snap courses did add esthetic accomplishment, producing a finer finish, broadened people, making them more useful to the community as players in the band, public speakers, or managers of children. Of course, the old answers implied that the arts were mainly for women and "artistic personalities" or misfits.

The old answers saw nothing essential in the arts. They were not necessary, merely secondary embellishments, like hobbies or trivial pursuits that would enable one to identify music on the car radio as Wagner or the columns on the bank portal as Doric. If not plain snobbery, the arts are certainly irrelevant for "real" issues like consumer protection, race relations, and the minimum-wage debate.

But the answer that emerges from my argument says something quite different. It says that without an exercised imagination there is an anesthetized stupidity in the public arena, a kind of sense-impaired response to the sensate world. We become insensitive to each other

and to our own sensitivities. We will have lost the ability to be es-
thetically persuaded. If the citizen cannot be moved by an editorial,
a politician's rhetoric, or an attorney's plea, then the Bill of Rights has
no effect. The freedom it enunciates assumes an imagining heart in
the body politic that responds in action. That sensitivity the Athe-
nians — where democracy first began — called *peitho*, the persuasive
goddess on whose ability to affect our souls depends free speech, fair
trial, free press, and elections.

Anesthetized responses are not simply unimaginative and insensitive; they have become merely mechanical reactions to stimuli. No
response means no responsibility. The anesthetized imagination becomes sociopathic and amoral. Without the enlivened imagination
there is no perception of insult and injury, no sense of injustice, and
so no sense of justice either. We are already in the slave camps of the
mind. Without the enlivened imagination there can be no comprehension of the issues at stake and no basis for ethical judgment or political
decision. Why are artists so often involved in social protest and so
protective of human rights? Why is their very presence so threatening
to the totalitarian state? The reason must lie in their dedication to an
imagination trained in silence: having exercised the first freedom, the
right to remain silent, they are acute to the other basic rights.

Hence, rights must be put into practice. As spiritual virtues they
exist *in actu* not *in potenia*. That is, unless we speak out, read, vote, and
assemble, these virtues are mere abstractions written into law but not
behaved in life. Silence, too, is not passively quiet, but needs to be
practiced whether in solitude or as a moment of internal echoing in
the midst of things. The counseling room is a place for this practice,
and therapy is as much an education in silence as in talking.

The ethical shocks now devastating our institutions need to be seen
in the light of our topic. The issues are not simply what rules obtain;
how to define a conflict of interest or an arm's length transaction; how
to distinguish between a tax shelter and a tax evasion, a gift and a
bribe; what precisely constitutes plagiarism, adultery, euthanasia, or
truth in labeling. A technical precision of ethics merely repeats the
same kind of thinking from which comes the disease, and remedies
cannot be concocted from a make-up course in ethics at a weekend

seminar. Ethical sensibility does not exist apart from the moral imagination. For, first of all, we must have that feeling that something is amiss, fishy, or compromising. We must be able to imagine wrong and what it might do to the soul.

Moral imagination is awakened and trained by confrontations with the great moral dilemmas of Abraham and Peter and the Greek tragedies, of Hamlet and Macbeth, of Anna Karenina and Madame Bovary. Novels by Hawthorne, Dostoevsky, Conrad, Faulkner, Orwell, and Roth way surpass the ethical instruction derived from case studies and legal precedents, because the study of great lives and literature opens the imagining heart to moral perplexity, rather than providing rules, conventions, and answers. If we cannot imagine honor, dignity, sacrifice, compassion, courage, loyalty, as well as ugliness of soul and the sins of avarice, how can we make an ethical decision or even recognize that there is one to be made? Besides, there is a morality of craft, the moral imagination of the hands, the ears, and eyes. The arts teach getting it right, doing it well, and an honest job that is truthful to the claim of the work.

If this be the case, then the new answer to the old question about the relationship between the arts and social studies goes like this. The arts are not an adjunct; the arts are rather the place where silence is fostered by reading, writing, throwing a pot, practicing the clarinet, or stretching at the barre. These activities in silence, by challenging collective anesthesia, activate the imagining person at the heart of all social and political life. Artistic activities are more than just worthwhile in themselves, because they ground the rest of the curriculum in a truly human agent.

This conclusion bears directly upon dyslexia and illiteracy. Why have we as a nation become more and more illiterate? We blame television and the computer, but they are not causes. They are results of a prior condition that invited them in. They arrived to fill a gap. When imaginative ability declines, other ways to communicate appear. These ways work even though they, too, are dyslexic in structure; simultaneity of bits, odd juxtapositions, messages that do not move linearly from left to right. Yet television and personal computers communicate.

Evidently, reading does not depend solely on the ordering of words or the ordering of letters in the words. Indeed, poets use dyslexic structures deliberately. Reading depends on the psyche's capacity to enter imagination. Reading is more like dreaming, which, too, goes on in silence. Our illiteracy reflects our educative process away from the silent grounds of reading; silent study halls and quiet periods, learning by heart, listening through a whole class without interruptions, writing an essay exam in longhand, drawing from nature instead of lab experiments. This long neglect of imaginational conditions that foster reading — Sputnik and the new math; social problems and social relatedness; me-centered motivation; the confusion of information with knowledge, of opinion with judgment, and trivia with sources; communication as messages by telephone calls, e-mails, and answering machines rather than as letter writing in silence; learning to speak up without first having learned something to say; multiple choice and scoring as a test of comprehension — has produced illiteracy.

The human person as a data bank does not need to read more than functionally. A data bank deciding yes or no on the basis of feedback (i.e., reinforcement) need not imagine beyond getting, storing, and spending. Just get the instructions right; never mind the content. Learn the "how" rather than the "what" with its qualities, values, and subtleties. Then the human agent becomes an incarnated credit card performing the religious rituals of consumerism. You need only be able to sign your name in the space marked "X," like an immigrant, like a slave, or a . . .

Or a psychopath. Descriptions of psychopathy, or sociopathic personalities, speak of their inability to imagine the other. Psychopaths are well able to size up situations and charm people. They perceive, assess, and relate, making use of any opportunity. Hence their successful manipulations of others. But the psychopath is far less able to imagine the other beyond a fantasy of usefulness, unable to perceive the other as a true interiority with his or her own needs, intentions, and feelings. An education that in any way neglects imagination is an *education into psychopathy*. It is an education that results in a sociopathic society of manipulations. We learn how to deal with others and become a society of dealers.

Neither the media, legal or illegal drugs, the education bureaucracy, nor the absent moral authority of parents are to blame for the ethical vacuum and our stupefaction. These usual scapegoats are the symptoms and, as such, are not causes but the presentation of prior invisible suffering. In fact, symptoms are failed attempts at a cure. The turn to crack and cocaine, for example, is partly in search of higher imagining to awaken the dead. The education bureaucracy arose to bridge the great gaps in imagination between the desire to learn and desire to teach. The authority of parenting faded long ago when esthetic skills, and thus sensitive responses, were considered inferior to moral rules. A morality literalized into rules is but a mechanized skeleton following commandments, incognizant of the moral struggle demanded by a life of imagination.

No, it is not the media that are to blame. Where the media may not accurately report the state of the world or the emotions of the family or the piety of faith, media do indeed report their audience. That television glass in the living room accurately reflects the psyche that sits before it. Television is a mirror showing us our own faces.

If we must blame, then let us blame ourselves. We counselors are supposedly the remedial force. Do we give our clients the right to remain silent or do we pump them up with more information? Do we assume a soul rich with native endowment within their depressive passivity or recalcitrant learning disorders? Do we encourage the client's fantasies and dreams with our speaking, or cut them down to the reduced size of our meager explanations? Do we recognize the inherent necessity of imagining in the human person as the guarantor of the person's freedom and the vitality of our political system? Do we stand authoritatively and administratively, or can we stand subversively, as did Freud, Jung, Adler, Reich, and Socrates and Jesus too. Those therapeutic educators are the founding figures of the helping profession, standing subversively against the state of the society when it is unethical, sociopathic, unimaginative. Or do we persuade adaptation to that society as we 'help" our clients to cope, get along, relate. Relate to what? Don't we ask them to adapt to a nonimaginal world at the cost of the silent, imagining, animal agent on whom the world's very life depends?

Conclusion

I will end with a final flourish of rhetorical politics. Counselors are the actual freedom fighters. We are freedom fighters not only because of our outrage over race discrimination and oppressions of sex and gender, over corporate exploitation and consumerism's poverty, over child spoiling and child neglect, drug corruption, callous pollution, abortion and contraception absurdity, textbook destructions, military machismo, bureaucratic pettifoggery; fundamentalist deceit and fund-raising hypocrisy, to say nothing of the staggering gamut of client tragedies that counselors must face daily. We are freedom fighters because we are the advanced guard of imagination as it tries to break into our civilization by touching its citizens through the symptoms of its discontents. And we are the advanced guard because we, like the artists, are the ones authorized to meet the symptoms by imaginal means.

We have been given the tools of art therapy, sand play, drama, dance, and clay, and rooms for conversation and silence. Moreover, we, unlike the artists, have been given a special authority to use these imagining tools with the civilization's victims, the symptomatically disenfranchised who are our clients. I would remind you especially of the disenfranchised children who carry so much of our civilization's disordered imagination, too conveniently, too rationally called "adjustment disorders" and "behavior disorders." In Nicaragua, Afghanistan, Sudan, Transvaal, Iraq, and places dropped from the news or not even noticed by it, children lie on the battlefield and die in hunger. Our nation's children wither in soul, victims of another attrition and another hunger: the systematic anesthesia of imagination in the name of development and achievement. The push forward, starting ever earlier, has kept them out of the halls of fantasy, depriving them of that great gift with which each child comes endowed: the wonder of silence.

Through them and our work with them in "silence, exile, and cunning"[5] the small beginnings of the freely imagining agent may subversively reenter the community and stealthily infiltrate the body politic.

"That civilization may not sink, / its great battle lost / Quiet the dog, tether the pony,"[6] for, as William Butler Yeats wrote in the same poem, "Like a long-legged fly upon the stream / [the] mind moves upon silence."

1. Adolf Guggenbühl-Craig, *Power in the Helping Professions* (Dallas: Spring Publications, 1971).

2. Seonaid Robertson, *Rosegarden and Labyrinth: A Study in Art Education* (Dallas: Spring Publications, 1982).

3. Howard McConeghey, *Art and Soul* (Putnam, Conn.: Spring Publications, 2003).

4. Mary Watkins, "Six Approaches to the Image in Art Therapy, " *Spring: An Annual of Archetypal Psychology and Jungian Thought* (1981), pp. 107–25.

5. James Joyce, *Portrait of the Artist as a Young Man* (New York: Viking Press, 1964), p. 247.

6. W.B. Yeats, "Long-Legged Fly," in *Collected Poems* (London: Macmillan, 1952).

7

Power *and* Gemeinschaftsgefühl

This is a rather remarkable, perhaps historical, event: a Jungian invited to be in your Adlerian community, to usher in this annual conference. Perhaps your hospitable invitation ushers in a new social feeling in the larger community; perhaps the classic schools, Freudian, Adlerian, Jungian, Rankian, Reichian, Kleinian, Lacanian, Kohutian — and there are even some Hillmaniacs out there — belong in a larger brother- and sisterhood. For we are all dedicated to the soul and its inalienable rights, attempting in our daily work to maintain a psychological perspective, the viewpoint of soul toward all things. What keeps our community a community despite all our differences is this dedication to soul. We are the only ones in the helping professions — teachers, ministers, nurses, developmentalists, activists, physicians — whose root metaphor is psyche.

I say historical because there has been so much division — all the schools and their advocates attacking each other. The way to overcome division is not merely to bury the hatchet and promote sweet harmony; rather, it would be to see the necessity in the symptom. What is the value of this phenomenon, division, as such, rather than we divide further over its causes and arguments? What's the purpose in this guiding fiction? What gains does division give?

For one thing, the dividing that goes on between schools demarcates them, not only as boundaries of territory, but also as boundaries

Delivered as an invitational paper at the 1987 annual meeting of the North American Society of Adlerian Psychology in Fort Wayne, Ind., and first published in *Individual Psychology* 44/1 (March 1988).

of style. Splitting is not only a power move, keeping what is mine from what is yours, nor only a logical one, arguing from different premises to different conclusions. Splitting is as well an aesthetic necessity. By means of radical cuts, we draw a hard edge, frame a canvas, end a sentence with a full stop, bring a concerto to a finale. Here, this ends. It goes no further. Sharp divisions refuse soft fuzzy eclecticism, false flabby unifications, watered-down holisms. Instead, an original vision formed by its constraints becomes a style, a school.

So we don't integrate Freudian drive theory into Adlerian psychology or Adlerian "as if" into Jungian commitment to the Self. Hard edges exclude and give definition.

The inner constraints determine the style of your work and prepare a grid by which you see things. Andrew Wyeth does not paint like Picasso, and George Gershwin makes different music from Stravinsky; but their dedication to the discipline keeps them in a common vision. So, I want to admit and stand for fundamental distinctions between the schools, between Jungians and Adlerians, each maintaining its disciplines, its style of thinking, feeling, and acting, just as the styles of artistic schools let us both express ourselves and keep us limited. Yet, at the same time, below the divisions flows the commonality of *Gemeinschaftsgefühl*, as among painters or poets who may vilify each other as rivals, but deeply recognize their common commitment to poetry and painting as such.

Let me illustrate this first point (that we do not truly integrate the viewpoint of another school try as we will with the best intentions) by telling you a bit about my own training at the Jung Institute in Zurich. This was in the 1950s; Carl and Emma Jung were both active. I was even examined by Emma Jung on "Theory of Dreams and Interpretation." One of our eight subjects for our oral exams, preparatory to seeing our first patients under supervision, was "Comparative Theory of Neurosis," and another of the eight was "Theory of Analytical Psychology," that is, Jung's theoretical concepts. Adler's Individual Psychology was included in both of these exams as it still is today, not only in Zurich but in the exams of other Jungian Institutes that follow the Zurich model.

We read Adler. We had lectures comparing Jung with Adler and Freud, following lines laid by Jung himself and his early pupils — who in the 1930s wrote at least three books that Jung recommended comparing the three schools.[1] And we were examined on Adler's theory of neurosis. Occasionally, Adlerians came to the Zurich Institute to explain his works more in detail and, later in the 1960s while I was Director of Studies of my *alma mater*, this exchange of thought continued. Rudolf Dreikurs, in fact, a very large fact, came to talk to us and we were immensely impressed with his assurance, his self-esteem, his wonderful practicality, and what seemed to us to be a true absence of an inferiority complex.

I say all this not to boast that I know Adler's work well, but to show that we were open to reading him, to coming to grips with his viewpoint. In this we were following Jung, who wrote, "No one who is interested in 'psychoanalysis' and who wants to get anything like an adequate survey of the whole field of modern psychiatry should fail to study the writings of Adler. He will find them extremely stimulating . . ." (CW 4, p. 756). In his *Psychological Types* Jung explains his concept of compensation (a major component of Jung's theory of dreams and symptoms) by acknowledging its source in Adler, whom Jung credits with the introduction of the idea of compensation into psychology (CW 6, pp. 693f.). In an earlier paper (1913), Jung says the "dream is a subliminal process of comprehension by analogy," adding, "on this particular point I find myself in entire agreement with the views of Adler" (CW 4, p. 553). In another paper (CW 4, p. 564), about the same time, he again agrees with Adler about the way the neurotic overvalues his or her infantile past, exaggerating its importance and thereby creating a fixation.

In 1948 Jung wrote an article, "Depth Psychology," for the *Lexicon of Pedagogy*, in which, after several paragraphs detailing Adler's contributions, Jung says (CW 18, p. 1154), ". . . the services rendered by Adler and his school to the phenomenology of personality disturbances in children should not be overlooked. Above all, it must be emphasized that a whole class of neuroses can in fact be explained primarily in terms of the power drive."

Finally, in 1950, when Jung was 75, he was asked in a letter why Freud and Adler divided. Jung answered, saying that, "Freud indeed couldn't see that Adler's views were justified by facts."[2]

Looking back now on all this, and the way we Jungians learned about Adler in the 1950s and 1960s in Zurich, I can lay it out in this way. What we do not have in Adler is the mythical grandeur of things, the highbrow mind, and the wide vision. No symbols, archeology, cultural anthropology, Eastern wisdom, Christian mysticism and theology, Latin and Greek terms, alchemical philosophy, theoretical physics — all those marvelous and sustaining fictions that hold one in Jungian psychology, all the mystical and shamanistic pretensions, as well as the Swiss earthiness.

What we do not find in Jung, however, is the main subject of our talk this evening, a subject so important that I could not resist your invitation — a social feeling, fellow feeling, community concern, *Gemeinschaftsgefühl*.

Just that social point was missed in our training. We were taught Adler through Jung's eyes. Our way of thinking was: arranging the career of your fictions was an ego-directed project and the ego was the ultimate arbiter. Jungians did not hear the other half of the Adlerian equation: aligning and adjusting the fictions to the social world, as if the social world were only the literal reality principle of Freud or a mere persona, just an "out there" that any neurotic would he having trouble with. We did not grasp the true depth in Adler's psychology and therefore declared it merely an ego psychology. We were continuing in the prejudice set up decades earlier by Freud and by Jung in letters to each other (F 147 and J 217) who each said that Adler was not psychological.[3] Freud and Jung had located depth in only one place. They did not gasp the true depth in the "out there," in the *Gemeinschaft*. And we were Jungians whose grid and style undervalued this *Gemeinschaft* as "only the collective" to which one adapted compromisingly, through the persona. It was not a true guiding fiction, like our "superior" guiding fiction: the individuation process. Only when that process advanced to an advanced, almost mystical, description would one be able to experience *unus mundus*, an ultimate unity of the inner depths with the outer world.

Later, I came to see that this unity is also a fiction. This unity of inner and outer itself depends on thinking in opposites, which in itself is a neurotic mode of thinking and like any neurotic mode of thinking maintains a defense and thus becomes a fictitious goal. Although there are plenty of remarks in Jung to show he, too, understood his goals as hypothetical ideas or signposts, not as achievements, we students who became Jungians were fundamentally defended against Adlerian depth of thought by our own concepts. Our concepts devalued the area, the *Gemeinschaft*, where Adlerian depth, it seems to me, actually lies.

So you see, despite good will, best intention, and honest training, our Jungian style of thought and perceptual grid did not allow us fully to see or feel Adler. And my point again is: eclecticism does not really work. There are, indeed, different schools. There are, indeed, distinctions and hard edges because a body of good ideas is a structure. It brings with it internal constraints that give the body of ideas coherence, vision, and style. As Stravinsky said, "Whatever diminishes constraint diminishes strength." Force, power, and strength derive from formed visions. You cannot just take a piece of this and add to it a piece of that without, on the one hand, importing the whole body into your new eclectic system or, on the other hand, without radically lopping off a bit so it is "out of context" and does not really make sense.

The best you can do, I believe, is to work more deeply within your own school, discover hidden recesses that can be worked further, enriching your inheritance and deepening your loyalty. In my work I've tried to do this with Jung, but also with Freud and Adler, not that they are my schools, but in as much as my community feeling feels for these three as the foundations of the field that has given me my philosophical outlook and professional life.

Let me go back a moment. I want to be clearer about Adlerian depth and why Jung and Freud could not see it. Where is this depth? What is its topology, to use Freud's term? You recall he said the unconscious has an altogether different topology; it has its own region with its own laws. It is in another *topos*, the Greek word for place.

From the beginning the unconscious was imagined as a deeper region, in the depths of the interior person's emotions, attitudes, wishes, fears, and images; or back in the depths of the forgotten past, in memory, personal or historical or cultural or linguistic; or down in the lower person, morally put down, evolutionally lower scale, or biogenetically or biochemically below. Only Adler, it seems, located this deeper other place out there — but not only out there in the singular you and your relationships, but out there in a plural you, all of the "yous" of human society and the deeper issues of common human concern.

Of course, both Freud and Jung, too, saw the importance of out there. Freud wrote of "the discontent of civilization," and the Freudian left in the 1960s declared that not much could change in the individual patient unless the unconscious out there, the psyche of the world, were to undergo radical change by allowing the pleasure principle and eros — shall we say *Gemeinschaftsgefühl* with a Freudian slant — to emerge from repression. Jung wrote many "essays on contemporary events," the very name of one of his books. Jung, too, recognized the plight of our Western civilization and the collective disintegration that threatened each individual.

Yet neither Freud nor Jung imagined far enough, fundamentally enough, into the disorder of the world of concrete things, government institutions, commercial practices—the physical, political, and economic unconscious — those symptoms and those pathologies. Freud and Jung and their schools internalize the world and believe it can be dealt with mainly in an internalized fashion. Clean up your own neurosis and that will clean up the world. Analysis for everybody: architects, politicians, teachers, lawyers, and then you will have better buildings, better government, better education, and better lawsuits.

I think an Adlerian must see things very differently. If the out there is a primary place of the unconscious, then the ways of the world must be tackled directly. Hence, we understand Adler's interest in teachers and tailors and in the socialist movement. Politics is psychology: depth psychology is also depth sociology; to go truly deep is to go into the soul of the world.

Yes, power conflicts operate between parts of the psyche. Yes, there is an internal struggle to master and suppress. But let us not forget the clash of powers in the psychic depths of the world soul disguised as political, natural, social, and economic. Moreover, this world soul, this depth psychology out there, is a symptomatic mess filled with insecurities and inferiorities, and this epidemic miasma, now called pollution, erosion, toxic waste, competition, defense, terrorism, scams and corruption, overpopulation and underdevelopment, unemployment, cannot but impinge upon each individual soul no matter how well analyzed, how pampered by the safe, enclosed space of the consulting room, a pampering called therapy that often may be a cover-up and substitute for disempowerment and separation from community with the world soul. For me, Adler's psychology today leads out of the consulting room into the world soul and its suffering. That is how I read him and that is why I am so happy to be with you this evening.

So, if time allows, a few further reflections along these lines. There is today a curious societal phenomenon that is worth looking at from an Adlerian perspective, because this phenomenon directly connects with disempowerment, inferiority, and *Gemeinschaftsgefühl*. I am referring to the new communities based on styles of personal suffering: Weight Watchers, Drug Abusers, Battered Wives, Rape Victims, Alcoholics Anonymous, Ex-Convicts, Parolees, Parkinson groups, AIDS groups, Exhibitionists, Vietnam Vets, Divorcees, Handicapped, Daughters of Alcoholic Fathers. We are joined by our pathologies and affiliate in terms of our symptoms. The symptom as admission ticket into a group: Hello, my name is Caryl and I weigh 285 pounds. Hello, my name is Harry; I have been dry 14 months today.

Therapists encourage these organizations by running groups of patients: why do they do this? Why did Jung, as early as 1915, begin the Psychological Club in Zurich for his patients so that they could meet one another in a social and educational setting, deepening by extending their common interest in analysis? Similar clubs formed wherever Jungian analysis took root: London, Basel, San Francisco, New York. Membership required having been a patient, having had at least fifty hours of Jungian analysis. Association occurs according with common interest.

Yes, but these clubs were also based in personal pathology, in the inferiority feelings and societal inferiority that one is a patient, a neurotic, whose neurosis is a badge of approval. Just here we see again the value of the Adlerian point of view. These groups were not set up to protect and pamper, to give a secondary gain to neurotics — or alcoholics, or overweights, or veterans, or exhibitionists who could not adjust to the "real" social world and so had to have a special one established for them by the good parent, their analyst. This might be partly the case, of course. Far more important is that the group welcomed social connection through inferiority, a new kind of societal connection that gives full place to inferiority. Empowerment to membership is given with one's inherent inferiority. Lions Clubs, Rotary, and professional organizations start the other way around. In these old models we are joined by success, by accomplishment, by persona. In the old clubs to be in therapy is a blemish. Inferiority is suppressed so as to appear "normal," where "normal" has come to mean striving for superiority, and is therefore a diagnosis of pathology, the one pathology omitted by the DSM III.

The new model arises from the age of therapy and carries therapy right into society. We are joined together by virtue of our inherent weakness. The new model may not be quite so new after all. I have to admit that it seems to echo primitive Christianism where one is joined through Christ's unhealed wounds, that eternal bleeding and one's own indelible sins, originally there, congenital, much like an organic inferiority.

These new groups, however, have all the strength and weakness of single issue politics. To view the world through only one window, the window of identity with my pounds on the scale, my drinking, my sexual proclivities, my physical inferiority — although this does admit inferiority — still does not come to grips with its roots, the roots in disenfranchisement, disempowerment. What notion of the world do we have that makes it a place only for the masterful? Why must being-in-the-world, as the existentialists would say, require the power of mastery, of superiority?

This notion of the world comes from Darwin, from Locke, from Hobbes, from Descartes, a notion of the world we have lived within for hundreds of years, a notion that has robbed the world completely of its depth and its soul. Out there is mere matter, objective, dead, said Descartes and Kant, echoing Jesus' "my kingdom is not of this world" and "render unto Caesar," a world of power plays with dead, objective things you can manipulate at will. Herbicides, landfills, river pollution,

strip mining, and other multinational agribusiness conglomerate horrors, even the litter in our streets begins not merely in the need and
greed of industrialized consumerism. The way we treat the world out
there begins in excluding it from the realm of soul, as if it were a
great Cartesian corpse. Dead matter does not matter. Our human superiority derives from the manipulation of the corpse by our technology — necrophilia. Our mastery over the world with dams, fertilizers,
pesticides, internal combustion engines, refineries, silicon chips, and
garbage barges is both a perversion and a delusion, for the world out
there is not a dead body of raw materials. It is a repository of soul.
To forget this world is to live already now in the nuclear winter. The
nuclear winter is merely the logic of our soulless world view followed
to the end; the ironically logical consequent of a world declared dead
centuries ago by our Western religion and philosophy.

Precisely here, in the face of world catastrophe, Adler's *Gemeinschaftsgefühl* offers so much. It offers so much not only for individual therapy,
but for the wider, more important issue of world therapy, therapy of
the soul of the world, the suffering of the *anima mundi*, as it has been
called by Platonists. I refer to the deep symptoms disturbing nature,
society, institutions and, consequently, our individual lives.

As some of you know, else you would hardly have invited me, I have
already devoted some thought to Adler's notion of *Gemeinschaftsgefühl*.[4]
This idea seems to be the abiding current of love in his work, appearing as the metapsychology in his thought and the feeling atmosphere
in his person that evoked such loyal testimony from his patients
and friends.

Just here, at the end of the century of which Adler was at the start,
we can carry his intentions further. I am speaking of that main feeling,
"of intimate belonging to the full spectrum of humanity."[5] If we follow
the ironic logic of *Gemeinschaftsgefühl* fully into community, community
does not stop with human beings. To stay there is to stay at the beginning of the century.

To stay there is to stay in Christian and Roman, and Cartesian scientific thought, which denied soul to animals and plants, as well as to
rocks and waters, and, of course, to everything made of matter. Adler
recognized "the general interdependence of the cosmos from which

we cannot abstract ourselves completely!"[6] So we may not reduce the cosmos to society, to human beings only. That interdependence today includes the rocks and the waters, the soil and the air, and all material things made by the human community as well — the buildings we must work in, the streets we walk, the foods we eat, and the clothes we wear. This world, too, has been disempowered by ugliness, distortions, and sham, inferior materials, inferior design, inferior quality, and above all by our inferior attention, our disregard of it as only an outer thing, throwaway, dead. Yet it is from these souls that we cannot abstract ourselves completely, these souls that impinge upon us daily in every unconscious way, from the styrofoam cup and underarm deodorant to the wasteland lots of suburban parking in which the world soul visibly suffers, a suffering shared in our souls and our patients.

The base of inferiority can never be resolved by human exertion in the human world alone. Try as we will, we succeed only in repressing aggrandizement with false modesty and hypocrisy. Instead of manipulating others, we manipulate ourselves into being good and kind: empowerment at the expense of ourselves rather than at the expense of others. Something else is needed besides a mutual social contract that merely repeats the old, and I think evidently failed, Christian moral duty to do unto others as you would have them do unto you. No, if inferiority is to be fundamentally resolved, inferiority must first be located not merely socially but, in a wide scheme of things, fundamentally cosmological. When the base of inferiority is set in a community beyond the human, then empowerment can come from beyond the human, our self-respect given not by others only. This self-respect is the empowerment coming from the mutual giving and receiving with a larger community feeling, feeling deeply into the suffering and beauty of things out there, in service to this larger vision of *Gemeinschaft*.

My basic inferiority is not due to your superiority, not due to my native organic weakness, nor to the power social forces exercise over me. My inferiority is truly native, given organically with the position of the human in the world, that the human soul is not isolate. It is in deepest community with the soul of the world. We must breathe its air and drink its waters, live with animals, insects, and bacteria as one animal kind among others, draw shelter and nourishment from the soil, and respond to all of them, each of them, with our hands and our speech. This is our cosmic dependence, our eternal worldly inferiority, a humility that grounds all humanity. And if, as Adler said, contribution is the true meaning of life,[7] then contribution could now be defined as service to the world soul, a service that practices inferiority rather than overcomes it.

As this country is moving from a productive economy to a service economy, we are already unconsciously recognizing new forms of empowerment: empowerment through service and rewards for service. We are moving from the necrophiliac, delusional superiority of the production-consumption waste cycle to the more inferior posture of nursing and caring and repairing and maintaining and teaching and guarding and counting in a community feeling with all things. By this attention, we restore soul to what had been mere matter of fact, mere data, feeling the "givenness," "the gifts," which *data* means. By taking account of each thing, we begin to find they count. Other creatures and things count and matter very, very much.

Therapy does not stop with the patient's psyche, for the patient's psyche does not stop with his or her skin, with his or her personal life. "We refuse to recognize and examine an isolated human being,"[8] As the borders of psyche cannot be limited, as Heraclitus said 2500 years ago, so therapy extends beyond its old constraints to a wider sense of service.

And service, after all, is what the word therapy, *therapeia*, originally means; attendant upon, attention to, caring for, in service of. It bears in it a religious feeling.

So, finally, I will not translate *Gemeinschaftsgefühl* with the term "social concern" or "social feeling" — but rather with our ordinary English word "common," as the village green in my New England hamlet was once a common for all bodies, human and nonhuman, to take part in common, care for in common, enjoy in common, common as ordinary, as common to all, this world so very common, so very dear, so much the source and the goal of our feeling.

1. Cf. W. M. Kranefeldt (1930), *Secret Ways of the Mind: A Survey of the Psychological Principles of Freud, Adler, and Jung* (New York: Holt, 1932); G. R. Heyer (1932), *The Organism of the Mind: An Introduction to Analytical Psychotherapy* (London: Kegan Paul, Trench, Trubner & Co., 1933); G. Adler, *Entdeckung der Seele: Von Sigmund Freud und Alfred Adler zu C. G. Jung* (Zurich: Rascher, 1934).

2. *C. G. Jung Letters*, eds. Gerhard Adler and Aniela Jaffé, Bollingen Series (Princeton: Princeton University Press, 1973), 1:557.

3. *The Freud/Jung Letters*, ed. William McGuire, Bollingen Series (Princeton: Princeton University Press, 1974), p. 235: "He is a theorist astute and original but not attuned to Psychology . . ." (Freud); p. 364: ". . . Adler for the total absence of Psychology" (Jung).

4. Cf. my *Healing Fiction* (Putnam, Conn.: Spring Publications, 2004), pp. 83–130 and notes.

5. Walter F. O'Connell, "Individual Psychology," in *New Catholic Encyclopedia* (New York: McGraw Hill, 1967).

6. Henri F. Ellenberger, *The Discovery of the Unconscious* (New York: Basic Books, 1970), p. 609.

7. Alfred Adler, *What Life Should Mean to You*, trans. Colin Brett (Center City, Minn.: Hazelden, 1998), p. 7: "True meaning of life depends on contribution and cooperation."

8. The Individual Psychology of Alfred Adler, eds. Heinz L. and Rowena R. Ansbacher (New York: Harper Perennial, 1964), p. 126.

8

Psychology, Self, and Community

The idea I most relied upon for much of my life and work, and have since become most suspicious of, is Individuality, Individualism, or Individuation. Curious, isn't it, that what one relies on most, one is also more distrustful of. Curious that Trust and Betrayal are such bedfellows. Or maybe not so curious for the paranoid schizoid personality.

When I entered analysis in 1953, I was completely taken by Jung's idea of individuation, of an immanent Self within the breast that urges each human being away from the collective fold into an individual destiny. The feeling of being a separate self, privately interior, protected, meant blessed — and anxious — with trust in an invisible force or luck unique to me — call it Puer Eternus, Mother Complex, American Arrogance, White Privilege, Narcissistic Personality Structure, or Sun-Moon conjunct in Aries — who knows? But how satisfying and congruent were Jung's ideas of an individuating Self that could give theoretical and even theological foundation to the despairs of seldomness, estrangement, and an actively-denied sensitivity.

The idea of individuation privileged me to live "my own style" of mental obsessions. I did of course those things my family had done before me and that one did in the fifties — big wedding, four children, long analysis, clinic, practice, publications — the keeping-up-and-at an advancing career. But all this was only the persona coat that kept safe and hidden the heroic isolation of a writing mind which turned

---

1 Adapted from remarks made upon receipt of the Recognition Award, Center for Psychology and Social Change, November 17, 1993, Cambridge, Mass. First published in *Resurgence* 166 (September/October 1994).

life into formulae. These "outer" things were only the necessary accompaniments or accomplices — the wife, the children, the patients — to the inner care of thoughts and images in the room of one's own, the room of individuation.

Switzerland was the ideal place for this: strange Giacometti, Honegger, Dürrenmatt, and Max Frisch. Near where I ate lunch, Lenin had been here in hiding; Dada was founded just down the hill; Wagner's apartment across from my office; Nietzsche in Basel; Einstein in Berne; Paul Klee; Corbusier in Geneva — the private secret banks, chronometry, precision tools — political non-alignment, mountainous refuge for Rilke, Hesse, Kirchner, Thomas Mann's final exit and grave, Joyce buried 300 yards from where I slept at night and, of course, Jung, and the psychiatry at Zurich's Burghölzli clinic — Bleuler, Adolf Meyer, Binswanger, Rorschach — and so on. Remember: it was in Zurich that schizophrenia was invented and in Basel, LSD. I stayed there until unable to differentiate individuation from alienation.

One of the cherished formulations that sustained me during the extreme asocial introversion of my 1950s and 1960s was this: when all collapses, what do I have ultimately to sustain me? What is the undeniable core from which one can live? The question reflected a social and political context which I, immersed in individualism, then did not recognize. (The very philosophy of individualism resists seeing social context.)

Now, however, I see this question about ultimate existential support within the climate of the post-World War II and the cold-war world. A context of ghosts of concentration camps, displaced persons, and stalags (Stalin died the week I had my first analytical hour), philosophies of Existentialism, tanks in Hungary, wars in Israel, the Bay of Pigs; ruined European cities, burning American cities; bomb-testings, bombshelters, and fall-out; Swiss mountain larders stocked with emergency rations; the riots in Algiers and shootings in Paris, Alabama, Arkansas, Mississippi; Korea, Prague, imprisonments, evacuations, panic, doom, and the increasing horror of Vietnam, so distant from Switzerland.

What if I were imprisoned? What does one have when all is lost and the soul is *in extremis*? Alone. There is only one's own inner world, the individuating process in the soul unfolding the meanings of its destiny.

Only your images remain. Only your inner voices, only the spirits that come to you in your cell. Nothing else can be trusted since nothing else is authentically individually mine. Inside are the repertories that legitimate reason and justify action — *an individualized center the only sustaining base when all else has gone.* So was how I thought; such was my conclusion.

That fixed center, called Self by Jung, and by many religious disciplines and philosophical traditions, also appears in Emerson's definition of the hero. The hero, said Emerson, is he who is immovably centered. Emerson gives voice to the long tradition, flowering in Protestantism and maintained devotedly by most varieties of psychotherapy, the faith in heroic individualism, man alone — and woman too — centered on a divine spark inside the breast that guides, and may even save. The right person, the hero, lives always centered immovably upon this spark.

And before we adjourn this evening, I shall raise some severe doubts about this individualistic ontology that was my faith and remains the silent faith of psychotherapy in general.

But first to adhere to our therapeutic tradition. I shall bring a case of utter isolation, a case that sets up exactly our question about the Self which sustains the soul *in extremis.* The case of Mr. Liu Qing as reported in the *New York Times* by Michael Kaufman, March 30, 1993.

The case I am using derives from the pathology of culture rather than from the pathology of the individual. I do this pointedly to free psychopathology from its enclosure in the individual self where it is attributed to personality development, structure, and reactions. If we of this Society seek ways to connect psychotherapy with social change, we must also *re*-imagine "case material." If we wish to release depth psychology from its confines in human personality and return study of soul, *logos* of *psyche*, to the larger world beyond the human, we must also draw our cases from pathologies in the culture such as the torture of living creatures, like Mr. Liu Qing, for the sake of doctrinal ideas in politics, but also in science, religion, medicine, and art. Mr. Liu served eleven years in Weinan No. 2 prison in Shaanxi Province where for some four-and-a-half years he was literally immovably centered, forced to sit without moving on a stool, eight inches high, from

8:00 am till 12:00, from 1:30 to 7:00 pm, and then until 9:00 pm. He could lie down at night. "I was not allowed to move or to talk to the prisoners watching me. If I did, I would be beaten."

The occasion of Kaufman's article is Mr. Liu's acceptance of a prize on behalf of his mentor, Mr. Wei, a dissident still in Chinese prison. It was because of Mr. Liu's activities and affiliation with this mentor that Mr. Liu was put in that jail and to that torture. After release, he married the woman who waited for him during the imprisonment.

Mr. Liu reports that while he sat those years on the stool staring at a wall he tried to kill himself by not eating; he played mental games; he conjured visions of food, counted minutes, speculated about astronomy and black holes, and much else.

Now to this important bit of data: "Mr. Liu said that he often considered escaping from the stool by signing a statement of self-criticism. People had come from Beijing and told me that all I had to do to assure a successful future was to sign a statement saying that I made some mistakes in my thinking. It did not involve naming anyone. As I sat there I would think 'it is a lie, and they know it is a lie, so why not do it and stop suffering.' But then I would imagine them coming into the cell, putting the paper in front of me and at that point I knew I could not do it."

Let us now understand Mr. Liu's remarkable endurance and refusal to sign a lie from the two contrasting ideas of Self. The first idea is from the heroic ontology of individualism, which I already described. The second from a definition of Self as "the interiorization of community," which I introduced and only sketchily elaborated in *We've Had a Hundred Years of Psychotherapy and The World is Getting Worse* (co-authored with Michael Ventura). What "in" Mr. Liu kept him from signing that paper? On what did Mr. Liu rely? And Mr. Liu is only one example among thousands of isolated individuals in similar jails in similar plights — even as we sit here together in comfort.

A classical Freudian reply is: the still small voice of the conscience prior to all contingencies. This super-ego is derived at root from introjected parental authorities. It sets the interior standards of inhibition. A classical Jungian answer is: the voice speaks like the famous *daimon* of Socrates. It told him not *what* to do, but what *not* to do, an inhibiting voice. It does not so much propose right action as prevent wrong action, thereby keeping a person from going astray, but remaining correctly centered. This is the inner truth of the hero archetype. As it did not prompt Socrates to escape from prison, so it did not press Mr. Liu to make false confession to relieve his suffering.

Besides the Freudian and Jungian accounts, there is a third. This view starts from the fact that Mr. Liu's refusal to sign was primarily an imaginal act. He *imagined* the paper he was to sign. Something to do with imagination, something imaginal did not allow the mock confession. This suggests that imagination can be a force, even a moral force; superior to external contingencies, because — I will now claim — it provides a community of beings who would not permit his betrayal of them.

I am trying to suggest to you that the heroic immovable center is less a single monad, an inner replica of a single God, than it is a group ethos consisting of the images of his also jailed mentor Mr. Wei, and the woman waiting, his wife, and the figures who embodied the principles, ideals, and values he shares, such as imagos of Truth, Justice, Dignity, Honor, that in Classic civilization were configured as persons with statues and altars, and perhaps also his dead ancestors on the other side of the grave as well as his dissident compatriots on the other side of the wall.

These figures are imaginal presences. Mary Watkins calls them "invisible guests." They were not actual people whose names Mr. Liu might have been asked to betray. Although "only" imaginal, they were more persuasive than his physical suffering. Imagine them as an interior platoon, a secret society, a tribal unit like an initiation group, a company of martyrs, an inner city of ancestors and descendents — and we, hearing the tale told by Mr. Liu via Mr. Kaufman, are further descendants in some strange way now associated with that company. Perhaps this is why it is so important to the soul to hear the stories of courage and glory, of beauty and faith, because these heroic remembrances strengthen and feed — not the immovable isolated center in heroic imitation — but the invisible guests. Hence, Homer and the epic tales of the Bible keep a human civilization going on by nourishing the inhuman spirits. They seem to love a good story; they especially seem to like to hear about themselves.

This interpretation of Mr. Liu's refusal invites reflection on the importance of ancestors who back you up. How do you observe them in your days? The importance of the groups you join, the loves you enjoy, the mentors you learn from, the figures you venerate, and the articulation of your ideals. Are you keeping your spirits alive? To what degree does the way you live your ideals foster an imaginal presence that might become a member of an interior community of a person, like Mr. Liu, *in extremis*? How do we imagine ourselves living in such a way that we become members of the spirit world, ancestors? And how does this question bear on the search for ethics which so absorbs our political world?

Mr. Liu's story further raises a research question for psychology. How does the Self appear phenomenally when a person is most alone? From Boethius thrown in prison in the sixth century to Admiral Byrd at the South Pole to the hostages blindfolded in Lebanon, there is plenty to examine regarding the interior support system of the isolated individual. A polar explorer and a solo 'round-the-world sailor have reported imaginal companions in the midst of unpopulated vastness.

So many new implications begin to arise which could lead me on and on that I have to summon one of a writer's two necessary angels, the God of suppression (the other is Fortuna, the God of stumbling on some bit of treasure). Only via suppression can we come to an end. The end that I am coming to takes us back to the shallow, measly example of my 1950s and 1960s. Though utterly different in degree of duress I, too, in my estranged individualism, was enacting the interiorization of a community: my first wife and our ideals; the idols of heroic mentors I had pasted on my bathroom walls; the Zurich Jungian community of fellow travelers; the idealizations of my spiritual and historical readings; the image of Jung in his tower and Freud's stoical pride in face of pain; the figures who came in my dreams; my two grandfathers who had risen from the bottom and climbed the torch of liberty — that is, what I believed then to be my individual Self was actually quite a crowd, an invisible society of imagination.

If my reasoning drawn from my personal pathology and Mr. Liu's extraordinary accomplishment holds water, then in that water is dissolved the cherished notion, perhaps delusional notion, of a private individual Self. We are never alone; not in solitary confinement, not in meditative contemplation, not on the death bed. No towers and no walls can keep the spirit out — and autism, too, needs new thinking.

We may then re-imagine the idea of Self as the focus or locus of visitations and semi-permanent residential inhabitants both dead and alive, both older than ourselves and not yet born, both of this world and of other worlds — and interiorizations as well of the various communities to which we give allegiance in daily life. They are communities not only of persons, but of values, figures, animals, ideals, places, and things. The freedom of the individual becomes his or her idiosyncratic way of enacting the ethos of that group in any particular situation in the full agency of personal integrity right in the midst of external abuse. Mr. Liu's noncompliance with the jailers' community and the Beijing authorities was made possible by his imaginal community. That compound Self of several voices in several rooms kept him a free man in the midst of isolation, degradation, and pain.

Mr. Liu's case is political, so we are obliged to draw a conclusion for political psychology. The ancient *polis* was founded on a cult of a dead hero. I used to think that the exploits of a hero, like Hercules, as told in the tales and enacted in rites and bound within a local geography, were the inspiring fantasy for the city, founding it again and again. All citizens could go back, I used to think, into the tale, and ritually perform anew the creation myth of their *polis* and claim their common descent as from a totem ancestor. The community derived from the heroic individual.

Now I think that the context of any community makes its hero. "Makes" in the Greek term *poiesis* for making myth. The hero does not so much found the city as the city's collective acts invent him or her as a collective focus. The hero is less a solitary fountainhead of the *polis* and rather the *"représentation collective,"* the personified nexus of its soul. Its citizens make him as much as he makes them. The communal soul epitomized as an individualized personification. The hero is simply the idealized interiorization of the community — hence the cult hero was always "dead," i.e., interiorized, not actual, alive only as image, as image of the community, living on in the city as embodiment of its ideals. Los Angeles recently found Mr. Reginald Denny to embody its feelings of justice and bring about the downfall of the tyrant police chief Mr. Gates.

How we imagine our cities, how we envision their goals and values and enhance their beauty defines the self of each person in that city, for the city is the solid exhibition of the communal soul. This means that you find yourself by entering the crowd — which is the root meaning of the word *polis* — poly — flow and many. To improve yourself you improve your city. This idea is so intolerable to the individualized Self that it prefers delusions of calm isolation and meditative retreat as the road to Self, I am suggesting. Self is the actual road, the city street.

I wish I could get this last idea clearer — but it still unfinished. Fortuna has left me stumbling and Suppression says "stop." But the intent of my deconstruction of individualism is an exhortation: we can never do enough for the city because it is, and has been since the Greeks, the heroic way of soul-making. That our cities today and our political life are in such disarray result from one profound *psychological* error: the internalization of the ideal hero into a personality cult of an individual self, which leaves the city without foundation and our therapeutic psychology deluded.

Thank you for awarding me your attention. Your listening is the most generous of recognitions.

9

Suicide and the City

Universal and ageless, suicide is archetypal; yet how we regard it is framed by time. So this book is bound by time and free of it — both. It bears traces of the mid-century when it was first conceived, the psychotherapeutics of the late fifties and early sixties still under the influence of medical models, a time altogether pre-soul of the late nineteen nineties.

It seems strange now: forty years ago "soul" was rather homeless, to be found only on city streets or buried in the sermons and cemeteries of religion. This book, in fact, resurrected "soul" from its reliquary in spiritual churchliness and instilled the idea with the passion-laden daily life of soul food, soul music, soul brother, soul sister, and soul death, it may rightly claim to have been the first to have brought "soul" to the center of clinical discourse, even emblazoning the word boldly into the book's title.

The elevation of soul into the title of a therapy book derives from Jung's famous work called in English *Modern Man in Search of a Soul* (1933). My book tries to carry his ideas of a soul-informed psychology into the most wrenching agony of therapeutic practice: the suicide of the patient. That is why it was written and why it continues to be read. It goes to the heart of therapy. Since we are each in a silent therapy with ourselves, the issue of suicide reaches into the heart of each of us.

Because psychotherapy of the 1950s was so medically minded, much of the book (Part Two) lays out the distinction between two

---

"A Postscript of Afterthoughts" to *Suicide and the Soul* (first published in 1962) and included in the 2004 reissue of the book.

contrasting attitudes — medical and psychological. The book as a whole carries this distinction further by radicalizing the cut between life and soul. It argues that the psychotherapist's primary task is "soul-making" (a term I later discovered in John Keats) and not life-preserving. Further, if life and soul may go their separate ways, the clearest paradigm for this distinction appears as suicide.

Even if this distinction is helpful in mind, in practice soul and life are not so easily divided; in fact in most of my subsequent writings on soul (and of course the work of Thomas Moore on the care of the soul in the world), show in some detail how life can be pursued without loss of soul, and soul can be made without forfeiting the calls of life. In earlier years I was not usually able to see this easy interplay, drawing the line between soul and everyday life even more firmly as in *The Dream and the Underworld,* in chapters on the *puer aeternus,* and in alchemical writings on the blue of melancholy and the imaginal white earth. Later, a counter-pull came from the side of life, witnessed by writings on urban design and habits, citizenship and ecology; one side or the other — oscillations between soul and life. Finally, a resolution arrived in 1981 by means of the concept of the *anima mundi,* soul of the world and in the world; and in that same year, the Eranos lecture on the "Imagination of the Air in Alchemy," which showed how soul moved out from the closed vessels of introverted secrecy to the public world of chemistry and technology.

Besides wishing to correct the first opposition — between soul-making and living life — another needs to be addressed. This book shows a bias against the medical model, even though in the context of the 1960s this animus was heroically valuable and valid. Psychotherapy had, still has, a medical shadow. This shadow is an introject of the cultural canon that elects psychiatry above psychology, body above soul, brain above mind, and science above art. So, the work of the psychotherapist is always shadowed by feelings of inferiority which fasten on the fact that he or she is "not medical." To come into its own, psychotherapy has to stand apart from its medical oppressor who speaks with the voice of materialism, scientism, and linear causality. Again, only later (*Healing Fiction*) I realized that the sense of inferiority is given with the soul and is not merely a result of the cultural canon and its championing of medicine as science. So, this book also presents its author's struggle with the medical shadow.

Because of this struggle, this heroism, this book overrides the truth that medical thinking can influence psychological practice along the path of virtue. Let's not forget that. For instances: the ethical code about privacy; the motto, *primum nihil nocere* (above all, do no harm); the Apollonic maxim of hastening to help which recognizes that therapy engage its practitioners in an altruistic enterprise. Therapy is other-centered. The medical model also takes into account public affairs — contagion, epidemiology, public health. This public concern translates in therapy into tending to the patient more widely than only as an autonomous singleton, a salient individual without background in the *polis*.

Another virtue of the medical model is the pathologized eye. The physician is steeped in pathology, in distortion, diseases, and death. This eye is attuned to shadows, attempting to discern the minutely complex movements of disorder. After all, what brings any patient to therapy has nothing whatsoever to do with transference, resistance, manipulation, repression, and all the other techniques of practice and dynamics of theories, but simply misery embodied often as illness. Something is no longer bearable and feels wrong.

The medical mind keeps present the primacy of illness, and an idea of illness must permeate therapeutic practice, anchoring it in the pain and patience of the human condition. Otherwise the consulting room of psychotherapy becomes a sealed chamber inflated with gaseous ideas of self-realization and spiritual transcendence, and the soul is back in church.

Let's remember, too, there are divinities in the medical model. For all its contemporary scientism and idolatry of drugs and machines, medicine has its godly backers — Apollo, Askiepios, Hygeia, Chiron, Machaon, Podaleiros, Panakeia, Dionysus, Artemis, Paieon. The entwined staff of Mercurius still signifies medical aid. Hercules was called a healer-savior; even Achilles could dress battle wounds. Besides the divine, medicine embodies a valuable human tradition of thoughtful observation and focused concern with the mystery of the human condition, a condition which medicine sanguinely knows does not meet the idealizations humans too readily fall for and which psychotherapy, without its medical background, may forget, even deny.

Despite this bow to the medical, I continue to stand up to what I wrote here thirty-five years ago. The soul does have affinity with death apart from disease and disorder which are not death's only messengers. And so death cannot be medicine's privilege. The inherent affinity of the soul with the underworld and the "other side" distinguishes the soul ontologically from any medical model that defines life and death in medical terms. Brain death may not serve as the full measure of death, and even that measure of sheerly physical death has been contested. What supports life can hardly be reduced to a life-support system. As long as the complexities and perplexities of death are confined to medical definitions, it is not easy to keep medicine and soul together. They fall apart and into opposition, as the former becomes addicted to hard-core pharmaceutical and mechanical procedures, the latter succumbs to spiritual serenity.

The basic distinction between soul and life that underlies the thinking in this book does not necessarily lead to that corollary also presented in these pages. By this I mean, it does not have to follow that soul is private and death the concern only of the individual. Perhaps years ago when the book was beginning to take up occupancy in my mind, Existentialism and its lonely exasperation had rooms in the same building. Camus, Sartre, Kierkegaard, Heidegger and his Dread and his Thrownness — these were the neighbors. Of course Jung had the whole ground floor from which emanated into my upper chambers his inspiring philosophy of the Self and its radical individualism.

Individualistic attitudes deriving from these philosophies insult the public sphere. It is conceived to be a senseless hell (Hell is Others, wrote Sartre), a mere "collective" in Jung's term, a term which describes the brutality of Soviet agriculture and the plagues and flies of Camus and Sartre better than it suits human society on which the soul depends for its sustenance and its pleasures. Of course Jung and the French writers were down on the collective. They had just come through World War II with its mass horrors, collaborators, SS, and death camps. Yet Caligula, Attila, and Cortez appear any time and any place, even under the pentacle of the Pentagon. After all, "the collective psyche" is nothing other than the *polis*. It is civilization itself and not merely the crowd, the masses, the mindless mob. By forcing individual and collective into a pair of logical antagonists, the individual becomes a stranger in his or her own city, that existential condition of estrangement. For this isolate self, death can only be imagined as bare and singular, logically and ontologically apart from any community of souls. Suicide is your own personal, private affair. It tortures the individual as individual in Hamlet fashion. To be or not to be must become the major question of each of us strangers, as Camus wrote.

If, however, "soul" refers also to an *anima mundi*, a world soul, then, as alchemists like Sendivogius and Paracelsus wrote, much of the soul lies "outside" the person. It belongs also to the world beyond your own authority. Then the decision about suicide does not belong to you alone. Maybe your body and its life is in your own hands, but your soul participates in the world. You may be the sole executioner, but may you also be the only judge?

A few years ago in a wide-ranging critique of therapy, I struggled with its excessive individualism, its neglect of the world. Why not, I proposed, define "self" as the *interiorization of community*? Why not give back to soul its cosmological importance, by definition embroiling environment and citizenship with our individuality? Why not grant attachment to be an ontological necessity, essential to the soul's nature?

Then, relationship between people as well as between people and things would be given inherently, no longer conceived as external connections between separated atomistic individuals enclosed within their skins. Then we would no longer "make" relationships or "work on" relationships; instead we would recognize, realize, and refine what is already given. Then therapy could discover that transference merely exhibits this innate and irreducible attachment. Once we have grasped that involvement is fundamental to the soul, we would be inescapably connected by definition, turning and twisting the threads of our fate with the souls of others. Others are entangled in your death as you are in theirs. Suicide becomes a community matter.

Old church decrees banned suicided bodies from burial in the common graveyard. Evidently it was believed that suicide severed your body and soul from the soul-body of the community. Suicide not only took your life: it took you out of your inherent attachments with others, cutting the threads with the *polis*. By taking your own life you were asserting that you were ontologically not a citizen, not a member, as if utterly free of any kind of cosmic participation.

Yet it is not the act that does the severing. It is the thought that my soul is mine, and so my death belongs only to me. I can do with my death what I choose. Because I can end my life when and how and where I please, I am wholly my own being, utterly self-determined, free of the fundamental constraint that oppresses each human's being — the uncertain certitude of death. No longer am I Death's subject, waiting on its will to pick when and how and where of its arrival. I have taken my death out of the hands of Death. Suicide becomes the ultimate empowerment. I am my own redeemer — "Death where is thy victory . . ." [I. Cor. 15:55] — the *superbia* of individualism.

This helps account for the common reaction against those who attempt suicide. They are not welcomed with sympathy by family, friends, or clinic, but rather are met with anger and disgust. Before we sympathize with a person's plight or pain that may have occasioned the attempt, we blame; we find ourselves spontaneously annoyed, outraged, condemnatory. I do believe this all too common response points to the enduring strata of the psyche that we all share, call it our archetypal humanity. We are indeed societal animals, as well as having individual destinies. Something insists we belong to a wider soul and not only to ourselves alone.

So, this postscript would disentangle suicide from individualism. I want to maintain the mystery which pervades this book, but now reflect that mystery in the mirror of a wider soul, its participation in the cosmos that is larger than my life, maybe than life itself. So large is this participation that boundaries cannot be found (Heraclitus). Because the boundaries of the *anima mundi* cannot be determined, I may not logically or morally justify my suicide as a call of my freely autonomous Self. Not soul and life are the fundamental contraries, but soul and the self-destructive freedom of individuality.

The arguments surrounding Kevorkian's assisted suicide restate the ancient issue: to whom does the soul belong? If it is mine, then I certainly have the "right' to go to Michigan and be helped to die by Dr. Kevorkian. If the soul belongs within a wider context — usurped now by the secular state and subjected to its legalisms — then my decision and his help are outlaw. Kevorkian presents the heroic position of the free, self-determining individual; the state, the dogmatic and oppressive authority of the collective.

On this tiresome level of individual vs. collective, the issue cannot be resolved. We need a wider context that embraces both. So, this postscript proposes the *anima mundi* as that context, and a definition of self as the interiorization of community. Suicide, literally "self-killing," now would mean both a killing of community and involvement of community in the killing.

Here then is my argument and a proposal.

If soul is essentially involved with the soul in the world, then any suicide must acknowledge this condition, else a decision to take one's life is not truly an act of soul, only an act of independence. The "world" of "others" must be brought into the decision, not deliberatively and literally, but ritually and symbolically. Some representative of the body politic, the so-called "collective," as an emissary of the cosmic invisibles needs to be summoned. The world must bear witness.

Once this role was carried by the rabbi, minister, or priest, though this figure could not authentically represent the *anima mundi* since any denominational religion was constricted by faith in dogma and not fully available to the signs of the fates. Nor can the judge in service to the secular state adequately represent the "others;" nor can the physician loyal to the medical model and the preservation of life.

The *anima mundi* could, I propose, be symbolically presented by some sort of community court — as legal, medical, aesthetic, religious, philosophical as well as family and friends. Not that this court would be authorized to grant permission or forbid, or even to facilitate or dissuade. The task of these others is *ritual*, simply to hold before the public the idea of suicide, to formalize its significance, to honor its value, and feel its power, so that death is not privatized. Then whether one commits the act alone or commits it at all no longer weighs so heavily. For the aloneness has been overcome by the ritual.

By bowing to this outside body and cooperating in the ritual, you would recognize that some of your soul is outside the body and its life, that it is by definition communal, and the invisible realities are also taking part in your death as they have all through your life. This contemplation of suicide before the act involves the world in a ritual gesture of closure with the world. It exonerates — not the "sin" of suicide which the act itself is not — but the *superbia* of individualism. The gesture gives the act its dignity, no longer a stealthy, shameful, and lonely preparation, a death smuggled and furtive — instead, a public display of honesty. Suicide comes out of the closet.

To take suicide out of the legal closet is what the Hemlock Society and Dr. Kevorkian have been trying to achieve. They have not, however, been able to liberate it from the psychological closet of individualism. Suicide still remains one's own personal *agon*.

Out-of-the-closet scares up new questions. No longer the moral one: is suicide right or wrong; no longer the medico-legal one: in which cases justifiable, how and by whom. Rather the question becomes more psychological: why the fierce resistance in Western civilization to opening the closet door? Why the persecutory panic when the suicide "threat" arises? — police action, lockups, criminalization of helpers, dosages to dumbness. Evidently taking suicide out of the closet of private individuality threatens the essence of private individuality. Bringing others into its profound questioning offers suicide an ancient background in Rome and a ritual one in Japan. Something other as well as my person is recognized. We step back as well into the metapsychology of Freud and the myth he restored to therapy. Freud declared Hades and his Underworld to be a universal force in the cosmos. He tied the soul ineluctably to the *thanatos* principle, the drive toward death, the drive of Death.

Freud was steeped in the Greek sources of psychological thought. His psychology insisted that death is not a matter of time, sheerly an end stage towards which all life moves. It is rather a drive itself. The soul seeks death as it lives. Death is always going on, and so we are committing suicide as we live. We call it radical change, growth, renewal, and we feel its concomitant loss and remorse. The soul contains both: a continuing spring of erotic reaching and a never-ending winter of grief and mourning. This universality of suicide, this *thanatos* within each soul's life, means that the members of the community court are not mere observing witnesses; they are participants in the *agon*. They bring to your individual plight not judgment but empathy.

Finally let's remember that individuality is an archetypal idea sustained by a myth. The idea obsesses the mind in many places and times. For instance the perplexities of Mediaeval philosophy: how to account for the principle of individualness, the differences among things, that each has specific quiddity. Individuality appears in Asian thought as a fundamental illusion, in fact, the most serious delusion of the separated mind. And the idea is crucial to the elevated notion of the person which feeds the Christian roots of Western values regarding the sanctity of each human individual, affecting our ethics, our political systems, and our notions of private property.

An archetypal idea, yes; but how hard to realize when feeling most "myself." How difficult to accept that the most preciously private "experience" of uniqueness is altogether a collective phenomenon available to anyone, anytime, anywhere. The archetype of individuality reflects itself in personalized consciousness which, if taken simply and literally, becomes the ideology of individualism and the mythology of monotheism.

If, as I am proposing in these afterthoughts and in the book as a whole, that suicide as a "self-killing" literalizes the desire to put this self to death, then the killing it seeks is the death of the archetypal idea of self that has imprisoned the soul in solitary confinement and convinced me of my individuality. The strength of the idea of singularity reflects the myth of monotheism — a self-contained, self-centered, self-motivated, and omnipotent One. If this be so, then the urge to do away with oneself may have its archetypal source in the excluded others: other Gods, other beings, their call to the soul. Their revenge may act out as my suicide, aiming to release my soul into a wider, fuller cosmos of participation with them. To restate the point again: the individual consists of more than his or her personal individuality. Something besides "myself" inhabits the soul, takes part in its life, and has a say in its death.

Whatever is essentially characteristic about "me" is given by my daimon (elaborated in my recent book, *The Soul's Code*) whose companion I am and who picked my life to inhabit. As Henry Corbin wrote, our concern should be with its individuation, the fulfillment of its call which our life serves. Thus the suicide question turns to your daimon for an answer, asking what does it intend by haunting you with a desire for leaving this world into which it seems to have wanted to come. Does it want to leave, go elsewhere; or are you the urgent cause? Only it can know, so it can offer responses you may not be able to imagine. Turning to it in despair and perplexity may begin a conversation similar to the very first suicide document human culture still treasures, the Egyptian New Kingdom papyrus translated as *Dialogue of a World-Weary Man with his Ba-Soul.*

Archetypal ideas may capture us. We all know this, having been in love, believed in our growth, hit the sky in victory, been flooded with fears and indecision, or been lost in bogs of doom. In these states of soul our consciousness becomes enslaved to a dominant idea, offering convincing testimony to the archetype that has seized us. So, too, we can become victims of individuality. We do not, however, have to get rid of ourselves in order to rid ourselves of the idea. Rather than seeing it through to our end, we can see through it to its end. Suicide fantasies literalize the attempt at *epistrophé*. To free the soul we do not have literally to leave the world to leave its worldliness, for world, too, can become an archetypal obsession. We need but see through the world outside and into its soul with which each daimon is bound and which claims our participation. For if we do not give back to the soul of the world some of what it gives us, will it not wither from neglect, the world becoming ever more soulless, and our urge to suicide ever stronger?

⟨∾⟩ ⟨∾⟩ ⟨∾⟩ ⟨∾⟩ ⟨∾⟩ ⟨∾⟩ ⟨∾⟩ ⟨∾⟩ ⟨∾⟩ ⟨∾⟩ ⟨∾⟩ ⟨∾⟩

10

The Heartbreak of America

In attacking psychotherapy for the last five years, I became more and more aware that there are other things going on in the world besides people's selves. The pursuit of the self creates more and more individualism and less and less community. So that the culture is trapped in trying to relate and talk about relationships, but the fundamental idea that makes relationships impossible is individualism, because if you are always creating stronger and stronger individuals, inevitably relating becomes the problem. If you start with community, then you do not have the problem of relating. We have got it ass-backward. So I have been very concerned with how to move the therapeutic system and the ideas of therapy away from the self, away from personalism, away from me and mine and my childhood, and move therapy toward an awareness of the political and social disasters that are creating the need for therapy. It is not the therapists; they are like the honest men in the trenches that are doing the work, but following a policy written by the wrong people.

The question we began with and it came up again and again: What is the conference about? What are we here for? And I think we are here about the broken heart. And whether we fret the broken heart in the personal stories of our marriages, the deaths in the family, the Vietnam War, or the relationship with the father, there is a broken heart. And it is the broken heart of America. It is the broken heart of our society. I don't think that we should talk about the healing of the broken

These remarks was delivered to close the Los Angeles Multicultural Men's Conference in Malibu, Calif., January 25–30, 1992. Privately printed.

heart, but to realize that it is there, and that is what love is really all about. That's where love comes through: the broken heart. Heartbreak is what it is all about. Heartbreak. What has happened here is the experiencing of the heartbreak of America. This has been something different than an "experience." We have been inside the heartbreak of America. It has been personal. We each have our own piece of that heartbreak. But we also *are* the heartbreak. Broken, our hearts broken and the heart of the country, broken into fragments which we call our neighborhoods, ethnic, colors, and so on. And what has happened here has been that the spirits and the images that live in the heart or come with the heart have met. And the souls have met. Maybe each of us, as embodied ego people, have not all met, and there are huge resistances in that meeting, but the souls have met and the spirits have met. It doesn't mean that they love each other. It doesn't mean that they all dance together, but they have met. And that keeps the heart alive because it is only the heart which is isolated or sealed or complacent or self-content that isn't feeling that it is broken. It does not fret the heartbreak and that is the danger. So what I want to leave with is not healing. I want to leave with that awareness of heartbreak. And I thank you for making me feel that intensely.

11

Loving the World Anyway

We spend so much of our modern urban time shutting out the world. We are busy "getting and spending" in Wordsworth's phrase. And we are depressed, focusing narrowly on our "problems." The world becomes a disturbance. It gets in the way of what has to be done today, or it breaks into our mood with its noisy demands. Rain is a bother; winter nights come too early; things break down and require attention. How can I possibly love a world that consists so largely in Muzak, traffic, and bad coffee? "All is seared with trade; bleared, smeared with toil," Hopkins writes. Besides, I am so preoccupied with my life that I can't follow David Ignatow. Everything I see becomes "a comment on my life." What do I feel about it? What does it mean? How can it do me some good? These reactions built into our psychological wiring show that "my" subjective self is bigger than Ignatow's mountain. I love myself; even meditate upon it to help its growth, to the exclusion of the world.

So how do we love the world anyway? Is there any way to bless it and be blest by it, to use the language of Yeats? Despite all my revulsions over its ugliness and injustice, and my bitterness over defeat at its hands, the world remains lovable anyway. But *anyway* also means any which way, any way at all, implying that there are many different openings out of self-enclosure and toward love of the world.

One way I've found into the world is through memory images. When I feel cut off and so preoccupied that the world around me seems dead,

First published as the introduction to the last chapter of *The Rag and Bone Shop of the Heart: A Poetry Anthology*, eds. Robert Bly, James Hillman, and Michael Meade (New York: HarperCollins, 1992).

I sometimes turn to recollections of years ago: the empty winter beach in South Jersey where I grew up, the gray sand, sea gulls cawing, and the wet wind coming off the breakers. I believe anybody can find a way into the world: some landscape, a particular room, neighborhood street, a building such as a barn with its smells, or a thing privately treasured, for instance, a baseball glove or a pair of shoes.

"All things are full of Gods" is an ancient Greek saying; "In my father's house are many mansions," a Christian one. These suggest that there is something divine even in the baseball glove and the neighborhood street. Pavese's poem "Grappa in September" reveals, even blesses, this divine quality of ordinary life, which comes to us through our senses. We see, hear, smell the world, and this, the poets are saying, is the true ground of our love for it. Our enlivened senses rejoice in it and bring praise to it.

Praise is an old-fashioned virtue. It goes much further than honor and respect, which feel like moral duties: you "should" love the world and show it respect. Praise, however, delights in the world and brings delight to it, as biblical psalms and old hymns praise the beauties and pleasures of creation. Hopkins in his adorations doesn't simply accept the world's strange deformities. He loves them and sings their praises.

Neruda praises a pair of wool socks, Ponge a door, McGrath bread, Simic the breasts of a woman, Merwin apricots, and Carl Sandburg the great bestial menagerie that inhabits each man's own chest.

How excessive some of these poems seem! It's as if once we begin to notice the world and enjoy it, we fall in love with its marvels. "The world is too much with us," Wordsworth says. But the "too muchness" of Hopkins's ecstatic celebrations, or of Simic's and Sandburg's exuberances, corresponds with the "too muchness," the extraordinary richness, of the world itself. Any thing you attend to carefully can bring blessing, like Neruda's socks and Yeats's empty cup.

The world's excess of riches tempts human ambition and also keeps it within bounds. "Old Song" from West Africa says, "Excel when you must," take the heroic course, "but do not excel the world." The world is always more than anything you do in it, to it, with it. No invention can surpass the creation, and no story can encompass the planet's history. The world sets limits to the heroic urge. Not only because the world is larger and older, but because of its supreme indifference. We would not need psychologists to warn about inflation and preachers to exhort modesty if we bore in mind the world's dispassionate habits as it goes its way; the days and nights, tides and seasons, which keep human actions in humbler proportion.

Auden's remarkable poem, commenting on Brueghel's painting of the fall of Icarus, makes the humbling indifference very clear. The puer-boy Icarus may perform "something amazing," flying and falling through the sky, but the horizontal world of earth and sea and daily work continue "calmly on."

Excess, exuberance, ecstatic adoration, yes, and also Creeley's rain falling, Auden's plowman, Martinson's earthworm, Frost's rough earth, Eberhart's groundhog, and Yeats's ditch. Loving the world's many ways.

Part Two

Politics of Beauty

12

On Culture and Chronic Disorder

I'm not going to begin by defining my main terms "culture" and "disorder," but shall start with an image. The image of the back ward in the state asylum, clinic, mental health home — and it doesn't matter whether today or when you were a child and there was a brick building for the criminally insane, the crippled children's home, the county asylum for the incurably insane, or whether your image be Bedlam, Bellevue, Brookhaven — there is a back ward. The retarded, the drugged, the indolent in strange postures; monuments of un-aging neglect, refuse, and decay, noiseless confusion, an underworld of benches and beds and ugly walls, glassed-in nurses, the defeated like ghouls under nightlights, odd clothes on shapeless bodies, odors unusual and sick, ridiculous the waste sad time stretching.

You may brighten the image with cheerfulness programs (youth in training), with occupational crafts and ward music, fresh pastel paint, little jokes on signs. You may have no chains, no mass showers, all replaced by tiny, glossy color-keyed pills. Still the back ward remains a fixedly recurring image — wherever it is located: on a Roman slave ship, in a Czarist drunken city, in Orwell's Paris hospital, a VA unit in hometown USA.

Now, let's move that image inside, as we psychologists are fond of doing. Let's move the back ward into our own backwardness. Let us envision our own retarded, crippled, "incurvature" as Robert Burton called our conditions as they age, the incurvature, the incurable, permanent conditions of human backwardness that cannot be cured,

Inaugural talk to the Fellows of the Dallas Institute of Humanities and Culture, given in 1981 and first published in the *Institute Newsletter* 1/2 (Dallas, 1982).

that cannot be endured. Here is our chronic disorder whether it appears in our marriage knots, family reactions, fears of the dark, erotic
fantasies, blank long depressions, inhibitions, compulsions . . . there is
a backward look, a terror of the back ward in us each which appears
in the chronic disorders of our human natures that bespeak the eternal
return, the *ricorso*, of primordial conditions.

The issues that now arise are these three:

a. how to look at this back ward;

b. how to deal with it;

c. what has the back ward (and how we look at it and deal with it)
to do with culture?

First, we may assume the chronic area is defective — sociologically
backward, deprived, underprivileged, underdeveloped — and owes its
nature to external forces. Or, we may assume a genetic defect, a hereditary taint, again owing its implacable nature to forces outside its own
condition. Or, we may take a Darwinian position that the backward is
the unfit. As Jung says, nature is aristocratic, profligate, throwing up
countless attempts, but only few seeds survive and even fewer rise to
genius or culture. Human life is a vast area of failed attempts. In this
view the back ward is as it is, a demonstration of nature, of natural laws
which have little to do with the individual case.

We could also regard the chronic area as cursed. This gives to the
natural laws a moral meaning. The back ward is a circle in Dante's
Hell, an area of the human soul as portrayed by Dostoevsky or in another mode by Graham Greene, in which God's purpose is working.

Further, we could imagine the place of irremediable disorder to be
the shrine of a specific God: Saturn, Kronos, Chronos. Here Saturn
reaches our lives and we would not find him otherwise but through
the retarded, crippled, unchanging chronic factor. Or, the God may
be Fate, the Furies, Ananke, that is, again in Jung's language, there is
a God in the disease (which is not to say that God is a disease, or the
disease is a God and must be worshipped as disease, for this is to idol-
ize disease and to limit the God to its shadow).

Each of these ways of looking at the chronic back ward implies *b:*
modes of dealing with it.

The first of these is heroism: let's get in there and do something. Let's not accept the chronic disorders to begin with. In American therapies, this notion appears in the refusal to accept any genetic governance of behavior, no hereditary taints, no karma — everything is changeable. It is a protean, mercurial view of the soul. All nature is subject to transformation by human will so that transformation tends to be equated with reformation.

We need to give time to this theme because for me heroism of this sort is a prime enemy of culture. Only in passing, then, let me characterize the theme: Heroism, and the American mono-myth of doing away with trouble; Heroism, and disappointment, or burnout and despair; Heroism, and move-out: the Sunbelt, New Frontier, Westward Ho! Get away from what drags — away, away with it. What actually is shot by troubleshooters? The heroic denial of chronicity seems to be a fundamental American tenet. "We must keep this nation on the move," say the slogans. And then the reverse: going down with your ship, for the flag, at the Alamo, a heroic stasis that leaves no culture either.

Heroism comes in a second style. Contrary to heroic redemption is heroic *suppression*. The chronic is accepted as it is: incurable, so let's not waste time on it. Let's stuff it away: euthanasia, concentration camp, ghetto, slavery — make it work for us, or get rid of it. Will power, control, clean the stables in one way or another. But keep it cost efficient.

A third way of dealing with chronic disorder we may call welfare. Here is our main modern approach, a fantasy of humanistic mediocrity, of democratic kindness and practibility. Welfare says the back ward is the price we must each pay for success, for our tough competitive ego. Some parts are weaker — not defective, but not quite able to keep up. So we must create a place for the chronic disorders, "remedialize" with programs the slower, stupid parts, and reintegrate, with halfway houses at the threshold, the back ward closer to the front-line, cutting-edge of the advancing civilization.

Welfare is both external in society and internal in the way we meet our individual backwardness. With the expectations of improvement, we administrate it, arrange for it, or "put it away." Mainly we have some sort of adjustment fantasy, progressivist, toward the civilized goals of conformism.

Welfare misses that the chronic is a different form, serves other Gods. The blind, the crippled, and the mad have other measures than unafflicted human norms. For that reason we can learn from them — the blind poet, the crippled artisan, the mad prophet. They imagine in wholly other ways. As Bachelard said, the imagination works through deformation; however, welfare works in terms of reforming and con- forming. Chronic disorder is precisely that which does not fit into progressivist humanism, precisely proof of the survival of the unfittest and that even the Platonic ideal of "fittingness" does not here apply. Hence there is the recidivism, the eternal return of chronic disorder in us and society.

Welfare fails and there is deep bitterness over its failure. "I've tried and still nothing worked . . . I've been decent, tolerant, kind." Wel- fare must fail because it remains within the heroic attempt to change, though this is a secularized, castrated heroism, subdued, adjusted, mediocratized — the heroic mission to *save* has become to *help* or to *improve*. Mission without mission and without hero. Mission becomes administration, institutionalized feeling. Welfare is finally a guilty-ego event, not an archetypal passion like an ascetic (burn it out) or a re- demptive jihad holy war (convert or die). Mere civility, mere good will and programmatic gimmicks.

We've now reviewed heroic redemption, heroic repression, and wel- fare or secularized heroics. Now we come to a fourth way of dealing with chronic disorder, and the one I recommend to your hearing.

If there is an archetypal basis of the chronic, if it has its own form, it then requires its own kind of handling. Let us imagine living with an incurable cripple. (Is that why freaks and cripples have been coming into prominence in our films and theaters — are we American heroes being reminded of chronicity?) This kind of handling is a caretaking, nursing, compassion, charity — charity rather than welfare. Recogni- tion of the God within the condition, a God not to be violated by cure or conversion. Drive out the Devil and drive out the Angel too. Sacredness of the back ward, for Hell belongs even in the Christian God's vision. Amelioration performed through charity (not tolerance) and compassion which says: "here is something to be lived with be- cause of its very difference, its utterly foreign alienness, which leads me to want to be closer to it for what it offers." The mission changes into a transformation, not of the disorder, but of my norms of order.

"The Elephant Man" affects the doctor and the actress because they have accepted his irremediableness, that his complaint is chronic, death the only cure. Irremediable does not mean unredeemable. Redemption would not change a condition, but blesses it for what is.

The first step of blessing the state-as-it-is leads to a second, interest in it, curiosity about its nature, desire to stay with it longer (becoming chronic oneself), that chronicity we call fidelity, to move it to show itself further, let it speak, enact, grow its wings. In other words, the ground of love is in the very irremediableness, its chronicity.

We are now led to my third question. First we tried various ways of looking at the back ward, and then we tried various ways of dealing with it. Now we ask c: What has the looking and dealing, and the chronic disorder itself, to do with culture?

Here I suppose you expect some notes toward a definition of culture. But all I want is to give the word a penumbra, a connotative atmosphere. It evokes "cult"; it evokes the "occult" (hard to see, deliberately hidden, esoteric, mystery); and "culture" also evokes fermenting organic forms that grow in intense, warm, richly fed unnatural vessels.

Culture takes us back to another place, another time, once upon a time, a golden age, beyond our usual existence, to forms in fermentation, and culture refers to fundamentals, traditions handed down. As such, culture is always trying to revive, reach back, attempt again by serving in cult, or to generate or resurrect as in a laboratory culture forms that do not simply happen in daily natural life.

May I here interject a quick distinction between culture and civilization (a risky thing to do, but others may make the distinction in other ways).

Culture evokes an intelligentsia or initiates — and these may be everyone in a society, not only an elite priesthood of "the cultured" — who appreciate, maybe even live in terms of, the occulted (like ideas, qualities, soul, virtues, forms). That is, *invisible values and the value of invisibles.* The occulted is not simply naturally given. It refers to something artifacted and thus becomes confused with art. But art is the visibility of the occulted, culture literalized, civilized, and does not necessarily indicate the presence of culture.

Here now some "hard facts" taken from *The Humanities in American Life* (Report of the Commission on the Humanities, pp. 113–28), published by the University of California Press, showing humanistic improvements and the advance of civilization. Are they also evidence of culture?

More than 750 new museums have been founded since 1969. In the single state of Wisconsin, there are more than 170 historical societies; in 1950 there were 59. Great book groups now number 2500 in the nation. In 1978, museums counted 360 million visitors which is six times the number of spectators attending professional baseball, basketball, and football games. More Americans attend performing arts events than spectator sports. In 1967 one million persons in the audiences of modern dance and ballet; ten years later there were fifteen million. Opera attendance has increased five times between 1950 and 1978, and there are close to 1000 opera companies in the United States today. In 1968 there were twenty-four professional theater companies; 1978, over 300. There are 1400 professional symphony orchestras.

These figures raise a question: what is the relation between humanities (arts) and culture? The name of this Institute includes them both; will it serve them both, as a "both"? Might this confuse them, substituting one for the other?

Culture takes place in closed, even closeted places, involving the alchemical *putrefactio*, or decadence as the body of fermentation. Generation and decay happen together; and they are not always easy to distinguish. What goes with civilization are irrigation systems, monuments, victories, historical endurance, wealth, and power as a cohesive force with common purpose. Civilization works; culture flowers. Civilization looks ahead, culture looks back. Civilization is historical record; culture a mythic enterprise.

They may interrelate, but they also seem able to do without each other. Civilization without culture is all around us. Culture without civilization? I think of the Tierra del Fuego Indians found by Westerners in the early nineteenth century, with hardly fire, clothes, shelter, tools or vessels, always starving, always sick, yet whose emotive songs and visions were rich myths of every sort.

Culture, as I have been speaking of it, looks backwards and reaches back as nostalgia for invisibilities, to make them present and to found human life upon them. The cultural enterprise attempts to peel, flail, excite individual sensitivity so that it can again — notice the "again" — be in touch with these invisibles and orient life by their compass. The key syllable of culture is the prefix "re."

To build an argument upon a pun, the back wards display the backwards toward which culture reaches. Here is a display of recurring forms that do not change through time and which repeat in every age and society. (All societies, by the way, have some conditions considered by them to be psychopathological.) This universality and chronicity is expressed by both the physical view, backward as "genetic defectives" and the moral view, backward as sin, fall, or eternal damnation. If the Gods have become diseases, then these forms of chronic disorder are the Gods in disguise; they are occulted in these misshapen, inhuman forms, and our seeing through to them there — in all forms of chronic disorder in ourselves and our city — is a grounding act of culture. The education of sensitivity begins right here in trying to see through the manifestations of time into the eternal patterns within time. We may regard the discontents of civilization as if they are fundamentals of culture.

It may be surprising to associate the diseased with the divine and culture with deformity. We do so want the Gods to be pristine models in marble on Olympus. But they are not without their shadows, their afflictions and infirmities.[1] As they are beyond time (athnetos, immortal), so these shadows of disorder that they portray in their myths reappear in those human events that are not affected by time, that is, in chronic disorders. Since we are shaped by their images, we do in time what they do in eternity. Their eternal afflictions are our human infirmities.

So, my point is coming clearer: it is in dealing with the back ward that culture grows. I do not mean going off to apprentice oneself in an asylum, to become a therapist — although I understand what students are asking for by wanting to enter a training program. Not merely to help people — that's the welfare reason. Rather it is to move from civilization toward culture. By being present with the chronic castaways of civilization, they become present to the timeless incurable aspect of the soul.

I may make this yet clearer to you if you think again of your own backward back ward. Nursing and sitting with it, dwelling upon it, tracing the invisible mystery in it, letting compassion come for your own chronic disorder — this all slows down your progress, moves you from future thinking to essential thinking about nature and character, upon life's meaning and death's, upon love and its failure, upon what is truly important, and upon the small things in words, manners, act, necessitated by the limitations of your inescapable disorder. We begin to hear differently, watch differently, absorb more sensitively. Confronted with the unbearable in my own nature, I show more trepidation — which is after all the first piece of compassion. In regard to others, my manners alter, my language more attuned and precise, I become more sophisticated and artful — as a cat steps, a bird perceives, a dog follows invisibles in the air. I look to art for understanding, to ritual for enactments, and to the lives of men and women of the past and how they came through. I need something further than community and civilization for they may be too human, too visible. I need imaginal help from tales and images, idols and altars, and the creatures of nature to help me carry what is so hard to carry personally and alone. Education of sensitivity begins in the back ward, culture in chronic disorder.

Finally, if you allow me one more paragraph, I come to appreciate the chronic itself. More than slowing down, more than an occasion for tolerance or instruction in survival, I come to see that things chronic are things that have nothing to do with civilized time, neither future time when it will be better, nor present time and adjustment, but rather the timeless structures of being, which accompany us, keep company with us, in forms that do not change and do not go away, seemingly so out of place, out of step with civilization and its courageous march toward its inevitable destruction. For civilizations do eventually decline and perish. Cultures by existing always in decay, in disorder, may continue beyond the civilizations that seem to hold them. In the shadows of the Gods are the very Gods themselves, their myths in the midst of what survives because it will not go away.

Borges said in a late poem ("Quince Monedas"):

Solo perduran en el tiempo las cosas que no fueron del tiempo.
(In time, only those things last which have not been
in time.)

1. Cf. my "Athene, Ananke, and the Necessity of Abnormal Psychology," in *Mythical Figures*, Uniform Edition of the Writings of James Hillman, vol. 6.1 (Putnam, Conn.: Spring Publications, 2007).

13

Aesthetic Response as Political Action

The coupling of aesthetics and politics, or beauty and city, seems in our times a radically adventurous idea. Yet it was common and basic in ancient Greek life and Renaissance Italy. Oriental potentates and European despots would bankrupt their treasuries to construct monuments of un-aging magnificence for the glory of their Gods, and themselves of course, but also to delight the people they ruled, and taxed. A turbulent populace was quelled by beauty, and the making of beauty — water gardens, summer palaces, fancy retreats, cathedrals, mausoleums, memorials, continuing as the great boulevards and massive edifices of republican nations. Aesthetic constructions gave pride in and confirmation of a political system, whether in Communist Moscow or Czarist Petersburg, Fascist Rome or two thousand years before, or in Washington, D.C, with its white marble temples to its secular heroes.

This mode of joining aesthetics and the city leaves the psyche of their relation unsatisfied. The aesthetic is reduced to politics; beauty serves an ulterior purpose: the concrete display of doctrine, propaganda set in stone.

I believe the relation between aesthetics and politics is more personal and psychological. It lies in our reactions to the world we live in. Every day, our sense of beauty walks through the world, accompanies us in the car, to the store, into the kitchen. All day long there is a continuing subtle aesthetic response to the world. We notice its images, we smell its sensations, and we imperceptibly adjust to its face.

Preface to *Politica della Bellezza*, a collection of essays and talks edited by Francesco Donfrancesco and published in Italian translation by Moretti & Vitali (Bergamo, 1999).

These adjustments, because they are subliminal, are where "the unconscious" lies hidden today. We are unconscious of our aesthetic responses. Although therapy's main task remains what it has been all through the twentieth century, that is, the effort of awakening, the focus of this awakened consciousness has changed. To become conscious now means more specifically — not of our feelings and our memories — but of our personal responses to beauty and ugliness. We have become unconscious of the impact of the world and our souls have become immured against it.

Foreshadowings of this more private psychological solution to the political implications of aesthetics begin to appear in my lecture at Eranos on Lago Maggiore in the summer of 1976. On that occasion I proposed a depth psychology of extraversion. Rather than conceiving "depth" to be only interior to the subject, depth could also be found in the object, in the images presented by the world. They, too, are faces to be read as displays of soul. I was then trying to free depth psychology from its introverted and subjectivist bias by introducing a basic idea from phenomenology and the psychology of direct perception; they both contend that depth is afforded by the surface, that is: the world is aesthetic presentation.

This turn toward the depth "out there" was shortly thereafter reinforced by moving, in January 1978, from Europe to Dallas, Texas. This most vigorously extraverted city was in the process of constructing its major public places, and the relations between politics, beauty, and ugliness were in everyone's eye, on everyone's mind.

But only in 1981 did a deeper psychological insight begin to form under the inspiring auspices of the editor of this book, Francesco Donfrancesco, and its dedicated translator, Paola Donfrancesco. Then, at the Palazzo Vecchio in Florence (October 1981) I was offered the opportunity to attempt the founding of depth psychology, and therapy, too, on the Renaissance Neo-Platonist idea of the *anima mundi* (cf. chapter 3 above)

If the soul, as Plotinus says, is always an Aphrodite, then it is always concerned with beauty, and our aesthetic responses are evidence of the soul's active participation in the world. Our sense of beauty and ugliness draws us out, into the *polis*, activating us politically. Simply by noticing what is about us and responding to it with naive recoil or desirous advance, we are involved. Our personal psyches are in tune with the presentation of the world's soul. The aesthetic response is immediate, instinctual, animal, prior in time and in ontology to the tastes that sophisticate the response and the judgments which justify it.

Any repression of the response is not only deleterious to our animal nature; it is an instinctual wounding as harmful to our well-being as is the repression of any other instinct. The denied aesthetic response, this ignorance of the psyche's aesthetic impulse, is also an arrogant insult to the world's presence. To walk right by an ill-designed building, be served and accept poorly prepared food, put on your body a badly cut and badly sewn jacket, to say nothing of not hearing the birds, not noticing the twilight, is to ignore the world. Yet this state of ignorance, this anesthesia, is largely the modern human condition. And, it is supported and promoted by our economics, our entertainment, our refrigeration, our modes of communication and transportation, and, of course our medications.

Because anesthesia — also called "psychic numbing" by Robert J. Lifton, the American radical investigator of collective catastrophes — is so common to our times, I suspect that it fosters the political passivity of the Euro-American citizen and thus favors the ruling powers to continue unimpeded on their ruinous course. If we citizens do not notice the assaults of ugliness we remain psychically numbed, but are still reliably functional as workers and consumers. We can still hurry to work, shop, and come home to TV, daily, dutifully, drudgingly — a cart horse with blinders — all the while erroneously believing that our personal miseries have their origins in our personal relations. Therapies collude in this false belief by insisting that the depression and aggression we feel come from abuses of past human relationships and not from present inhuman abuses of our aesthetic instinct. Therapy misses its mark when it loses sight of Aphrodite's daily significance for the soul.

By denying the reality of the *anima mundi* and its reflection within our personal soul, we take all suffering on ourselves, *mea culpa*, and remain oblivious to the suffering in the world soul — how tortured its structures, how it is exiled in a nihilistic wilderness and how it longs to return to a cosmology that gives first place to its beauty.

We all know how to engage in political action: to campaign, to march, to protest, to resist. We know the courage action demands and the risk it entails. But we no longer know that we have other means of action that too require courage: the courage of the heart to stand for its perceptions. And unless we stand and speak in behalf of our aesthetic sense, the pall of numbing conformity deadens our language, our food, our work-places and city streets.

Small acts of protest and praise break through the numbed condition. We can each be heroes of the heart, for this kind of personal response, simple as it seems, goes yet deeper than the usual protests about genderism, racism, environmentalism. There is no "ism" here, no ideology. You are in service to the soul's unquenchable desire for beauty. Remember? Psyche in Apuleius's tale was imagined to be the most beautiful figure in all classical myth.

I do believe that were the public to awaken to its hunger for beauty there would be rebellion in the streets. Was it not aesthetics that took down the Berlin Wall and opened China? Not market consumerism and Western gadgets, as we are told, but music, color, fashion, shoes, fabrics, films, dance, lyrics, and the shapes of cars. The aesthetic response leads to political action, becomes political action, is political action.

14

Aesthetics and Politics

We all know a lot about protests, marches, voting rights, equal opportunity, and affirmative action. We also know a lot about how to get involved, and that involvement usually leads, after a few months or many years, to burnout, disgruntled bitterness. Something psychological is missing. Yet we all know a lot about therapy, about self development, growth, empowerment, self esteem, and that this also leads, after a while, to burnout, or at least disenchantment.

It seems not to connect enough to the real gripes, the real injustices, and the real impoverishment and victimization experienced in the political arena. So how put politics and therapy together? How achieve psychological activism? And what is a psychological activist?

I want to answer the question today with this proposal, and I call it the "aesthetic response."

The ethical response you know. Injustice, oppression, corruption, we see it and react against it. What do the strikers say on their placards and sandwich boards? "Unfair," unfair to workers; to women; to minorities. But do they ever say, "Ugly"? Do we ever protest and go on strike because of the insulting, repulsive, and just plain ugly places of our work? Of our malls and strips? Of hospital buildings and government decor? Of the materials we handle, the lights we submit to, the "workstations" we are confined within, the lecture halls that we must endure? Yet these aesthetic oppressions affect our bodily feeling, our emotional

Originally a talk ("Can There Be Ethics Without Aesthetics? — Aesthetic Responses as Political Action") at the *Tikkun* Summit for Ethics and Meaning, Washington, D.C., April 1996, and published in *Tikkun* 11/6 (November–December 1996).

well being, and we must ward ourselves from their influence, the despair they produce, and the exhaustion. Ugly environments cause us to repress our reactions, and repression is exhausting. One of the first old ideas of Freud: repression takes up a lot of energy.

We deny our aesthetic responses by closing down our senses, our perceptions, and we anesthetize ourselves with loud music in the ears, with Advil and Xanax, with sleeping pills and caffeine and Prozac, with alcohol, with ice cubes before every meal so that we've already anesthetized our tongues — we hardly can know what we're eating anyway — and high sugar and high salt. Who can get through a day with senses fully awake and responsive? Too much overload of junk input. Too much ugliness.

Our aesthetic responses come as outrage, as repulsion, as insult, if not assault. A heightened irritability; sudden moments of irrepressible rage at the post office; being held on the phone; waiting in line; stuck in traffic; with the shoddy thing you bought. And the rage comes up like mad.

Psychotherapy does not take these aesthetic frustrations into account. Example: I'm a patient, and I'm on my way to my therapist in Boston. I drive some fifty miles to get there on the Turnpike. I'm in my modest little Hyundai, and the great eighteen wheelers pull out and thunder by. Dense traffic, potholes, jagged metal obstacles, road kill — by the time I've got a parking place and walk in for my session, I'm a wreck. "Tell me about it," says the therapist. I start in with the threat, the noise, the fumes, the ugliness, the chaos, and the fear; he says, "What's it remind you of?" And soon we leave the highway, leave the trucks, leave the actuality, and find the nervous anxiety to be within me. My relation with my father, represented by the big trucks. And my frail ego, thin-skinned and fragile, represented by my Hyundai. Maybe truck drivers have bigger dicks. Trucks are not disempowered. My low self esteem, my falling so easily into victimization — and I am being analyzed. And analyzing myself, and finding all those problems in me.

All the problems of the outer world, and what has actually made me upset, could be the beginning of a political action about toll roads and long-distance trucking, and food contracts of supermarkets with California growers at the expense of local suppliers and oppressed migrant labor, of construction graft and speed limits. All this is nipped in the bud by the internalization of the emotions to my inner problems.

Fear recognizes danger — fear is a mode of perception. If you didn't have fear, you wouldn't be able to get through a day. It keeps you on the curb when the traffic goes by. Now fear has become anxiety, translated, internalized, and anxiety is a condition, by definition, without object, a wholly internal state. All mine, and therefore all my fault. And in fact, if it *is* fear, it becomes phobic, and then it's in the DSM.

Other emotions that report directly to us about the state of the world are also internalized by therapy and made "mine." And of course some of this is necessary. For instance, I'm deeply affected by the increasing destruction of the natural habitats. Each day, I see images on television of forests burning, land ripped open, animals vanishing, rivers polluted. This is all registered by my soul, and even more things than I see are in pain and dying in the soul of the world. I am affected unconsciously as well. Of course I am in mourning for the land and water and my fellow beings. If this were not felt, I would be so defended and so in denial, so anesthetized, I would be insane. Yet this condition of mourning and grieving going on in my soul, this level of continual sadness is a reflection of what is going on in the world and becomes internalized and called "depression," a state altogether in me — *my* serotonin levels, *my* personal history, *my* problem.

And the drug industry, to which we do not say "no," and government health agencies and insurance companies are in general agreement: You must become even more anesthetized. Take something: Depression is a disease and weakens the economy. It is announced that way; there are statis tics about how many workdays are lost because of depression and how much that costs the nation.

In our book *We've Had a Hundred Years of Psychotherapy and the World's Getting Worse*, Michael Ventura and I challenged these notions in therapy: its neglect of the world, and the sabotaging of political consciousness by therapeutic theory. I'm not attacking individual therapists, who are in the front lines trying to mop up after the huge destruction left by neglectful social and environmental Republican policies.

I want to emphasize that the way the world gets to us is through sense perception — what the Greeks called *aisthesis*, from which comes our word aesthetics. By suppression of our aesthetic responses, we leave the world to itself and isolate ourselves from its plight. No amount of relating and community building will restore us to the world, and restore the world, unless we trust our aesthetic responses.

Therapy says "connect, only connect," I'm saying sense, see, notice, react, only react.

Let us put some solid stuffing into this word "aesthetic." Especially since it is usually employed to mean only aesthetic — pretty, decorative, and quite free of moral and ethical value. We can redefine "aesthetic," connect it with ethics, and finally, connect aesthetics more profoundly with the cosmos itself.

First, about aesthetic judgments — how can we trust them? Isn't beauty in the eye of the beholder? Merely a matter of taste? This is the subjective view, and it has been held for many, many years by many eminent people, including the philosopher David Hume, who maintained that since there are such differences of opinion, it becomes a matter of taste. The arbiter, then, is the one who has the best taste, says Hume, the educated taste. In our culture, that would be the gallery owner, the critic, the museum director, the expert. Eventually, the auctioneer at Sotheby's. So that in our day, the subjective view boils down to money.

Opposed to this subjective view is the objective view of beauty. As with most everything else in our Cartesian world, it's either objective or subjective — that's all the choice we ever get. The objectivists hold that there are definite formal properties of a painting, a musical score, an architectural plan, a poem, such as rhythm, balance, scale, proportion, complexity, unity, finish, and so on. And these are recognizable, inherent in the thing judged and combined to make the thing pleasing, so that we call it beautiful. Santayana defined beauty as pleasure attributed to an object.

Now I'm not either a subjectivist, saying it's just personal raste, nor an objectivist, saying it's inherent in the form. In between is something more psychologically instinctual, which is the soul's reaction. I think we have an immediate sense of attraction to things. They seduce us and they repel us. It is how we read the world how our animal nose and ears and eyes read the world. Cultural norms and habits may sway us this way or that, but beneath these social criteria is the instinct, the aesthetic response itself, which makes selections and draws back from ugliness as Plotinus wrote 1700 years ago: the ugly makes us withdraw, shrink into ourselves, turn away.

This is what we do all day long, assaulted by environmental ugliness. What do therapists meet in the consulting room? Precisely those souls who have shrunken into themselves, turned away, withdrawn. We call them narcissistic now, and schizoid, and unrelated but could they not be suffering from a surfeit of ugliness? Therefore, my statement that aesthetic response is political action. Let me carry this forward in another way.

The individual citizen is less stupid than we believe and are told to believe by opinion polls, with their simplistic questions that make people seem stupider than they are. Even if our ability to articulate complexities, or to remember historical information, or discriminate the relevant from the dross is limited, our emotions have an intelligence in them. Emotions, like fear, keep us from being hit by a car; emotions like pity reach toward the other in need; emotions like silent, stubborn truculence recognize being used and being shoved around. So we have all sorts of emotions every day — of outrage, of anger and insult and revulsion — about the sensate world we must participate in. I say *must* participate in; you can't walk away from the shoddy materials used to built your condo, the cheap switches installed in your lamp, the design of the cafeteria or the hospital waiting room. You must participate in this oppression.

One of the oldest Western ideas was that the soul was the form of the body, that is, the form of things present their soul in a material way. Living among ugly things makes for ugliness of soul as a consequence. How many of the problems therapy has to deal with — the rage in households, the hatred in the workplace, the frustration in families and the draining depressions truly come out of the woodwork, out of the closets, out of the materials and designs we live with. I believe that many of the problems that sap the economy — absenteeism, slow-downs, addictions, sexual harassment, careless quality control, nagging, underperformance, ill health, resentful lawsuits — are architectural problems that have become psychological problems.

The toxicity of the chemicals and air systems we read about, we know about. But I'm talking about the soulless forms and the visible ugliness. We already know about sick buildings, but do we understand the sick psyche of the building? And there's no escape. A building is thrown up on the street corner that blocks the sun, causes vicious down-drafts, invades the perspective, places the pedestrian against a giant wall as if for an execution. This building, a public nuisance, stands there on a street corner anonymous, unsigned — you don't know who its contractor was, or its architect, hardly its owner. No accountability for that building. If I made too much noise, or took off all my clothes on a street corner, I'd be arrested as a public nuisance. But the building stands for decades, making even more psychic noise and displaying even more in-your-face insult.

In the Greek world, the good and the beautiful could be together in one word, *kalokagathos*. The beauty of the world was the smile of the gods, hence the gods were believed to be smiling, which showed their beauty and their goodness. Hence, too, the idealized forms of classical sculpture, which presented virtue as well as beauty. Christianity made it very clear that goodness and beauty were to be separated — to separate this world from the next world. If there is beauty, then the best kind — and our Puritan reformers made and still make a great point of this — is internal beauty, moral beauty. Not the beauty of outward show. Ethics not only coopted beauty, but repressed it. This was one of the many ways that Christianism could get rid of Aphrodite and other pagan goddesses.

Much later, religious thinkers such as Kierkegaard placed aesthetics lower down in value than ethics. One progressed morally through aesthetics to more profound values of a moral nature. Nietzsche's work makes an even stronger separation: He shows the bloody, the horrible underside of Greek beauty, the evils and the destructions that accompanied it.

As well we can see that many good things can be ugly — look at Socrates, the ugliest of men and the most virtuous. Look at Pandora and Eve, so beautiful, yet all the troubles and sins started with them. The Nazis murdered, and played Mozart. Clearly, ethics and aesthetics can be separated.

By now, in Western history, aesthetics and ethics occupy separate compartments in our minds, just as they occupy separate compartments in our universities. But Plato and his brilliant followers down through the ages, including the great Romantic poets like Keats, insisted the two belong together. If ethical virtue does not *show* in the way a life is lived, then how claim that it is good? How judge unless there is visible presentation? The question of their relation often comes down to the practical versus the ideal. Many philosophers consider beauty useless, and therefore opposite to the practical. Whereas I've been arguing that it is the most useful and practical. For any practice that is not at the same time idealistic, that does not have a a further vision, that does not attempt to realize some image of beauty, loses its practical goodness.

You don't just fix a car to fix it, but to restore it to its best functioning, to its ideal image. Burnout comes when practice does not have a vision, and you don't really know what ideal you're putting daily into practice. Or burnout can come when you have a vision that cannot reach into practice. Ethics is the realm of practice; aesthetics, the realm of sensate images. Therefore good ideas in tiresome language, dense pages of dense prose does not awaken the vision. You need sensate images, rich language, aesthetic sensitivity. Moral suasion touches guilt, but not the deeper desire for loveliness and grace. Ethics without aesthetics will not hold us for long. We get earnest, driven, obstinate, and eventually ugly.

I'm suggesting that all our ethical concerns for justice and fairness, for decency, require as well an aesthetic vision, such as images of the biblical and classical ideals of Jerusalem, the city on the hill, Zion, the restoration of the Temple, the image of Athens and its Acropolis, the cities of the Renaissance like Florence and Venice, images of Paradise, of Eden. America itself was such a vision of harmonious beauty — the Peaceable Kingdom. Those great aesthetic images are behind the American Dream.

A tyrant may build beautiful oases and pleasure domes; beauty is no guarantee against tyranny. Aesthetics does not replace the ethical. But aesthetics must give ethics sensate images that direct our longings toward ideals, a vision to contemplate, and seduce towards it.

How does your own particular aesthetic response connect with the cosmos? To begin with, *kosmos* is originally an aesthetic term; it does not mean vast and empty outer space through which sealed-up cosmonauts fly at great cost. It meant the right placement of things, fittingly, becomingly, nicely. *Kosmos* was used especially of women with respect to their embellishments. And this meaning continues in our word "cosmetics," which owing to our disparagement of the aesthetic, we see only as superficial, as in "cosmetic surgery," makeup, false front. Whereas "cosmos" means that all things are on display, show themselves, and are presented to the senses which respond to them with feelings of like and dislike, approval and disapproval, and with a varied and differentiated judgment of their value. Thus your aesthetic responses are cosmological, not merely personal. They are signs that you are here and taking part in the entire world order, which is from the beginning set out as a pleasing aesthetic display. The world is first of all an aesthetic phenomenon before it is mathematical, logical, or theological. So the most basic reaction to being in the world is aesthetic. That word, *aisthesis*, goes back to a root that means "I breathe in," like sucking in the breath when struck by beauty or horror. Our aesthetic responses are inherently related to the actual world and to the primary way that we take part in it. To suppress these responses is to cop out of the political, that is, out of the common, shared world.

My final point is that ethics alone is not enough to make a change in the world. Alone, ethics without aesthetics doesn't hold. For instance, the environment: We're not motivated to fight for it simply because we ought to. Of course we are ethically responsible for our patterns of consumption, and we are guilty because of consumerism. Nor are we motivated solely by high principles of Gaia, and deep ecology, and future generations, making amends, atoning, sacrificing. The motivation must come from *below* the superego, from the id of desire. We must first be moved by beauty. For then, love is aroused. When you love something, then you want it near, not to be harmed. Then you are a little blind to its faults and risks — no question of cost effectiveness, of balance sheets, of worth assessment.

What evokes love? As has been said in many places in many ages and felt by any one of us: beauty evokes love. An aesthetic perception draws forth our ethical care. First awaken *aisthesis*, breathe in the beauty of the cosmos — the meticulous crawl of an insect, the heave of the frosted earth as winter yields its grip, observe the composite complexity of an ordinary stone, the eddies in the sand as the tide recedes, or hear the early morning bird call. Beauty astounds and pulls the heart's focus toward the object, out of ourselves, out of this human-centered insanity, toward wanting to keep the cosmos there for another spring and another morning. This is the ecological emotion, and it is aesthetic and political at once.

15

Natural Beauty Without Nature

The image we shall hold before us is an archaic urban phenomenon, or rather an archetypal urban phenomenon, because it is so universal and so powerful and so self evident: the City Wall. It is curious that human kind has more or less universally constructed cities apart from the natural world. Are cities therefore unnatural? Are they merely human inventions without Gods and without soul? Is soul only on the other side of the wall to be found only in nature or in human nature, but not in the city, and certainly not in its walls? Does the city wall mean that cities have no souls, or if they do have souls, then what sorts of souls exist in this city? What is an urban soul?

We cannot come easily to an understanding of the soul of city until we first unburden ourselves of some very common prejudices, especially that basic idea common to most of us, that cities are human constructions different and separate from nature. The city wall stands as a symbol of the separation between civilization and nature, between what is man-made and God-made, between two kinds of beauty — civilized beauty and natural beauty. Owing to this extreme distinction, we commonly believe that we must go to nature to find beauty and to commune with soul.

Transcribed from tapes of an invited lecture at Leslie College, Cambridge, Mass., 1995. The first version was presented at the symposium "Past Tense, Future Perfect?" under the auspices of For the People, September 1982, published in a report of that symposium, edited by P. Gunter and B. Higgins (Land/Mark Program, Dallas, 1984). A fuller version was published as "Natural Beauty Without Nature" in *Spring 1985*.

Moreover, we commonly believe that there is an untouched innocence about nature, whereas the city is polluted, corrupted, and evil.
As early as the first novels of the United States, in the late 1700s, the
city was the place where the innocent farm boy became corrupted.

That was Philadelphia, which even now, according to *USA Today*, is
the evilest city in the country. Our common view holds that goodness
resides — as does beauty, truth, and soul — in trees, rocks, streams,
mountains, flowers, but not in streets, offices, garages, airports, and
apartment houses. Our sense of soul is restored by a tree or a stream
and seems to be lost in a parking garage. So to find soul again we try to
import it within the city wall by making a garden, a fish pond, a bonsai
tree or an art object to remind us of natural beauty and therefore to
feel soulful.

I will challenge these usual habits and usual experiences, stemming
from this usual prejudice, because if we do not begin to examine our
usual experiences, the cities we live in will become more and more
soulless and alien and our lives and personal souls more and more victims of contemporary urbanization. The occasional islands of beauty
in giant noisy, smog cities like Manila, Cairo, Mexico City, and Osaka
do not resolve the major problem of our urban existence. Some other
thinking and feeling is required. What I am touching upon has echoes
in lives all over the world. Our problems are similar: the extension of
airports into farm land, the protection of smaller farmers against indus-
trialization, the concretizing of the world, increasing slums, high rises
that block the sunlight, the mass tourism that despoils rural places in
the search for beauty, the retreat of individual citizens from the urban
world into private sanctuaries of transcendent meditation, psychotherapy, alcohol, and entertainment. Collectively, these problems keep the
soul numbed to its dilemmas.

The bitter political fights and technical arguments over wilderness,
pollution, and energy have grounds that are not only ecological. They
have, as well, deep aesthetic grounds in the necessity of the soul for
beauty. The psyche's need for beauty is fundamental. All people have
modes of beautification: enhancement of their bodies, their utensils,
their movements in dance, their speech, and in poetry. When satisfaction of the urge to beauty is located in nature, and nature is threatened

with destruction, it is human to feel a soul loss and we are driven to extraordinary measures of conservation. The aim is not to preserve the snail darter and the whooping crane as such, but to preserve the soul's need for beauty and the satisfaction of this need by nature.

Our Western tradition has long condemned nature as a machine, an enemy, or a lifeless, soulless extension of objective matter for exploitation. Consequently, we realize that our philosophy made stripmining possible because our Western philosophy had declared matter dead; therefore, you can do what you want with it. This same arrogant, tough-mindedness has paradoxically retained a tender-minded association of beauty with nature. The lazy creek and white waterfall, the wide clean sky, a sunset, the far hills, and great trees — these have been our models for beauty and so refuge for the soul.

It was not always so in our civilization's history. During many periods, nature — or the physical world "out there" including the seas, and the mountains, and the forests — was considered demonic. A great deal of scientific literature from the early days of this country insists that the forests be radically cleared to allow more sunlight to dry the air and thereby improve human health. The forests were places of miasma, of disease, of pagans — read it in Hawthorne — of all kinds of bad things. What we now call "nature" was not a good place. The wilderness was for centuries dreaded. Only during the Romantic period did British puer young men first climb the high Alps. Our language still bears traces of this vilification of the natural: "heathen," "savage," "wild pagan," "boor," "peasant," and "clown" as terms of opprobrium are derived from natural landscapes. These words originally mean wooded, rocky, hills, of the soil and so on. The natural is not necessarily the beautiful and the beautiful not necessarily natural.

Let us further this distinction between the idea of beauty and the idea of nature and explore what may practically result from our inquiry. Philosophers have already noted at least sixty different connotations of the word *nature*. Perhaps Heraclitus, at the beginning of Western thought, was right when he said, "Nature loves to hide." At least it is as

elusive as the mythical nymphs of nature, or illusory as the Hindu idea
of *lila*, nature as a playful and ensnaring display. To use the word nature at all ensnares us in nostalgias, fears, fascinations, and devotions.
"Natural" embroils us in its history, not of nature as vegetation, rocks,
or un-thought behaviors, but in the history of an idea with its shifts
of affect-laden images. Kepler's astronomy, Linné's botany, Goethe's
Farbenlehre and *Urpflanze*, Darwin's species and the contemporary Gaia
hypothesis, present parables of the mythic imagination, which act
upon consciousness as creation myths. In other words, imagination is
perpetually creating nature and recreating it in a new guise; nature is
archetypically psychological. There is not a thing called nature, there
is an idea of nature.

I am trying to suggest that we cannot take nature just "naturally,"
unconsciously. We tend to use the words "nature" and "naturally" to
mean unconscious and unconsciously, as if nature referred to a purely
physical environment of air, water, earth, and fire; animals, plants, and
minerals; planetary bodies, motion, substance and their shapes, colors,
temperatures, and tastes. We think of a world "out there" not invented
by human minds or constructed by human hands, a world without consciousness of any sort and before all consciousness as its ground. To
be natural has come to mean to be simple, un-self-conscious, without
art. Just plain given. We call it data — purely objective. This as well
implies that nature is objectively pure, without subjective artifice. It is
genuine, and therefore the one remaining place where truth, beauty,
and goodness abide.

This givenness, this priority of nature, is often expressed as "God-
given," and opposed to human or "man-made." This quality of God-
given is longed for by the soul in its turn to nature to find beauty. But
this turn leads to a major shadow: by turning to nature, to God-given
nature for soul, we leave the City, thereby fostering more urban devastation. Neglect and ugliness consequently increase in the places where
we pass our days and do our work.

Let us realize the seriousness of this topic. Otherwise, we merely
continue as before, imagining the soul has only two possible locations:
either in natural things — streams and trees and rocks — or in human persons and among human persons in their relationships. Because

we identify soul with nature, the desire for nature becomes desperate. Anything that represents nature, such as sexual body, tropical fruits, wild animals, memories of rural places, even audiotapes of ocean waves or bird songs, become idealized and passionately clung to. A vast area between nature on the one hand and human persons on the other is considered soulless. What is considered void of soul is the realm of constructed objects, the things we live with daily. Our entire surrounding imagined to be only material, that is, functional, is soulless and dead. So, of course, the environment, toxicity, immunity, and allergy are the problems of our times. Our cities have become great concentration camps, almost cemeteries, where people go about their lives longing for escape.

Perhaps the strong contrast between nature and city can find a background in contrasts between several Greek Gods, those whose cults find locations mainly in the city and those outside. The Greeks said, "all things are full of Gods," so therefore the Gods are everywhere. At least five figures are to be found mainly in what we call nature, outside the city walls: Pan, Ares, Poseidon, Dionysus, and Artemis. We have also to mention Aphrodite, the Greek Goddess of love.

Pan's places are among rocky hills where goats and sheep graze. He is the God of the isolated shepherd (somewhat like the Japanese figure Oni, a red-faced figure, with horns, bearing strong animal attributes). Pan is wild, he makes his music with shepherd pipes; his impulses are sudden and sexual. He was the God who invaded civilized life with nightmares and the frightening demons of sleep. He still appears in the word "panic." He was the most favorite Greek figure in nineteenth-century Western poetry; he appeared more often then any other of the Greek figures during its turn to romantic wild nature and its turn away from industrialized urbanism. Pan is decidedly outside the walls.

Ares, the battle God, is not well spoken of in Greek literature. As a war God, Ares urged humans to fight and rage, but he protected the city. He was to be kept outside the city, as for instance in Rome where Mars, the Roman equivalent of Ares, had a special place in the field of

Mars outside the walls. Armies were not allowed in the city of Rome until after Julius Caesar, so dangerous to the city was Mars.

Another figure of great power was Poseidon. He was one of the three brother Gods who ruled the cosmos: Zeus above, Hades below, Poseidon the waters. These waters referred to all the surging, rushing, disquieting phenomena, the restless and stormy seas as well as the rivers coursing toward the seas. He was the God of earthquakes. It was Poseidon who gave horses to humans. One tale about Poseidon and the horse shows that the issue we are discussing today, city vs. nature, is not new. There was a fierce argument between Athena and Poseidon. She was the patroness of all cities and of the greatest city perhaps ever, Athens. On one side, Poseidon; and on the other, Athena, both claiming they gave to human beings the horse. Finally, it was decided that Poseidon gave the horse, but it was Athena who gave the bridal and the reins. The power of the horse is natural, the control is civilized.

The fourth figure on this short list of city outsiders is Dionysus. Inside the city, Dionysus's place was the theatre for he was a God of tragedy and comedy and the presentation within a civilized form of the deepest natural forces that rule human fate. In fact, he was simply called *zoe* or the life force. (Our Western languages still have the words zoo and zoology indicating the connection between Dionysus and instinct, beyond civilization and beyond domestication.) He ruled natural conditions such as intoxication from wine and excitement, from sexual mystery, and the deep descent to underworld depression beyond the polite world of urban manners.

Just as Dionysus could be discovered within the city, through deep emotions, as in the theater or in drunkenness, the Goddess Artemis also was in the city, but only in an emotional way. Her places were outside the walls. However, she was in the city for women in the pangs of childbirth. This lady of the beasts, as she was called, was the force of nature in a women's body as she gave birth. Otherwise, Artemis was distant, remote, a Goddess of the animals of the forests, a huntress that had to be alone. She would find the crowds of the city unbearable, because the very word for city in Greek, *polis*, for which we still have political and police, and metropolitan and polite, means originally throng or crowd, like a flowing press of people in a city street.

You could imagine how miserable Artemis would feel holiday-shopping in a strip mall.

I have not mentioned Aphrodite. One must always take great care inviting the Goddess of love into your conversation because her strength is so mighty and her rules so irrational. We can never tell in advance what might happen. She is not bound by city walls and therefore cannot be said to belong either inside or outside. For the Goddess of love can appear anywhere and something about her does not like walls at all, for they make separations where she makes new unions. Nonetheless, her temples were located often near the seaside and she herself was born from the foam of the salt waves. Further, many of her temples were near rocky promontories, overlooking the majestic and forceful landscapes, attesting, as one scholar has written to the irresistible and terrible power of love, a natural power beyond the control of civic order.

If these Gods and Goddesses are mostly found outside the city or within the city only at special ritual moments, like theatre or child birth, drinking celebrations, or the rush of sexual desire, then much of nature is considered to be (at least to the Greek mind which originated the very notion of city in Western culture) destructive to the city. Perhaps city walls and the division of city and nature are the only way possible to imagine cities. Perhaps the Gods themselves wish to keep a separation. However, I am insisting that the quality and experience of God-givenness does not have to be restricted to shoreline and canyons, grasses and birds.

We are now caught in a problem: do the Gods themselves want to keep these two things separate, which would mean that God-givenness is only out there in nature? The solution here is to look again at that word "natural." Natural, as well as prior, and God-given could be deliterized to mean far more than only the physical world out there. "Natural" could also mean lawful rather than willful; rightly formed, rather than freely expressed; systematically ordered, rather than random. "Prior" can also mean given first place to anything other than my subjective self, that is, nature as it comes first.

"God-given" can also be sensed as belonging to an object. For example in animism where any object can be animated to have soul.

Any little thing could be considered to have soul: what you wear around your neck, the keepsake you bring back from vacation or the little stone you pick up on the beach. These, too, would have soul. Any stone, whether in the ground or held in the hand or carved into a statue, used as a tool, or respected as an amulet can be a soul-speaking object, that is, a totem or a fetish, depending upon where it is placed, how it is cared for and ritually regarded. All sorts of things can afford the sense of beauty, even mundane, everyday objects, depending less on their origin in nature than on their treatment by our hands and minds. One of the virtues of the pop art movement has been its ability to restore the sense of wonder to the banal things of life, like a Brillo box, or a comic strip. The ordinary world can release the experience of God-givenness. Once we are released from identifying that experience solely with nature, with what human hands did not make, then "all things are full of Gods" becomes quite obvious.

We begin to see that what we go to nature for can be distinguished from the natural world. We begin to see that the natural world does not necessarily afford this experience, because in various times in cultures nature is not the place of beauty. Finally, we begin to see that nature as a primary given cannot be separated from basic ideas about nature found in the human psyche. "Nature" is always somehow human-made, if not directly with our hands, certainly with our minds. We are always constructing nature one way or another. How difficult it is to keep this distinction because a fixed idea of Nature is already in your mind. It is that rock out there. However, that rock out there is what we have defined to be nature, and where does nature stop? The great question now, in psychology, is *where* is the subject, not *what* is the subject, but where does the subject stop? Where does the unconscious stop? Where does the psyche stop? Does it stop inside my skin? Does it stop in my relationships — just you and me? Does it extend into the room, into the furniture? Where does psyche stop?

If I ask two questions: first, what comes first to your mind with the idea of beauty? Usually it is a physical, natural phenomenon. Then if

I ask: what best nourishes your sense of soul? Again, the reply is usually some aesthetic experience. A moment of beauty, a moment of music, a moment of seeing a fox suddenly in the forest, a painting, or a moment of communication with another person that went deep. Something you would call "beautiful." In the city we try to fulfill this longing by importing beauty and placing it in a special reserve: a museum, a concert hall, a garden, a temple, or art treasure in a special place in your private room. This kind of beauty does not permeate all of life, and so the city remains generally untouched. Beauty remains sequestered and objectified into precious places, times, and things.

As you know, beauty is nourished differently in many tribal, non-industrial societies. There, songs and stories, and dances and decorations and rituals, enhance much more of every day. The Balinese say that they do not have art; they simply make each thing as beautiful as they can. In some so-called "primitive" societies, two-thirds of waking time passes in "non-productive" aesthetic ritual. In other words, they spend their time talking, telling stories, getting ready for a feast, decorating their bodies, cleaning up after a festival, arranging a huge celebration, a hunt . . . not in the labor of growing food and selling things. Most of the waking time passes in aesthetic ritual.

Industrial cultures — European, American, Asian — however, seem to treat beauty in the special secluded way, walling it off from the world in general. Why this wall, why the walled garden, that classic symbol of the *hortus inclusus*, which we find in Muslim architecture, Persian poetry, Catholic symbolism, as well as in the superb examples of the enclosed garden in Japan? My concern, as I said at the beginning, is to disrupt our habitual thinking and so to look for ways of getting out of the garden. By getting out of the garden, I mean releasing beauty from enclosure in special preserves.

The sacred preserves which protect beauty are usually religious, or revered with religious emotion. Today, museums with paintings by great masters and concert halls for great performance artists are places of secular religion. They have become temples of beauty and our relation to art objects has become a kind of religious piety. The forty million dollars that a Japanese businessman pays for Van Gogh's *Irises* or the money spent on rare exquisite manuscripts, violins, Persian carpets, and contemporary sculptures attest to the high value we place on beauty in a secular world were money states value. High price is a secular way of appreciating the divine quality of an object — *kami* in the Japanese sense, *theos* in the Greek.

High prices show a religious homage to beauty, attesting again to the need of the soul for beauty. But a problem remains. Although these religious emotions recognize the high or religious quality of art, because art inspires and delights the soul, these same religious emotions tend to segregate art with a secluded and protective reverence: alarm systems, humidity control, and restoration to keep each art object safe from touch and from time, eternally preserved as if forever young. Michelangelo's Sistine Chapel has recently had cosmetic surgery.

Beyond these protections, there exists a psychological attitude that an art object is itself somehow holy, and therefore sacred and separate from the mundane. As if each moment or thing of beauty is itself a walled garden. Now the precious seclusion of beautiful art should be blamed not only on egocentric artists or vanity and curators, greedy gallery owners and collectors. The desire to sequester beauty seems to arise from the soul whenever it encounters something precious. In a world where beauty is so rare, this desire to keep beauty behind lock and key is especially strong. We feel this protective urge about a rare tree as well as about a rare drawing by a master hand. Psychologically, we feel a protective urge in a similar way about our precious loves, our rare and important dreams and cherished memories. We tend to wall them off and allow, only on special occasions, someone special through the gate into our private garden of intimacy.

So you see the problem with the wall confronts us again. First the wall between city and nature, then the wall between secular and sacred and now a third wall — the one which the soul constructs to protect its treasures.

Now I am quite at a loss. I intended to lead beauty from exile out of the garden back into the city. Instead, I am finding her increasingly walled in. Moreover, it seems as if the soul asks for these walls, this protection, as if beauty itself asks to be enclosed. Must we conclude that the soul requires the seclusion of beauty? If it is the soul that insists upon protecting beauty, then does opening the wall to allow beauty to enter into the world mean we are violating the soul's own wishes? Does it mean that our intention to restore beauty to all the daily things of the city would result in a loss of beauty? Is this move into popular city life soul-destroying rather than a soul-making enterprise? Must not we protect rarity rather than dissipate it? Is not one exquisitely perfect cup made of nearly transparent porcelain more significant than thousands of very well made ones?

The answer to this aesthetic question once again goes back to those Greek Gods. This time to a God who definitely belongs more to the city than to wild nature, the God Apollo. As you will recall he was the young God of sunlight, of male perfection, of rational clarity, purity, and eternal tranquility, away from the turmoil of ordinary life — a God of the elite. He upheld correct action, correct form, and noble ideals. He was a God of youth, and his temple stood off in high places, in rough terrain, signifying his opposition to the wild powers of earthy nature. In Western culture, Apollo was particularly associated with and became the patron God of the arts, even medicine and science. In short, from the heights of Athenian civilization, through Rome and the Renaissance to the Neo-classicism of the Enlightenment, an Apollonian idea of beauty dominated Western culture. The art of the people was considered only folk art or ethnic or primitive or regional or parochial or amateur or outsider. The restriction of art to high art of masters, we owe to an Apollonian defini-tion of beauty. This is one reason why art by women rarely received ac-claim in Western culture. Women were not part of the Apollonian vision of life, and Apollo's own mythical relation with females was frequently and usually a disaster. Apollo had appropriated beauty for himself so that art objects, art criticism, and art theory reflect Apollonian ideals, until the various rebellions against him by followers of other Gods such as the Dionysian romantics, the Demetrian feminists, and the Hermetic con-ceptualists, and so on. And not only Western culture. Apollonian atti-tudes, even if not called such in other cultures, dominate all sophisticated urban civilization where art is associated mainly with higher values of an elite class and where beauty is sequestered.

Curiously, the myths of Apollo tell of attempts to objectify beauty and fix it in a natural place or moment. This cuts off the rarified instance from nature. Much of what we today regard as nature has suffered this objectification and seems to be a projection of sophisticated urbanism. Consider this: most supporters of environmentalism are people living in cities. Thus, before we can restore beauty to the city and the soul to the world, we must free our notion of beauty from Apollonian ideals. Then beauty could be freed from objectification and seclusion and we might still have our precious objects and walled gardens, but not as the only locus of beauty. Beauty could find definition in many other styles: office buildings and office furniture, traffic highways and gasoline stations, neon signs and TV advertisements could also be imagined as places where beauty might "naturally" appear.

The casual graffiti on buildings and subways, the strange disharmonies and words of pop music, the clever consumerist advertising, the sarcastic and aggressive disillusion of the avant-garde, are each ways of tempting aesthetics away from the eternal perfection and purified ideals of the Apollonian mode. For example, some years ago in Singapore's extremely Apollonian structure, graffiti was a serious crime. The pop modes at first seem cheap, destructive, and careless. Nonetheless, they make an opening with humor and vitality for the soul to find beauty back in the streets. Let us remember the Berlin Wall, the symbol of so many walls of our time, came down partly because of these very same, cheap, sarcastic, graffiti-like impulses in the common citizens. Pop music took the wall down.

The two main ideas we have been developing — freeing the definition of nature from the narrow limits of natural things and disentangling the need for beauty from the need for nature — have consequences for our daily environment. First, we would no longer have to split the natural from the urban. If God-given and man-made are an unnecessary, even false, opposition, then the city made by human hands is also natural in its own right. Surely it is as "natural" to human beings to make burial grounds, marketplaces, political and social communities, and to erect structures for worship, education, protection, and celebration as it is for them to gather nuts and berries, trap animals, or hoe the soil. Cities belong to human nature and nature does not begin outside the city wall. Therefore, the beautiful City does not have to copy the green world, a habit that puts a premium on suburbia, each citizen with his or her private tree, turf, and Toro mower. Urban beauty would not draw its standards from approximation to wild nature, requiring potted trees and trellised vine interiors, noisy water-walls that impede natural running conversation. The sounds of the water in imitation of "nature" drown out a "natural" conversation. Further, there would be no need for plastics that fake the look of bark and stone. Again, pop art and sculptural forms have revealed the simple genuine givenness of plastic masses that do not imitate anything prior to themselves.

Second, if we take back the experience of God-givenness from its location only in nature, then we might be able to find this experience elsewhere. The great cathedrals of Europe were God-given and man-made both, and built at a time when the wider outdoors was usually felt to be haunted by evil. The soul's need for beauty was met mainly by urban events such as pageants, music, contests, and feasts centered upon the huge cathedrals and their walls. What we now turn to nature for — inspiration in the face of might and majesty, wonder over intricacy, rhythms, and detail — could as well appear in our constructions. Skyscrapers, power stations, airports, market halls, and hotels can be re-imagined as structures for the soul to find beauty, rather than conceived merely as secular and cost-efficient service functions.

Third, the imitation of nature would change. We would imitate the process of nature rather than what the process has made. We would imitate the *way* of nature rather than the *things* of nature. (Scholastic philosophy differentiated *naturans* from *naturata*.) It would be less a matter of building a false river through a mall — the Disney sort of way of doing things — than of building a mall so it reminds us of a canyon or a streambed. It would be less a matter of planting trees along a sidewalk than of making the sidewalk itself meander organically as if it were growing along irregularly. It is the way nature makes things, rather than imitating what nature has already made. However, we go on making imitations of what nature has made, vinyl to look like wood.

Hotels and malls pay large sums for the care of the artificial plants. Rather than copying, we would remember nature in the way we construct so that nature echoes in the constructed object.

An example from Texas is the Fort Worth Water Garden: a majestic, descending torrent of water running through a place that hasn't a single leaf, a single loose pebble; an utterly "unnatural" mix of stones, cement, hidden piping plunked down into the usual downtown wasteland. Yet that construction completely overwhelms with the experience we expect from natural beauty. It is a wild adventure of encompassing grandeur. When you are in this cemented place, with no trees, no leaves, no imitations of any sort, you may be overwhelmed by its power. You experience the way nature itself works in a canyon: a rush of water going through a dry streambed. Likewise, when you are walking down Fifth Avenue in New York, perhaps you may get the experience of inspiration from the towering structures of glass, steel, and aluminum — hardly an imitation of mountains.

The imitation of nature can well employ technical means as it has done for centuries in the arts. The garden, after all, is not nature but art, or rather, it is nature imitating art. The restitution of the natural environment would not require the literal transplanting of whole biospheres "parked" into set-aside preserves, but would rather suggest miniature biospheres all through the city such as hybrid dwarf shrubs, song-birds in cages, window boxes and vegetable plots, fishponds, insect vivariums and terrariums. Botany and biology would be honorably represented on the staff of City Hall instead of serving only academia and servicing the drug industry. I am suggesting the imitation of nature as a miniaturization of nature such as the Japanese practice. I am suggesting a reduction in the scale of awe from a romantic and sublime immersion in vastness — the American way — to joy in pondering the particular.

Fourth, if art moves out from behind the secluded wall, then why not the artist too. Why not imagine the artists as citizens. The artist is a member of the *polis* whose life, as with any other citizen, is partly in service to the city. We would no longer regard the artist as the most independent of all persons, but rather as the one most involved and most engaged in meeting the needs of the soul and therefore most caught in the issues of the community.

Fifth, we would ask leaders and politicians to declare their aesthetic policy and not only their economic, foreign, environmental, and agricultural policies. We would want elected officials to reveal their taste regarding all public projects, architecture, parks, conservation, education, and so on.

Sixth, we would expect all private and public construction in the city, in the planning stages, to submit to aesthetic review by artists. Art would not just be added to a project as a decoration like a huge wall painting in the entrance lobby of the bank or City Hall. Rather, art for pleasing the soul would be inherent to the project from its very beginning. A project from inception would be designed for the sake of the soul. (I'm begging a question here as I'm suggesting that artists already have a sense of soul.)

Seventh, we would require city officials, when letting contracts for purchases, to take into account their design, the quality of the materials, and the role of artists in their production. In this way, city government becomes a regular patron of the arts in the simplest purchases for offices such as printing and for whatever equipment government has to buy. As a result, city officials would have to account for the aesthetic design of what its officials are buying, and not only the price.

Eighth, every city would have its guardians of memory. This is rather similar to the notion of historic preservation in the United States or the national trust in Great Britain. The guardians of memory would have veto authority over all demolitions, all remodeling, and all reconstructions. Their concern is the preservation of memory, which is located not merely in the human brain but in the physical structures of the City. Cities become amnesiacs when their old towns are destroyed. They lose the physical representations of their memory. Again, not merely ancient monuments and national treasures hold the memory of the city, but all sorts of minor designs, structures, shops, doorways, and signs.

Ninth, we would encourage that great Japanese virtue, miniaturization. Instead of expanding the green belts and increasing the park areas to bring nature into the city, we would rather imagine small details like drinking fountains, fish aquariums, singing birds as bits of nature within the city. We would further attempt to devise the buses, the machines, the public toilets and trash containers, the lights, and rail-ings and parking places and their meters in such a way that these small events of daily life gave pleasure to the soul.

Tenth, we would no longer let the National Parks Service, the Sierra Club, or God take care of our need for beauty by protecting or fostering wilderness. We could come to a more psychological notion of wilderness, following a definition inherent in the rules governing wilderness areas. Enter and enjoy, but make no mark. Disturb nothing, pollute nothing, and leave no trace, not even a footprint. This definition, psychologically, implies that wherever we tread with the attitude of "no trace," we are creating the experience of wilderness. When we move with senses acute, listening, watching, breathing in tune with the world about us, recognizing its priority and ourselves as guests, witnessing its God-givenness, then we have made a wilderness area or moment. The restoration of the pristine starts in a fresh attitude toward what is — whatever and wherever it is, not necessarily out there in nature. I know of school classes that start their discovery of nature by first exploring the city with ears and eyes alert and only then do they go into the countryside. Awakening to nature depends on the attitude brought to a place by the observer, and not only upon the place where the observer goes.

Idealizing wilderness and placing it in Idaho and the Adirondacks casts a shadow on our daily world, trashing it yet further. Beauty is elsewhere, so what is here becomes desolate, uncultivated, waste — exactly what was meant by the ancient idea of wilderness: the place of Cain and the scapegoat in the Bible. By worshipping one kind of wilderness in the high Sierras, we create the other kind in the backyard: the city as scapegoat, as place of Cain. Instead, the sense of beauty that we seek in the idealized wilderness can be fostered by the attitude of walking the world without injury to it, leaving no trace, no leftover actions to be dealt with by others, giving priority to the physical thing over the subjective will.

Finally, eleven, we come to psychotherapy. We would recognize that therapy as it is now conceived does not include the repair of the world's loss of beauty and therefore is inadequate to meet the needs of the soul. We would ask therapy to reinvent itself as an aesthetic activity. There could be profound shifts in therapy of soul. Soul could be reclaimed from soulful places out there filled with God-given beauty, as if soul were given to us automatically by osmosis when we stand beneath a redwood or hear the waves on the shore, as if all you need to do is to get out there in nature and your soul is filled again. Once we recognize that the need for beauty must be met in many places and not just in scenic, physical nature, we would take the soul back into our own hands. Then we might better realize that what happens with it is less given and more made — made through our work with it in the actual world by making that actual world reflect the soul's need for beauty.

Yes, a last footnote recommendation: every week or so the lights of the city would be doused at two in the morning for two hours, perhaps except in emergency areas, so that the citizens would be able to free themselves from light pollution and once again turn their gaze to the sky of stars.

16

The Repression of Beauty

My desire is to show why an idea of beauty is useful, functional, and practical. Too often and for too long when the words *bella* and *la bellezza* appear they raise us to lofty thoughts. This high style, of course, has been declared to be a function of beauty: it inspires, reminds us of our wings as Plato would say, lifting the mind to permanent values and eternal truths. This higher idea of beauty, shown immediately by the effect it has on our rhetoric the moment we begin to enter into discourse on aesthetics, would not be disputed by either classics or romantics. And it is also this higher idea and lofty rhetoric that often makes the discussion of beauty stupefying, *noioso*, narcoleptic.

The narcoleptic effect of the usual discussions of aesthetics, the disguised moralism that beauty is "good for you," is even good itself, have turned an entire century against anything to do with beauty, classic and romantic, and have banned beauty from painting, music, architecture, and poetry; and from criticism, too, so that the arts, whose task once was considered to be that of manifesting the beautiful, will discuss the idea only to dismiss it, regarding beauty only as the pretty, the simple, the pleasing, the mindless, and the easy. Because beauty is conceived so naively, it appears as merely naive, and can be tolerated only if complicated by discord, shock, violence, and harsh terrestrial realities.

I therefore feel justified in speaking of the repression of beauty. "Repression" indicates that we are engaged in a profound question, not

---

First presented at the Seminar "Repressione della Bellezza," Centro per l'Arte Contemporanea Luigi Pecci, Prato, February 1991, and published in *Archivo* 2 (Museo Pecci, Prato, 1994).

only regarding the arts, psychology, and the theory of aesthetics, but as I intend to show, regarding the world we live in and the condition of its soul and ours.

To speak of beauty today, so soon after the Gulf War with its apocalyptic devastation, could seem precious, elitist, even fascistic. I assure you this is not the case. Discussions of beauty during most of this century have been perverted by the totalitarian appropriation of the subject too often neglected by the humanist and existential concern for democratic social improvement. The political right took over fields left untilled by the political left. If we do not boldly open this question, it remains not only repressed, and worse: subject to totalitarian misuse. So what I am hoping to do today is make one small step towards reclaiming for the democratic tradition some of the abandoned terrain — much as I have tried on previous occasions regarding Greek myths and Romantic thinkers. For, let us be quite clear, fascism today is not where it was fifty years ago; nor is it here in our reclamation of this theme. Today, totalitarianism is on television, its glorification of war equipment, the technology of destruction, the suppression of human feeling with uniform language, and the mass patriotism stirred by the letting of blood.

Psychology — by which I mean of course a psychology that is true to its name, *psyche logos*, the study of the soul, psyche, and anima — has been influenced by theories derived from scientific medicine, from physics, chemistry, physiology and pharmacology, from anthropology and linguistics. Psychology has been influenced, however, also by aesthetics, particularly by the very denial of beauty which appears in psychological discourse as an absence, a repression. Beauty is not a category in psychotherapy or a factor in considering the language used, the style of the patient, the taste displayed by the therapist, the preferences in the arts of the patient, or that we all live, one way or another, within aesthetic ideals: imagining ourselves in terms of the lives of dead artists or as figures in their works, or in present films, or enacting moments in our lives that consciously repeat in recollection leitmotifs from drama, music, novels. We choose fashions, decorate our rooms, search for restaurants, and judge our friends.

This curious refusal to admit beauty in psychological discourse occurs even though each of us knows that nothing so affects the soul,
so transports, as moments of beauty — in nature, a face, a song, an
action or dream. And we feel that these moments are therapeutic in
the truest sense: make us aware of soul and make us care for its value.
We have been touched by beauty. Yet, as I say, therapy never discusses
this fact in its theories, and the aesthetic plays no role whatsoever in
therapeutic practice, in developmental theory, in transference, in the
notions of successful treatment or failed treatment, and the termina-
tion of therapy. Are we afraid of its power?

To conclude from this fact in my own field, I shall claim that the most
significant unconscious today, that factor which is most important but
most unrecognized in the work of our psychological culture, could be
defined as "beauty" for that is what is ignored, omitted, absent. The repressed therefore is not what we usually suppose: violence, misogyny,
sexuality, childhood, emotions, and feeling, or even the spirit which
receives its due in meditation practice. All these themes are common in
daily conversation. No, the repressed today is beauty.

With this in mind, let us attempt now to show how beauty affects
our contemporary practical concerns beyond both psychology (my
field) and the arts, yours. You notice of course that I am postponing
any sort of definition of beauty, any move to make it clear what beauty
is. I ask you to hold this question in abeyance, and to feel instead
whatever idea of beauty you have, letting what I say resonate with the
recollections of beauty and feelings of beauty that have established
themselves in your way of life.

The first of these concerns is the world itself: ecology. One approach in general today has turned to the mythical figure of Gaia.
The Gaia Hypothesis of deep ecology holds that the world is a living and breathing organism, even the magma and rocks at the earth's
core, Gaia's basic stuff, shall be imagined organically. This hypothesis, which interconnects the whole world, is the triumph of feminism
and organicism. The hypothesis that the world is alive represents a
complete reversal of values, an *enantiodromia* from the paternalism of
God the Father and his instrument on earth, the Pope, as well as the
doctrines of higher spiritualism which sees the world as an act of

creatio ex nihilo and the matter of this earth as merely dead, Cartesian *res extensa*.

Nonetheless, the Gaia Hypothesis of deep ecology reduces the puzzles of the world to interacting functionalism; Darwin up to date. Our wonder in face of the world's complex magnificence attends less to its sensate presence than to its subtle interactionism — microorganisms, ozone layers, virus strains, methane, tropic heat evaporation, chlorophyll, gene pools, interdependency of species. Our ecological wonder remains scientific — as it should be since the Gaia Hypothesis was formulated by Lovelock and Margulis, both physical scientists. The world of deep ecology remains *physis*. But is this vision enough to draw us toward the world? That we feel an obligation to the world is clear enough. Great Mother Nature no longer provides our support; we are now obliged to care for her. Nature today is on dialysis, slowly expiring, kept alive only by advanced technology. What can stir our depths equal to the depths of ecological need? Duty, wonder, respect, guilt, or the fear of extinction are not enough. Only love can keep the patient alive — a desire for the world which affords the vitality, the passionate interest on which all other efforts rest.

We want the world because it is beautiful, its sounds and smells and textures, the sensate presence of the world as body. In short, below the ecological crisis lies the deeper crisis of love, that our love has left the world; that the world is loveless results directly from the repression of beauty, its beauty and our sensitivity to beauty. For love to return to the world, beauty must first return, else we love the world only as a moral duty: clean it up, preserve its nature, and exploit it less. If love depends on beauty, then beauty comes first. Separated from beauty, love becomes a duty. Love thy neighbor becomes a moral obligation, almost a commandment, and the world's alluring face becomes a temptress. In the pagan pre-Christian world, love follows attraction, ever further extending and deepening possibilities of love led on by beauty. Beauty before love also accords with the all-too-human experience of being driven to love by the allure of beauty.

The second of our major concerns which calls for a practice of beauty is economic. This may seem surprising. For usually beauty is imagined as an accessory, a luxury, beyond the scope of economics. If, for instance, a public plaza is to be constructed, town planners first arrange the traffic question then the accessibility for shopping and other commercial uses, last comes the "look" of the place: a commissioned sculpture, a fountain, a little grove of trees and flower beds, special lights. The artist is brought in last and is first to be eliminated when the project begins to go over budget. Beautification costs much. It is uneconomical.

Contrary to this usual view, ugliness costs more. What are the economics of ugliness? What is the cost to physical well-being and psychological balance of careless design, of cheap dyes, inane sounds, structures and spaces? To pass a day in an office under direct glaring light, in bad chairs, victim of the constant monotonous hum of machine noise, looking down at a worn, splotched floor cover, among artificial plants, making motions that are unidirectional, push-button sagittal in-and-out that repress the gestures of the body — and then at day's end to enter the traffic system or the public transport system, fast food, project housing — what does this cost? What does it cost in absenteeism, in sexual obsession, school dropout, overeating, and short attention span, in pharmaceutical remedies and the gigantic escapism industries of tourism, wasteful consumer shopping, chemical dependency, and sports violence? Could the causes of major social, political, and economic issues of our time also be found in the repression of beauty?

The third repression of beauty we find in depth psychology. Today, our field is characterized by an intense subjectivity of self-reflection: introspection, reminiscence, reconstruction, feelings — the cultivation of personal interiority. The mirror has become a favorite metaphor, adolescence and childhood the major topics, resulting in a contemporary syndrome, a character disorder, relatively unnoticed in the first sixty years of psychoanalysis: I am, of course, referring to the diagnosis of "narcissism."

Narcissism had classically been described by Freud in 1922 as an absence or disturbance of "object libido," that desire reaching into the world "out there." Instead, desire flows inward, activating one's isolated subjectivity. The beauty of the world holds no allure, no echo that draws our noticing because the world's beauty does not call. I seek and find that beauty in a self-concentrated gaze. This is Narcissism and, as the word itself betrays from its origin in the Ovid tale, *narcissism is a beauty disorder*, the face of the world unattended, the libido objectless, turned toward the narcissistic subject, disordering his character. Narcissus was captivated not by himself, not by reflection, but by beauty.

If we wish to be practical and therapeutic in regard to Narcissism, supposedly the most prevalent syndrome affecting the younger population of Western society, this narcissism that prevents relationship and citizenship, displaying itself as self-centered immature escapism in alcohol, gambling, drugs, consumerism, fashion, and celebrity worship, then we may do better considering the syndrome a disorder in the realm of beauty, a result of its repression, rather than a disorder in the realm of individual patients. For the anaesthesia in the soul of the individual cannot be separated and treated apart from the anaesthesia in the soul of the world and its *Zeitgeist*.

There is yet one more arena where the restoration of beauty could be practically valuable. I am thinking of contemporary philosophy Generally, philosophy has never been noted for its passion or compassion in regard to the actualities of life lived; but today it seems more cold and callous — shall we say "anesthetized" — to the plight of the soul in the shipwreck of the world than ever before. I recall a conference a few years ago entitled "Philosophy — Where Are You When We Need You Most?"

This anaesthesia, what Robert Lifton calls "psychic numbing," shows in philosophy in several ways: In cosmology where speculation on the origin of the cosmos invents big bangs, black holes, and gas storms without a thought about its stupendous beauty visible, for instance, each night in the sky. Anesthesia shows, also, in death-of-god-theology and in the disguised apocalyptic of chaos theory. It shows in postmodern deconstructionism which relies on the semantics that have severed the signifying gift of the human spirit from the significance of the world within which it moves. We are left with the fractals and wittily named particles (by definition non-sensate) of theoretical physics, the puns and parodies of architecture and the language games of philosophical analysis resulting in a severe dissociation between what is thought, said, and written and what the senses see, the heart feels, and the world suffers.

We have not yet said what beauty is. This evasion is deliberate: we want to enter into the heart of the subject before we are snared by the rational defenses against the subject. We must beg the question because a major part of the repression of beauty has always been an inability to find for it a rational definition. We cannot talk about beauty since we cannot define what we are talking about.

The usual definitions fall in to the usual subject/object dispute. The subjectivists, Hume for example, say beauty is in the eye of the beholder: *De gustibus non est disputandum.* If there are conflicting judgments about the beauty of a painting, each viewer perceiving beauty in his and her own light, the resolution lies in acquiescence to superior enlightened taste cultivated by those who are experts. Eventually the expert person of cultivated taste becomes the influential art critic, the academy judge, the museum director, the gallery owner, so that subjectivism finally degenerates, as in our time, to commercialism where price determines taste and substitutes for value. Beauty for sale at the auction house.

The objectivists maintain that beauty is not in the eye of the beholder or if so, then only because of the formal properties of the artwork and seen there in the object: composition, variation in unity, color, line, contrast, complexity, finish, tension, subtlety, resolution of internal conflict, proportion, accomplishment of intention, balance. Beauty is reduced to conceptual formalisms.

Instead of these dilemmas, suppose we were to imagine that beauty is permanently given, inherent to the world in its data, there on display always. This inherent radiance lights up more translucently, more intensively within certain events, particularly those events that aim to seize it and reveal it, such as art works.

If we use mythological language for this inherent radiance, we would speak of Aphrodite, the golden one, the smiling one, whose smile made the world pleasurable and lovely. She was more than an aesthetic joy; she was an *epistemological necessity*, for without her all the other Gods would remain hidden like the abstractions of mathematics and theology, but never palpable realities. (Abstractions, by the way, require proof and belief; they must be made convincing by argument or believed in by faith; whereas Gods that manifest their qualities to the senses require no such mediation.) Owing to her, the divine could be seen and heard, smelled, tasted, and touched. She made manifest the divine mind. And we respond to her radiant presence in things with words like "divine, marvelous, gorgeous, superb, wonderful, amazing, heavenly, delightful, out-of-this-world" — words which attest to the divine enhancement of any ordinary thing, whether the feel of a fabric, the fall of a woman's hair, the taste of a wine.

Just here a passage from Plotinus (*Enneads* IV, 4.37) will be useful, for it has to do with the power of ordinary things. After all, is that not the great puzzle: that ordinary things — the *objet trouvé*, the collage of newsprint, wallpaper, and postage stamps, the light glinting off the icicle — can exhibit the invisible power of beauty? Plotinus argues that, "We do not habitually examine or in any way question ordinary things, but we set to doubting when confronted with any display of powers which are out of the ordinary, and encounter the extraordinary with astonishment, though we should be astonished at these ordinary things, too, if we were unfamiliar with them and someone presented a detailed account of them and explained their powers."

Plotinus is saying that we take ordinary things for granted, and that they are "ordinary" precisely because we do not examine them carefully enough in detail which does not allow the power of their aesthetic smile to appear. The artist, of course, does indeed reveal the extraordinary in the ordinary. That is the job — not to distinguish and separate the ordinary and the extraordinary, but to view the ordinary with the extraordinary eye of divine enhancement. Is this not the intention of Pop Art? For, as Plotinus goes on to say in the same passage, "We must admit, then, that each particular thing has an unreasoned power . . . has share of soul . . . "

This sense of the world as the presence of Aphrodite is already given in the Greek word *kosmos*, from which come our cosmology and cosmonaut. *Kosmos*, when translated from the Greek into Latin, became *universum*, betraying the Roman penchant for general laws, the whole world turning around one (*unus-verto*). Cosmos, however, does not mean an all-embracing system; it is an aesthetic term, best translated into English as fitting-order, appropriate, right arrangement, so that attention to particulars takes precedence over universals. *Kosmos* is also a moral term, as for instance *kata kosmon* (disordered) in the *Iliad* (8:179) means "shamefully." *Kosmos* embraces meanings such as becomingly, decently, honorably. The aesthetic and the moral blend, as in our everyday language of craft where straight, true, right, sound imply both the good and the beautiful. Another group of connotations are discipline, form, fashion. *Kosmos* was used especially of women in respect to their embellishment, decorations, ornaments, dress, and the word is descriptive of sweet songs and speech. "Cosmetics" is actually closer to the original than "cosmic," which tends to mean vacant, gaseous and vast. The Stoics used *kosmos* for the *anima mundi*, soul of the world — quite different indeed from "universe" which has no immediate aesthetic implications. Plotinus (*Enneads* I, 6.2), because he was immersed in the Greek implications of *kosmos* or fitting-order, could therefore state as a definition that "ugliness comes from an insufficient mastery by form and reason (*morphes kai logon*)."

If the cosmos itself implies beauty, if we live in an aesthetic world, then the primary mode of adjustment to the cosmos would be through the sense of beauty. For this reason alone the repression of beauty has cosmic proportions. No wonder civilization is in disarray and no wonder the terrible burden on the individual artist to find his or her way back to the innate demand that the cosmos places on an individual talent. We are each out of order and in need of therapy because we have forgotten that life is essentially aesthetic, cosmologically so. In Whitehead's words, "The teleology of the universe is directed to the production of Beauty." [1]

The Aphroditic notion of beauty as sense perception or *aisthesis* raises display to the primary mode of knowledge and replaces belief in the unknowable with trust in the visible. Rather than analysis into the microbits of science or abstraction into the comprehensive laws of mathematics and theology, display of the world reveals its truth.

Moreover, by shifting back from the Roman universe to the Greek cosmos, beauty, too, shifts its locus from the universal to the particular. We hardly realize how "universe" has favored science, mathematics, theology, and law and has disfavored the arts which are concerned with each particular body made evident in a painting, a dance, or a song. The arts are no more general than is nature. Even if nature presents panoramas and *bella vistas*, these remain particular images. Each star in a galaxy of billions has its locus and magnitude.

Cosmos does not present itself as an all-embracing whole, but as the appearance of fittingness of each thing as and where it is; how well, how decorously, how appropriately it displays. Its beauty is that very display; cosmos in each, as each, grain of sand. Different indeed from the idea of beauty in a universe where artworks are signified by a whole beyond themselves — Church art being a prime example — becoming representations of abstract symbol systems, thereby devaluing the displayed immediacy of the thing at hand and its sheer decorativeness which does not have to gain its power by pointing to a larger conceptual significance.

Animals bear the most apparent witness to the cosmological importance of display. Adolf Portmann, the Swiss zoologist of genius who died some years ago, gave evidence in many publications for the primacy of display. According to Portmann, the exterior coat of the different species is laid down in its genetic structure and develops prior to the eye which can see the coat. Moreover, there are small oceanic creatures living in the interiors of the larger deep-sea creatures, or living below where light can penetrate, yet which present vivid colorings and symmetrical markings that can never be perceived in their habitat or by their own species which have no optical perceptive organs. These patterns bear no useful purpose, neither for camouflage against enemies, attractions for breeding, signaling messages, staking territory, nor lures for prey. This is "sheer appearance for its own sake," or, what Portmann calls "unaddressed phenomena." Animal life is biologically aesthetic: each species showing itself in coats, tails, feathers, furs, curls, claws, tusks, horns, hues, sheens, shells, scales, wings, dances, songs. If, for "its own sake" how similar to the aesthetic idea of "art for art"; and, if "unaddressed" and therefore nonfunctional, how similar to Kant's idea of the aesthetic as "purposiveness without purpose."

To conclude with these theoretical reflections derived from the idea of cosmos and the idea of animal display, I hope I have been able to suggest that we can consider beauty from a vantage point altogether outside the dilemmas of subject and object, altogether outside of the human restrictions on the theoretical imagination. If life itself is biologically aesthetic and if the cosmos itself is primarily an aesthetic event, then beauty is not merely a cultural accessory, a philosophic category, a province of the arts, or even a prerogative of the human spirit. It has always remained indefinable because it bears sensate witness to what is fundamentally beyond human comprehension.

We ought now to find ways to lift the repression and invite the return of beauty. But one caution before we can begin: lifting the repression cannot be done directly, as if solely by beautifying, by applying what we believe to be beauty directly with our hands, bodies, or voices. This direct road does not lead there because the very repressing function — that which denies, refuses, ignores — would be the very instrument we would employ. We would still be relying upon the power of the personal rational will, what psychology now calls "ego" to do the job, whereas it is this very same ego that is the instrument of the repression. It would first itself have to become beautiful, that is, affected by beauty. Only likes can beneficially affect likes, *similia similibus curantur.*

To escape from this dilemma — that the repressor of beauty in its attempt to make beauty will only make more repression — we must move indirectly. The road to beauty means for the ego to enter conditions like those of beauty. The first of these is *pleasure.* George Santayana — who belongs among the great Mediterranean forefathers, like Plotinus, Ficino, Vico, Ortega — passed his aging years in Rome where he died some thirty or forty years ago. Santayana defined beauty as *"pleasure objectified."*[2] "Beauty," he said, "is pleasure regarded as the quality of a thing . . ."[3] We do not see beauty as such; we perceive pleasingness, delight, and sensual joy. Pleasure subjectively is a psychological experience; pleasure objectively is what we call beauty. To me there seems little doubt that the innate link Santayana proposes between beauty and pleasure indicates that Santayana's thought is informed by Venus, that his theory is not Apollonic, i.e., formal qualities, such as we find in the classic aesthetics of Winckelmann.

For us it means that the road to beauty begins in pleasure, opening the soul's body to delight, which anyway is implied by that sensate word *taste*. So, the lifting of the repression necessitates a prior lifting of Puritanism and its denial of pleasure.

The second indirect road derives from the familiar idea that beauty arrests motion. For example: you draw in your breath and stop still. This quick intake of breath, this little gasp — *hshshs* as the Japanese draw between their teeth when they see something beautiful in a garden — this *ahhhh* reaction is the aesthetic response just as certain, inevitable, objective, and ubiquitous, as wincing in pain and moaning in pleasure. Moreover, this quick intake of breath is also the very root of the word aesthetics, *aisthesis* in Greek, meaning sense-perception. *Aisthesis* goes back to the Homeric *aíou* and *aisthou* which means both "I perceive" as well as "I gasp, struggle for breath," and *aisthomai, aisthanomai*, I breathe in.[4]

Does this not suggest that if beauty is to appear, we must be stopped still; the eye's roving perceptions, the body's habitual forward thrust, the mind's ceaseless associations arrested? The arresting of motion has long been consciously used in painting, for instance in the static riveting gaze of Coptic portraits and Greek orthodox icons, in the still life or *nature morte* in which the very name of the genre states the arrest of organic motion, in photography where the snapshot frames and holds a moment as if in eternal presence, and in the gigantic color field paintings of the 1960s, which completely immerse the viewer stopped before them, embraced within them. By stopping the forward motion of the mind, body, and spirit, the soul may become receptive, as in the Annunciation paintings where Maria is surprised by an angel, startled, suspended.

The moment of attention does not last; it breaks the flow of time for an instant, but time returns. Continuity seems stronger than eternity. So, Yoga and Zen disciplines attempt to extend the grace of the aesthetic moment described in T.S. Eliot's words in *Four Quartets*: "The stillness, as a Chinese jar still / Moves perpetually in its stillness / Not the stillness of the violin, while the note lasts." Like Rilke's line "Rose O Rose:" in which the "O" is the arrested moment. Not the rose as such, that customary symbol, is beautiful. It is beautiful because of the stopping "O," and then the repeating, respecting, going back to see again, as the only motion possible, the motion to recapture the evanescent epiphany.

At the end now I want merely to list briefly other suggestions that lift the repression. I suggest them as key phrases for our consideration, and with an invitation to you to make further suggestions. For one thing is certain, lifting the repression requires all our attention and the more the better, since there is surely no limit on the number of roads.

One is the courage to abandon irony. Another is the courage to be afraid. If beauty does have to do with naked power of imagination, the divine power of Venus and of Mars, then there will be mortal fear in closing with the beautiful. Defenses against beauty are often defenses against the fear of its power, and these defenses are some we saw: wit and parody, appeal to the mind before the senses, sentimental literalism, sweetness, slickness without complexity, surface without depth.

A third road comes again from Plotinus (*Enneads* I, 6.2): "When the soul falls in with ugliness, it shrinks back, repulses it, turns away from it as disagreeable and alien." Does this not suggest that whatever we turn from and deny becomes thereby ugly? And does this not as well suggest that what we turn toward may become beautiful? The painting of this century especially has followed Plotinus on this road. It turned toward African sculpture, toward old chairs and old shoes, toward machines, toward rusty steel and plastic, toward slabs of dead meat and distorted human bodies, toward ordinary manufactured objects, warplanes, celebrity cheapness, toward crude matter of mud and barbed wire and broken glass, and with such success that we hardly today can imagine that once these materials and these subjects were not always the focus of painting. The turn toward and not shrinking from is quite clearly a way to beauty: think of what Constable did for the disapproved topos of landscape, of what Goya did for images of war's horror, and of what Toulouse-Lautrec, George Grosz, and Otto Dix did for the ruined discards of society, what Mapplethorpe did for the sexually outcast. The work of art allows repressed districts of the world and the soul to leave the ugly and enter into beauty.

Another requirement that I urge is to risk gorgeous or exquisite intensity, that is, to risk excess. Whether this is a baroque, romantic, or eccentric prejudice of my own you may decide, but let us bear in mind the value of prejudices, for if allowed to go to extremes, that is, if we drive the prejudice for excess to become excessive, then it may show its final intention. The violent prejudices of Blake, of Mondrian, and of Cézanne too, perhaps, is what drove them to the extreme limits, and not their search for idealized beauty.

Also on my little list is this thought from the Platonists: do not neglect or forget the Gods. This was the essential commandment of the Hellenic world. Humans were not asked to have faith as with the Christians or to obey the law as with the Hebrews. The "pagans" were asked not to forget or neglect the Gods. Surely this caution has some relation with the role of beauty in Hellenic culture. But how? Perhaps, it means that art, as anything else we humans do, remembers the non-human and immortal powers, as the Gods were defined in antiquity.

Then we could lift repression from beauty by anchoring the mind in non-human values. For surely the humanist program is not enough: social protest and political concern, the exploration of self-expression and the full exploitation of the materials, the reaction of one school or movement to another school or movement, to say nothing of the drive for fame, career, and money, are not satisfactory anchors of the mind's intention in the making of art. Beauty cannot enter art unless the mind in the work is anchored beyond itself so that in some way the finished work reflects the sacred and the doing of the work, ritual.

Perhaps ritual is the best way of grasping Kant's phrase that the aesthetic shows "purposiveness without purpose." We perform ritual with cool formality, a "disinterestedness" that is anything but diffident and yet with intensely passionate devotion. The timeless repetitious character of ritual suspends the forward motion of will and ego toward some fixed purpose. Instead, a dedication to the powers served by the ritual.

If there is time for one last reflection, let it be this. That gasp of which I spoke comes from the chest, which in the Kundalini Yoga is the place of the heart chakra. There, the sudden unexpected comings and goings of feelings are imaged by the fleeting gazelle glimpsed only rarely in its quick, startling movements and its absolute frozen stillness as it stands watching and listening, senses acute. Unless this chakra comes to life, unless the heart is opened and the gazelle awake, we remain deaf and blind, repressing despite our best intentions, simply because the organ that perceives beauty, that emits the gasp of the aesthetic response has not been stirred. The gazelle hides in the dense thickets of the soul or sleeps in innocence. In the thought of the heart lies the key to the practice of beauty and the end of repression. So, above all else I have said — and I have said far too much too fast and too crudely — let the heart be stirred.

1. A.N. Whitehead (1933), *Adventures of Ideas* (New York: The Free Press, 1967), p. 265.

2. George Santayana (1896), *The Sense of Beauty* (New York: Dover, 1955), p. 55.

3. Ibid., p. 31.

4. R.B. Onians, *The Origins of European Thought about the Body, the Mind, the Soul, the World, Time, and Fate* (Cambridge, U.K.: Cambridge University Press, 1954), pp. 74–75.

17

Segregation of Beauty

I am calling this hour with you the Segregation of Beauty, because something like apartheid operates around the facts and ideas of beauty. Beauty is permitted to make its appearance only in certain scenes — high fashion, cosmetics, restaurants, art galleries, museums, beautiful food. Further, it is allowable closeted in the privacy of homes — house beautiful with beautiful collections.

But beauty hardly gets into downtown, to the lunch counter or cafeteria, the shopping mall and the parking lots around them. Moreover, the retail strips, the industrial parks, commercial zones — forget it.

Nor does beauty get into psychology. Amazing to say, it is not mentioned in our training programs, in our case reports. Not only does the patient's hair, shoes, the patient's taste in furnishings that the patient lives with day to day, the patient's likes and dislikes in music, reading, color and language come into the therapeutic sessions. Except most rarely, everything to do with beauty, aesthetics, seems simply to have dropped from consciousness. That is why I have been claiming for the last years that the great repression today is beauty — not family, not sexual habits, not childhood, not violence or misogyny or incest, not memories and abuses which make it to the talk shows regularly — even Satan and aliens day in and day out — but where is beauty? Have you ever turned on a show where the topic was beauty? Are we too afraid of it?

Perhaps we are. An analytical patient once told me something that happened to him in London. This man was intelligent and sensitive.

A talk delivered at the Ninth Annual Meeting of International Skye, New York, December 1995.

He worked as an editor of high-quality technology books, so had exposure to beauty. He was seeing me for worries, depressions, exhaustions, and panics. He said he was in London, down in the tube. There, a trio of musicians who earn money playing at the station were set up with the hat open for contributions. He, being urbane and hip and cool, said to himself — "no, not this crappy stuff, this kitsch . . ." and then the trio struck the first notes of Bach. It pierced his heart. He could not take it; and he fled from the platform, back up the escalators. It was too beautiful.

Nothing stirs the heart, quickens the soul more than a moment of beauty. We stop. We flee. We gasp. A passage in a song, a scene in nature: the person's face, eyes, hair, a bird suddenly seen, suddenly gone. Sometimes it is almost too much, and like that patient, we flee up the escalator to stay untouched, unmoved.

Plato was the first to show the intimate connection between love and beauty. He said love desires the beautiful — or to put it another way, the beautiful arouses, awakens love. Just as each of us knows that when we fall in love with something, someone — everything becomes beautiful. For me, this means that maybe we fall in love in order to find something, be in touch with something even more important than love: beauty. "A thing of beauty is a joy forever," said Keats. Beauty offers that "forever" — something beyond, and perhaps that is why we are afraid and do keep beauty segregated. It is too much.

Still, it is a most strange fact: this segregation of beauty. Did you know that in the art schools — and some of you may recall this having been to art school — the idea, the word, beauty, is almost a taboo. Beauty does not enter the conversation. It has come to mean only pretty, easy, simple, sweet, and sentimental. It is without power, intelligence, complexity, or originality. Art works are not looked at with an eye to their beauty — that they might take your breath away, make your hair on your neck rise, give you goose bumps, and bring tears to your eyes. Art works are discussed in terms of expression, technique, derivation and influence, media and materials, formal properties.

So, if beauty cannot get into our public life of cities, into psychology of the soul, or into art — the one calling dedicated to its realization — little wonder that we live in a civilization that critics, especially foreign critics, find ugly.

So, my question for this morning: why is the USA so ugly and what might be done about it? I am of course begging a question here, and perhaps you do not concur that the USA is ugly. In the Greek world, beauty was Aphrodite. She put the whole world on display so that it could be touched and smelled and enjoyed. Because of her, mighty Aphrodite, the world was desirable. Moreover, her absence left things in disorder, even ugly. Temples and altars were raised to her, flowers and animals offered. Her temples were often by the sea. The Greeks wanted to be sure that she did not desert their towns, their homes, and their private lives. For Aphrodite — the embodiment of beauty itself — brought pleasure and made people and things attractive.

Perhaps mighty Aphrodite has not departed altogether. She still appears in advertising, in packaging, keeping our consumerism alive with unfulfilled yearnings. In fact, perhaps the segregation is only of the deeper aspects of beauty. Whereas, in the USA, the superficial, seductive part has been completely appropriated as in no other culture. Beauty, or Aphrodite, still appears, but only in part as seductive, luring, sexy, catching. What the Greeks called Aphrodite Pandemos (popular and sort of pornographic) — and they had no trouble with that, so long as the other part was also remembered — the Aphrodite Urania as the heavenly haunting aspiring that enhances all things and lifts the soul with other sorts of joy, other styles of desire. One way beauty is kept out of conversation is by forcing a definition. "Well, what do you mean by beauty?" I think it best to leave it undefined, and for you each to connect the term with some moment, some memory, some place or thing that gives that word significance. Justice Potter at the Supreme Court said this about pornography when asked about a definition: "I know it when I see it." You know when you have been struck; you know that catch in your breath, the physical shiver.

The usual accounts of beauty take one of two forms. Like so much in our culture, it is either subjective or objective. The objective position says there are formal laws that make something beautiful: proportion, rhythm, closure, scale, balance of dissonance, integration of parts, finish and workmanship, etc. This is true, whether in music, architecture, painting, or a garden. These formal values are there and can be objectively appraised, calculated, even taught by classical schools. Beauty is a formal quality, objectively given in things.

The subjective position takes an opposite stance. Beauty is not in a thing; it is in the eye of the beholder. This is why so many different things from so many different cultures and periods are beautiful, and then at another time found no longer to be beautiful. It is a matter of taste and about taste there can be no dispute — to each his and her own. You like Hummel statuettes, I like Japanese Raku; you raise orchids and have rare tree peonies; I like trellises with climbing pink rosebuds, and over there my neighbor does gladiolas and keeps her forsythia hedge clipped tight.

To decide authentic beauty we must turn to experts, since there are no objective universal criteria, say the subjectivists. This was the philosopher David Hume's argument: beauty could be called such only by an arbiter of taste, a man of good taste who has spent a life with music or sculpture or poetry, critics and patrons of the arts who shape the notion of beauty. Who does that today in a society where money defines value? The expert — Hume's man of taste — becomes the gallery owner, the influential critic, the appraiser at Sotheby's or Christie's, and the subjective finds a new definition of beauty in commodity value. Now I am not going to concede beauty to either the formalists or the personalists. I think there is a way out that is neither private and subjective nor universal and objective. I propose beauty to be an aesthetic response, given to each individually, but as a universal instinct.

You can recognize this aesthetic response as a gasp, a sigh, a star-tle. The Japanese suck in breath through their teeth. We say: Whew. Ah! Wow.

Curiously, the very words "aesthetic" and "anesthesia" (or numbed, insensitive) derive from this instinctual gasp or sigh. Aesthetics comes from the Greek word *aisthesis*, to sense, to perceive, and it is rooted in *aisthomai*: I breathe in, and further back to *aiou, aisthou:* "I perceive."

So we might say that there is an aesthetic instinct, a sense of beauty given with our biological being. It is a potential in everyone like an appetite, like a reaction of fear, or a desire. Moreover, like an instinct, it needs to be fulfilled — for some, more strongly than for others.

In addition, it can be depraved, abused, and perverted when it is attached to other instincts — for instincts are malleable — as a hunger, and we get the hyper-aesthetics of gourmand eating. Alternatively, it can be repressed and denied, like sexual desire in a religious discipline. The aesthetic instinct can become anesthetized because we are exposed to so much noise, color, stench, and ugliness that we shut it down, with pharmaceuticals, close our ears and do not respond.

As there can be sexual disorders and eating disorders, so there can be beauty disorders, and if the world has become as ugly as I am claiming, and we are shutting down our aesthetic responses, then why not consider that many of the problems we meet in therapy might well be rooted in the repression and segregation of beauty.

I should point out that animals, of course, share this aesthetic response. They must, if it is instinctual. Animals present themselves as an aesthetic display — colors, forms, symmetry, gaits, and gestures decorative attributes, like horns and hair patterns and tails and spots and stripes, and all sorts of smells and sounds we do not perceive.

Animals are always on display. The Swiss biologist Adolf Portmann explained that even at tiny levels of primitive organisms, all animal life has a "coat," an outer appearance, even those that swim in the sea bottoms where there is no light to see them.

The way creatures size each other up is aesthetic — how they show themselves. And the world is a vast presentation to the senses asking for aesthetic responses.

I want to come back now to our main theme: the segregation of beauty. And I will tie that theme to what was just exposed: the aesthetic response.

Another main way our culture keeps beauty out of the daily world is by contrasting beauty with usefulness. Beauty may be a lovely luxury, a decorative accessory, something rare, dear, and special, for the elite perhaps, but it is not functional, and especially not economically functional.

Look what it costs to put on an opera, to keep a symphony orchestra going for a season. Trimming the budget usually means cutting to the bone, and the bone is never imagined to be beauty . . . that is skin deep.

So when the office high-rise is planned, the budget is laid out: first considered are land costs, developer fees, taxes, architects, and so on. And finally a bit of art: a sculpture for the lobby, a mural for the stairs.

If the project goes over budget, these reminders of beauty are the first cut and last included. Beauty is imagined only as beautification: a decorative touch to something that is primarily functional by which is meant profitable, cost-effective.

Besides marginalizing beauty, I want to make an additional claim: only beauty can save the planet. Let me explain. Our ecological psychology and the environmental movements are caught in old ways of thinking. For instance, in economics we hear it makes sense to scrub fumes from factories and power plants because it is cheaper to prevent than clean up.

For instance, anthropocentric arguments: We are urged to fix the ozone holes and save tropical forests to prevent human skin cancer, or to find curative medicinal plants.

For instance, ethical moralisms: We should save the trees for children; we should spare the animals because they are God's creatures too; we should clean up as atonement for past greed.

But even the strongest combination of guilty feelings, economic reasoning, and scientific evidence are not enough to turn the tide so that our planet's life may continue. Nevertheless — and here is where beauty comes in — if you love something, you want it to stay around and stay close, and keep radiantly well. And it is precisely beauty that makes you fall in love, makes the world desirable, gives you the feeling that what is here is to be treasured and not misused or harmed, and certainly not to be regarded in terms of functional usefulness or economic return, for such is to look at the world as a slave or a whore.

So, ecology depends primarily on this aesthetic response to the entire environment — natural or urban — a response, which approaches the world first through the idea and feeling of beauty. This implies that neither economics, nor moral principles, nor scientific evidence is enough to keep us going. Beauty is the ultimate bottom line.

If we follow that thought along, it becomes a citizen's duty to awaken and stand for his and her aesthetic responses. This stand could be to collaborate in the physical improvement of your township, to protect regionalism and biodiversity, to insist on arts education in schools, to support conservation of good buildings, and above all, to work to protest actively against ugliness wherever it appears, or threatens to appear. These are not matters of personal taste, and subjective opinion, but belong to a citizen's duty. Otherwise you remain "anesthetized" — without *aisthesis*, without the awakened aesthetic response — passive and compliant with whatever is going down, and among those responsible for our culture's going down.

In projecting a series of slides of nineteenth- and twentieth-century paintings of arranged flowers in bouquets and vases and of constructed bridges, I am intended to evoke your aesthetic responses. While you were looking, you may have felt a stirring. let's review empirically what happens: *What does beauty do?*

1. It awakens longing — a sense of need, desire.
2. It awakens ideals — for something, some state of perfection.
3. It slows: Thomas Aquinas said, "beauty arrests motion:" opens into stopping, regarding, more close looking, respecting, and contemplation.
4. It touches the great themes of heart: melancholy, romance, death, worship, peace, and mystery.
5. It activates: I want to have that. I want to do/make something. I want to share/give something.
6. It remains fleeting: "keep beauty fleeting" as in the words of Hopkins, Yeats, Shakespeare, or Goethe.
7. It is softening, yielding, smiling: is this Aphrodite's effect?
8. It makes us surrender: when we stop segregating beauty, the soul of the world moves inside us and we move inside it.
9. It evokes remembering, imagining.

18

The Cost of the Ugly

There is always a danger when addressing our topic, beauty, a danger of going up in a hot-air balloon, soaring above the streets, looking down on the ordinary world. Beauty beckons beyond, inviting contemplation of higher things, loftier thoughts. We suck in our breath, gasp, a pang strikes the heart. In fact, the very root of the Greek word from which we have our term "aesthetics" means "I breathe in."

Beauty is inspiring, inspiriting. One leap of the ballerina, the steel arcs suspended above the river, the melodic phrasing of Mahler, coming through a hedge into a garden and our breath leaves us. We are seized, lifted beyond ourselves, transported for a moment into a state of being that the soul seems, most of all things, to long for. As Plato said, beauty gives wings to the soul. The idea of beauty belongs to the airy realm. So, we will not be able to close on it; it eludes our conceptual grasp, evaporating into feelings that ask the arts to express. Hence the discussion of beauty tends to merge with discussion of the arts.

This risk of its call away from the ordinary world must account for the contemporary repression of beauty in art departments and art criticism. "Beautiful" and ugly are not terms that enter the vocabulary of teaching or thinking about the arts. The very basis of what the arts were once understood to serve no longer enters as a factor in their making. In those schools and that criticism beauty has been demeaned to mean the pretty, the easy, the pleasing, the mindless, the simple,

A talk delivered at the conference "Beauty in Civilization," Asia Society, New York City, December 2, 1997.

and especially the old-fashioned and naive. Because beauty has been so naively conceived, all sorts of attempts are made to violate beauty's sweetness by shock, assaulting discord and terrestrial crudities — as if 'true art" must prove itself immune to the seduction of beauty. It uses naive ugliness to counter the naive notion of beauty.

Repression of beauty, keeping it out of the conversation because it is always so inflating, cannot be an approach approved by a psychologist. So I will be taking another tack altogether. We'll sail right into the eye of the storm inquiring into why does aesthetics always invite high-falutin, elitist preciousness? What is inherent to the discussion of beauty in our culture that makes inflated rhetoric an ever-present danger? Is there an archetypal force that forces this rhetoric on us so that we tend to speak in the language of transcendence and ideals?

Could we avoid the rhetoric of beauty neither by avoiding the subject, nor by being ugly, loud and crude, but by engaging the subject in a down-to-earth manner? Could we be practical, even speak of aesthetics usefully?

"All art is quite useless," said Oscar Wilde, his witty way of summarizing Kant's notion of the aesthetic as disinterested and purposeless. If this tradition of uselessness be followed, then our presence here these two days may be entertaining, even informative, but quite useless.

As I said, this is not my tack. I'm going to take on Wilde and Kant too. Damn the torpedoes — full steam ahead. I intend to demonstrate that the beautiful and the ugly is a thoroughly practical topic. We could hardly be engaged in any topic more relevant, more serious. For our theme today bears directly on our collective societal distress and our personally psychological syndromes. I'll stake this claim for aesthetics in four specific areas where aesthetics are immediately practical: the four are depression, urban youth, electronic technology, and fourth, the environment. I hope these four demonstrations will show the cost of ugliness.

Let us begin with depression, that condition of soul once called melancholy before it was clinicalized and secularized. For once it belonged to Saturn rather than Eli Lilly. Depression today is the number one psychological syndrome in America. It has been declared endemic to our nation. That is, whether you know it or not, feel it or not — and there are tests that can discover it for you — millions of our citizens are depressed, justifying of course the use of anti-depressant drugs.

But my target here is not medical psychology. Rather it is architecture. I want us to think that our problems originate not only in our private selves and their pasts, but are reactions to our public spaces, our physical worlds. I'd like you to entertain the idea that our habits and habitations, our psychic interiority and interior design are deeply correlated, much as it was believed for centuries that the soul of the person and the *anima mundi* or soul of the world are inseparable. Our soul life takes place in actual places — on highways in traffic, in houses with hot air blowing onto our dreaming beds, in malls and airports, in open offices — where, by the way, in the past ten years the amount of space per person per cubicle has shrunk some twenty-five percent.

Let's consider ceilings for an example of the cost of ugliness in architecture and interior design.

Now what does meet the eye looking up? Today, this basic human gesture, that also raises the head and lifts the person, has become so acutely unpleasant that our glance instinctively retreats. We lower our sight. What's up there is tacky, unarranged: scattered islands of air vents, smoke detectors, sprinkler spigots, loudspeakers, perhaps a red exit sign, perhaps a TV monitor eye, and the ubiquitous track lights pointing every which way, recessed cans, or fluorescent tubes in mesh cages. The material is often acoustic board, often askew from repairs, stained with leaks.

What statements are these ceilings making? What are they saying about our psychic interiors? If looking up is that gesture of aspiration and orientation toward the higher order of the cosmos, an imagination opening toward the stars, our ceilings reflect an utterly secular vision — short-sighted, utilitarian, unaesthetic. Our heads reach up and open into a meaningless and chaotic white space.

Moreover, you do not want to raise your eyes, to look into florescent fixtures, at the bright bulb in the track can. You keep your head down — a depressive posture, outlook limited to the horizontal or the downward stare. In such light what does the soul do with its shadows, where find interiority? Does the soul not shrink into even deeper personal interiors, into more darkness, so that we feel cut off, alienated, prey to the darkest of the dark: guilt, private sins, fears, and horror fantasies. (Cf. chapter 22, "Ceilings," for a fuller exploration of this theme.)

I am suggesting, by means of ceilings, that our buildings are not truly inhabitable. I am suggesting that many of our social evils and psychological troubles — and even economic ills, such as inefficiency, absenteeism, sexual harassment, job turnover, quality decline, on the job addiction (whether valium, alcohol, coffee, or soda pop) — are psychological results of interior design. Until we recognize the design of interiors on our interiority, we shall be living in a kind of Orwellian repression, that is, disguised and unnoticed, like living in his book *1984*.

For repression is never where we believe it lies. That's its very meaning. We cannot be aware of it; it is unconscious. So, the repressed today is not where we think it is, in our sexual feelings, racial prejudices, family knots, and hidden motives. Today the repressed is outside of us, and we are anesthetized and tranquilized to the world we inhabit, what has been called "psychic numbing," which refers to every detail of soullessness from our Styrofoam cups to the sounds and light and air, the taste of water, and low maintenance clothes we put on our skins, discomforting but so easy to maintain. By repressing our reactions to the basic ugliness of simple details, like ceilings, by denying our annoyance and outrage, we actually encourage an unconsciousness that estranges and disorients the interior soul.

If the first cost of ugliness is depression, the second cost may be the degradation and violence of youth owing to anesthetized school budgets, budgets that cut back or cut out the arts. I will hold myself from analyzing school buildings, school food, and school bureaucratic language as exhibits of this anesthesia. I want us to focus only upon arts education — as it is called.

So long as education in beauty and awareness of ugliness is considered accessory to making a living, that is, accessory to making a life, music appreciation, rhetoric and elocution, poetry and drama, studio hours that open the eye and instruct the hand will also be elective, accessory, not core to the curriculum because not core to the culture.

So long as construction of schools — their classrooms and halls, cafeterias and buses, the actual physical world where our youth are forced to spend their most wakeful hours — follow principles that place function ahead of form, aesthetic considerations will only be accessory. If form follows function as modernist architecture insists, then utilitarian functionalism is actually forming dysfunctional children. Their syndromes of dysfunction may be ascribed to the environment that forms their school hours. And this dysfunction is costly. The swelling numbers of students in remedial classes, on prescribed drugs, as well as the violence in these functionally formed schools may well be neither a teaching problem nor a learning disability, but rather due to aesthetic neglect. Again, a cost of ugliness.

But really! Come on now! School is for kids, and what do they know about the higher realms of aesthetics, about beauty and ugliness!

Well, if there is no beauty in school they find it in the streets. Look at the gangs — not with the eyes of fear that sees only swagger and danger. Look with the eyes that would discern beauty. Appreciate the display: the hairstyles, tattoos and piercings, the attention to dress, the value of shoes, of jackets, the rapid transit of fashions. Listen to the beat in the language; watch the dance in the walk, the formalities of greetings, the words that indicate an eye for style, elegance, display. Show for its own sake. Aesthetics.

Watch where the money goes: not for pots and pans and windowsill plants of domestic tranquility, but, like our military spending, entertainment spending, science spending, for exaggerations of show. Notice what happens to the used cars: rebuilt, repainted, baroque, neon-lit; low riders; joyrides of aesthetic purposelessness, the transubstantiation of mass-produced consumer goods into chariots of delight.

Notice, too, what happens to our blank bank walls and office buildings, the merely functional fortresses of the international style and their cost-effective, low maintenance, impersonal facelessness. They become refaced — though we say defaced — with graffiti, signatures, monograms, declarations of love, territorial markings, glyphs of sprayed colors; humor, daring, inventiveness. Public anonymity reclaimed by enterprising privateers.

There is something else, and most curious, that I'd like you to notice: gangs exhibit in their exhibitionist bravado the classic link between the aesthetic and the ethical. Perhaps not your ethics, or mine, for ours tend to live in the modern divorce between duty and beauty. But in the gang and the hood and the street, there is a code of honor, of truth telling like it is, of heightened sensitivity to insult and dissing, and where attitudes of pretension are seen through. There the emperor wears no clothes. Too dangerous to fake it.

The importance of shame, of dignity, of pride, of honor, loyalty, neighborhood, and family — the very moral qualities praised by Bennet's prissy book of virtues go hand in hand with the aesthetic way of being.

If the aesthetic way of being of youth is not recognized by society as basic and necessary to youth, it will not be fostered by society. Instead society imposes a work ethic with long-range abstract goals that say nothing whatsoever to youth's explosive experimental power. Ethics alone cannot hold the violence since the ethics imposed are severed from aesthetics. You are told to be good, but not beautiful, to be honest but not glorious, and to be ambitious but not adventurous. I am saying: to curb the violence bring back beauty. Remember Orpheus whose music tamed the wild beasts?

A gang member is held by the image of himself and as this image is displayed to others. His life-support system as a human being is not the social system. It is the imagination. At the edge of death, where so many he knows and has known are hooked or wounded, doing time or already shot dead before twenty, there is no future, no planning, no schedule. Nothing but today's rhythm. Those who report on these youth at the edge say the only means of entry to them, and of them to society, is what they are already engaged in: rituals, not reasoning; aesthetics, not therapy. Singing, constructing altars and gardens, murals, drums, processions, ceremonies, and mournings. Methods of imagination.

All the while we rational folk on school boards and budget committees reduce the place for imagination. We do so to make room for
electronics, to upgrade our workforce to strengthen our nation's competitive economy. Upgrading the workforce? Or is it degradation?

It could be different. We could start with music. The Greeks — on
whose culture our culture still rests — placed music in the first rank
for educating the citizen. In the decade between eleven years old and
twenty-one, nothing seems to hold the spirit more compellingly and
lastingly than music. Who does not recall the tunes, dances, and lyrics
of your adolescence, of your generation?

American music from the spirituals and blues through tin-pan alley,
jazz, bebop to rap is perhaps America's most influential contribution to
the world culture. It was not Gorbachov's *glasnost* or Reagan's arms ex-
travagances that melted the Berlin Wall: it was the transistor radio playing our songs. But music appreciation, chorus, free instruments, and
instruction is cut back. Schools without song; dumb; anesthetized.

So kids are left to their own resources. The opportunities to expand
musical range, to sophisticate taste, and focus the young person's own
musical desire and proclivity go by the board. The kids find other
musical mentors — disc jockeys and commercial pop producers, imprisoning their musical potential within the narrow frequencies of free
market consumerism.

Let's shift now from music to spoken sound for my third demonstration. Let's think about the computer and the Web. Let's call up what we
have been told and sold regarding what's coming down the pike, the
next millennium of Internet and cyberspace with everyone online.

A brave new world waits. Isolation and parochialism vanish; censor-
ship and paranoid possessiveness impossible; an open society of equality based on equal access, for each one can have his and her computer
and thereby interact with anyone anywhere as well as accumulate a
vast bank of data.

Sitting there, booted up, right hand on the mouse, in control of this
treasury of opportunity, what is the cost, what is the loss — since for
every gain something is always lost?

First, the body: you can stay in that rolling workstation all week
long, without bathing, without dressing, without shaving or fixing

your hair. Naked, if you prefer, with popcorn and candy bars at your left hand's reach. All the while the screen before your eyes displays marvels of color and form, even images of sexual lubricity. You're in touch with everything in the world but your own physical self.

Second are social skills. No manners, no apologies, no innuendoes. You need but plug in and be there, instantaneous contact without the inhibiting delicacies of approach. No age differences, color, or gender. What is lost? What is the cost? Think of a party: the preparations, the food and flowers and drinks, the dog at the door, the chat and cosmetics, the sight of smiles, of old faces, new faces, the waves of silence and conversation, the sound of laughter, the formalities of leaving and thanking. Communication at the cost of what civilization has taken centuries to refine. Think of the perfume.

Third is the sound of human voices beyond information, beyond even words:

> What we do get in life . . . is the sentence sounds that underlie the words. Words in themselves do not convey meaning, and to [. . . prove] this, . . . let us take the example of two people who are talking on the other side of a closed door, whose voices can be heard, but whose words cannot be distinguished. Even though the words do not carry, the sound of them does, and the listener can catch the meaning of the conversation. This is because every meaning has a particular sound posture . . . Just so many sentence sounds belong to man as just so many vocal runs belong to one kind of bird. We come into the world with them and create none of them . . . We summon them from Heaven knows where with the audile imagination . . . it is no use trying to make them, they will not rise. We can only write the dreary kind of grammatical prose known as professorial. (Robert Frost)

> I wanted to write poetry in the beginning because I had fallen in love with words . . . What the words stood for, symbolized, or meant, was of very secondary importance.

What mattered was the *sound* of them . . . I did not care
what the words said, overmuch, not what happened to
Jack and Jill and the Mother Goose rest of them; I cared
for the shapes of sound that . . . the words . . . made in
my ears. (Dylan Thomas)

Poetry of many kinds . . . gave me great pleasure, and
formerly pictures gave me considerable, and music very
great delight. But now for many years I cannot endure to
read a line of poetry. I have also lost almost any taste for
pictures or music. My mind seems to have become a kind of
machine for grinding general laws out of large collections
of fact, but why this should have caused the atrophy of
that part of the brain alone, on which the higher tastes
depend, I cannot conceive. The loss of these tastes is a loss
of happiness, and may possibly be injurious to the intellect,
and more probably to the moral character, by enfeebling
the emotional part of our nature. (Charles Darwin)

To answer our question: the cost of the electronic miracles may well
be more ugliness; the loss, poetry.

We come to my fourth and final demonstration by turning to the
environment. I assume we are each concerned, maybe panicked, about
environmental degradation, and that we are each doing something
about it — with money, with political action, with practices of preservation in our daily lives.

And yet we know the tigers are going and the rhinos, and the frogs
and butterflies, and millions of irreplaceable trees. Soils wash away, the
hillsides turn barren, insecticides, pesticides, and herbicides become
our human suicides. That we must do something is clear enough; nature cannot do it for us. Great Mother Nature can no longer even take
care of herself. She is on dialysis, slowly expiring, kept alive by our
advanced technology.

What can stir our depths equal to the depths of ecological need?
Guilty atonement for our human wrongs? Fear of cataclysm and extinction? Religious devotion to the planet as a mother? Ecological sci-

ence to restore a balance? Nativism, Feminism, Vegetarianism, Green Activism — these energetic campaigns require the same willpower, the same Western ego that propels the problem they try to solve.

None of these is as useful as love. Why? When we love something we want it to stay around and keep close. We want to do for it, care for it, and serve its well-being. And we can let it be as it is, not mess with it, respect its existence for its sake and not ours. Yet love cannot be commanded as a duty — despite Christianism's imperatives.

What does evoke love is beauty, an idea as old as antiquity, as vital as the Renaissance, and as fresh as your feelings: what you love you apprehend as beautiful. And when you find something beautiful, love pulls you towards it. Its beauty holds you and you move quietly from attraction to contemplation. As Thomas Aquinas wrote, "beauty arrests motion."

This connection between ecology, love, and beauty means that an awakened aesthetic sense is the most practical way of defending the environment. First beauty, first aesthetic sensitivity, first recognizing the world's beauty. This evokes our love for it and our desire to keep it well and forever. Beauty first accords with pagan philosophy rather than Christian, for it returns our longing to this world rather than to another, not here, not yet.

The path to the apprehension of beauty seems to go by way of ugliness. Recoil may well be the primary sign of coming to our senses. Pain instigates quicker reactions than pleasure; its lessons last longer. Renaissance theory of image-making held that the distorted and frightening image made more impact on memory than one of calm harmony.

So just here, the cost of ugliness gains a further meaning. Ugliness costs us pain. We hate it, we are shocked, dismayed at so much ugliness everywhere. We find ourselves outraged, emotional life in disarray. But this pain to our senses may be the entrance fee, the cost required for attaching ourselves to the world, re-finding our love for its beauty. It costs ugliness to awaken our contemporary anesthetized consciousness.

Before we close and invite discussion, I do need to speak more clearly about the ugly. I've found the most instructive, even if tantalizing, approach to the idea of ugliness neither in *formalism*, that is, ugly means disproportion, cacophony, carelessness, nor in *moralism*, that is, disregard in a work for ethical intent and a work's obligation to truth (i.e., beauty becomes ugly when severed from its ancient Platonic sisters, the true and the good).

Nor have I found that the ugly can be reduced to contextualism, that is, to merely a matter of subjective taste and historical time, so that the ugly reduces to what is disliked, neglected and out of fashion.

Rather than these usual ideas of the ugly, I turned to the Greek philosopher Plotinus whose one book from the third century AD, *The Enneads*, is arguably the greatest single work of philosophical thinking in the Western tradition.

Here is what Plotinus (*Enneads* I, 6.2) says about ugliness, *kakon aischrotes*, which also means evil, bad, turpitude, shameful, obscene: An ugly thing is something that has not been entirely mastered by form (*morphos*).

In other words, mastery of the medium and the material is essential to eliminating ugliness. But that is not all. More significant still, I believe Plotinus is saying an ugly thing has no encompassing and profound idea of what the thing wants to be. The ugly is lacking in contemplative thought about itself. It therefore cannot be truly what it is. It is not true to itself, and consequently it cannot be beautiful or do good.

In another passage Plotinus says: ". . . ugliness is going over to another order." [*Enneads* V, 8.13] I understand this to mean we move toward the ugly when we desert the aesthetic position, when we employ the aesthetic as decoration, say, only secondary to principles given more importance. Such as public opinion, political program, cost accounting, market value. This kind of ugliness goes on every day: a major construction goes up midtown. The plan and the budget include murals in the lobby, a fountain in the plaza, landscaping. Then, cost overruns, higher interest rates force downsizing. The first to be eliminated are the murals, the fountain, and the plantings. We have gone over to another order, aesthetics submits to economics. When the aesthetic integrity of anything at all can be compromised by cost accounting, then the accountant rules the architect and we have gone over to the other side. And the true cost is ugliness.

A third statement from the *Enneads* speaks directly to the psychological cost of the ugly: "When the soul falls in with ugliness, it shrinks back, repulses it, turns away from it as disagreeable and alien" (*Enneads* I, 6.2). Here he describes the innate aesthetic response, that immediate uninhibited cringe away from aesthetic insults whether in objects, in sounds, in manners, in timings.

Plotinus is here describing the psychic condition of so many patients who come to therapy: the psyche shrinks within itself, turns away from the world, is out of tune, alienated. Could not our collective malaise for which individuals seek personal therapy be more likely the result of having fallen in with the ugly, compromised with and adapted to another order? And this makes the soul sick.

What is the other order but that of economics — whose laws and values dominate the entire planet. The bottom line has become the one great God who subjects all other principles to secondary satraps. The new world order is economic monotheism. That is our cosmology, our main explanation for why things are as they are and why we do what we do each day.

This cosmology, for whom beauty and ugliness are contingent if not irrelevant, finds support in the biosciences and information sciences that take their start in an accidental big bang and find their end in an inevitable black hole, senseless and nihilistic from start to finish. Since our lives — like the planet itself — are accidents, the best we can do is manipulate things to suit ourselves, that is, technology, in accord with the only moving force in life this cosmology recognizes — the predatory, willful, and selfish gene.

This dominant cosmology betrays the very notion of cosmos. That word, cosmos, believe it or not, is an aesthetic term! It means becomingly, appropriately, fittingly, as the planets and stars move in their spheres, as all things have their place and do belong. Cosmos was used of women and their adornments, so that "cosmetics" is closer to the original sense of cosmos than "cosmonaut," an insulated tinkerer in frigid, empty space. Cosmology, the logos or study of the cosmos, means that neither scientific method nor economic calculation reveals the essential order of the world, because the world is primarily and always an aesthetic phenomenon with which our animal senses and innate reactions are attuned.

Finally now, the innate aesthetic response that turns away from the ugly is also a political act. To refuse to fall in with the ugly, to protest against it, to react to aesthetic insult not only asserts the will to survive as an individual. That response is essential to being a citizen, not shrinking away, not alienated from the world. The aesthetic response lifts the repression, counters our anesthetized numbing.

Let's make no mistake: the aesthetic response does not mean surrounding oneself with high art and high fashion. It does not mean beautification, adopting a highway, tinseling the tree. Our task is less with beauty than with ugliness. For us today, who are psychically anesthetized and encouraged to be literally numbed by the pharmaceutical industry, our aesthetic response to ugliness restores our responsibility as citizens. The citizen as a watchdog of ugliness, ready to bark wherever another order encroaches upon the aesthetic terrain.

We can trust the responses to beauty and ugliness by remembering they are our primary way of being in the world. They tie us in with the world because they are cosmological in nature and in import. If the soul, as Plotinus insists over and over again, is an Aphrodite — his actual words — then our psychological life is inherently concerned with beauty. Our awareness of beauty states our devotion to her, Aphrodite, and to the world which long ago was imagined to be her smile. Our small, individual responses can keep the world smiling. Otherwise the cost is the soul, and the world itself.

19

Justice, Beauty, and Destiny as Foundations for an Ecological Psychology

During the final months of the twentieth century the modernized world went through a preparatory ritual. The presence of the unpredictable, the invisible loomed. We called this presence "Y2K" and devoted immense concentration and tedious labor to the minutiae of prevention. Imagination focused on what could go wrong; catastrophe, apocalypse.

The fact that nothing happened, that the evening and morning of the new millennium dawned and passed as usual into another day, another year, another century, without incident affirmed to the intelligentsia of science, business, government, and academia that we could rely on reason and human will. The defeat of Y2K reconfirmed the triumph of the Western mind. It was not "at the end of its tether" (H.G. Wells). Apocalyptic catastrophe was merely a myth.

Could we snatch some defeat from the jaws of this victory? Could we draw another, different lesson from that midnight anxiety, the preparatory rituals and the countdown of a winter's night?

This paper integrates two short addresses: "Laying the Table," a keynote talk at the Psychology at the Threshold Conference, University of California at Santa Barbara, 2000, and published in D.P. Slattery and L. Corbett, eds., *Psychology at the Threshold* (Carpenteria, Calif.: Pacifica Graduate Institute, 2001); "Justice and Beauty: Foundations of an Ecological Psychology," a keynote speech given in Rimini, Italy, October 2001, and published in *Il Fuoco nel Cristallo*, vol. 1 (Verucchio: Centro Ricerche Pio Manzù, 2001).

We might have learned how inextricably interdependent is the world for its daily existence; that the machinery to which we have delivered our life-support systems can suffer massive breakdown; that we must devote more and more of our lifetimes to servicing systems we neither control nor even understand, yet on which we depend. For without these systems we are left isolated in tall buildings, cold, dark houses, tangled in directionless traffic; food, water, and shelter depending on the kindness of strangers, reduced overnight to that condition Hobbes (*Leviathan* I, 13) described: "solitary, poor, nasty, brutish, and short."

We might also have learned that "signal moments" of the calendar must be heeded. For the calendar is a divine, perhaps divining, instrument opening to mythical powers whose movements it attempts to record in numbers. The schedule book and weekly agenda cannot keep out the Gods. Holidays, Holy Days, even the days' very names remind of their presence all week long. Their breakthrough or break-in is always possible, and rituals acknowledging them always necessary. We have been closer to the recognition of the power of myth during the last frantic days of 1999 than in the triumphal ignorance of January 2000.

At the turn of the century catastrophe was still in the air. But the catastrophe averted is not the monster slain, and it is in the presence of the monster and the terror of helplessness it evokes that the archetypal psyche recovers its great myths of creation, of survival, and of a heroically founded civilization.

The questions we now address in psychology are placed in this calendar period. We are "after the catastrophe", a phrase I take from C. G. Jung. With what questions does psychology engage now; are its foundations adequate to that dreaded midnight? What revision must psychology undergo in practice and thought when catastrophe is kept in mind as the cradle from which this century's psychology emerges?

The maladies and issues psychologists presume to be today's currency — family, relationship, spirituality, diversity, violence, gender, consumerism, addiction, community — are remnants of the last phase of the last century. The language in which we encase our cases belongs to a time that already seems strangely distant: conscious and unconscious, projection and integration, ego and self, feminine and masculine, opposites and wholeness, development and regression, transference and counter-transference — how professional and technical they strike the ear, how tired and jaded and worn away with overuse, and how very far from carrying any of the menace of the monster or an adequate response to the power it can constellate.

Something grander is needed; foundations of vision and value that offer universal validity, else so-called depth psychology will be dibbling around in the topsoil of our personal gardens while "after the catastrophe" is shifting the tectonic plates on which our private plots rest. Psychology is called by the monster to reach beyond itself, its techniques, its models of thought, its language, especially its language, so as to realize itself as a defender of civilization, adventurer of culture, and advocate of soul. Depth psychology after all arose at a high point of central Europe's culture, its practitioners highly civilized, and its name proclaims it the psyche's thoughtful advocate.

Robert Sardello, Wolfgang Giegerich, and Mary Watkins have already seen the narrow paucity of psychology's self-conception: its obsession with subjectivity. Each has made a major turn: Sardello to differentiated spirit; Giegerich to relentless thinking; Watkins to societal oppression. I share with them a common discomfort that ignites into passion. We would release the imprisoned psyche from confinement in its own definition.

To the question, what is psychology after the catastrophe, my response is to go back, as did the Renaissance, back to the catastrophe that calls itself modern psychology. I stumbled towards this move backwards, this jailbreak, in the Terry Lectures, by "suggesting a poetic basis of mind and a psychology that starts neither in the physiology of the brain, the structure of language, the organization of society, nor the analysis of behavior . . ."[1]

Were we now to dream this suggestion onward, we might come to altogether other grounds for psychology that are more true to the soul's desires and the culture's wants than the piddling sentimentalities of mental health, relieved relationships, self-development, or even heightened consciousness.

A great consensus of beings, regardless of their deliberative capacities and linguistic abilities, sense in varying styles and degrees that this planet, their home and the home of their ancestors from the beginning, is now so severely threatened that its viability, and therefore theirs, may not endure into another century.

What role has the discipline of psychology in the widest sense played in the progress of this hastening deterioration, and what part might it play in slowing this progress, or better, altering its course? I believe this is the only important question for psychology today — psychology which still attracts hundreds of thousands if not millions the world over of bright young students into university classrooms, experimental laboratories, and even more numbers of all ages seeking help in clinics, counseling centers and private consulting rooms of therapists of every stripe. What bearing has psychology on the environment, and can psychology become ecologically effective?

The record is not encouraging. Here we must admit that psychology from its beginnings in German universities, French and British asylums and Viennese consulting rooms is fundamentally flawed. It entered the world with a birth defect. It bore the ancestral curse of Cartesian rationalism, which divided the world into subjects and objects, conscious human minds and dead material things. The actual world was not psychology's province.

The compound word "psyche-logos," declares that psychology is the study of the soul; yet since the very inception of this discipline the psyche has been confined wholly to the human, placed inside the human skin, and denied existence anywhere apart from the human. Not only has the psyche been identified with human subjectivity and interiority, but as well the *logos* of *psyche*, its method of study, has been restricted to, and by, scientific method. An early maxim of the discipline stated: "Whatever exists, exists in some quantity, and therefore can be measured." In this way everything unmeasurable was ruled out of existence, and the method applicable to the Cartesian *res extensa*, the extended world of materialized objects, became the only method allowed for the study of the soul.

Restricted to a science of the personalized individual subject, psychology as conceived and practiced has placed itself outside the "planetary dilemma." Insulated by the self-reflecting mirror of its worldview, psychology is quite irrelevant to the anguish affecting the great consensus. Even that anguish and those dilemmas are internalized into personal psychological "problems" to be resolved apart from their source in an ugly, unjust, and unhealthy world.

The ecological result of this inheritance is double. First, psychology is anthropocentric. Its definition of consciousness, for instance, declares it impossible, *per definitionem*, for anything but humans to be conscious. The self is still imagined like a pineal gland, a self-enclosed atomistic unit, neither inherently nor necessarily communal. The planet is an alien place, essentially nihilistic, into which the individual human is thrown, estranged and anomic.

Second, human-centered psychology fosters a disordered, senseless, and enslaved planet. By ripping the human soul from its womb in the *anima mundi*, the world soul, this mother of all phenomena becomes a corpse, reduced to measurement, experimental dissection, and cannibalization of its body parts. Rivers and rocks, flowers and fish defined as soulless can find value only by human assessment. For many centuries of our history and in most other cultures, an idea of the world soul endows all phenomena with meaning and intelligible intentions and their own individual inwardness. Depth of soul lies not just in us; it resides in the planet's own nature.

Clearly, we need to start again. We need principles that start not in the human mind but are given to the mind with the world. We need to imagine an ecological psychology that takes its starting point not in human concerns only, but in the planet's concerns and its beings concerns, which we humans serve with our mental capacities. That is, we do not dig in our philosophy, science, or theology for principles, nor turn only to our human experience; rather we can attempt to formulate the principles already at work within the cosmos, grounding the value of all participants.

I propose three universals for founding psychology after the catastrophe: Justice, Beauty, and Destiny. They more accurately qualify the "poetic basis of mind."

I am not turning to science for foundations. I am not seeking principles of explanation, but of value. Explanations like complexity, evolutionary genetics, and microphysics give cold comfort. Nor are my
three alternatives for or fungible with familiar trinities like body, soul,
and spirit; black, white, and red; faith, hope and charity; the good, the
beautiful, and the true. Justice, Beauty, and Destiny offer universals of
archetypal strength, that is, they are recurrent in time and ubiquitous
in place, cross or trans-cultural, immensely fecund; they muster emotive and symbolic expression and are instantly recognizable in daily
affairs. They are universals on which cultured communities and human dignity rely and aim to further. Without them, existence becomes
Hobbesian — nasty and brutish. With them, psyche finds itself in a
moral, aesthetic, and intentional cosmos, and psychology becomes
the study of the ways any phenomenon, including human beings, measures its place in the world.

The very words — Justice, Beauty, Destiny — inspire. They evoke
ideals that can neither be defined nor achieved, yet which bespeak yearnings of life-sustaining motivational power. Even as ideals, Justice, Beauty,
and Destiny offer practical touchstones for assessing the behavior of any
phenomenon: where does it belong; what is it; what qualities is it showing; what is it attempting to fulfill. And we first recognize the presence
of these principals in the usual way — through pathologies: the fury at
injustice, the recoil from ugliness and the despair of aimlessness.

My empirical source for these fundamentals is suffering, that perennial source of depth psychology. No matter the ontologies offered for
grounding the field of psychology in physics, in evolution, in spiri-
tualities, its actual starting point is complaint, disorder, suffering. As
Freud sought the ground of suffering in archetypal principles — Eros
and Thanatos — beyond the personal case, so suffering can find poetic
understanding in the *poesies* of tragedy. Tragedy is an old word for the
slouching beast, what Yeats foresaw as "anarchy," "the blood-dimmed
tide," "darkness drops again," from *The Second Coming*. Our feeling reflects tragedy, not energy, not the psychodynamics of opposites and
the psychodramatics of struggle, but the tragic composted with its co-
relative, comedy. To live with the perpetual nihilism of the slouching
beast always at the threshold, there must be some justice, some beauty,
and some sense of destiny.

The wound to humanistic hubris inflicted by Nietzsche, Marx, Darwin, and Freud cannot be repaired by even the best of wounded healers until they would be led back to the universality of tragedy, intimated by Y2K, as the self-inflicted destruction of civilization owing to the flaw of its hubris.

An idea of Justice has hardly been important to psychology, which has proceeded as if Justice could be ignored. Yet Justice is the ruling principle of society, perhaps of the natural world as well, formulated as natural law. The Greeks considered Justice (Themis) foundational. She was a great earth Goddess, like Gaia whom Zeus, too, had to obey. She lies in the roots of the *polis*, the city, making structural cohesion possible, giving each its rightful place, allowing it to belong, yet not overstep its bounds. Ostracism, banishment, exclusion for transgressions have long been punishments based on Justice's cohesive inclusion.

Justice is inherent in society for making society possible and inherently necessary to individual survival in society, so Justice is inherent in the individual person, perhaps in all creatures maintaining their claims to mutually dependent existence. Justice lies so deep, feels so innate — it works like an instinct. Transgressions spring quick to the eye; injustice stinks and its wounds long fester. A sense of Justice comes with the newest soul. The smallest child cries: "that's not fair!"

Justice makes possible an inherently co-related society of beings where mutual dependency is based not on mutual usefulness and economic exchange, but on the bare fact of participatory existence. If all beings belong, then all are needed and useful, and justice prevails for each and every.

Psychology has come upon justice indirectly. Empowerment, entitlement, victimization — all miss the archetypal dimension that re-values these feelings as ethical and political claims. When Justice is foundational then injustice becomes a primary syndrome, a diagnostic category perhaps, and a primary focus of therapy. The justification of one's life becomes more significant than its individualized meaning. The pursuit of Justice leads psychology toward moral and political philosophy.

And to aesthetics: *le mot juste.* Justice insists on the right use of language, the right gesture, rhythm that bespeak the psyche's basic poetic requirements. Of all the injustices that psychology ought to rectify foremost is getting its words to fit the case, and the case is always the soul. Getting things right — that is where ethics and aesthetics converge, which now leads us to Beauty.

"Divine enhancement of the earthly world,"[2] that neoplatonic idea of Beauty overwhelms with its beautiful simplicity! Divine enhancement — that's what strikes the heart, stops us up, catches our breath, calls us, and can shine forth from suddenly anything, anywhere, anytime. No wonder the Greek word *kalos* (beauty) also bears the meaning of "call." Beauty calls: we fall in love, we buy the painting, the restless search to know thyself falls away as knowledge gives over to perception and appreciation. A hope of joy forever is all you need to know.

Besides its calling power that draws into the world, making it desirable and waking our love for it, besides the pleasure and vitality it affords, Beauty offers one advantage as a psychological foundation: it vanishes before capture in literalism. When Destiny is taken literally, it becomes determinism, and Justice, legalism, so Beauty taken literally becomes aestheticism, either programmed or formalized or symbolized or kitsch. As an *a priori*, Beauty remains the sheer enhancement of things, not a thing itself and therefore ideal, visionary, wholly immanent. First principles must remain prior in every sense so that they can stand as priorities of value toward which culture tries to move and for which the soul yearns.

This longing for Beauty, its effects so deeply transformative, its universality in the presentation of nature and in human culture of body, of food, of place and tools, to say nothing of the arts whose calling is to bring that immanent enhancement to sensible perception — what could be more fundamental? Incredible that psychologies of depth and their therapies remain so insulated from these everyday facts. At least psychology's anesthesia makes one thing clear: we need to cross over, quite out of captivity.

A lack of Beauty as everyday fact, as clinical condition, was also described by the neo-Platonists: "Let the soul fall in with the ugly," said Plotinus, "and at once it shrinks within itself, denies the thing, turns away from it, out of tune, resenting it."[3] Don't tell me an archetypal psychology is not clinical!

Of Destiny there is scarce to say. Is it not simply the mythical sense of life, that we are both chained to and carried by forces we pretend to understand. Their power emerges in our awareness as necessity — Ananke. And this archetypal necessity translates into a sense of personal destiny, moments of feeling necessary. Something is meant, something is wanted, and something is living alongside my life, nudging, urging, sometimes seizing the wheel and setting another course.

Unless a sense of destiny is built into the foundations of psychology, it becomes essentially anemic, lacking *poesis* that envisioning force to engage the despair, the drifting loneliness and panic that psychology is called on to encounter. Without an idea of Destiny, psychology fails its own destiny.

The study of these forces we pretend to understand, this process of investigation is what makes psychology's activity interminable. It is an activity of faithful observation, which brings the breadth of mythical powers into the small world of the little people who whisper in the grass. Notice, listen and appreciate: something is always speaking. Observation becomes a daily practice of observances.

As a psychology founded upon Justice becomes ethical and political, and founded in Beauty must be sensate and aesthetic, so Destiny requires psychology to be observant, that is, religious and animistic.

I suggest that these three archetypal ideas can transport psychology across the threshold by affording a vision to uphold the psyche in the face of catastrophe, whether environmental, technological, or apocalyptic. As more cultural ideas than purely psychological ones, they prevent psychology from isolating itself as a specialist's discipline or a professional practice. As the soul belongs to no province of inquiry, the ideas on which psychology rests may not be provincial. That has been the thrust of an archetypal psychology from the start. Depth psychology, after all, is only one manifestation — late, minor, and mainly Western, wealthy, and white — of culture. So our base must find itself in culture's principles, and culture attempts always to articulate its destiny by revealing beauty and upholding justice.

Archetypal psychologists have always known in our hearts that suffering is never more mollified and the menace of breakdown better endured than when ugliness and injustice can be averted, when there is a glimpse of beauty, some justice in the offing, and when destiny gives to a blow of tragedy the value of importance.

I have been trying to lay the table for the next threshold of psychology as an "adventure in ideas" (Whitehead) for a value-based psychology, ideas that might possibly serve to urge psychology into the peculiar terrain with its peaks and vales of a yet unknown century.

I submit these principles are basic to cultures everywhere because they are given with the cosmos itself, and, since primordially given, they are ecological guarantors. Psychology's task is to rebuild its learning and its therapies on these primordial principles, so that the great wide world and its beings can never be outside its purview. Because Justice, Beauty, and Destiny are not merely humanistic, religious, scientific, or regional, they allow many modes of implementation, yet transcend all implementation with an ideal claim of transcendental value, inspiring artistry, dignity, and respectful care, and prompting lasting rectification of ugliness, wrong, and lost ways. For precisely ugliness, wrong, and lack of engagement are the major causes of a suffering planet, that blue ball wrapped in a whirlwind, so fragile, afloat in a sea of stars.

1. J. Hillman, *Re-Visioning Psychology* (New York: Harper & Row, 1975), p. xvii.
2. R.H. Armstrong, "The Divine Enhancement of Earthly Beauties," *Eranos Yearbook* 53 (1984), pp. 48–81.
3. Plotinus, *The Enneads* I, 6.2.

Part Three

Places of Practice

20

The Street Corner: Gods, Disease, Politics

Joseph Campbell once said that the gods are not in Greece, or in books about myth, but instead are right on the corner of Broadway and 42nd Street in New York, waiting for the light to change. They are facts of everyday life, not merely the glorious and frightening images printed so beautifully in Campbell's own massive works.

This observation of Campbell's leads us to a very old question that has haunted those interested in myth, and that is: have the gods truly fled? But there is an even more necessary question: can they leave the world? If they are the world — as the powers within its variety — how can they be separated from it? Are they not the immortality of the world, giving every item of this world its inherent transcendence, its sublime enchantment, imagination, and beauty that is at once also fearful, cruel, enigmatic, and profoundly un-understandable?

Why has the modern age accepted the thesis that the gods can simply up and go? Certainly their absence, if that is the case, cannot be due to our having deserted their groves and altars, failed their rituals and sacrifices, and forgotten their mysteries. They surely cannot be that dependent on what we do or don't do. How could they claim their superhuman authority in the cosmos if their presence or absence depends on our behavior regarding them? The gods of myth would then be nothing more than what both orthodox religion and secular relativism insist: fictions of human fantasy.

Opening Talk, Mythic Journey Conference, Atlanta, Ga., June 2004. First published in *Parabola* 29/4 (Winter 2004).

So the question turns again: who and what benefits from declaring the ancient gods dead, or fled? Who wants them gone and with them gone as well all pagan feeling, all pagan forms of consciousness? One thing sure: both historically and logically the absence of the gods allows the world to become *res extensa*, as Descartes called it, a mathematical space, calculable, adrift with the litter of soulless objects. All soul, mind, and consciousness condensed inside the human brain, putting nature at the disposal of the human will. The absence of the gods is not only an efficient secular convenience, an industrialist opportunity for exploitation, a hubristic inflation of mortal humans, it is more: the declaration that the gods have fled is also a Christian convenience. Their absence leaves the world open, with plenty room for the presence of Jesus the savior, who gives his own redemptive, apocalyptic answer to the needy times.

There have been many scholars of religion and history, of myth and literature, of arts and philology, who have intimated that the survival of the pagan gods is hidden within the Christian mythos where they remain as disguised presences despite the official and evident absence. There have been, as well, many who have attempted the revival of the pagan gods by imitation, invocations, and interpretations.

I myself have followed a method that springs from two famous sentences, often used by and quoted from C. G. Jung. The first comes supposedly from Delphi. It is a saying, cut in stone on the lintel over the front door of the house where Jung lived and worked for most of his long life: *vocatus atque non vocatus, deus aderit* (called or not called, the god will be present). The second sentence reads, "The gods have become diseases; Zeus no longer rules Olympus, but rather the solar plexus, and produces curious specimens for the doctor's consulting room, and [often not included in this sentence but also from Jung] disorders the brains of politicians and journalists who unwittingly let loose psychic epidemics in the world." (*CW* 13:54)

The interiorization of divinity, the move from transcendence to immanence, has already been argued by Spinoza. This move is further articulated by Heinrich Zimmer, the Indologist and Joseph Campbell's first mentor, who said, again famously, "All the gods are within." These assertions — from Jung, Spinoza, Zimmer — are each different, and different again from Jesus: "The kingdom of God is within you." It is important to recognize the crucial twist that Jung's psychology gave to the immanence of the gods: it indicates that the gods have been interiorized into pathology.

Jung tells us that the myths live in behaviors, demanding recognition and observances. They bear new names borrowed from the textbooks of psychiatry and abnormal psychology. Their refuge is no longer the altar and temple *fanum*, the site of oracle and mystery cult; instead they inhabit the psyche, where they make themselves very present indeed as the irrepressible powers in the background of the soul's infirmities.

Since the repressed returns in the strangely inventive form of symptoms (after all, symptoms are extraordinary inventions), the gods are indeed present, whether invoked or not, right on the corner of 42nd Street. Jung is neither the only nor the first to indicate this confluence of the mythological and the pathological, the gods and diseases. Already in 1900, Wilhelm Heinrich Roscher interiorized Pan into our nightmares. Concurrent with Roscher, Freud interiorized Oedipus from a theatrical figure to a drive in one's personal, intimate body. As well, Freud elevated the mythical personifications Eros and Thanatos to the dominant gods of all psychological happenings. It is fashionable today to bypass or surpass Freud for all sorts of reasons — sociological, feminist, scientistic — but one gift from Freud we ought never neglect: his return to the sources of culture in Mediterranean myths, rooting psychology not in the brain, or genetics, or blind evolution, but in the poetic basis of mind, whose imagination is structured by mythical configurations, or *universali fantastici*, as Vico called archetypal presences.

The recognition of the intimate and subtly differentiated connection between myth and pain, between the gods and diseases and politics, is the greatest of all achievement of the Greek mind: the perfection of tragedy, which demonstrates the mythic governance of human affairs within states, families, and individuals. Only the Greeks could articulate tragedy to this pitch, and that achievement has not been equaled since.

In the Greek sense, we are today [in 2004] in just such a tragedy as Thebes under Oedipus Tyrannos: the king is sick. And in the madness of his sickness, in his profound unconsciousness, the tragedy of the nation lies — its poverty, wasted youth, the degeneration of its crops and soil, its water and forests. This was the condition of Thebes at the beginning of Sophocles's first Oedipus play: "The city wastes in blight. Blight on the earth's fruitful blooms and grazing flocks, and on the barren birth pangs of the city women. The fever-god has fallen on the city and drives it."

The fever-god today is the same as the one named by Sophocles, line 191 of *Oedipus Tyrannos*: the fever of the god of war, Ares. And all this because the king is blind to his own nature. In other words, the facts of our collective condition must be laid upon the king. As Shakespeare ambiguously says:

> Upon the king, let us our lives, our souls, our debts, our careful wives, our children and all our sins lay on the king!
> (*Henry V*, 1.248)

I do not want to overlook the fact that the psychological method I am pursuing, following from Jung and Campbell, gives scant attention to the historical time frame of the myths, to their geographical locations, to the philological analyses of the texts or where they are recounted, or to the authenticity of their transmission. The revelations, which an archetypal psychology seeks to uncover, are ancient myths in behavior, in the phenomena we all unthinkingly absorb as usual reality and utterly unmythical. We ravage the scholarship of others and pilfer whatever we can, justifying these violations in the name of bringing deeper understanding to psychological afflictions.

Archetypal psychology attempts to connect present experience to historical culture — something sadly lacking all through the culture today. Hoping to open a closed door long bolted from two sides — history and its scholarship bearing witness only to the dead and gone, and psychology utterly contained within the painfully present and personal subjective soul. Jung and Campbell, and those of us who work in this tradition, attempt to show how Western antiquity can be relevant to the life of the psyche, and how psychic life can vivify Western antiquity. When scholars speak only to documents and psychologists only to patients, culture languishes, its soul shallows, unrooted in historical knowledge, and historical knowledge without soul.

Let's go back to 42nd Street. Behavior; action; myth as it moves along, unspoken, for myth is action, or, as some theories say, myth follows from ritual or is embodied in ritual. Moreover, myth gives the certitude of action, as we easily recognize when possessed by the goddess of sexual love or blinded with martial fever.

This very idea is made clearer by the work of Vico, that extraordinary man and one of my dearest heroes, who lived and worked in Naples in the early half of the eighteenth century. Maybe it was the fall he suffered at the age of seven that cracked his head and, keeping him from school for three years, freed him from church dogmatics and the science of the time, its education and ideas of truth — freed him from Newton and Descartes and Galileo — and allowed him to find the mind in myth and lay out another idea, that of certitude versus truth.

Certitude is the concrete engagement with life, and it precedes all principles, theories, and interpretations. The facts of 42nd Street precede our verification of them in thought or law. We live myth before we declare it to be myth. The existential engagement is already a certitude — the certitude of immediacy; my urge to fly sunward above it all with Icarus; my unknown union with my mother, like Oedipus; my unapproachable distancing, intactness, like Artemis; my aggressive attack on dirt and bestial monsters, like Hercules; the unworried smile and the charming allure I bring to every encounter, like Aphrodite. Before verum, or truth, and all arguments about truth, myths are the ongoing fantasies concurrent with our behaviors; myths are enacted in the ceremonies of habitual performance and daily patterns of expression and perception embodied in human behavior.

We need to look again at Sophocles's *Oedipus Tyrannos*. Myth is certainty or certitude that goes on unthinkingly in each of our actions. As Isaiah Berlin says when talking about Vico, it is myth that gives us the sense of reality: reality is not the absence of myth, or the contrary of myth; our immersion in myth is reality. Early in the play, Oedipus the king says, "Well I know you are all sick, and in your sickness, none among you as sick as I. Your pain comes to none other than myself."

Oedipus, the king, has taken on the city and its people as himself. He calls them his children. He identifies his condition with theirs.

He is the city and people. We are dealing, however, with something beyond the symbolic significance of kingship. There is an interpenetration of sickness among the *polis*, the city, people, and the individual. All are sick together; private and public cannot be separated. The gods do not affect individuals and their families alone, only human beings; they affect the crops and the herds, and the institutions of state. A city, too, can be pathologized by mythical factors — exactly as Jung said in "Wotan" in 1936, looking at Germany. The gods live in the *polis*.

How does a city act when it is sick, whether Thebes or New York? What notions of remedy arise from a sick city? The play gives us answers. First, the sick city calls upon the leader to find a remedy, equating the king with the city: the government is responsible, the people are children. Second, the leader calls upon Apollo to reveal the cause and the cure. Oedipus says: "I was sent away unto halls to find what I might do or say to save the state." The government turns to Apollonian consciousness, Apollonian means of diagnosis and correction, and the government speaks in God's name: "God proclaimed now to me, for me and God and for our land." Third, the city purges. Oedipus says, "I will disperse this filth." Oedipus speaks of purification, expulsion, punishment. He curses those who would not obey him: "I forbid that man, whoever he may be, my land, and I forbid any to welcome him, or cry him greeting, or make a sharer in sacrifice offering to the gods, or give him water for his hands to wash. I command all to drive him from their homes, since he is our pollution." Fourth, the sick city makes edicts. Oedipus says, "I forbid, I command, I invoke this curse." In the early passages of the play, he speaks as the voice of the city. Oedipus the king is the state, an utterly public figure.

These four remedies are actually manifestation of the city's sickness, diagnostic signs. The solutions imagined by a patient for his illness belongs to the image of his illness. That is why therapists listen closely to what patients want at the beginning of therapy: how the patient imagines remedy and what measures he is already pursuing show how the patient is constellated by his condition. The solutions to the problem of Thebes present the problem of Thebes. The simplicity of Apollonian solutions to America's disease is part of the disease itself. The classically ritual solution could only be sacrifice of the king. And sacrifice of the king means more than the capacity to admit a mistake, although here in our kingdom even that is missing.

I have turned to one basic tragic tale, Sophocles's *Oedipus Tyrannos* to expose the myth in which we are now struggling. There are others, such as the story the exclusionist followers of Jesus are absorbed by, the story of Armageddon that envisions the final chapter of life. What we can and must learn from Joseph Campbell is that myth is all about us, on every street corner. Myth is reality, and recognition of this certitude, and the analysis of myths at work among us, may keep us from falling prey to the blind belief and the disasters of delusion, for we are in a collective madness.

21

City, Sport, and Violence

. . . the most practical advice we offer to readers is that they had best reconcile themselves to a continuing life with hooliganism in football and elsewhere. [1]

I. Martial Violence

All too familiar, the shocking reports, the press photos: Brazilian football stadiums surrounded by moats, chain fences, police with attack dogs; Italian tifosi (rabid with typhus); some forty or more killed in Brussels by rioting Liverpool followers; five hundred injured in a race melee at a high school game in Washington, D.C.; similar stories from Central America, Turkey, Argentina, Peru, China, the Soviet Union, Egypt. When Brazil won the World Cup in 1970, two million people celebrated the returning team: forty-four dead, 1,800 injured. Urban sports spectacles, even local minor contests, result sometimes in deadly violence. This is a worldwide phenomenon.

What does an archetypal psychology say to this? By "archetypal" here I mean ubiquitous, passionate, ever-recurring, inescapable patterns bearing value and religious depth. "Archetypal" also implies "necessary" patterns which govern behavior because they are rooted in psychic life. If the psychic life of human beings is by nature political, following the premise of Aristotle, *anthropos physei politikon zoon* (man is by nature a political animal), then what necessary and essential political purpose could be served by the archetypal phenomenon

A lecture delivered at the Villa Montalto Hochberg, University of Florence, 25 May 1990. First published in *Psyche and Sports*, eds. M. Stein and J. Hollwitz (Wilmette, Ill.: Chiron Publ., 1994).

of urban sport violence? How might we understand our theme, both psychologically *and* politically? In fact, might it be possible that sports violence provides the very bridge for exhibiting the innate relation between the deepest animal forces in human nature and the life of the *polis*?

To begin with I shall stake a major claim by extending Aristotle's statement to say that sports belong to the political nature of human being and that violence in sports, as inherent to sports, is therefore also political in significance. Fierce physical contests are neither only contingent nor mere accessories and diversions, simply circuses for the proles and plebs. I want to claim them as basic component of political existence.

Second, my method for this archetypal investigation shall follow from Jung's famous dictum: "The Gods have become diseases." We no longer look to Olympus or only to ancient cults, temples, and statues of the past for the Gods, nor even to their mythical narratives and dramas. Instead, the Gods appear in our disorders, private and also public.

The very first lesson we learn from Oedipus is not what Freud taught — a lesson about the private disorder of the erotics of family — but a lesson about the sickness of the city with which the tragedy of *Oedipus Rex* opens and which is the concern of Oedipus when answering the Sphinx and when seeking out the evil that scourges Thebes. Oedipus would save the city. This is his first concern, as I believe it cannot help but be for depth psychology, following from Freud's vision of Oedipus as the basic myth of our field. As well, this concern for the city must be the focus of any psychology of soul since the soul of the individual is located within the wider scope of the *anima mundi*. Saving the city remains the concern of Sophocles at great old age with his *Oedipus of Colonus*, ending that drama by having Oedipus die in a place that blesses the *polis* of Corinth. Yes, the Oedipus myth sets the course for depth psychology, not merely toward the private sickness of family, but also towards the public sickness of the city. By turning an archetypal psychological eye toward urban sport violence, we are merely continuing Freud's mythical approach, in fact his Oedipal approach, to psychological disorders.

We are also following Jung by searching out "the God in the disease" of sports violence. But — which God? That question, "which God?" echoes the standard request put to the oracle in antiquity: To which God or Goddess or Hero do I sacrifice?"[2]

To name the power responsible is already the beginning of remedy. To be told the altar at which to lay the trouble places it and gives a particular significance to the disorder. For the troubles of Oedipus, it was Apollo; for the troubles of Hippolytus, it was Aphrodite; for our troubles in the soccer stadiums, it is Ares (Mars).

That competitive sports constellate the incursions of Mars has long been attested. Even horse racing! As late as 1822, the British journal *The Annals of Sporting* suggested that spectators go armed to Epsom and Ascot[3] since violence might break out at any time, as, for instance, when a favorite gentleman jockey, having disappointed his followers by not winning, was set upon by the crowd and whipped. Look at today's tennis. A doubles match: four persons, usually in white, on a carefully rectangular ground with white lines, requiring a total of at least fourteen linesmen and judges to keep the decorum and prevent disorder.

Although Giovanni de Bardi formalized and aestheticized *calcio* in his *Discorso* (1580), earlier writers had called *calcio* a "battaglia." *Gioco della pugna* and other games such as the annual stone fights at Perugia played by hurling rocks, later condemned by Savanarola, attest enough to a wide recognition that Mars indeed was, in earlier Italian times to say nothing of the Roman period, the God in the disorder we now call urban sport violence.

Here we must keep quite clear about two things regarding Mars. He is a God neither of strategy nor of victory. Neither the thought of fighting nor its outcome is his province. Mars appears in the red-faced fury, the intoxicating fever (hence *tifosi*) of actual combat like a sexual or drug rush, an unstoppable transport to another condition that makes humans passionate about physical combat, addicts them to it, since they are then, during these moments of battle rage, in the embrace of a divine energy.

The epithets of Mars say much about his effects. He was called Mars *moles* attesting to massive power and his power as a mass phenomenon. He was called *caecus*, blind, and *furibundus*, raging, and *ferus*, wild or untamable Other more ancient terms (Vedic, Avestan) analyzed by Dumezil[4] that were given to the warriors of Mars were "headstrong young man," "mighty hero," "giant," and also "dancer." Words for anger, fury, and to kill also belong in this complex.

Although we may have forgotten the Gods, they do not ignore us. We are still subject to their archetypal possession. Perhaps, then, the first benefit of the violence that we are now examining is that it forces us to recognize their continued presence, no longer externally in the overt obeisance of our bodies and souls to their rituals, but now as psychological "diseases" in the body politic and soul of the city.

The mythical fact that Mars is always in love with Venus tells of his Venusian component, his Venusian other side which loves beauty as much as battle. This, Giovanni de Bar and his Florentine sportsmen favored and displayed. Just think for a moment upon the velvets and silks, brocades and armors, the banners and scarves, the orange vermilions, the scarlets, and the empurpled sleeves worn by the children of Mars whether in the Renaissance or in any sports event today.

And just imagine Venusian love, so sensate, precise, and refined, exhibited by the Sons of Mars in their care of actual weapons of war, hunt and sport, the blades, edges, points, teeth, metals, hammerings and tempering in the variety of knives, swords, spears, pikes, halberds, sabers, battle-axes, skinning knives, rapiers, daggers, lances that have been lovingly honed with killing intention. Remember the music: the drums and fifes and pipes, the trumpets and bugles, the marching songs, marching steps, marching bands, brass, braids, and stripes. Remember, too, the parades and the legions, the military decorations, the feathered hats and ivory-handled pistols, the medals and honors; and recall the great fortress walls and bastions designed with violence in mind by Brunelleschi, da Vinci, Michelangelo, and Buontalenti.[5] Even today, as Dunning, et al., remark, spiked fences and cages have transformed the majority of British football stadiums into "fortress-like constructions."[6] As well, young fans feel themselves to be defenders of territory at home and adventuring invaders in rival cities.

I ask only that we not forget that Mars governs a great range of the human psyche and human history from the glories of heroism to the assaults of hooliganism. In Florence itself, wasn't the Battisterio originally a temple to Mars; didn't Giuliani de Medici present himself, after a joust, in the pose of Mars; and did not the fictional fighting between the Blacks and Whites occur under a statue of Mars?

We may conceive Venus and Mars not merely as opposites, but rather as interior to each other. That lovers fall into the mad fury of Mars does not surprise us. The reverse is just as true, just as evident. The world of Mars enjoys close physical contact, display of body, aesthetic delight in style, instinctual release, passionate impetuosity; all in all. Mars and Venus share a lust for life as well as a life of lust.

The difference between martial heroism and hooliganism depends largely on three kinds of discipline: the discipline of beauty of which we have just spoken and shall return to again; the discipline of bonding about which I shall say more towards the end of my remarks; and hierarchical discipline. These disciplines provide the ritual that can enclose into the human sphere the transcendent infiltration of the Godly martial power.

The obsessively severe rituals of hierarchy that require instant obedience, as on the battlefield, still show in the soccer stadium, both in regard to the unquestioned authority of the team manager or coach over the players and in the supreme authority of the umpires and referees over all participants. In a sandlot game played by children in a neighborhood, hierarchy quickly establishes; a captain emerges. Violent urban gangs enforce strict hierarchal discipline as well. Where Mars is present so is hierarchy, which suggests that the feminist attempt to dissolve hierarchy to promote literal equality, as if that were the key to democracy, actually invites Mars rampant, disobedient, unordered, and blind. Hierarchy protects the God from his fury. I would even suggest that hierarchical discipline is less a repressive constriction owing to a patriarchal Saturn than it is the *spiritus rector* within the archetypal figure of Mars, whose own violent spirit invents hierarchy to save the God from his blind and wasteful spending in senseless eruptive violence. After all, the Gods, as the Neoplatonists insisted, are intelligences. We must assume they know what they are doing, inventing their appropriate requirements.

Some examples may help my point about hierarchical discipline. Both Japanese Sumo wrestling and our Western Olympic sports, fencing and Greco-Roman wrestling, are intensely competitive and physically demanding, calling forth the martial heat of explosive man-to-man combat. Yet, the spectators are usually quiet. Order reigns owing to elaborate ceremonial discipline. Whereas the Golden Gloves boxing tournaments are noted for violence breaking out in the audience, because, I believe, these tournaments are a kind of democratic free-for-all. Only one side of Mars, his battle rage, has been allowed, to the neglect of his requirements for hierarchal formalities.

Because the violence, whether heroic or hooligan, derives from divine incursion, it can never be fully explained by Marxist, Freudian, sociological, psychological, or symbolic structural interpretations. We may speak of mob psychosis, of an *abaissement du niveau mental,* of the crowd and its power; we may talk of the revolt of the masses and the impotence of the oppressed classes, of the loss of the father who gives authority and order, of the passive-aggressive behavior fostered by the media, of urban despair and anomie, of exploitation and displacement through the commercial manipulation of sports . . . but never can we account for the madness of Mars. What takes place in urban sports violence is more like what takes place suddenly on the battlefield. Though we call it "hooliganism," this very transgression of all civic norms tells us that what is going on is not simply "sick" it is also mythic. Where myth now operates most vividly, showing the transcendent to the power of the Gods, is precisely outside of usual reason, just there in the inexplicable behaviors we call psychopathology.

II. Testosterone

Mars lives on the Areopagus, his hill in Athens; and he lives in the Campo de Marte outside the Roman city. He was always recognized as a danger to the civis and this because he lives inside each citizen's bloodstream, where he is called "testosterone." The virility of Mars is also a phenomenon of the glands. The Gods live not only on Olympus, not only in the heavens of myth and the shrines of antiquity; they continue to inhabit our bodies.

Again and again studies repeat that the attendees at urban soccer matches are mainly teenagers. This is especially true of the newer, third-world nations where the population age-median is lower than in Western Europe, but even in Cologne, research shows that over half of the spectators at regular matches are 21 or younger and, of course, 88% male. The riots have been called "delayed puberty crises," and even thought about in terms of young males seeking initiation through physical risk.

At the onset of puberty testosterone secretion suddenly increases thirtyfold. The effect of this male hormone is stupendous. In the moose, for example, the rack of antlers on its head grows to a breadth of two meters in only 120 days. Nearly 90% of the food the male moose takes in goes solely toward its magnificent display of aggressive male pride. Testosterone produces prolonged and intensely exhilarating experiences, a "male high," and it can occasion violence. Testosterone levels are reinforced, not reduced, by violence. No amount of moralist preaching by city elders and sports commentators, or police control, or feminist ideology can affect this natural force, this Mars in the bloodstream. It must be reckoned with. So let us look more closely at the psychological situations that raise and lower testosterone:[7]

- Anticipation of a challenge.
- Competition and success in competition.
- Increase of status: a successful response to trial.
- Anticipation of sexual encounter and success in sexual activities. Testosterone levels rise before and after sexual activity.
- Anger.

It is therefore not unexpected that a judgment call perceived as unjust or an unpunished foul that sets off anger in the crowd will trigger an escalation of fury owing to the increased testosterone levels. And it is not unexpected that already before a sports event, the anticipation of it prepares for a riot in the bloodstream. Nor should it be surprising that when the game is over, there is no falling off of excitement and that after a victory, an even higher potential for outburst.

Of these five factors which raise testosterone levels, anger deserves especial notice since it is a major component of sports violence and because anger belongs both mythologically and symbolically to the traits of Mars. Psychology, however, will not help us here because it often loses the specific value of anger by clumping it together with hostility, aggression, rage, fury, and hatred. Yet, the different words show, these states of soul are each different feelings, different behaviors, different significances. Our lack of differentiation of the martial emotions results from a long history, particularly Christian. *Ira* (anger) and *cupiditas* (desire) were long considered the two great enemies of Christian life. *Ira* and *cupiditas* translate into scholastic concepts the primal powers of Mars and Venus, so that in the concept lies concealed the Christian fear of the pagan Gods.

Rather than repress these impulses because they are "pagan," they can be refined. As the amatory arts improve the skills of desire, so sports improve the skills of anger. The coach, for instance, before each game speaks the rhetoric of Mars and unleashes a raging exhortation to impassion his team with the spirit of fight. So, too, the glaring stare of the boxer. A player in every opponent sport must learn, first of all, the skills of anger — how to let it rise, contain it, not "lose" it or "choke." Also, how skillfully to provoke the anger of the opponent so that he or she makes errors and commits fouls. Even solo sports such as golf, downhill skiing, and car racing require the skillful management of anger where the explosive charge upon which successful action depends never crosses over into blind attack. "Instrumental" violence used purposefully as a means to an end (as is the intention, usually, of hooliganism) must not fall into "expressive" violence — whether the expression is on the playing field, in the stands, or among the police deployed to maintain order.[8] Mars always strains at the leash of discipline which checks expression for the sake of instrumentality.

When we remove anger from the personal field, detaching it from hostile and aggressive traits, and instead attach it to the archetypal figure of Mars we can then see its necessity. Mars is the initiator, the beginning — like March at the start of the year, and April, his month, opens (*aprire*) the way, like a butting head of a ram. Anger is the first emotion off the blocks, the spontaneous combustion that originates (*oriri*, to rise) action. How often do the deeper explorations within personal

relations start off as angry battles? Disturbing yes, but without anger, the other cheek turned, there would be no sports at all, not even
ping-pong.

Again, the testosterone factor is not something new. At Carnival
time in twelfth-century London, young men of the city played ball in
the open fields. Senior citizens and local elders spectated the contests,
as if to recover their lost youth, "their natural heat seems to be stirred
in them at the mere sight of such strenuous activity and by their participation in the joys of unbridled youth."[9]

This "natural heat" (or Mars or testosterone) rises through mere
spectating. If this be the case, then sports are certainly not cathartic.[10]
The spectators are more charged afterwards than even before they entered the stadium. And so we also see why an entire city is rejuvenated
when its team moves toward the Cup finals. A ritualized revival is in
the offing.

In the case of losing we have another picture. For testosterone levels fall when one suffers: defeat; humiliation, failure, loss of status;
denial of sexual access — the Lysistrata phenomenon; isolation — it
is depressing for vital energy to be separated from the body politic;
inescapable punishment, so the usual formula for reducing male exuberance is cooling off the "natural heat" in a jail cell, which combines
isolation, humiliation, and punishment all together.

Since loss lowers testosterone levels and is equated with depression,
impotence, and isolation — that is, social anomie — events that can
raise testosterone levels favor the communal vitality of the body politic. The testosterone factor is merely another, more physiological, disruption of what civic celebrations such as triumphal parades, victory
arches, brass-band military concerts, running the bulls at Pamplona,
and the Palio horse race in Siena — and soccer matches — have long
recognized: a vigorous city must honor Mars.

The close relation between aggressive competition and sexual appetite, which studies of testosterone show, restates in psycho-physi-
ological language the mythological relation between Ares (Mars) and
Priapus. You may remember that Priapus, the God of phallic enormity
and seminal fertility, teaches boy Ares to dance. Only after he is trained
to be a perfect dancer does he become a warrior.[11] Tribal youths in the

first flush of puberty must learn hunting dances and war dances so as to make more erotic, aesthetic, and fertile the direct blood-letting called for by Mars. Priapus teaches Mars — besides evoking his Venusian potential — that sexuality shall be *danced*, shall be displayed before women and the community, and shall be a beauteous pride prior to violent aggression.

Dance occurs spontaneously. It breaks out. The leap, the stomp, the swivel and sway with arms raised, hands reaching for a high-five — all the exuberance after a goal show the Martial impulse to dance. Yet, recently the bodily joy expressed by a player after scoring a touchdown in American football has been forbidden, and over-doing the "spiking" of the ball subject to penalty.

Permit me to read you a passage from a recent interview with a British hooligan in the *Corriere della Sera*. I read it to show that a life without dance, without proud display, without the arts Priapus teaches, leaves to Mars only the imagination of violence.

Gilles, a 26-year-old porter in a large London department store who is about to go to Italy for the World Cup explains his behavior. Gilles says he is not racist and has never taken drugs, though sometimes he drinks too much. He enjoys "physical confrontation."

"Why does he like physical confrontation?"

This is Gilles's answer: "Because it's lovely to have fear and to overcome fear. And to make a bit of a ruckus. The newspapers go on about our being super-organized. It's not true. The chief of our group gets picked right in the stadium. Whoever is most in form becomes chief. Look, I do my portering all week long. I am no one. Maybe in ten years I'll be head porter, if all goes well. I'll still be no one. At the stadium, with my friends, for one day I am someone. You get it?"

There are echoes here all the way back to the Iliad and the Bible where captains and heroic chiefs emerge spontaneously according to their form; the martial spirit calling them at some specific moment.

Right here in Florence (as well as in other thirteenth-century Italian cities) a Captain of the *popolo* (people's civic militant guild) was the one "more likely to have quickness, ardor, flash, color, and emotional following, especially as pageantry and symbolism were exceedingly important. This was more a visual than a literate society."

III. Spectating

I am sure that you have been noticing that I am not making the usually strong distinction between active sports players and passive sports
spectators, heaping praise on the first and blame on the latter. That division between players and spectators is psychologically false since the
God Mars invades both and testosterone levels rise in both. Watching
the match prone on the couch before a color TV in a tenth-story cement apartment nonetheless excites the martial fury; I feel it in my
pulse, hear it in my voice, and find it in my behavior toward my fellows
and the women who are near.

Moreover, studies show that actual spectators of sports events —
bicycling, soccer, tennis, baseball, bowling, whatever — are also those
who play sports. The active person is also the watching person; the
inactive person neither plays nor watches.

Let me speak in defense of spectating. Nothing more belongs to
city life; a city is the place of spectacle and pageant, the display of
the imagination at its most nobly complex. Whether in and around
the cathedral, the market, piazza or in front of the city hall, spectating the performance of others, watching others as players, is a major
part of what draws us to cities. For cities are where the great fires take
place, the public executions, the new buildings arising, the wedding
and funeral processions, the accidents, strikes, and demonstrations. In
the city we may catch sight of a celebrity. To all this the citizen is
a spectator, even if today spectating becomes nothing more than an
amble through a shopping mall or a sitting at a cafe table, "people-
watching."

The pleasure of watching must not be underestimated. The scopo-
philia or voyeurism, that erotic flush in the city street, the fantasies
released, the speculations derived solely from spectating, are perhaps
more the true reason for the flourishing of cities than the usual reasons
such as protection, commerce and exchange, communication, culture,
industry, opportunity, changing class, etc. Therefore, anything in the
schedule of civic events or in the architecture of urban planning that
promotes spectating fosters city life and may, moreover, remove spectating from its concentrated focus in sports events.

It has been suggested that New York City, so extremely in debt and with insufficient police force, should abandon its great parades on holidays, parades which commemorate the ethnic groups in the city, in order to save the expense of crowd control. If, however, my argument holds that an essential aspect of civic life is spectating, then these huge pageants of color, music, and fantasy may actually be more cost-effective in bonding the body politic than sober restrictions. Spectacles satisfy the citizen's need for participation in the civic throng.

The etymology of the word *polis* shows it related to such words as *plenus, plerus, plebs, palus, plus* (or overabundance, evermore). It is a Dionysian word. In the midst of the many, packed into the stadiums, individuality melded with thousands of spectators, I am more in and of the city in its root meaning than when I am alone in my apartment behind my locked door. Yet, behind that door, alone, watching the game on TV, I am still more a political animal in city life than when not spectating. Again, therefore, whatever promotes throngs and crowds and the temporary dissolution of individualism fosters city life.

Here I need to take an example from American cities. It has been written that the great cities of the United States became homogenized metropolises in the nineteenth century owing to three surprisingly mundane factors. American cites, in their beginnings, were a hodge-podge of ghettos: the wealthy, white, and well-established in their reserves, the older immigrants in theirs, and the newer arrivals from Southern and Eastern Europe, and the so-called "coloreds" and Asians, in theirs. Food, language, ceremonies, holidays, churches, even clothing styles, as well as political loyalties, were ethnically determined. These groups did not meld easily. The actual "melting pot," as the American city has been called, came about only when the disparate factions were drawn together in a common *Gemeinschaftsgefühl* — feeling of community.

One of these was not education, though it is fondly believed that the American democratic free public education system did bring unity. The education system arose perhaps as a consequent of three principal factors: first, public transportation which allowed people of all sorts to venture cheaply and easily from enclosed neighborhoods; second, the department store which attracted people from outlying districts into a downtown where they could jostle and mingle and eventually even fall in love with an exogamous stranger; and third, the city team, especially baseball. If the first two, transport and department stores, encouraged the moving and mixing of bodies, the third, the city team, forged the feeling of the ethnocentrically separated and rival ghettos into a town spirit.

Although spectator hooliganism misuses the city spirit as a rallying banner behind which hides battle lust, the city nonetheless gains. The violence reminds the city that it is a living organism grounded not simply in commerce and culture but in trans-human factors that still demand blood. The violence has many complicating p sycho-social factors that are possible to expose and condemn, and hopefully to correct. The basic point I wish to make here, however, is that the source of hooliganism lies neither in eruptive compensation for passive spectating nor in intense civic pride in the symbols of the team.

IV. Ritual

Where, then, does the problem lie? I have said that urban sport violence cannot be blamed upon the exuberance of team spirit or upon passive spectating. I have also maintained that the urban throng fostered by sports is essential to city life, and I have refused to agree with sociological, Marxist, and other psychological explanations, which all too often use their explanations to condemn the phenomenon they would explain. Instead, I have been claiming that the madness is Martial, a divine fury, and that it has physiological constituents which arise in specific situations. In other words, I am saying urban sport violence is an innate, natural potential, belonging archetypally to the human being as a political animal and to the city as the abode of this political animal. I have further been maintaining that hooliganism is aborted ritual. I consider it to be a demand of the God in the populace for recognition and obedience to his power. The martial God in a secular city finds no aegis for his fury. And so, his power dissipates in secular random violence, turning against the very members of his cult, the spectators and fans, who in their unwitting attempt to honor this power only provoke a more stringent repression.

Since we are now on the threshold of the World Cup in soccer (football), inviting a divine madness and expecting that "fury and fierce civil strife shall cumber all the parts of Italy," (Shakespeare, *Julius Caesar* III 1), we had better understand something more about young men and their need for rituals, about testosterone, and about Mars. More police, fire hoses, attack dogs, and the resort to flogging serve repressions, but we have learned from Freud that the repressed always returns; besides, can Mars be repressed? Would we not do better to imagine in terms of ritual?

Turning Mars over to the military and young men over to gangs, prisons, drugs, the senectitude of colleges and universities, and testosterone over to motorcycles, pop concerts, and cocaine does not meet the need for ritual. Condemnation does not invite the elders to reflect upon initiation of their younger fellow tribesmen. Rather, these moves abandon youth, even attempt to get rid of it as a "problem." Despite the condemnation and repression, even the murder, of youth by the negligent elders, the "problem" does not go away, manifesting most obstreperously in hooliganism. Hence the righteous concern — and fright — in the elders. They realize that the secular norms cannot hold the divine fury, and that rituals are actually taking place in the gangs, prisons, the riots, the rock concerts, as if the God, despite the elders, is forcing youth into initiations regardless of their profane and inadequate form.

Societies, for centuries, have been more concerned with the initiation of their youth — the honoring of the "litima" (Gisu of Uganda), or violent energy, in their young males, the successful channeling of testosterone and the introduction to that God we call Mars — than with almost anything else in their worlds (cf. Michael Meade, *Men and the Water of Life*). The preparation of ceremonies and the enactment of rituals constituted the major part of the waking life of most tribal peoples. Initiation went on for years and years, just as ritual was carried into all of life as it was lived, not merely something set apart and called "a ritual." I am not suggesting now, with René Girard, that violence is sacred or that it is necessary to the sacred and that the sacred is built from violence. I am, however, suggesting that a more sacred view toward this disorder may honor the God therein and may invite him to reveal more of his deeper intentions with our culture that treats him as outlaw, even as it devotes a preponderant proportion of its industrial potential and export agenda to the service of war.

So I am calling for a turn to Mars with a fresh awareness of his significance as a dominant in psychic life, in civic life. Only that God who brings a disease can take it away. Like cures like.

V. Clinical Recommendations

As a clinician of the soul, and especially of the soul of the city, who has made a differential diagnosis that our disorder is due to a specific God, I feel obliged to conclude with recommendations for treatment. Treatment begins with recognition of the God in the disease and consists in prescriptions that, we imagine, may more satisfactorily honor the God's intentions.

One: bear in mind that civic sports events are dedications of the spirit of the city to the violent force of Mars. They invite Mars to be present, so they must be conceived with solemnity and pageantry: more martial music, banners, songs; more officials, judges, patrons; more parades, costumes, ceremonies. Take a page from Giovanni de Bardi.

Two: rituals especially for spectators. Do not treat them as sheep, for then they become a mass. Rather invite them into the arena as participant players in the larger performance. Allow them individual or a small-group heroic entry. Invent a more ritualized *rite d'entrée* and rite de sortie so that the God who rules the stadium is contained within the sacred space. Repressive crowd control only becomes necessary once spectators have become a "crowd."

Three: remember Venus — and not only with cheerleaders and pom-pom majorettes. There would be special prices for women, and special prizes for women's fashion. Dress for the event. Men too. Let there be dancing on the field after the game. Display. Beauty.

Four: less conception in terms of numbers — the gate, the cost, the crowd which reduces the spectators to mere "number," which only furthers the anonymity that fosters chaotic violence.

Five: more media attention to the public as people, showing off their display to TV viewers. Let TV spot individual women spectators, their clothes, the cosmetics, their hats.

Six: less humanism. Less translation of the heroes of sport into human terms, as if they were really just ordinary guys with nice little families, who drink milk and eat burgers, who have smiling wives and drive the same make of car as you. Their role is more than human. As Sons of Mars the mystery of their superhuman prowess must be maintained and even ennobled so that they fully become ritual figures, awaking awe, respect, and distance. This goes for Daughters of Mars, too.

Seven: less monetary evaluation. They are paid in cosmic figures not because they are so superior to those just below them in ability, but because they are emblems of another world; Stars, belonging to Fama, favored by Fortuna. The exalted salary recognizes their otherworldly worth. Their earnings should not be imagined in terms of ordinary mortals.

Eight: increased competitive intensity in all matches. Sports always at the extreme edge of eruption. For the display of managed force, of controlled extremity, demonstrates the capacity of ritual to transform Martial violence into Martial art. I believe that violence, intensified and formalized at the same time, diminishes the capacity of epidemic contagion.

Nine: more hierarchy. A general rule seems to hold in sports: the more hierarchically structured the sport, the more reinforced is the sacred container which keeps the influx of energy within bounds. Hierarchy means rankings, officials, roles, penalties, protocols, captains, divisions — a constant eye for procedural order.

Ten: more aesthetics. A greater appreciation by sportswriters, media cameramen, and citizens of the beauty brought to the city by their champions. Rather than final scores and winners, let us dwell on the "dance" of the game — passes, saves, artistry, style, movements. For the game is where the ordinary person is lifted by the epiphanies of physical beauty, moments when Hermes passes, a miraculous turn, a sudden, swift, impossible save, the whole culture of the plebeian lifted from their seats, lifted by a vision to another dimension by the radiant fire of Mars.

So with these prescriptions, the doctor sits down awaiting the game, once again a spectator.

1. E. Dunning, P. Murphy, and J. Williams, *The Roots of Football Hooliganism* (London: Routledge, 1988).

2. Cf. H. W. Parke, *Greek Oracles* (London: Hutchinson, 1967), p. 871; and *The Oracles of Zeus* (Oxford: Blackwell, 1967), p. 111.

3. A. Guttmann, *Sports Spectators* (New York: Columbia Univeristy Press, 1986), p. 68.

4. On Mars and Ares see "Epitheta Deorum," in W. H. Roscher, *Ausführliches Lexikon der griechischen und römischen Mythologie*, vol. 7 (Hildesheim: Georg Olms Verlag, 1993); G. Dumézil, *Archaic Roman Religion* (Chicago: University of Chicago Press, 1970), vol. I, pp. 205–45.

5. Cf. my "Wars, Arms, Rams, Mars" in *Mythical Figures*, Uniform Edition of the Writings of James Hillman, vol. 6.1 (Putnam, Conn.: Spring Publications, 2007); see also my *A Terrible Love of War* (New York: Penguin Press, 2004).

6. E. Dunning, et. al., *The Roots of Football Hooliganism*, p. 235.

7. I thank Michael Meade for the digest of the testosterone literature.

8. Cf. *The Roots of Football Hooliganism*, pp. 236–38.

9. Guttmann, *Sports Spectators*, p. 50.

10. Ibid., p. 155.

11. K. Kerényi, *The Gods of the Greeks* (London: Thames and Hudson, 1951), p. 116.

22

Ceilings

I am a psychological analyst. I speak to the private issues that lie inside the public forum, in the soul of the city. I am less a developer than an underminer, following the leaks of gas that cloud and poison our personal relations, the drain of strength in insomnia, impotence, addiction, the little mice of impulses nibbling away in the corners of our interior space, the power failures of despair. This interior city is private and unspeakable in the forum. Yet we can connect this interiority, our soul-life, with the interiority of our public life. In fact, we may discover a correspondence between two kinds of interior. The conditions of our psyches, I will suggest, reflect the interior of our rooms. There are relations between our habits and our habitations. And that is my theme and my method now: the relation between the inside interior of our lives and the interior inside our living places.

Most city *talk* is about major buildings, planned public spaces, transit. In the mind's eye the word "city" conjures a panoramic shot like the opening of "Dallas" coming in from South Fork Ranch, the city through a car windshield, on a TV screen, glass, of course. This is all seen from the outside, the exterior city: skyline, skyscrapers, windy squares. That kind of city has more to do with planning boards, tourists, and TV shows than with its actual nine-to-five inhabitants.

Actual city *life* is interior: inside rooms, sitting on chairs. We push through doorways, go down passages. We wait at elevators, rummage in drawers, stare at walls. Much of the time we are in fact looking

Lecture delivered at The Dallas Institute Forum, 17 May 1982. First published in the *Institute Newsletter* 2/1 (Dallas, 1983).

down at something on a desk, focused on an electronic device, a piece of paper, or across at another face. No matter how tall the building or magnificent its skin and front plaza, inside, that soaring feeling is reduced to individual rooms, corridors, compartments, cubbyholes with an eight-foot ceiling. You step out of the elevator on the forty-eighth floor, into a corridor whose ceiling you can almost touch with your fingertips: we are still in the same tunnel like the underground garage. Let's turn our attention to those ceilings. Let's look up, for I want to encapsulate all I have to say about the psychology of interior design and the design of it upon human interiority by a brief psychoanalysis of the ceiling.

Looking Up

But before we look up: consider this curious psychological fact. There is no visible top to our heads. What we see of ourselves upwards are perhaps our eyebrows, a lock of hair in some fortunate cases. There is no limit upward to our self-experience of the head. As the bottoms of our feet touch the ground, the tops of our heads enter the sky. The ceremonial tonsure of monks and priests that open the scalp to heaven remembers this fact; so does the cranial position of the 1,000-petaled lotus of awareness in Hindu mysticism. So does the Platonic reading of the newborn baby's still unclosed skull — it is still open to the upper world whence it supposedly comes. So, too, the Jewish and Islamic custom of keeping the head covered at all times, in prayer, and indoors. Because there is no natural separation upward between human and heavenly, the ceiling of a hat remembers the distinction and is a sign of human humility. We have to have ceilings — not just for practical but for psychological reasons. The atrium opening straight up extends our heads into hubris and inflation, no cap to the skull; inspiration gone manic, the sky's the limit.

Now what *does* meet the eye looking up? Usually, today, this basic human gesture, that also raises the head and lifts the person, has become so acutely unpleasant that our glance instinctively retreats. We lower our sight. What's up there is tacky, unarranged; scattered islands of air vents, smoke detectors, sprinkler spigots, loudspeakers, perhaps a red exit sign tucked up high, perhaps a TV monitor eye, and the ubiquitous track lights pointing every which way, or recessed cans, or fluorescent tubes in mesh cages. The material itself is often acoustic board, taped with silver masking strips into rectangular blocks, often askew from repairs, stained with traces from pipe or roof leaks.

What's up there refers to fire, smoke, bad air, loud noise, theft, accidents, and the repairman: the ceiling as service center, a covering for wires, cables, tubes, ducts, immediately accessible for maintenance, Here is one more instance of interior designed not for the nine-to-five inhabitants of that interior, but for the maintenance crew, not for pleasure of use, but for occasions of breakdown. It is like choosing your clothes in the morning to wear for an accident.

I want now to claim that the ceiling is the most neglected segment of our contemporary interior — interior in both architectural and psychological senses of the word. Whether oppressively close and ugly as just described, or removed altogether in vaulting A-frames or atriums to the roof, the ceiling is the unconsidered, the unconscious, presenting interiority without design, with no sense of inherent order.

What statements are these ceilings making? What are they saying about our *psychic* interiors? If looking up is that gesture of aspiration and orientation toward the higher order of the cosmos, an imagination opening toward the stars, our ceilings reflect an utterly secular vision — short-sighted, utilitarian, unaesthetic. Our heads reach up and open into a meaningless and chaotic white space. The world above has merely a maintenance function, God the repairman called on when things break down. Curiously, however, the *perspective* from above still remains. Look at our usual blueprints, our usual models. They are drawn from above as floor plans; the view is down from the ceiling. The place from which the Gods have fled is now where the planner sits. We must remember that renewal of spirit occurs within an enclosed space, under some sort of ceiling. Ancient Kings, as far back as the Pharaohs, placed themselves under a canopy, a tent, a dome — walls were incidental — and thereby the interior man, the soul, received renewed vitality. The ceiling did indeed refer to heaven, to *ciel,* as our popular and mistaken etymology of ceiling continues to insist.

Etymology

For ceiling doesn't come from *ciel*, French for heaven, sky. Covering the room, enclosing it, that feeling of interior designed space — that there is design to the interior, and this design renews the human spirit — is the true root of the word. It derives from *celure*, via Middle English (*celynge, silynge, syling,* and *selure* [*celure*]) for tapestry, canopy, hangings, finally coming to cell, meaning "to line with woodwork" (1400–1600).

Ceilings became white only during the Enlightenment, the eighteenth century, with the refinement of the plasterer's art. Previously all the detail was exposed: joists, beams, the reverse of the floor above. Then the detail was enhanced by carving the beams, painting, gilding, stucco, plaster, so that looking up fed the imagination. The eye traversed an intriguing pattern of rhythmical and inherent relationships — where function (joists, floorboards) and beauty were inseparable. Ceilings emphasized design — and I do not mean only the magnificent ones painted to represent the heavens and the Gods.

Inside the Latin root of the word itself (*celum, caelatura, caelo*) is the idea of design as burnishing, chiseling, engraving. The upper aspect of our interior space is an intricately fashioned and figured design. The ceiling is a place of images to which imagination turns its gaze to renew vitality. The true ceiling, then, as derived from the word is not a flat white rectangular space studded with incidental equipment, but a magnificent artifice of imagery. The ceiling up there corresponds with the richness of human imagination. It is this that our heads can open into and find protection under.

Ceiling Lights

This brings us to the quality of light and ceiling fixtures. We all feel the difference when the overhead light is turned off and standing lamps, table lamps go on. You know the kind of interior that emerges — like a Vuillard or a Bonnard room, an effect used in the movies to change the atmosphere toward intimacy and interiority. Single uniform brightness gives way to shadings of color, reflection, and the sense of nearness to the light within the reach of the hand — as to a candle or a fireplace.

Overhead lighting belongs originally to large state halls, banquet rooms, exhibitions, factories, and markets, where very high ceilings and expansive floor plans demanded flooding of light from above. A splendor both marvelous and functional; indoors, yet lit as the sun-filled world. The light fixtures became objects of awe. They have of course given way, in most cases, to what the maintenance crew can get at and clean up, as low-cost as possible.

Now, we apply the same overhead lighting in the smallest cubicles with the lowest ceilings. We sit bathed in a merciless, shadowless enlightenment, democratically falling on all alike, straight down — a spotlight like that used to break criminals into confession, a brilliant clarity like for an anatomical dissection. The light does not group the furniture, encircle it. Instead, each thing is distinct, isolated from each other thing. Interiority is gone: the flickering feeling of the cave, lighting that makes this piece of room here different from that over there. The room receives the massive doses of illumination of summer outdoors: uniform, bright, cloudless. And timeless; it is always noon indoors. We cannot tell because of these ceiling lights what time of day it is, what the weather, what the season of the year.

Moreover, you do not want to raise your eyes, to look into flourescent fixtures, at the bright bulb in the track can. You keep your head down — a depressive posture, outlook limited to the horizontal or the downward stare. In such light what does the soul do with its shadows or where to find interiority? Does the soul not shrink into even deeper personal interiors, into more darkness, so that we feel cut off, alienated, prey to the darkest of the dark: guilts, private sins, fears, and horror fantasies? I am suggesting some of our most oppressive psychological ills come out of the ceiling.

Moldings

Now to conclude this psychoanalysis of the ceiling — a word on moldings. At the retreat of the Dallas Institute on Architecture and Poetry, Robert Sardello gave a remarkable, thought-provoking paper in which he examined the place of the right angle in the design of modern cities. He pointed out that the right angle is an abstract expression for the ancient archetypal directions of heaven and earth, Sky God and Earth Mother, the vertical and horizontal dimensions reduced to a simple pair of intersecting lines, much like the tool used by carpenters, the square, the Greek word for which is *norma* (from which we have norms, normal, normalcy). The simple right angle normalizes our entire world from the grid plan of city plats to the graph paper on which we calculate and display the living curves of economic activity.

Modern Bauhaus design exposes this conjunction of father sky and mother earth. The joint is laid bare. Moldings resolve the shock, the violence of their direct rectangular conjunction. Moldings provide a skirt, a curtain covering the exposed pornography, the crotch shot of ceiling joining wall in bare fluorescent light. Moldings are not merely a Victorian cover-up, a delicate discretion — they are an erotic moment in a room, a detail that softens the vertical, letting it come down gently through a series of ripples, heaven into earth, earth into heaven, the secular and the divine, not cut apart and placed at right conflicting purposes, a leap, a gap (as we often see a black line at the ceiling's edge where the two directions have receded from each other, the sheet rock not quite meeting, the taping and mud inadequate).

The problem of how to conclude a ceiling, its edge or end, was a particular concern of Islamic builders, who had to set circular domes on square rooms. Squaring of the circle and circling of the square, the meeting of two worlds, gave rise to extraordinarily ornate corners rich with embellished moldings. Rich fantasies develop at the juncture where the ceiling descends into the living space of everyday.

Let's now come to a close. I deliberately chose a small subject because in this city of Dallas we all think so big and bold. I chose ceilings for this exhibition of interior design because just these minor forgotten matters are the more psychological. But now let me be bold: it doesn't so much matter how tall and what color the next huge building is downtown or what the library, the symphony hall, the museum look like from the outside. These considerations seduce us into staying outside, playing planner and developer ourselves. It's what's inside that counts, says the psychologist. And the very interest in the exterior of projects — the arts district, the malls — reflects the exteriorization of our inner concerns. Human beings adapt to their surroundings, and we shall have human beings designed like our interiors, human beings of gold and silver and glass, with hollowed atriums, uniformly illumined by shadowless light, without upper orientation, and with only the crassest, simplest right-angled norms and straight rules for connecting the principles of the heavens with the ways of the earth. These shall be the inhabitants if these be our habitations.

I am suggesting, by means of ceilings, that our buildings are not truly inhabitable, that we must become a certain kind of person with strange habits of soul in order to stay in such rooms under such ceilings for the major part of our conscious life. I am suggesting that many of our social evils and psychological troubles — and even economic ills, such as low productivity, inefficiency, absenteeism, sexual harassment, job turnover, quality decline, on-the-job addiction (whether valium, alcohol, coffee, or soda pop) — are psychological results of interior design. To believe still that our psychological problems have economic causes and economic solutions is not only crude materialism, it is crude to the soul, psychologically unsophisticated. I am saying that until we recognize the design of interiors on our interiority we shall be living in a kind of Orwellian repression, that is, disguised and unnoticed, like living in his book, *1984*.

For repression, as Freud discovered it — and he considered repression the greatest of his discoveries — is never where we believe it lies. That's its very meaning. We cannot be aware of it; it is unconscious. So the repressed today is not where we think it is, in our sexual feelings, racial prejudices, family knots, and hidden motives. We are far more aware of these interior events than in Freud's day. Today, the repressed is less in our interior life, and to search still for it there only furthers the main repression: our unconsciousness regarding the interior psychic reality of the external world. Today the repressed is outside of us, and we are anesthetized and tranquilized to the world we inhabit. This has been called "psychic numbing," which refers not only to possible nuclear catastrophe but to every detail of soullessness from our styrofoam coffee containers to the sounds and light and air, the taste of water, and low-maintenance clothes we put on our skins, discomforting but so easy to maintain. By repressing our reactions to basic simple details, like ceilings, by denying our annoyance and outrage, we actually reinforce an unconsciousness that estranges and disorients the interior soul.

I am not calling for more potted plants, for sweeter manners, for longer coffee breaks to humanize the interiors of the office. Nor am I beating the antique drum, going back to old ways: historic preservation, nostalgic inspiration from European palaces, ceilings like that in the Sistine Chapel, Disneyland imitations, Red-North-Valley-Center-Preston-Wood Mall. We don't need to build them like we used to — we can indeed build better, as the slogan goes. Restoring and preserving the old, worthwhile as it is, remains a lesser concern because it can become a literalization of what we truly are after: preservation and restoration of the human tradition, the tradition that shapes in replication of the cosmos, where the roof over our heads brings heaven into our minds.

The interior sense always seems a minor matter when compared with the public arena — whether to build aircraft carriers and what kind, whether the deficit should be 90 or 120 billion — these abstract issues that seem so mighty are really the advertising campaign of governments to keep us buying their product, that is, government, to keep us believing that it is dealing with the important issues of "reality." The reality of the soul, however, must be affirmed again and again in this city, for the city is an invisible, spiritual city, not of buildings only, but of small sensitive things that give life to its soul as a city of soul and spirit, of sensitivity and inspiration.

So, my intention has not been to suggest how rooms should be built — even if I have drawn attention to moldings, lights, ceiling height, arrangement. My purpose with these physical details is to make a psychological point. I want to preserve and restore the simple gesture of looking upwards. If our society suffers from failures of imagination, of leadership, of cohesive far-sighted perspectives, then we must attend to the places and moments where these interior faculties in the human mind begin. Remember the Psalm: "I shall lift up mine eyes — from whence cometh my help." That primordial gesture toward the upper dimension, that glance above ourselves, yet not lofty, spacey, and dizzy, may be where the first bits of interior change take place. This change of soul can take place inside our ordinary rooms.

23

Walking

From archaic times through antiquity and the Renaissance and right into the early twentieth century, basic human postures — lying, sitting, standing, and running — have remained the same. Body movements, such as bending, reaching, holding, leaning, squatting, and dancing, more or less go on through the ages, differently, but with continuity. Today we may sit more and stand less or sit more than crouch and kneel. Our beds and couches may alter from historical period to period. But basic human movements have changed radically only in walking. We not only walk less than did our ancestors; we have almost eliminated the need to walk. It has become obsolete. Locomotion has become mechanized, from remote-control devices to, of course, automobiles.

Automobiles do more than locomote us. Dutch psychologist Bernd Jager has observed the differences in facial expressions in the newer western and southern cities of the USA that depend on cars, and the older northern and eastern cities, where there is still jostling in the streets, subways, buses, and pavements. Jager concludes that the more uniform, bland, ad-like faces of people in the Sun Belt result from the increased use of the automobile and the fact that one does not need "to prepare a face to meet the faces that we meet," as T. S. Eliot says. Our face belongs to others as well as ourselves, and results from others. How we countenance others, engage them with our expression, open up or close ourselves off — all this shows in the face.

First published in the pamphlet *The City as Dwelling* (Irving, Tex.: Center for Civic Leadership, University of Dallas, 1980).

As humans become faceless under their blown-dry hair and cosmetics, cars pick up more distinctive names and fronts, those personalized expressions by which even small children can at once discern the make and model. But the face of the driver within the car is generally vacant, glazed behind the windshield. Strapped in, door locked, listening to a tape, staring ahead, passively registering motions of objects out there or subjective emotions in here, worries and desires, it is not an interpersonal face, but an isolated face — its expression does not matter.

The face of the city block, bazaar market, and alley is wily, vivid, canny, and as expressive as the gestures and language of those engaged from morning till night with other people. The Greek word for city, *polis*, originally meant flowing, throng, crowd. A city is a jostling of bodies in the street of common people.

So, the absence of meeting faces absents us from our own faces; it also absents us from the city as it was original imagined: a congregating crowd of human faces from all "walks" of life.

Views from designers' boards and developers' plans rarely show a crowd. Instead, couples stroll under trees; persons emerge one at a time from cars under canopies. It is as if there were a polyphobia, a fear of the many, facing and being faced by others. I believe that the fear of violence in city streets correlates psychologically with the sense of oneself as a depersonalized, defaced object — a sitting duck or victim — placed in an empty abstract street like a little figure in a designer's plan.

I have found in my psychological work with people that during periods of acute psychological turmoil, walking is an activity to which one naturally turns. This was of course in Zurich, Switzerland, where I practiced for some twenty-five years before coming to Dallas. Walking doesn't come as easily in a North Dallas suburb. In Irving or Plano, a person walking up the street stands out more oddly, more suspiciously, than does a winded jogger in red warm-up suit, yellow-striped shoes, and earmuffs. Walking can be meditative therapy — not an idyllic hike by the ocean — but simply around the city for hours in early morning or late at night. Can our city allow this psychological self-cure? Or would we become prowlers or victims in the eyes of our fellows?

Walking calms turmoil. Prisoners circumambulate the yard, animals exercise back and forth in their cages, and the anxious pace the floor — waiting for the baby to be born or to hear news from the board room. Heidegger recommended the path through the woods for philosophizing. Aristotle's school was called "Peripatetic" — thinking and discoursing while walking up and down; monks walk round their closed gardens. Nietzsche said that only thoughts while walking, *laufenden* thoughts were of value — thoughts that ran, not sitting thoughts.

One goes for a walk to get the stuck, depressed state of mind or its whirling agitations into an organic rhythm, and this organic rhythm of walking takes on symbolic significance as we place one foot after the other, left-right, left-right in a balanced pace. Pace. Measure. Taking steps. With the soul-calming language of walking, the dartings of the mind begin to form into a direction. As we walk, we are in the world, finding ourselves in a particular space and turning that space by walking within it into a place, a dwelling or territory, a local habitation with a name. The mind becomes contained in its rhythm. If we cannot walk, where will the mind go? Will it not run wild, or stay stuck, only to be moved by the rhythms of pharmaceuticals: uppers and downers, slowers and speeders, calmers and peppers? Is not a city that offers no walking also a city that offers no dwelling for the mind? Simply said: We may be driving, literally *driving*, ourselves crazy by not attending to the fundamental human need of walking.

There is probably an archetypal cure going on in walking, something profoundly affecting the mythical substrata of our lives. When we are most in the grip of anxiety, as in nightmares, we are often unable to move our legs. There is a long association between flight and motion of the feet — the word for fright in German, for instance, means to leap or jump up. Could it be that the less we move our legs, the more subject we are to anxiety; that by not moving, we are already living an unconscious nightmare?

Walking also brings me in contact with my animal nature. I am as I move: catlike, nimble and stealthy, bullish, stiff as a stork, waddling like a duck, strutting and prancing like a young buck. There is an animal display in our motion by which we are known. When this animal of our nature is neglected, it tends to be compensated by external accoutrements: cars (cougars, rabbits, eagles), city teams (tigers, birds, lions), hairstyles, jewelry, labels on clothing (the fox or alligator now sewn on the shirt). These static emblems are designed for sitting persons in a car, at the conference table, over lunch, where only half the body appears. We watch talking heads or fast-paced motion on TV. Walking does not suit TV: we can see violence, excited jumping up and down, running to each other, escaping from each other, sports, dancing, exercises, but where are the persons ambling along the street? Lying or sitting as we watch TV, its sympathetic magic turns us into talking heads, Muppets watching Muppets.

Two centuries ago, during that calm and rational period of the eighteenth-century Enlightenment, there was a good deal of walking in Europe, especially in and around gardens. The art of garden-making reached an apogee. We can learn something from those gardeners. They were the great developers of that time: whole prospects were raised or levelled, streams diverted, vistas opened, mazes constructed. No sooner a duke or count imagined a landscape than shoulders and shovels went at it. Those developers then were moved by aesthetic considerations, ours more by economic ones. What they left behind became national treasures for the community; what ours are leaving behind results in personal wealth for individuals. The history of property and land development ought to be part of every developer's consciousness and conscience.

The art of the eighteenth-century garden considered it essential that both the eye *and* the foot be satisfied: the eye to see, the foot to travel; the eye to encompass the whole and know it, the foot to remain within it and experience it. It was equally essential in this "aesthetics of dissociation," as Robert Dupree describes it, that the eye and the foot *not* travel the same path. The poet William Shenstone writes that when a building or other object has once been viewed, the foot should never travel to it by the same path which the eye has traveled over before: "lose the object (from sight) and draw nigh obliquely." Further, says Shenstone, the worst design is one that creates a "strait-lined avenue where the foot is to travel over what the eye has done before . . . to move on continually and find no change of scene attendant on our change of place, must give actual pain to a person of taste."

Cityscapes today — the malls, streets, building complexes — seem built for the eye only. The foot is forced to travel over what the eye has done before so that walking becomes indeed a pain. In Shenstone's scheme, walking is a mode of discovering new prospects. Walking in our layouts is merely a slow and inefficient way of moving us nearer to what the eye has already seen. The foot is slave to the eye, which makes walking boring, a matter of covering distance. When we can maintain the tension between foot and eye, we embark on a more circular, indirect approach. Foot leads eye, eye instructs foot, alternating. Walking takes on the movement of soul because, as the great philosopher Plotinus said, the soul's motion is not direct.

The eighteenth century took care of this need of the soul in a canny manner. Into the walking areas were constructed what the common people called "ha has": surprising sunken fences, hidden hedges, boundary ditches which, when come upon suddenly, called forth a "ha ha," stopping the progress of the walk, forcing the foot to turn and the mind to reflect.

How strange this is to us today: imagine, while walking from your parked car toward your visual objective, being blocked by an open culvert trench or a chain barrier that you had not previously perceived. Your 'ha ha' would be fury — a public complaint, a lawsuit. When we walk today, it is mainly a walking with the eye. We want no maze, no amazements. We have sacrificed the foot to the eye. Older cities often grew up around the traces of the feet: cow paths, corners and enclosures, crossings. These cities followed the inherent patterns of the feet rather than the planned designs of the eye.

Clearly, the automobile seems a further development of eye consciousness — rather than foot consciousness. Despite an old word for the car, "locomobile," its locomotion is a visual experience. Hence, walking on a highway because the car broke down is a horrifying, depersonalizing experience. "Out there" is revealed to the foot as burrs, weeds, holes, trash, and roaring leviathans at one's back. Of course new cities have pavement problems since the foot is ignored. The streets soon become criminal regions: roll up the car window, lock the door, don't linger. Street crime begins psychologically in a walk-less world; it begins on the drawing board of that planner who sees cities as collections of high-rise buildings and convenience malls with streets as mere efficient modes of access.

Development planners have radically affected our notions of cities leading us to forget that cities spring up from below; they rise from their streets. Cities are streets, avenues of commerce and exchange, the low-country world of physical thronging, a congregation pounding the pavements in curiosity, surprise, and encounter, human life not above the melée but right in it. Cities depend on walking for their vitality.

Let me end with a modern fairy tale — and a recommendation. The tale comes from *The Phantom Tollbooth* by Norton Juster. A little boy named Milo comes to a city where people hurry about, eyes to the ground, fixedly knowing exactly where they are going. But there are no buildings and no streets. They have all vanished. Milo is told the reason why: "Many years ago on this very spot there was a beautiful city of fine houses and inviting spaces . . . The streets were full of wonderful things to see and the people would often stop to look at them."

"Didn't they have any place to go?" asks Milo.

"To be sure," he is told, "but as you know, the most important reason for going from one place to another is to see what's in between . . ."

Then one day someone discovered that you could get faster from one point to another if you looked at nothing and took short cuts. The people became obsessed with getting there, rushing and hurrying, "eyes on their shoes," as the storyteller says. And because "no one paid any attention to how things looked . . . everything grew uglier and dirtier, and as everything grew uglier and dirtier they moved faster and faster, and at last a very strange thing began to happen." The city began to disappear. "Day by day the buildings grew fainter and fainter, and the streets just faded away." They went right on living there just as they always had done, in the houses and buildings and "streets which had vanished, because nobody had noticed a thing."

Our buildings are surely not vanishing. More are rising all the time. Although they stand there, gold and silver in the sun, maybe they are fading in another sense. Maybe they are losing their sensate, aesthetic reality, becoming non-buildings that nobody notices, buildings for neither foot nor eye, but simply an available office, warehouse, or convention space, abstract numbers transformed mathematically into concrete, metal, and glass, great seamless Mason jars. And this happens principally, I believe, because these buildings are not made for walking. Only emergencies allow us to use the stairways between levels; the atriums are traversed with escalators and elevators; the uniform hallways are shortened to improve intra-office connections. When we minimize walking within a building, we are minimizing interior motion, the life of the soul within the building, thereby diminishing the building's interior and the interior of the lives of all who dwell in the building.

What can we do? May a psychologist question proposals for malls without foot-imagination, and may he raise doubts about underground tunnels for pedestrians, or recommend interesting downtown pavements rather than glassed-in walkways? May he propose things that are noticeable to the eye and yet draw the foot into exploration — like complexities, nooks, water courses, levels, shifts of perspectives? It is surely not the psychologist who lays out the span between parking lot and building, for if he did it might be more a mode of encountering faces, with posters and paintings, places for pausing, rather than an eerie cement-grey space to hurry through in fear, where place is remembered neither by eye nor foot but conceptually — a code-lettered stub clutched in the hand. Yes, I suppose the psychologist would build "ha has" in the paths of progress, wanting every design for a street project to be imagined not only in terms of getting there, but also in terms of being there.

I am not beating the antique drum of romance: a stroll under street lamps and leafy sycamores, across clean-swept pavement towards the ice cream parlour where there is always an empty table; balloon men, vendors . . .

Rather, I am urging what the city itself has always urged by its very name — with crowds, walking in the streets, the city is a place of soul because it allows our souls their legs, our heads their faces, and our bodies their animal styles. In all things we think of for the future of our city, let us keep our city on its feet. We dwell not only in rooms behind doors, in chairs at tables, at jobs behind counters. We dwell on earth also in the freedom of the legs that give freedom to the mind.

In the temples once we were blessed for our "coming in and going forth." The blessing took into account the human as a moving being, a soul with feet, a physical being in the midst of a physical world made to walk in, as Adam and Eve walked in Eden. That garden is the imagination's primordial place of the nostalgia which recurs unconsciously in all utopian dreams. And that garden was created, you will remember, by a walking God. That image says that there is walking in Paradise; it also suggests that there is Paradise in walking.

24

Transportation

The invitation extended so courageously, maybe foolishly, to speak today — about a topic that is far from my area of expertise — intended a contribution that might move the question of transportation from a level of practical problems to a level of psychological reflection and insight. As a psychoanalyst or depth psychologist in practice, I don't, I can't, make this split between practical problems and psychological reflections. In my work we regard anything that is practised as always a psychological expression, just as the jokes about analysts imply: "Good morning," says the elevator attendant to two analysts going up to their offices, and one says to the other, "What did he mean by that?"

Our method works rather like this joke: on the one hand, daily practical events contain psyche — a fantasy image, private idea, or deeper emotional meaning. On the other hand, invisible ideas, emotions, and fantasies are also being practised somewhere in our public lives. For us private and public sectors connect; we assume every problem has a private sector to it and that fantasies appear first in the public sector as hard, tough, real, thorny, weighty, and urgent problems. "Problems" are simply the dense outer shell in which fantasies are wrapped. They cannot be truly solved until we have uncovered the fantasies nourishing them from inside.

Let me show you how the practice of psychotherapy operates. When a problem is brought into the consulting room, we listen to it very carefully, attempting to hear through it for fantasies. How is the problem

First published by the Center for Civic Leadership, University of Dallas, Irving, Tex., 1979.

constructed: how does it shape itself in words, what constructs does it come in? Let's begin with transportation. We ask the patient:

What is this problem you call "transportation"?
Moving people and goods in and out of the city, or around it, or between it and other cities, as efficiently as possible.

Hmm. That's a pretty large order . . . you mean like between Dallas and Fort Worth, Dallas and Chicago, even to Berlin and Stockholm?
Well, yes, but I guess for this session we can limit it to just in and out of the Center City. I mean that's where it's most acute.

How about that word "efficiently?" What do you want to say with that?
Quickly, cheaply, smoothly — few bugs, minimum negative spin-off on the world transportation is moving through, easy access for loading and unloading, convenient, and democratic.

Like a good marriage or the perfect job! Why not tell me more first about how you actually experience transportation?
But that's just negative — we shouldn't think in negatives — I don't want just to complain.

Complaints are what bring you to a psychologist, not ideals; so what's wrong?
I mean stuck in traffic, high cost of parking, the car always in the shop; I mean insurance rates and those repair bills and feeling gypped, and that waiting to get a new sticker. Then there is the guilty feeling about burning up rubber and gas, and the profligate using of prodigious energy to manufacture and maintain a car. I mean my whole life oriented around the car, the whole nation car crazy, picking up the kids, running here and there, the ugliness of the strips I drive through, trash, the rumble and the

smell, and my fear on the freeways and thruways, those trucks and the holes. I could go on and on — the ruin of nature and neighborhoods with more and more cement. Even the trees are dying. And the future looks doomed: Center City like a cemetery or a ghost town after 5 p.m.; no more gas, no more money to maintain the roads, the whole machine struggling to its death in the last traffic jam, ourselves dead from exhaustion. You know, I don't even like driving any more, but I can't bicycle — it's too far, and who takes a bus, even when there is one?

I sit and wonder: how did the patient get into this condition and why has it not dawned before, this fear and rage, these fantasies of waste, lost time behind the wheel, guilt, being poisoned and poisoning others. What has happened to a consciousness that it puts up with a condition so much like war (imminent arbitrary death, time-waste, ugliness and ruined nature; the sense of being caught in a great impersonal machine that leads to doom.) And I wonder is transportation looking only for patch-up solutions? Can we get into the problem more radically, or must a breakdown first occur?

Therapeutic precaution dictates that we attempt to go deeper into the problem so that the breakdown won't be necessary. Therefore we must examine the basic constructs that transportation uses in telling about its problem. These words contain the fantasies which are shaping the problem in its present form, so let us look at some of them.

The first one to note is the division between private and public. We call our systems "public service," "mass transit," "interstate." The word "bus" comes from *omnibus*, meaning "for all" — not for each. Cars, however, are private vehicles with private registration numbers that may even encode personal initials and nicknames. When I go by car to town, I am a driver, driving. The wheel is in my hands. When I ride a bus to town, I am a passenger, a word which first means fleeting, transient, spread out all over, a bird of passage (like the bus itself with its indirect route and occasional stops) and with conjectural origins that connect passenger with passive, pathetic, pathology — suffering.

Facts hardly affect fantasies: though public transport may in fact be more efficient in the many ways our patient wants, giving the privacy of reading the paper, eating and drinking, writing and dozing, while being cared for. Or on a train, walking, chatting, or simply resting with my eyes closed. Nonetheless, my repose is still dominated by the larger fantasy of ego control versus passivity, the difference between driving and being driven, active versus passive. Our minds do not readily associate "getting there" with "sitting back," "going" with "resting." Private management and enterprise just do not fit together in our minds with "being taken for a ride" in a mass, public conveyance, being "railroaded," whereas it does indeed fit with the construct of "private drive."

The words on which we drive help to drive us: thruways, highways, freeways. These descriptive terms reinforce fantasies of unburdened freedom and liberty when we are driving our vehicles measured by horsepower. So, at any intersection where we may meet others, we must be cautioned to "yield"; relationship is put in the language of submission as if in a contest. Furthermore, stopping or resting is in terms of inhibition of drive, i.e., curb or park (originally a demarcated enclosure, paddock, pen.)

For public transport to gain more adherents, would it not have to meet the dominant fantasy of self-determination and goal-directedness which governs our notions of work, individuality, and dignity? We do believe we are more dignified and individualized behind the wheel of our own car in a stream of ten thousand other such cars than sitting in a bus or train. Perhaps our bus lines need more individualization — colors, numbers, and especially names like the "streetcar named Desire," like the curious, even romantic, image-rich names on the buses in Dublin, London, and Paris, so that the routes and vehicles would reflect the symbolic psychology of the persons who travel them.

These names refer to places; and now I would like to contrast "place" with "space." Whereas place governs our experience in the city, space tends to rule our thinking and planning about it. Sometimes, space takes away our sense of place — and we get lost, need signs and lines, as in a parking lot, airport, under tall glass skyscrapers, or on a thruway. Place — like piazza, place, plaza — is a self-limiting locality, characterized, qualified, with a name and a face. We have images of places, whereas space is an abstract concept, best presented geometrically, a kind of formal spirit in the mind. When we think of transportation in spatial terms, we are at once into charts and graphs, concepts of direct lines, axes, vortices, miles per minute and minutes per mile, highway speed. Our patient, remember, judges efficiency by speed. The root of the word "speed" is cognate with space, Latin *spatium*, and also the Latin *spes*, hope, as in our "prosper." The Shakespearean "God speed" meant "may you prosper": success and speed trace further cognates back to words for increase and growth.

It is surely no news to transportation planners that space and speed — miles and minutes — are co-relatives. Now we also realize that the space-speed fantasy is intimately tied with a notion of prospering that requires a hoping, growing city. As long as we determine growth by increase, by quantitative measure rather than by qualitative distinction, we are forced into the speed-trap: quicker equals better. Even if growth has at last found its limits and is becoming a backwards idea (suggesting cancer more than strength), once we have begun to identify the success of our city with its spatial increase, or even to describe its success and its hopes in spatial terms (charts, graphs), we must become speed freaks, addicted to the measuring of "good transport" in terms of traffic flow.

I can't resist pointing out here that the traditional symbolism of green — our "Go" color — has always signified hope, growth, youth, and an unimpeded burgeoning of optimistic desire.

Possibly some of the cure of our patient lies in the transformation of our notions of a region from geometry of space and a mechanics of acceleration to topography of places, a city as clustering places. Where space tends to propel us into future fantasies (space-age utopias, a word which means "nowhere"), places tend to remind us of history, of ethnic and earthy differences that cannot be homogenized into the universal sameness of our contemporary utopias, the nowhere everywhere of our shopping centers and roads to and from them.

City originally refers to community, a fellowship of persons in places. But our patient has come to speak of it as a center, "Center City." Center, too, is a geometrical notion. It is not geography, for the word comes directly from *kentron,* the Greek for that prick-point made by a compass in tracing a circle. Its earlier verb form means a spoke, a stick for striking, a goad or spur to make a horse or ox "getta going." "Stimulus" and "instigate" are the exact Latin translations of the Greek *kentron.*

So the city conceived as a center is where it happens, "downtown that's where the action is," where we are stimulated and spurred, and the center beats us forward like beasts of burden, even if paradoxically the actual center city is a static place of parking lots and windswept fronts. My first recommendation to the patient is: remove from all roads all signs saying "city-center," let nothing be called "central." It is sure to be choked by its own hurry and exhaust(ion).

Our maps tend to show cities as centers, as focal points — big round circles and bold capital letters. Our map-thinking soon draws imaginary lines, like the interstate highway system, connecting the centers. The location of the center in its region, its actual placing in physical geography, is abstracted by the larger vision of centers surrounded by empty spaces, dotted by peripheral minor satellites, much like an astronomer's chart of the heavens.

Cities conceived as centers — rather than as named places, personalities, embedded in physical earth — influence even our eating habits which further complicate our transportation problem. The loss of regional embeddedness makes us forget that cities rise from the earth, from land with local produce. Map-thinking favors long-haul trucking, neglecting what belongs right here at hand. Instead, food from a thousand miles, unrelated to season and locality — and taste.

These constructs so important to the way we conceive transportation also create a world with little place for slowness. It has been banned from the city to the country. For classic and medieval man, nature was demonic; now the city is demonic. We flee from it via express lanes and nonstop flights to take us to where we can slow down and stop. We vacate. In order to re-imagine transportation we would as well have to revision the city as a place of rest and leisure, of nature's elements, water, fire, and earth, refuge, paths in the shade, temple gardens, . . . we might then be less eager to get away.

In conclusion now, most of our "case study" has involved the idea of motion. This is surely the deepest fantasy in the transportation problem. Motion has been essential to the Western idea of God who has been defined as the self-moved mover, and the Western idea of nature which defined the universe by laws of motion (for "Greek and modern are agreed that the most universal characteristic of this world is motion.")[1] The idea is essential to the soul which, since Aristotle, has been considered the motion of the human person. We are either quick or dead.

We are forced to recognize that transportation awakens profound fantasies about motion, and that transportation plans are attempts to rationalize motion. Driving to Center City, covering space with speed, my foot on the accelerator, puts me automatically into the fantasy of motion as an *actual experience* that before our automotive age was imagined more in terms of Gods, stars, and atoms. For centuries motion stayed still; it belonged to the harmonic rhythms of the cosmos, replicated by the left-right tread of the foot over ground. Napoleon's troops marching to Moscow did not cover more ground in a day than did Alexander's millennia before. MPH on the roads began to accelerate only in the early nineteenth century (bicycles, better carriages, and road surfaces), then jump-started in the twentieth with the automobile.

Today, the driving "I," the modern secular ego, is the self-moved mover, which is precisely what the word "auto-mobile" means. Moreover, wheels, including the steering wheel, reflect the ancient Celtic and Mediterranean symbol of the wheel of death. As long as I am driving, the wheel is in my hands; no matter the facts of death on the roads, my fantasy assures me I have death in my control. To meet our patient's complaint, to restructure the relations between private driving and public service, means coming to terms with this gigantic fantasy of our godlike power over motion and death.

This fantasy that identifies the control of motion with the control of individual fate makes it so difficult to conceive transportation as a service required by a community, much like justice and education, fire protection and public safety, water and sewage, lighting and cleaning. Instead, we imagine transportation from a private viewpoint as if it should pay its way, part of free enterprise, competitive. Where stree lighting, street signs, and street repair may belong to our community life and be supported by taxes, we resist paying for public conveyances through these same public streets. Public transportation seems to infringe upon our identity as self-moved individual — so that we pay for the "auto-mobile" fantasy with every sort of tax without protest. But we are unwilling to invite, and to pay for, public transport, the collectivity of the omnibus, the tracks and schedules of trains, which take the wheel of fate out of my hands.

My ending note is dark. But our depth psychological tradition is not known for optimism. We don't point ways out of problems; rather we search for ways more deeply into them. In this case I have tried to show the inherent link between the city transportation problem and an egocentric conceptual model that constructs a world in which the problem fits and is inevitable. Our patient cannot cure one isolated symptom, transportation, without a deeper change in character structure, which means our view of ourselves in the universe. If we would move the transportation problem, we must also shift the fantasies in which it is embedded. This shift begins by attacking the strategic problem on a tactical level — localized qualitative improvements. I am suggesting a place-age imagining of *values* rather than a space-age planning of projections and thinking spatially in terms of lines, speed, and numbers. Then we will have begun a shift of perspectives not only from space to place, but as well from city center to community, public to persons, homogeneity to differences, geometry to geography, from quick and easy to slow and interesting, from private driver to civic passenger, that sense of transience, which accepts that the wheel on which we turn can never truly be in our own hands.

1. R. G. Collingwood, *An Essay in Metaphysics* (Oxford: At the Clarendon Press, 1940), p. 216.

25

Further Consideration for MARTA

Ideals: The vision needs to be communicated to the users of the system and the citizens as a whole. Communicated without boosterism (to increase ridership), without self-congratulatory boasting. The system is an emblem of city pride. It shows what Atlanta can do, has done, is doing: finding solutions for congestion, modeling urban integration, reducing pollution, regenerating inner city. These are major issues of the coming century in many cities, both older and newer fast-growing ones.

Density: At the beginnings of Western thought the Greek philosopher Heraclitus said, "Souls take pleasure in moisture." Heraclitus did not merely mean actual wetness (ponds, moats, canals, fountains). Moisture also meant "flow." Cities flow: *polis,* the Greek word for city ("political," "police," and the prefix "poly") means throng, flowing crowd, the many *(polloi).* It connects with *palude* (French, for swamp), pollution, and Latin *pleroma* (filled, full) and *plerus* (more, many). Cities arise not only to separate human life from wild nature and to protect against enemies (walls, ditches, moats). They also arise because souls take pleasure in the flowing throng. We feel this each time traffic gridlocks, stopping flow, each time we go to an event and the seats aren't all filled, the restaurant has not enough diners.

Discussion presented to a broad panel of stakeholders in the construction and development of a new transit station, Metro Atlanta Regional Transport Authority (MARTA), Atlanta, Ga., 29 April 1999.

Trees: In many cultures trees are sacred: residences of powers. There are founding trees, peace trees, trees where saints sat, trees that spoke oracles. In Western psychology trees symbolized the individual soul, and are used (for instance the Tree Test, or Draw-A-Tree) for diagnostic purposes, especially for small children and their serious illnesses. They give an image of a person's sense of self. Trees require respect rather than being only used for decoration or functional shade or to remind, with street names like "Peachtree," of green nature among cement and steel. They deserve the high maintenance that they ask for. They call for radical thinking, departing from usual trees as in usual urban designs. Not an imitation of nature, but with an eye toward Japanese design of the garden as "artificial nature" that surpasses nature. Non-symmetrical; mixed varieties. Clumped, or uniquely singled as landmark.

Signage: Disorientation is common not only for the first-time users, tourists, visitors. It belongs to the perceptual dysfunction of some types of persons, always. Directional signage is best when it has an image, makes an image, is recalled as an image. Words and conventional symbols are not sufficient for all kinds of people.

Archeology of Place: Modes of singularizing each transit stop as a "place," with descriptions written inside transit cars, on plaques at the stop. Personalities associated with the locale of the stop. Battles. Ancestors. Heroes. Events. Historic buildings. Covered-over roads, waterways. Poems for riders to read among the ads over the cars' windows. Facts about construction of a particular stop. Flora and fauna, geology of the locus. Connection of a place with nature and environment.

Threshold: On emerging from the car (whether above or below ground), there is a need for a clear demarcation that one is coming out of one kind of place into another (and vice versa on entering MARTA). This is a ritualized moment (concretely represented by the turnstile) of changing "zones." Thresholds need not be elaborate or costly or difficult as impediments — but should be marked visually and/or physically (turning the body, changing texture of flooring . . .). Threshold prevents the beeline, the anxious hurried state that propels people ahead of their bodies and out of where they actually are.

Individualization: Whatever can be done to individualize the transit lines (the different stops and their character names, etc.), the cars' interiors, the "feel" of the different lines (not merely North, South, etc.) by means of images, colors, names gives the rider a more individualized experience, and raises the consciousness of the citizenry, who are subject every day to more and more massification and uniformity. Individualization is important for a democratic form of government and provides internal security against "mass psychology" and mass movements. Every means could be considered that prevents MARTA from being "mass transit" and a "people mover" only.

Fear: Class stratification. Racial segregation. Sectionalism. Factionalism. Age/youth demographics. These factors underlie resistance to MARTA and need to be brought consciously and conscientiously into the light of day. Denial and repression of fears undermine the entire project. One law of psychoanalysis still holds after one hundred years: the repressed always returns.

26

Moisture

The mind has a marvelous reach. We can sit here in downtown Dallas, May 1984, and imagine buried aquifers under the high western plains, the imperial gardens in China, and a gleaming Town Lake in the year 1999. The mind can even reach out and touch old Heraclitus, 500 B.C., before Plato and Aristotle, an extraordinary psychologist who said, "Souls take pleasure in moisture."

Heraclitus wasn't merely meaning your ordinary pause that refreshes. He was referring to a system of elements or humors — the moist and the dry, the warm and the cool. These elemental qualities of water and air, fire, and earth compose our bodies and souls and everything else in the world, visible and invisible. For the invisible nature of people could be preponderantly earth, immovable cold clods; or hot-tempered and overheated; or like a deep pool, or a sap, a drip, a wet rag. But always essential to the healthy psyche of a person or a place was the right proportion of the moist humor.

That fragment — souls delight in becoming moist — meant, of course, that water symbolizes with the arousal of desire: swept away, dissolving, your knees go liquid, your juices squirt, unstoppered, going with the flow, and breaking through the dam.

Commerce and advertising know about the delight of moistening. We do buy moisture: plants all over the house, waterfalls in the restaurants, each receptionist under her tree, gallons in the flush toilets and shower heads, bigger bathrooms, spas and pools, liquid

A talk delivered in response to the Dallas Town Lake project. Published in the Dallas Institute of Humanities and Culture's *Institute Newsletter* (Fall 1984).

diets, free drinks, sappy teenagers gurgling sodas, cats purring over moist foods, flow charts not dry statistics, melts, soft drinks, even abstract art is runny and drippy — and of course the ultimate article of faith: the trickle-down economy to increase cash flow to build the affluent society.

A common manner of moistening the soul is by dreaming. Dreaming is a nightly dip, a skinny dip, into the pool of images and feeling. Dreams solve problems because all dreams are wet: they dissolve the mental constraints of the day-world in the flow of imagination. And they affect your humor because they are full of humor themselves.

Not only do they make you laugh, if you let them, but dreams often have refreshing images. You have probably sometimes dreamt images such as these: entering a pool and feeling the freedom of effortless swimming, going deep and finding something never seen before, drawn to the water by beautiful bathers, or making love under water, being close by a lake and feeling its stillness, or a river and its fullness, walking the margin of the sea.

Water in dreams has different effects and means different things. It may be a sobering cold shower after a hot night; it may offer cool reflection or wash away the stuff we cling to; bringing new thoughts in gushers, doom with floods — that is, flood us with doom forebodings; drown us in hysterical turbulences or provide a body of clear doctrine that holds us up when we immerse ourselves in it fully naked as a believing child in its greater body.

Above all, water is seductive. Aphrodite, the goddess of beauty and pleasure, is born from the sea, and Dionysos arrives from the waters. Travel posters of Cancun, even Fort Lauderdale, continue to lure us, just as the mythical nixies and mermaids tempted our ancestors into enchantment. Waters were alive, living beings, and one had to know who was living in the water: a dragon who could suck you in the maelstrom, a nymph who could drown you in her embrace. These fears of capture by water still echo in our fantasies of pirates, of the great white shark, the giant clam, the enwrapping squid. I wonder what dream figure and what mermaids or dragons inhabit our Town Lake project? What is its allure? Are we being sucked in? Over our heads? Too deep to get out? Will the taxpayers take a bath?

The dreams in the people of a city are its waters; they make any city an affluent watering place — even Dallas. I suggest to you that Dallas is dry not because it has no mighty river or bay, but because whatever it dreams, it right away places into dry concrete, continually actualizing. Town Lake could make us drier simply by being built, by losing the dream in the project.

If we look closely into the roots of the Greek word for city, *polis*, we find that these roots draw from a pool of meanings related to water. The Sanskrit-Indo-Iranian-Aryan syllable of *polis* goes back to words meaning pour, flow, fill, fill up, swim . . . The very word *polis* locates city in the wet regions of the soul. For the true meaning of city is full, pulsating with folk, streaming, subject to waves of emotion, tides of opinion, ripples of gossip, and always feeling too full, too crowded, flooded. The flow must go on . . .

Does that mean that Town Lake will make Dallas more of a city? Here a word of psychological caution: to a psychologist, a project also means a projection — something thrown out of the psyche and forward into the future, made concrete and visible. Is the dream of Town Lake a projection of our own internal place of reflection, our darker moods and rippling emotions, to become the surface glitter of a new project, another hopeful happy hoopla, only eight feet deep?

I suspect there may be a peculiar law in the progress of our American civilization. The more its dreams are outwardly realized, the poorer it tends to become in soul culture. The more we have located education in schools, the less literate we have become. The more we have externalized into museums our muses and our culture, the less internal musing. The more we write morality into laws and regulations, the less internally governed we are. The more we broadcast religion and construct churches, the less internal piety, and the less grace and mercy. The fatter our civilization, the thinner, it seems, becomes the soul culture of the individual.

So I worry about collecting the moisture of Dallas into one literal place, laid out in another huge development. Dallas needs another kind of development — the moisture that gives pleasure to the soul is the flow of life, of people, of juices, of ourselves crowded with dreams, our streets pleromatic, full of folk. The lake we need to build is a lake in the soul of the city, following this path of water, ever downward, ever spreading out to moisten the lowest reaches of the *polis*, the body politic.

I believe the Town Lake project is a projection of hope for a flowing, mingling, and humor-full city that is also a deeper and reflective city. The project projects a wish for a democratic potential that has yet to be built. Whether Town Lake will bring that democratic city, whether it will be built at all, I do not know. But from my experience as a psychoanalyst, I do know that the longer one can hold in any projection — that is, contain that lake within the levees of the mind and find out more about its nixies and demons, the subtle meanings in it, the dreams of water hidden in the arguments and figures — the more chances there are for figures to appear and make clear what this city truly needs.

27

Goals for Dallas

I must congratulate you for this meeting. What an extraordinary thing — the unknown faceless bureaucrats of City Hall, the administrators and all-powerful paper-pushers meeting with the absentminded professors, the impractical useless fuzzy arcane academics. You are the hard-boiled and we the eggheads. You know that ever since the Middle Ages there has been a running war between town and gown: between government and university. Actual battles in the streets between the students and the honest citizens. Even as late as 1973, when I was at Yale, the university and the city of New Haven were in litigation with each other over taxes and property.

What we are doing reaffirms the oldest notion of city, *civitas*, community, not only a geographical place, but a psychological "place" called Dallas that holds us in community, as the place or our common interests. Of course there are meetings similar to these: there are seminars with technical experts and there are retreats with spiritual leaders. But those meetings — technical or spiritual — have very fixed goals. You are meant to learn something, to come away at the end programmed toward more efficiency whether in technical knowledge or in spiritual inspiration. Our goal today is to let imagination loose, to loosen our minds and hearts without fixed notions of where we are going to end up.

I do believe that our kind of meeting results partly from the *Goals for Dallas* initiative. This initiative is hugely successful — not by the

---

A talk delivered to the Department Heads and Subheads of the City of Dallas, June 7, 1979.

measure of what it may have accomplished, but by measure of what it has prompted: meetings such as this which require us to reflect and fantasize, to inquire into basic notions about the city for which you work and in which we all spend our life on earth. *Goals for Dallas* makes us ask questions even about goals themselves. I want us to consider *what goals we pursue,* how they work psychologically.

There are two major psychological views of goals — C. G. Jung's and Alfred Adler's. And as is usual in depth psychology, these two main views seem to contradict each other. Jung's view is that every event in the human soul whatsoever is purposeful, always moving towards a goal. Goals are absolutely necessary for the human spirit. We must have goals. Without goals we become cynical, lazy, aimless, purposeless, and neurotic. We have no star, no leaning toward, no "where" to head for, nothing to do but busywork, and so we look backward for causes, complaints, blame, what went wrong.

Adler's view starts off very similarly: all human life strives upward toward some kind of idealized image. But Adler says these goals are all fictions, "guiding fictions" as he calls them. They guide, but they are not realizable and to believe so, to take one's fine high goals literally and to strive to attain them in actual life, is neurotic.

Thus, from Jung's viewpoint, each department must have its goals in order for the spirit to work purposively. But from Adler's viewpoint we must remember the goals are necessary, but they are fictions, so as not to take our goals too literally. For then we become fanatic, dogmatic, and lay out schedules of progress toward the goals, like Soviet Five-Year Plans, programming ourselves, our lives, and our cities into *ideals.* This is a realistic attitude, a pragmatic view of goals. They are to help us, guide our fantasies, not to program us.

The important point is not what goals we have but in what way we take up these goals. Dallas for example: the goal of easier movement between North Dallas and Downtown. Nothing is wrong with that goal. Goals are noble and worthy. But when we take them too literally, the goal becomes narrowed to increasing the capacity of the single artery, the Central Expressway. And the more literal the goal, the more fixed into one image of it and the more fanatically we fight for it. Working together, the cooperation within a department or among departments or between departments and the city council, is more often a matter of agreeing upon the same goals, being on the same side of an issue and aiming for the same thing, than it is having the same freer attitude towards goals themselves.

Those who share the same view of goals have less trouble with each other, even if they are on opposing sides of an argument, than those who think differently about the idea of goals. For them the difference is like between one man a literalist, who says fish or cut bait, and another man whose idea of fishing is just that — just fishing, which does not mean for him directly to catch a fish, even though that may be his goal indeed as he goes about doing many things related to fishing without ever directly getting to the lake.

Literalists take that goal of easier movement in and out of downtown according to one specific plan — whether bus travel, light-rail transport, doubled-decked expressway, widening parallel streets, etc. — and then the fight goes back and forth over which of these plans achieves the goal of improving the connection between downtown Dallas and North Dallas. The goal is no longer a guiding fiction but a fiercely fought program — and we even forget what the goal is. Whereas "improving connections" offers a wide enough ideal, a purpose that can be worked in many ways and which go far beyond fixation on Central Expressway — more inner city housing, satellite office areas, new thought about South Dallas instead of North Dallas, car pools, staggered office hours, integrated localized neighborhoods, etc. The less literally we take the goals, the more inventive we become, searching and trying alternatives or exploring wider horizons and new images. It is hard for the literalists to understand the fictionalists — if we may call them that. The looser way seems to lack all conviction. To the literalist mind the fictionalist becomes a hypocrite. In order not to be a hypocrite, in order to show how strong is one's belief in the goals, literalists redouble effort and lose sight of their goal — the very definition of fanaticism given by the philosopher George Santayana.

Another example is the billboard issue. *Goals for Dallas* says: "Elimination of all billboards" — that's the ideal goal. Well, let's bear that in mind as a guiding fiction. Let's work at the purpose intended here: no eyesores, no traffic hazards, and no cheapness. Let us keep an aesthetic sense towards what we see around us, a steady pressure in consciousness about commercialism as part of urban ugliness, a mind to finding ways and means with the billboard question. Then, instead of arguing for or against billboards, ways to tax them and ways to defend them, court battles; instead of this literal, fixed, narrow "eliminate billboards," we may realize that they are such eyesores that they are already being eliminated in the citizen's mind and, in fact, billboard signs may be working against the very products they advertise, useless, unnoticed. Or we may discover new sorts of billboards, alternative designs, interesting styles, other locations — the billboard as a Pop art, much like the painted murals on brick building walls.

The difference between literal, fixed goals and goals as guiding fictions boils down to this: is it *Goals for Dallas* or *Dallas for Goals?* Goals serve a city by giving it aspirations, guiding its thought and imagination toward searching out alternative solutions. But a city serving its goals becomes a city programmed to set purposes, enslaved by its own objectives, coercion through legalism, directives, and ordinances. City Hall in the name of the people against the people. None of us want this. So the best goals are those that cannot be fulfilled, but remain ideal; necessary fictions that keep our sense of purpose alive. I would like to present a goal that can't be directly realized, and therefore is already a guiding fiction. This goal is rarely stated, but it is a goal which could be useful throughout your work whatever you do, wherever you live. And this goal's purpose was instrumental in the building and maintaining of our ideal cities: Athens, Florence, Washington, Paris, and Petersburg. I mean an *aesthetic* goal, or what was once called the Idea of Beauty.

Now let me make clear that by aesthetics and beauty I do not mean planting petunias and cleaning up the beer cans. Aesthetics has been literalized into specific beautifying acts, beautifying the city — plant trees, buy a statue, enlarge the museum, and eliminate billboards. Aesthetics has been departmentalized, as if only the concern of landscape-gardeners, preservationists, and artists — a wholly segregated and externalized notion: adornment, cosmetics; bring in the decorators. Beautiful things — quite separate from the practical, the economic, the efficient. Not basic to government or to business.

It is common to treat aesthetics in this way. Nowadays, we tend to treat most values this way, localizing and departmentalizing culture into museums and theaters, religion into churches, health into clinics, and education into schools. We all know better: we all know that religion takes place in the way we drive, that health takes place in the way we consume, and that education takes place in the way we speak with each other. So beauty is woven through anything we do. And it does indeed belong in Government.

To show this, I could refer to the past, to classical times. Then, what was well, what was good, showed by its beauty. The root of the word beauty itself means good, well. Good government and public welfare would also be beautiful, which at the same time meant beneficial. How far from our sense of welfare today, which seems the very contrary of beauty: welfare as drab, flat, stale.

But if we stick with our own sense of ugliness, we may be getting closer to how aesthetics is actually at work in our daily world. For I want to show aesthetics to be something going on under our noses and not only in the department of parks or in the museum.

First of all, aesthetics, as the philosopher Kant said, is a judgment independent of logic. This judgment comes spontaneously as a reaction to ugliness: "I can't stand it." "I hate it." "It's awful" — a gesture, the sight of something, a tone of voice, a report, a meeting, the way someone comes on. Or we feel the contrary, something good, marvelous, beautiful. We feel it in our chest; it opens us up; it catches our breath. It feels like love. All beyond reason, yet a definite judgment formed by the aesthetic sense, indicating that aesthetics is at work. We need to trust these automatic judgments and develop them further even though they are illogical, if we are to let our work for the city have an aesthetic quality.

Second, in addition to being a faculty of judging, beauty is a sense of form. Form appears not only in buildings and statues. We are each forming things, putting things in better shape, making order every day, from the filing cabinet to laying out a schedule. There is a sense we each have of "doing something right," of finishing something properly (as we speak of the *finish* on a piece of wood or jewelry), handling something fittingly and skillfully — which is what *art* originally meant — artfully, like an artisan.

We can hardly expect the visible world around us to show beauty if the way administrators, who originate or approve what eventually becomes the world around us, do not have an aesthetic sense of form. What is formed out there in the street is also first formed in here in the mind. See! Administrators are not mere technocrats, civil servants. You, too, are the "beautiful people" by the way you form what you do.

We are all suffering from form deprived of aesthetic form as formalities, as formalism, as those dreadful things called business forms, government forms, paperwork, mere forms. There is that creeping nausea, that paralysis of delay, at having to fill out one more form. Nothing could be more unaesthetic.

Again our nausea and resistance must be trusted. William Styron and George Orwell, the novelists, and Hannah Arendt, the thinker, in writing of the Nazi holocaust and examining the question of totalitarian evil, have come to the conclusion that evil is not only what one expects: cruelty, moral perversion, power abuse, terror. But the deepest evil in the Nazi system is precisely that which made it work: its programmed single-minded, monotonous efficiency, its bureaucratic formalism, the boring daily service, standard, letter-perfect, uniform. The danger we must each watch for is not the man in uniform; it is our own insidious uniformity.

Here our individual aesthetic sense is a watchdog against the Devil who, as has always been said of him, slips into our lives where we least expect, dressed in the most ordinary disguise. In administration, we find the Devil in the in-basket — office memos, official-ese, routines and meetings that dull the mind, dull language, dulled hours, copied and recopied, screaming for coffee. Urban sprawl, litter, pollution, and blight right at our desk. These things happen in the mind and soul as ugliness of style, gesture, and language, long before they happen out there. Where a government works for the welfare of the city, it may, at the same time, be wrecking that welfare by the very means it uses — standardization, monotony, boringness, uniformity. I believe contemporary rebellion against government forms and procedures is not just the old rebellion of free enterprise versus control. It is also an animal voice against ugliness, an aesthetic rebellion of sense against a kind of evil that is so hard to see. Boredom and monotony are such soul-destroying experiences because they are the very devil. When we are bored we are in his hands, and our aesthetic sense is waking us to this fact.

It is important to have the courage of one's own aesthetic sense, one's own taste. The aesthetic rebellion against soul-destroying procedures, memos, meetings, language, formalisms, is even more important than objecting to wasteful procedures on the basis of rationality or efficiency. We have been trained to see waste and encouraged to make suggestions to minimize it. But taste — whether good taste or bad taste — has been neglected, as if it had only to do with which tie to wear, which color matches. Whereas the courage to speak from one's taste may lead to more far-reaching reform and serve the goal of a good city than will our habitual concern with rationality and efficiency.

An essential criterion of the aesthetic, again according to Kant, who is widely acknowledged to have been the most penetrating mind on the subject, is that the beautiful combines the purposeful with the purposeless. Kant's idea is quite similar to fictional goals rather than literal programs. As soon as a goal becomes a program, the sense of purpose has become defined and narrowed into a specific end. Programs are therefore unaesthetic. They cannot help but be boring, standardized, monotonous — hence evil, like a Five-Year Plan. They have forgotten the essence of the aesthetic: that it is purposeless purposefulness, a vision of a goal that refuses every fixing of it into a rigid scheme. We want to do something right, handle it well, beautifully, but once we have established the standardized method and can plan it as a form, that which was once artful becomes a formalized routine.

Finally, in addition to spontaneous judgments and the sense of form, beauty appears as imagination. By this I do not mean imagining beautiful plans, layouts with gardens and gleaming buildings. I would like to return imagination to something that is already going on in us, just as our aesthetic judgments come automatically, just as our revulsion to forms and formalities come spontaneously. Unfortunately we tend to think of imagination only as an act of will: now I am going to dream up something. Create. Be imaginative. But we are already imaging without sitting down at the drawing board. We are already working under the influence of images.

Professor West Churchman at Berkeley, one of this country's leading philosophers of systems research — whether federal, state, or private, in regard to land use, highways, energy, education systems, food distribution, airports — has made the suggestion that every new proposal, every memo on what to do, lead off with an image at the top of the page: a sketch, a dream, a verse or ditty, indicating the imagination is operating in the mind and is formulated by the concepts of the plan. A rational proposal is the reformulation of half-conscious imagery. If we grasped more fully these images, our imagination would play a more vivid part in what we are doing and there would be more aesthetics and less boring uniformity and evil. There would also be more consciousness.

For instance, what are the mythic images governing our notion of a City: is it a specific city somewhere in history, a utopia miniaturized in an architect's model, a paradise, or New Jerusalem? What image do we have of development itself? Growth like a tree, branching out until it comes to natural limits, or a gas-filling balloon — bigger and bigger until it bursts; or is growth a larger or fuller can of worms? And what are our fantasies of order? Are they mainly negative: no noise, no dogs, no fires, no traffic? What specific images and fantasies come to mind with such words as efficiency, optimizing, enhancing, improving?

We need another meeting like this one in which we tell each other just what imaginations are going on in our thoughts, just what ideal visions inform what we say and work toward. The definition of purposes cannot be merely held by such narrowly fixed goals, worthy as they may be, as a new subway or downtown housing, new industrial base, merit pay, or even by such broad concepts as "citizen involvement" and "improved human services." We need to discover what images are behind these goals. Then, from the images come spontaneous aesthetic reactions: "Oh no!" "Beautiful!" "I love it!" We can be grabbed by an image, fall right in love with one, cherish it devotedly. And when we know each other's images, then we can better understand each other's minds, what we are after, what we mean with what we say, what we really have in our minds or what images really have us. Then we enjoy being citizens, because each event we are engaged in is jammed full of imagination.

28

Imagining Dallas

On my last trip back to Zurich, friends would say to me, "So you've moved to Dallas . . . Imagine that!" "Imagine living in Dallas. I can't imagine what it's like." And then I would reply: "Well, it's not like what you imagine at all," or I'd say, "You can't imagine what an amazing place it is."

All these common expressions of imagining refer to having or making an image of Dallas. In order to imagine Dallas, we must have or make images.

Image-making is a different procedure from thinking, planning, projecting, and conceiving. Thinking can go on without images by means of pure abstractions, operations of pure thought, like thinking to logical conclusions or thinking in numbers. Twelve and three, less seven, times two, equals sixteen can run through the mind without images, and, in fact, when we do put in apples and trains and yards of cloth, these images intended to help thinking often make thinking harder.

I am quite able to conceive of Dallas doubling its population within the next two years without actually imagining this conception. I can project it onto a flow chart, a mathematical progression. I can think about it in logical steps: so many more births per month, requiring so many obstetrical facilities, and so many more deaths per month, requiring so many more funeral parlors and burial plots; as well as housing units, utility lines, additional fire trucks, police cars, ambulances, and so forth. I do not have to imagine moods of births and deaths, their scenes in hospital rooms, or hear the ambulances, and the fire trucks.

Originally published as "City Limits" in *Imagining Dallas*, ed. Gail Thomas (Dallas, Tex: Dallas Institute of Humanities and Culture, 1982).

So, too, the months of frozen January, green and blooming April and scorched July, its peaches and pools, can be replaced by the numbers one, four, and seven. Dallas itself can be replaced by The Metroplex, DFW region, or just "D."

Because projecting and conceiving Dallas can happen without images, plans are well-served by electronic data processing; computer programs work without images, without imagining, and without emotion. Program, you know, is a bad word in art. We have to take care that computers serve our images but not replace them or determine them.

When planning, projecting, and conceiving do make images, they are images of what we have already planned or conceived — two-dimensional graphs or photographs, three-dimensional miniature models of buildings and highways. But these visual aids, as they are called, are aids of a projected program. They are different from images in that visual aids are *illustrations* of ideas or demonstrations of projections, rather than acts of imagining. The difference here is like that between advertising copy or background music written to capture and present a concept, rather than a scene in a novel or movement in a concerto which sets the mind imagining. Visual aids attempt to program the mind rather than let it fly or sing. One of our most successful philosophers of practical wisdom, Muhammed Ali, said, "Ken Norton's got no imagination. I got imagination. I can fly."

I have labored this difference between imagining in images and visual aids for conceiving and planning because when we try to imagine Dallas, we may be substituting for our individual spontaneous imagination of the city visual conceptions pre-programmed for us. We need to test these visualized programs against our own memories, fantasies, and imaginations of daily life in our bodies in our city. We have to take these concepts — Town Lake, Roseland Parkway, Central Expressway — and make the effort to enter them imaginatively, taste and feel and breathe them, try ourselves in them with our hearts and bodies.

I have also labored this difference between imagining and conceiving to emphasize that images do not have to be optical, things for the eyeball. They may be verbal, or musical, or sculptural for the hand. Imagination evokes our whole physical being. It especially reflects the heart — like those peaches and pools in July, like the bird sounds on an early March morning.

The classical locus of imagination was the heart. In the Renaissance and for the Romantics — from Michelangelo, quite a city builder himself, through Goethe, consultant to the royal court on mining and road inspection — images derive from and spoke to the heart. Imagining Dallas also means feeling Dallas, imagining it from the heart as a place for the heart.

By "heart" I mean nothing other than what our common language has always said: heart of courage and generosity, heart as place of emotions, especially loving kindness, heart as longings, heart as the place of hidden truth, deepest soul, and inner conscience. I know there is another language of the heart today: heart as muscle, as pump, with valves and walls, as place of attack, pacemaker, and bypass. These recent words for the heart remarkably reflect a conceptualized, mechanized city. This change of heart from feeling speech to technological speech affects the way we regard our city's heart, its downtown.

Restoration of the heart of the city requires restoration of the image of the heart itself. Imagining Dallas calls for re-finding the heart in ourselves, our values and longings, conscience and courage, our trying out the programs presented inside our own hearts, taking the city to heart so that our images of what grows in our city are rooted in the heart.

Before we go on, I must go back to the notion of growth so fundamental to all our imaginings of Dallas. Growth comes in many fantasies. For some it may mean simple extension of boundaries, like a balloon; for others it may mean evolutionary progress, as the word "development" in land use — an upgrading from soil to cement, measurable in dollars, growth as a rising line on a chart. Growth can also mean maturing into a full idealized form like a child becoming an adult, a sapling into a full mature tree. Or it may refer to differentiation into more detail, like a mosaic: an increase of tension and sophistication, a qualitative refinement and relation of parts, like the historical growth of a musical instrument, the piano, for instance. Growth also tends to stand for life over death: the dead cannot grow. When these images are not distinguished, we tend to believe that expansion equals health, or that a rising curve of financial development equals maturing, or simply that bigger equals better. When speaking of the growth of Dallas, we need to know just which fantasy of growth is working through our minds.

Each of these notions of growth is backed by an image. Expansion outwards is like a balloon, filling in, and differentiation is like a mosaic, the fit of bits and pieces; maturity is like a tree. Balloon, mosaic, tree — these images portray a primary characteristic of all images: they have limits, boundaries, frames like a photograph or painting. These edges may be soft, as the shading of a dream image, and only sketchy, as a lyric image conjures a person by mentioning only fair ankles and golden hair, but they hold the mind to a definite focus. An image presents a moment of time and forms it like a sculpture; even musical and dance imagination is limited to a particular phase, its completed breath, and its inherent limit. Images come to an edge and have a stop. Imagining is self-limiting by its images. Images provide limits.

This takes us back to the beginning, to my friends in Zurich who cannot "imagine Dallas." They are quite right, for how can we imagine it when, as the man on the phone said the other morning when I called for the Republic Bank time: "Dallas is a city with no limits." The sky's the limit — don't fence me in. No limits means no image.

The external limitlessness of Dallas is what strikes one first on arrival here from Switzerland: where are the hills, the little streams, washes, drops in elevation? And the immense relentless sky so opened out. Not much to force geographical boundaries. Moreover, there are also few internal edges that divide the city within itself: economic, racial, historical, ethnic, religious hard edges. Democratic toleration keeps sectarianism to a minimum, but from another perspective, sectarianism has often been the bones of a city, the ground of sharp definition and sectioning. I'm not talking about prejudice, but of pride — giving that deep internal structure that makes a city a place of passionate neighborhoods, ethnic rivalries, class loyalties, and religious communities.

The absence of both external and internal natural borders leaves a city without those obstacles and hindrances that force reflection. Nothing to come up against that turns us back on ourselves — total availability, endless action to the horizon, the spirit of Texas space. A seminar such as this, emphasizing reflection through different viewpoints, in search of images, reminding the city of its psychological interior, already helps give more definition to the city's limits.

This question — what determines limits — is perplexing not only in the growth and death of cities. Boundaries also trouble science. For instance, it is a question in physics as to what determines the edge of an object so that its outside molecules do not combine with its surrounding. Mathematics has invented the term "fuzzy sets" for certain kinds of indeterminate relations. In biology: what keeps a yellow pine or a magnolia to its limits, so tall and no taller? Psychology, too, tries to find out just what factors determine the limits of intelligence. And for medical research in cancer and aging, limits and their absence or breakdown have become crucial issues.

One of the greatest minds to have worried over this problem of limits was the German genius, philosopher, scientist, and poet: Goethe. For him form was the answer. Each natural and artistic event has its inherent form and limits itself by its own image, which, as we would say now, is laid down in its genetic code. This form or internal image appears at the borders of things giving each thing its visible shape. These edges are not rigidly fixed, but breathe in and out, like the heart's expansions and contractions, a beating rhythm of life.

There is a remarkable second step in the Romantic idea of self-limitation through image. A tree, for instance, is limited not only from within by its genetic code, but the form of a leaf, say, or of any growing thing, is limited by a kind of negative capability, a negative invisible pressure. As the leaf unfurls into space, it is as if space shapes the leaf into live oak, or mulberry, or holly as if sheer emptiness exerted an image-shaping force, keeping each thing to its dimensions.

This idea of negative form is much like the oriental one of the void. Emptiness is not mere absence, nothingness, but is the determining invisibility at the heart around which the potter forms his bowl. The shapes of things — jars, bottles, vases — or those in oriental paintings are determined by the voids out of which come the visible forms. In psychotherapy we follow this oriental respect for the void: we are always very careful with a person's void and empty place, his or her feeling of nothingness, considering it as the invisible image which determines the way in which, and in response to which, that person's future form takes shape. We do not rush in to fill this emptiness with programs, "things to do," suggestions, advice. We let the emptiness imagine itself out. As it does so, it begins to define the person's self-development according to a specific quality and direction.

When we go about "imagining Dallas" in search of its native form, its definition, so as to discover what form it must take and how it will grow, we are obliged — if we follow the thoughts that I have briefly sketched — to search for those aspects of the city which correspond to this negative capability, this factor of emptiness, these shadows that are the actual shaping power in our city's unfolding.

This means that the greatest drawbacks of Dallas are its blessings in disguise, for these are the obstacles and the nothingness that draw us back to reflecting and imagining. For instance, the natural emptiness, flatness and aridity of our geography become a perpetual challenge to which we continually imagine new responses. Trees, lakes, landscaping emerge from within their arid absence. The cultural dearth leads to intensification of cultural fervor — theatre, music, museums, Channel 13 and KERA, restaurants, and universities. These responses to the challenge — Toynbee's formula for the movements of civilization — are the way human imagination generates culture within its sense of lack. To keep the culture alive we must keep that sense of lack, those feelings of geographical barrenness and cultural inferiority. To ignore our emptiness and deprivation, to cover it over with promotional boosterism or abstractions in numbers fills the holes that must be felt for imagination to prosper.

Another example of negative capability shaping our image is the lack of historical roots and the flood of rootless new urbanites from outside Texas (as far away as Switzerland!). This lack shapes a Dallas of nostalgia for whatever is old and local, antiques as antiquity, an archeological fantasy of a city imagining into its own roots — preservation, Fair Park, the Vineyard, Swiss Avenue. Or downtown, this more desperate problem for our planners, its desolation and void at evening, its five o'clock shadow, is a negative form continuing to shape new images for the heart of the city. Its very failure can draw our city's greatest efforts of creative imagining. So to do away with the void with a new master plan of new structures is not the answer because it is a programmatic response which fills the void rather than respecting its potential. Rather, we would have to let what is already there spontaneously develop qualitatively toward more definition.

The all-the-sameness of any city — I mean its uniformity without a rich variety of ethnic peoples and dialects and customs — is another such formlessness and impoverishment which could make us imagine and value even more the few ethnic differences that we do have. For they give internal differentiation and add to the city's imaginative richness.

And last, the very hugeness of the Metroplex reminds us of the value of intimacy, personal relations, knowing each other. The social formalities of Dallas give it form: fashion, manners, style in speech, rhythm, respect for the heart's charm, grace — these belong to the image of Dallas and provide definite patterns and limits.

I think we are led to the conclusion that growth in size is neither objectionable nor dangerous. No need for protectionism — city walls, keep them out, tight little Dallas. Size is a function of form, not an independent factor in its own right. An elephant must be big because its form demands it; so Dallas must have the size appropriate to its image. That the size of anything is a quality given with its image was already convincingly argued by Plotinus in Rome at the beginning of our era. This implies that the size of our city will not run away with us as long as it is governed by imaginative forms, by the limits of its images. It can grow proportionately only when it is imagined. I *can* imagine Dallas when I focus particularly upon the very reasons I *can't* imagine Dallas, for these negative factors — aridity, dearth, inferiority — are precisely what stimulates imagining.

When we abnegate the task of imagining, when we lose heart, we get size without imagination — once called titanic, now called urban sprawl, overdevelopment, strips and blight, inflation, cancer, proliferation — or, conveniently, "Houston." The more size, the more need for imagination, for images that give internal articulation and differentiation. The more expansion, the more care we must take with form; and the more success, the more valuable become the obdurate hindrances, the failures and inferiorities, the shadows that will not go away and which keep the megapolis from megalomania, inhibiting its strength from Titanism.

We can find our city limits in the courage with which we can abide in negative capability, in our hesitant unknowing and searching of shadows — not only searching for solutions — in activities such as this seminar which attempts to face the negatives as capabilities without programming them, thereby keeping imaging alive in the image-making heart of the citizen, that heart where the future of the city resides.

29

Imagining Buffalo

This is a marvelous event — we can have a purposeless day's talk about City! No single issue is to be debated, no partisan political action committee, no attempt to raise funds for a cause — just a coming together to talk and listen, to feel, think, and imagine about the spirit of our home on earth, the City. What could be more important? I wonder why we aren't doing this all the time. Perhaps, in fact, we are doing this sort of thing, unconsciously, when we gossip, complain, argue an issue, judge our officials and comment on their projects, or rally around Buffalo's teams.

Today, however, we will be intensifying this feeling, thinking and imagining so as becoming more conscious of the invisible spirit of place, what antiquity called the *genius loci*. We want to see the shape and hear the voice of the particular genius that makes its home in Buffalo.

What we are doing affirms the oldest notion of city, *civitatis* and community as a psychological activity that holds a place together in a common sense about the common interests. We could even imagine that this building where we are meeting is the old village common.

Of course there are meetings similar to these: seminars with technical experts, retreats with spiritual leaders, encounter sessions with psychological counselors. Those meetings have fixed goals. You are meant to learn something, to come away at the end programmed toward more efficiency whether in technical knowledge, in spiritual inspiration or human relationship. Our goal today is different: we want only to let imagination loose, to loosen our minds and hearts without fixed

A talk delivered at a citywide conference in Buffalo, N.Y., and first published in *Buffalo Arts Review* 2/1 (1984).

notions of where we shall be ending up. The end, in fact, has already been achieved: that we are all here participating, bringing dedication to the City.

As you know, I come from Dallas. Buffalo and Dallas: poles apart. Dallas so often looking toward the year 2000 and the next century; Buffalo so often looking back at its glorious last century. Of course they do have in common the assassination of Presidents — that is, both are marked by mythical events of national proportions. But what I believe they hold in common is this concern with their cities, the attempt by a few enterprising citizens to work on the spirit of the place. It is as if the City itself, in Dallas and Buffalo, tries to become conscious of itself, puts itself through a psychoanalysis of its symptoms, of its parents and its childhood (early days), its case history, its fantasies and typical behaviors, its dreams and nightmares. It wants to know itself.

Now we are speaking of City as if it were a living being, a body with a soul, a dreamer. This organic, vital aspect of City shows in how we fall into physiological language when we speak of it: traffic as circulation, the parks as lungs, the downtown as heart, the congestion of its arteries, the feeder lines, dying neighborhoods, the foot of a street or the bottom of a street — and of course, a distasteful body part for the City's "pits" that my discretion keeps me from mentioning out loud.

But one word especially shows this organic thinking, this feeling that a City is alive: *buildings*. Why not, as Robert Sardello has said, call them *builts* or *buildeds*? The word that is used for the most characteristic structures of a city, so solid, so walled, so fixed, indicates that the imagination of City goes on as an organic process. A City is more than a spirit in a place; City is a spirit of a place in process.

To get at this spirit of your city, to define it by feeling its specific quality, we first have to get out of the way some absolutely basic perceptions of City itself. That word, City, already has meanings in our minds. It produces images and ideas, so that the imagination of City affects our feelings and views about any actual place, such as Buffalo.

If we walk around with unconscious ruinous thoughts about the archetypal City, then the city out there becomes what we expect of it. Psychology calls this self-fulfilling prophesies. Psychology says that cities, like bosses, like children, like spouses, like quarterbacks, enact our deeper notions of them. They perform according to our conscious expectations. Cities partake in and are even ruled by the images they unconsciously carry.

A very simple example, usually disguised as an economic issue: the whole Dallas area is over-built with millions of square feet of empty office space, condos, and hotel rooms. Yet Dallas is still building more. In Buffalo, on the prime street under which the subway runs, a street already partly revived, it is hard to find offers for what Dallas developers would consider must surely become a prime business district. Manic excitement and momentum without limits rules Dallas, depressive anxiety and inhibition rules Buffalo. For Dallas, too, has its bankruptcies. Interest rates are just as high there, and many Texas banks are in bad shape. There are all sorts of grave problems in Dallas: education, transportation, neighborhood preservation, water, ethnic oppression, and crime, to mention only six of the worst. Yet Dallas' self-perception, via its ideas and images, sees only golden sunshine. To effect change in any city we need to become more psychologically aware of the ruling ideas and images affecting our perceptions, especially of City itself, especially if these ideas and images are ruinous.

There are three major ruinous thoughts about City that we inherit in our culture, ideas that we pick up with the air we breathe, the words we think with. They are like a psychological inheritance passed on unconsciously for generations, subtly poisoning our city life.

The first of these is *City versus Nature*, urban versus rural. On the one hand, nature is imagined to be good, godly, and ordered. Peace resides in nature (so we each want to have a bit of suburb with hedge and grass and tree). On the other hand, City, ever since the Bible, is the place of Babylon and Ninevah, Sodom and Gomorrah: vice, disease, unnaturalness, corruption, danger, perversion, fanciness, usury, luxury — and bad for children. "Children" — our way of speaking of the growing and creative — would be better off in "nature." These ideas are sometimes called Romantic, sometimes attributed to Rousseau, but they are deeper and older than that and they still affect us profoundly.

They make us lose sight of the fact that the City is as natural as human society, as the exchange of goods, as perimeters and boundaries (walls and ditches), as conversation and news, as organization and construction. All these natural human activities go on in cities. Lewis Mumford said, "The city is a fact in nature." So we must watch out for the ruinous divisions between City and Nature, which sentimentalizes Nature and denigrates City.

The second of these ruinous thought-models is one expressed by St. Augustine: the City of God versus the City of Man. This does not originate with Augustine, for already in the New Testament there is an opposition implied between the world of Christ and the world of Caesar. Christ's Kingdom is "not of this earth." Hence, from the earthly city there is to be expected only power (Caesar) and the corruption that goes with power: hierarchy, bureaucracy, paternalism (Caesarism), oppression, and poverty. The economic view of life itself is part of this division, since money, as the same New Testament passage says, belongs to Caesar. What is here and now, the human City, is merely human and built by sinners. The good City and the real City is the heavenly one.

So again a caution: watch out for oppositions between heavenly, ideal, otherworldly hopes for your city opposed to the mean and sordid everyday world. For the two Cities co-exist and continually affect each other.

Practically, this means that the desire for perfection will affect every city project. Nothing built or made, nothing thought or said about Buffalo, goes on without some heavenly counterpart in mind. Practically, this also means never leaving behind the real city streets with their messy insoluble problems in order to achieve grandiose schemes that would tear down and throw away (urban renewal) the Sodom and Gomorrah of actuality. Heaven is not on earth, for that is what Heaven means.

Now the third ruinous thought does make that mistake. It attempts to realize literally the ideal Heavenly City right here on earth. Plato tried this with his Republic and the city of Syracuse in Sicily. It became tyrannical. Marx tried it, too, by removing Heaven altogether to have the ideal City on earth. Here begin theocracies and utopias, 1984 and the thousand-year Reich. A city without shadow becomes all shadow.

This should caution us to watch out for idealizations of Buffalo. There is no ideal community, no ideal plan, that adman's dream or planner's playhouse of glassy towers, consumers strolling under exactly spaced trees, sprinkled like parsley along the waterfronts and river walks, inoffensive sculptures and pretty awnings — and no trash, no kids, no winos, no cars with busted mufflers, and nowhere a snowstorm.

My point so far has been — not what is the right or the wrong way to imagine this city, Buffalo — but that an imagination of City already exists full bloom in our historical-cultural mind. We already inhabit a psychological City before we enter any actual city at all. The City of the Psyche builds the actual cities we live in, so it is of first importance to attend to our notions and fantasies, our dreams and words before we unconsciously actualize them in our streets, subways and schools.

I want now to expand this third ruinous thought—the idealization of the City, the attempts like Plato or Marx, to build the Heavenly Jerusalem right here on earth. And I want to expand on this in terms of Art, the arts, and artists.

I beg your patience here: you may think there are more urgent matters than arts. Politics. Economics. Schools. Crime. Justice. Jobs. Interest rates. Race relations. In a city everything is urgent. That is what is wonderful about Cities: everything is immediate, pressing, desperate. But I want to suggest that nothing is more immediate than Art.

The way a city handles art reveals a great deal of its imagination of itself. When the City is imagined to be unnatural and therefore sinful and ugly, art is brought in to beautify and uplift. In the Marxist and Platonic states, the arts serve the state's purposes — or they will be suppressed. Even in our nation today, art objects are conceived to decorate and refine the city plazas and banks, the walls of its hospitals and schools, to embellish the only functional with the purely aesthetic, as a cultural overlay, a cover-up of Caesarism.

So developers plan in their budgets, as the last step in construction, for some wall art and some landscape art and maybe even a monumental sculpture to be added on at the end when the whole project is in place. As the budget estimate usually doesn't cover actual costs (overruns), the add-on of art is then lopped off. The issue here is neither bigger budgets for art nor tighter budget controls. The trouble begins with the notion of art as an add-on. It begins with the relation in our imagination between City and Art.

I do not know if this view of art as add-on has been or will be the Buffalo way. It has been too often the Dallas way. In Buffalo there is the Albright-Knox Art Gallery, the cemeteries, and good old houses, the avenues and solid industrial remnants, the jazz and poets and critics, the preservation of ethnic sensitivities, so that probably this add-on, decorative view of art, art to beautify the ugly city, does not hold. I hope not, because this view actually degrades the city by imagining City from the beginning as merely functional and ugly and in need of decoration, and it degrades the arts by perceiving them as decoration.

We all know that art — writing, painting, composing, and sculpting — is not decorative but disruptive. We all know that art hasn't anything to do with decorum. It disorders, upsets your fixed perceptions and fixed notions. It doesn't present the ideal but rather exposes what is not ideal, thereby reminding indirectly of the ideal. Often, art is at war with both the earthly City and the Heavenly City: things as they are and things as they should be. Yet art abounds in cities, derives life from cities and exists for cities. Art is the response of the City to its own psychological condition; Art expresses how each city senses itself. In fact, art is its common sense.

I am not saying that artists must be disordered or disorderly persons. But rather, the way they do things disorders our habitual laziness and what they see and say discomforts our anesthetized daily life. The ideal City would be comfortable, smooth, anesthetized. No breakdowns in Heaven. But the artist discomforts, always breaking down our usual sense of things because of his or her aesthetic sense — aesthetic, which means sensitized perception. No wonder Plato's rational Republic would either ban them or keep them under severe control. No wonder artists in dictatorial Eastern Europe are so often dissidents. No wonder in our Capitalist nation they are so often broke.

If artists are like the City's watchdogs, the barking guardians of immediate unanesthetized noticing, then a first priority of any city is to increase the participation of its artists and to make life for them more possible — not "easy," or recognized or successful, merely possible.

By "artists" please don't hear me to mean professional entertainers in orchestras and ballet companies, or those who hold down professional aesthetic jobs in museums and universities. I am not referring to those with professional artistic skills. They may not be the watchdogs at all. (In fact, sometimes they are more like pussycats or pet parrots.) No. The artist that a city needs to favor is anyone whose perception and action embodies subversive, discomforting, aesthetic noticing — preacher, journalist, photographer, humorist, thinker, investor. Any citizen at all is an artist when he or she cuts through cant, demands quality, and refuses to be anesthetized.

Artists are not those who have taste, but those who do taste, taste and see the world. They do not have special senses, sensibilities, sensitivities; they simply sense as men and women of sense, sensing what goes on, and responding 100% to the city, to its discomforts and outrages by being equally discomforting and outrageous.

The artist furthermore — and you are beginning to see that what I am calling artists others might call citizens — is always altogether engaged. Everybody into everything. The artist is the 100% turnout. That person on whom popular democracy depends. Nothing in his life or hers is specialized, nothing divided into fractions: he or she is both labor and management, servant and master, prosecutor and defendant, work time and free time, functional and aesthetic, practical and ideal. What happens in the street, what he or she smells and touches has no less importance than Major Policies and Great Ideas. The artist leaves nothing to George, and nothing to Sam. He or she is the eternal busybody.

This 100% response, this transformation of the notion of citizen into artist, corresponds with the notion that the City itself, as Louis Mumford has also said, is the greatest work of art, of all art of all times. We each live inside this artwork, and to live in it rightly is to live in it as an artist.

Allow me to conclude with a private piece of my own imagining of the Heavenly City. We cannot help idealism coming in. The New Jerusalem infects every Buffalo, every earthly City with its vision of something marvelous.

Until that day when each citizen realizes he or she lives within a work of art and recognizes his or her aesthetic reactions, that is, admits to being an artist, there would have to be what are now called artists on every single decision-making board. Not merely women and blacks and Latinos and handicapped, not merely in the name of justice, not merely to save artists from their inflated ivory towers and depressed garrets of poverty or the mediocrity of university posts. Not another Federal program. No, the artist would be there as guardian of common sense, to keep the city sensible, in touch with realities of image and ideas as well as realities of the senses. Artists would be brought in from the beginning — planning the subway (not merely decorating its stations), selecting textbooks (not merely for the subject called art appreciation), working on crime prevention (not merely as occupational therapists), studying the traffic flow, supervising hospital management, analyzing interest rates, and advising on business loans. Artists in the fire department, waste disposal, emission controls, building codes, utility rates . . .

The arts would no longer be separated out — Art Councils, Art Endowments, Art Reviews, Arts and Recreation. Instead, artists would be counseling, endowing, reviewing and re-creating everything going on everywhere in the city. You would soon not be able to tell a citizen from an artist. And think of the money we would save on "arts programs."

Imagine that! Imagine Buffalo like that! Not even Nelson Rockefeller got this far . . . that's my outrageous story for this afternoon of stories of Buffalo. Call it science fiction, call it political science, and call it the aesthetic revolution. But do let it discomfort and entertain your imagination. For that purpose we are all here today.

30

Pittsburgh: City as Patient

The only possible reason for your inviting me to speak must be because my work is psychoanalysis, a psychoanalysis among whose patients are cities. Not only the patient in the consulting room, but the consulting room in the much larger patient: the City. For cities, too, have souls. They are not merely piles of concrete and steel, buildings, sewers, bus routes, and school systems. Cities, too, have repressed memories. They have forgotten ancestors. They come with a case history. They have potentials for development and suffer the pains of past failures, past violence. Cities have ambitions and destinies, periods of latency, flowering and stagnation, and they have faces, habit, and styles. Also, cities exhibit classic syndromes of psychopathology. About the psychopathology, I shall soon have more to say.

It's easy to see these psychic conditions and syndromes in large nations: France and the French psyche with its grandeur, its love of the word *Gloire;* Ireland and the Irish psyche with its poetic heroics; Boer-Dutch South Africa and the Afrikaans psyche with its senile paranoia and repressed puritanical rage. Images, stereotypes, jokes, and emotions come quickly to mind. We can see these psychic conditions in some of the states here at home. California is more than a geographical and political entity: it is a state of mind. Euphoria makes its home in California — 30 million people eating health food and having a nice day. And megalomania makes its home in Texas; and idealizations in Minnesota; while Indiana, Kansas, and Nebraska seem captivated

Public lecture given at the University of Pittsburgh (sponsored by Urban Redevelopment Authority, the Carnegie Institute, and the C. G. Jung Center), 1 May 1987.

by that major American syndrome endemic throughout the country — the syndrome of normalcy. People move from place to place according to the soul of a state that suits the state of their soul. For decades most Californians were not native born, but they were born "Californians." Texas drew "Texans" to it from Michigan, Arkansas and Tennessee: extroverts out to make it big. Jobs and climates are not the sole determinants in moving: we move according to soul affinities, according to fantasies, which speak of the soul of a state and city.

I say all this to put a *viewpoint*, not to put people and places in a diagnostic nutshell — that shell game of my profession that creates nuts by putting people in tight shells. I am mainly saying that the psychology of persons extends beyond individual persons. There is a mind-set, a soul-state beyond our personal selves. C.G. Jung called this wider, more embracing level of the psyche the collective psyche, and this collective unconscious affects whole areas and groups, giving to a region, a place, a crowd definite common characteristics and patterns of reaction. This view helps us imagine a city as a soul-place inside the physical place, a complex psychic condition inside its economic conditions, a fantasy activity going on inside its social problems.

The value of imagining cities this way is much the same as in psychoanalysis. Problems, choices, arguments, symptoms are analyzed into their fantasies — the fantasy, we believe, creates the people, the choice, argument, symptom. As Jung said, "fantasy creates reality every day." And we analysts believe that if you can change the fantasy, the reality changes too: The problem is imagined differently, so it is perceived differently, and then lived differently.

Loss and Change

A rule we work with in psychotherapy says: no change without loss. Even growth is not mere acquisition. There is always a sloughing off, giving up, taking away at the same time. If there weren't this equilibrium between change and loss, we would become grandiose, deluded by feelings that everything's going my way: loss would be the other fellow's and gain only at another's expense. The psyche neatly protects us from megalomania by the feelings of loss. Some cities miss this point: Dallas, Orlando, San Diego, Virginia Beach. They change so fast that they do not notice what is lost: old neighborhoods, small street shops, lots and alleys, fields and trees, ethnic sections, churches and synagogues left isolated without congregations, and especially the charm of aging buildings built of good materials. Dallas represses its loss, claiming itself a city with no history, so there is nothing to lose. The solid downtown buildings recording its history as proud land-marks of the southwest are imploded on Sunday morning or at night so the citizens will not see, will not feel, will not regret.

Continuing our parallel between city and psyche, if there is to be change, there will be loss: lost jobs, lost industries, lost neighbor-hoods, lost ways of life, and there will be a mood of bleak regret and sadness amid looking backwards at the city as it was "before the flood," a condition called depression in psychology.

Mind you now, depression has become an economic term — de-pressed areas, depressed ghetto, as if the term meant only low income, poor housing, high crime. Originally depression was a psychological term referring to the feelings of dejection, low in spirits, and only 150 years later around 1800 did depression begin to refer to busi-ness conditions. (Of course, business and banking and economics has usurped a big chunk of psychological language: interest, value, credit, trust, bond, liquid and flow, safety, security, enterprise, goods, support, gain, balance, benefit, profit, labor, liability, and of course, the word "loss" itself.)

Economics has so taken over the language of psychology that we have to look at economic news to read our national mental state. In-flated or depressed? Sluggish or expansive? Which way is "interest" going? We watch the charts and hear the prognostics to discover what the collective soul is feeling.

The psyche is literalized in economics. The basic moods and values of the soul become the bottom line. Right here I want to break into my talk, interrupt myself with an attack on bottom-line thinking, which is part of the new fundamentalism that has the nation in its grip. All value reducible to cost. Cost efficiency as decisive. Some years ago the high priest of bottom-line thinking was David Stockman, Director of the Budget Office. He was once a divinity student. Hear his argument on acid rain concerning the 170 dead lakes in New York state (4% of New York's lakes): "does it make sense to spend billions" to control emissions in Ohio (and probably here too) for these few fish, and for the recreational and commercial value of the lakes?" The fish and the lakes, in Stockman's view, have only human value — not a value to a wider ecology, nor to the fish and lakes as living bodies — and this only human value is further narrowed to the literal area of 4% which is then reduced into dollars.

Cost efficiency most simply defined is to get the most for the least. The principle is fundamentally unethical. On other occasions, in other situations we would consider getting the most for the least to be a con trick, cheating. Look what happens when value is reduced to cost: euthanasia of the aged and retarded is cheaper than nursing homes and special education; execution of convicts is cheaper than long imprisonment. Bad education is cheaper than good. Neglect of property is cheaper than repair.

I think we are now entering a new civil war, not between genders and races, classes and regions or policies, but a more important one than these, a war about values. What happens when price determines goods, when cost determines values? Cheapness becomes the bottom line, and the huge cost is aesthetic, ecological, psychological, spiritual — the very quality of life, the soul of life.

Cost efficiency replacing value means the cheapening of quality. So that the war to be fought — and you can tell I feel strongly about this one — is against bottom-line thinking, thinking that the literalisms of economics are the true, real, hard facts and that life is based there. From the economic perspective, loss is only literal loss, on the negative side of the line, and the change that accompanies loss can only be a change for the worse so that the value of loss itself is canceled out.

This rule — no change without loss — can be turned around the other way: no loss without change. Then we might have another way of looking at our civic and our personal depressions. These losses are announcing changes, and not merely changes for the worse. That would be to see things only with the dark eye of depression. That eye interprets data always glumly.

For instance, a few years ago before the oil and gas bust, Dallas was all glitter and Buffalo all gloom. Now, of course, to the glee of the rust belt, that glitter is tarnished and a new name appeared for the formerly successful Texans: they are called the "nouveau broke." Dallas, then, could not see even the smallest cloud on the horizon. Office buildings were going up at a phenomenal rate although there were already 30 or 40 million feet of unused space. See-through buildings, as they were called; land turned over from day to day in speculative mania. Land, earth, soil had become property; property in large amounts of dollars. People could only see change and change only as growth.

In Buffalo, despite the reinvigoration of the city in many subtle and visible ways — downtown, the subway, the arts and intellectuals, the lakefront banking — no one would invest in properties along the subway's main street. So caught were they in loss — the decline of the port and grain shipments, the shutdown of Lackawanna Steel — even new events were imagined through a depressive eye. They saw change only as decay so that even their assets — the level of education, the ethnic strength, the plenitude of water, the art collection and the rich architecture, political history, skilled work force, the city's grit and guts — were simply overlooked. Remember, the characteristics of serious clinical depression are no future, no hope, black moods, looking backward with remorse and resentment, feeling of rot, poisoning and decay, everything getting worse, slowing down, narrowing of focus, physical immobility, increased dependence. And fear of blackness becomes fear of blacks. In fact, the feeling that a city does not control its own fate but depends so much on outside forces — Harrisburg, Washington, Wall Street — belongs to the depressive clinical picture: victimization by and dependence on outside forces.

The images I have sketched of Dallas and Buffalo show not only two cities, but two sides of the manic-depressive syndrome lived out in the boom/crash cycle of economies. But do notice one thing: the depressive fantasy in Buffalo did create a new reality — the subway! The imagination went down into the depths and built a new bottom line. Dallas, by the way, does not have many cellars. Most houses are post and beam construction. Basements are rare. Skyscrapers, however, since the 1920s have been its pride. The manic boom fantasy does equate with success, for bankruptcy has struck Dallas; and depressive/ crash fantasy does not equate with failure, for Buffalo — and we could say the same for Newark, St. Louis, Hartford — have not rolled over belly up. There is a way of working within any syndrome. Even fragmented chaos can yield a city, as it is said of Manila, Hong Kong, São Paulo, and Los Angeles. It's not whether or not the fantasy is normal, ideal, or healthy, but that one discovers how the imagination works the fantasy into urban, civic realities.

This psychological approach offers a variety of imagining: loss of population, of industry, and losses of the Pirates, the Panthers, and the Steelers. Am I saying loss is good for you, so learn to take it? No! Not at all. I am saying that the moment you experience loss, the psyche is making way for deeper changes — is actually going through a change. Instead of depressively only stuck in the loss side of the events, changes in values, in habits, are coming through the openings left by loss.

This move leads me to the heart of our topic: the Open City. There have been several stories of open cities. Paris and Rome during World War II were open, meaning that they would not be defended so as to be spared destruction. Another sort of open city is the free port, a city without customs barriers, servicing the free traffic of goods in and out. Yet another sort is the city, open as a refuge, like Amsterdam in the sixteenth and seventeenth centuries — a city welcoming every kind of person, all kinds of philosophical, religious, and political ideas and artistic currents. To suggest that Pittsburgh declare itself an "open city" intimates some of these meanings of the term, but of course none of them literally.

Paris and Rome would say to Pittsburgh: you save yourself from destruction by letting the invader in. Amsterdam says you take on your distinctive character by freely admitting all the crosscurrents, the ethnic and racial, religious and political spectrum. Danzig says don't specialize with a specific product or identify with production. Facilitating is already enough.

What makes the open city so remarkable in the history of cities is that a city so often starts out as an enclosure, a sacred perimeter of walls, distinct from nature, separated off by a ditch, a moat, e.g., Fort Pitt. Cities originate as closed places, forts, stockades, and military camps with gates, customs barriers, and watch towers often perched on hills, e.g., Duquesne. It imagines the outside as hostile — the very meaning of the word hostility derives from the enemies outside the walls. Early cities, and those of Greece and the Italian Renaissance like Venice and Florence, were often city-states, self-asserting states of mind, rivals to others, with their own warriors — like the Steelers and Pirates against Philadelphia, Cincinnati, Buffalo, and Cleveland. A city imagined itself as autonomous and able to determine its own course in face of the world around it. The city was essentially paranoid, proud — and afraid. Still today, most of the people in the great cities of the world stay inside its perimeters and never go elsewhere in their whole lives. They never cross the moat.

Today cities no longer have this self-governing assurance. Harrisburg and Washington determine what happens in Pittsburgh. Conglomerate takeovers, federal grants, money center banks, state education systems, interstate commerce regulations and national labor unions all disempower a city from determining its own course. Suddenly a decision is made in Delaware and a plant closes — citizens laid off. Suddenly your team is sold to another city, your department store, medical center, and newspaper become part of a chain — your corporation dissolved, losing its name and identity to a set of letters headquartered anywhere, but not here.

These seem to be the enemies of autonomy, and a city feels powerless. The walls have been insidiously tunneled under by a buyout, by the State House, by Washington, D.C. Centuries ago the wars in Greece and Italy were between city-states trying to gain hegemony over each other. In colonial times the same sort of fight between cities; Boston and Philadelphia contested domination, as did the larger colonies, over the location of the new capital — not to be in Pennsylvania after all but closer to Virginia. Today the struggle is often between new cities and old ones for locating plants and hubs, for federal funds, for art collections and research centers. How can a city retain individuality? Pittsburgh evidently has succeeded to everyone else's amazement. The most livable city in the USA! I am not proposing the paranoid defense: Keep 'em out! As Idaho and Colorado have tried to turn in on themselves, as the people in Oregon were saying about their southern neighbors . . . keep them out; we don't want to be Californicated.

The paranoia index rises. With it come retrenchment, xenophobia, parochialism, and racism. City pride takes on a defensive feeling. The pie is shrinking and everyone grabs "my share." In the imagination, the moat and walls and watchtowers are going up again.

The idea of the open city may come to our rescue here. And the model might be Chinese. When Yang is blocked — when expansion has reached its peak — let in the darkness. So all invaders and conquerors were absorbed by the old Chinese way. Whether the political top changed from Mongol to Manchurian, to Japanese, or European, little changed in the life of the daily round. Chinese culture received invasion, absorbed it and did not yield to it. Openness does not mean loss of essential individuality. How did the ancient Chinese do it?

Besides ancient China's excellent bureaucratic organization and the native formalism of the people, there was constant attention to their culture: remembrance of ancestors, respect for learning, ecological stolidity — that is, the images and language and rhythms of the earth and nature permeated all they did. Their individuality as a culture was rooted in what architects also call the vernacular, a term that applies as well to the great variety of local dialects and kinds of cooking.

Translated to Pittsburgh, this would mean resistance to buyout and takeover and close down, resistance to becoming but a corporate hub or member of a chain. Resistance occurs in each act that strengthens the *vernacular*, fortifying all that is particular and native to the culture of your city: keeping close to its geography, remembering its ancestry, its style of contribution to learning, its festivals, its food, its dialect, its care for older people — the actual ancestors. Perhaps this sense of locality is already so basic to Pittsburgh that this is one reason why Pittsburgh is such a good place to be. Perhaps its greatest strength is its openness, its absorption capacity. For Pittsburgh has shown an amazing capacity to be hurt, from its very origins in a lost battle. This is the city that can say, "George Washington lost here" — for let us remember that "open" does not mean only unlimited, free, and clear in the Dallas sense. It also means vulnerable, surrendered, exposed, hurt — the suffering that gives enormous strength. And this city has the capacity to take the punches, absorbing the most radical violence of the left and the right opened to the very richest and very poorest, the Scotch-Irish and Ukrainians, the Jews and the Catholics, the pig

iron workers and the micro chippers. Its very geography above a confluence of streams bespeaks this city's individual character — letting
things come in, mix together, and flow by.

City in Service of Ecology

We have talked about a city open to loss and change, about a city open
backwards to its tradition, and now I want to talk about a city open to
nature. Let us say an ecological city, a city in mature relation with the
world around it.

Ancient city walls signified the hard-edged division between city
and nature, so hard-edged that in our minds today urban and rural,
city boy and country boy, slickers and hicks, traveling salesmen and
farmers' daughters are fixed in our folklore. Much of the American
dream says nature is good — cities bad. The earliest American novels, *Wieland, Arthur Mervyn,* and *Ormond,* by Charles Brockden Brown,
published in 1798 and 1799, depicted cities as dens of evil, fallen to
sin. Drinking, gambling, whoring, corruption, and disease — that was
City. Brockden Brown's terrible city, by the way, was Philadelphia.
And the innocent country boy fell prey to these desperate, crowded,
ugly, rude, brutal, urban ways. Generally, immigrants to America came
to work the land, to build homesteads — not to found cities. A colony meant farming and the trade of produce. Whereas in the ancient
Greek world, cities were what the hero was to found. We still retain
an idealization of the land and nature and a view of cities as places
of money, crime, dirty politics, viciousness, rackets, gangs, and dope.
The terms "rust belt," "ghetto," and "smokestack cities" continue the
same fantasy.

What has made our cities ugly and evil was not merely industry,
Frick and Carnegie, the productive rise of America after the Civil War
in which Pittsburgh played a huge part. No, it is an attitude toward
cities, perhaps given by the self-enclosed meanness and suspicion,
the paranoid pathology of the City conceived apart from Nature that
gives a city a dark vision of itself. This fantasy is carried on to this
day, as Holly White shows in his careful examination of contemporary downtown corporate buildings: buildings as bastions, three-story

walls like fortified castles, cold stone, repelling glass, hard-faced metals and concrete. The corporation itself is a self-enclosed city, turning its physical back on the larger city around it. This fantasy of City as dangerous, mean, corrupt, and ugly further splits it from nature as idyllic and healthy. Yes, fantasy creates reality every day, and fantasy has created our everyday reality called Pittsburgh. Change the fantasy and you change the everyday reality, the actual city.

There is another way to imagine the connection between urban and rural. City, too, is a natural phenomenon. That is, the urge to build cities, to collect in market places and exchange, converse, project, and plan, to construct walls and arches and roofs, to honor Gods, construct monuments, and store goods against hard times — this all comes with the nature of human beings. Lewis Mumford considers the city as the greatest of all cultural achievements of humankind — the great artifact, the work of art — more than a symphony, more than religion, more than science, or government and its institutions. City is the one great human creation comparable with the creations of nature, with a life of its own like nature, a beauty and a terror like nature, and because of this very likeness to nature, has often been opposed to nature.

The split between urban and rural — going back surely to the Christian division between the city of God and the city of Mammon, Christ vs. Caesar — reached its final apogee in the industrial city from the 1860s to the 1950s, a hundred years that coincide with Pittsburgh's pinnacle. And this split exploited nature in favor of cities: cities as power plants, railheads, truck hubs, refineries, mills, smelters, rock grinders — cities as vast consumer maws that ate the world. Nature, an indefatigable provider, a huge nurturing beast.

But that great mother who has sustained our cities is depleted, exhausted. Great Mother Nature has gone senile. She can't manage anything on her own anymore. The oceans, the air, the forests, the rivers and lakes and wells, the plants and bugs and birds, the very soil itself, require our maintenance, our constant attention. Nature no longer works on its own. And, like a senile patient, she strikes out in sudden destructive rages. Our great mother is no longer independent and neither are we. We will need her air and soil and water, and her ice and tides and bacteria. City and nature are utterly bound together in a new mutually caring relation. A new fantasy is creating a new reality — the reality of mutual service. And the United States, rather than being behind the Japanese or Swiss or Germans in production and exports, may actually be ahead because it has moved in the ecological era to the service economy.

To illustrate my hope for practical thinking about harmony between city and nature, city as open to ecology, let's talk about hamburgers. I suppose you know that well over 40% of the beef eaten in the United States is eaten as hamburger, and that figure is predicted to rise well above 50%. Maybe it's there already, as home stewing and roasting of beef declines. A great part of that hamburger beef is imported, and a great part of that imported beef comes from Latin America where the United States is having trouble with uncollectible debts, political enmity, cocaine economies, and in the larger scene, disasters in the soils, forests, and atmospheres on which much of the world depends for oxygen replenishment.

This is rather standard information, but maybe it has not been tied enough to hamburgers, fast-food, take-out, and bottom-line eats. Now the virtues of hamburgers are not for discussion — including their contribution to our civilization by supporting prime-time television programs. Hamburgers nourish the nation with protein — are the ritual food for popular communion at the temples and shrines along our roads, provide jobs for the young, unskilled, and unemployable who do the service. Under the sign of the burger our cities gather the family; and a mark of advancement out of infancy occurs when a tot can swing a lip over his first Big Mac or Whopper. Hamburgers are essential in American communal life, and as the hamburger spreads its domain, they have become essential even to European and Third World urban life.

Let us connect hamburgers to physical nature and to Pennsylvania's rural problems in particular. Small farms are in a shambles: bankruptcy, foreclosures, rural poverty, and this affects smaller towns, banks, mortgage institutions, and so on around Pittsburgh. The small farms cannot compete with cheap food imports and the giant multinational agribusinesses. When farmers cannot care properly for their land, then what follows is erosion, pollution, deforestation, water-table problems. In response, let us entertain this fantasy: the city gives permits to hamburger stands only if meat is purchased from regional farmers, not from agribusiness feedlots, not from imports. Suppose the city rigorously inspected the raw burger meat for disease-carrying organisms, for additives and adulterants, in order to improve not only the consumer's health, but as well to raise the quality in the rural economy. This fantasy would help struggling small farms sell beef cattle locally. And suppose — to open the city yet further toward the ecological world — no hamburgers were allowed to be grilled or fried from animals grazed on former Latin American forestland.

All this sounds incredibly fantastic. And what would it do to the bottom line and what might it do to the sale of Heinz's ketchup and relish? Why a Pittsburgh burger would cost twice the national average! How could we guarantee the steady supply of local beef to equal the local appetites; how could we meet the inspection costs, or face the retaliation from agribusiness and the great chains? And wouldn't this be just more protectionism hurting Latin Americans who need to export to pay us the same dollars back?

Expensive? Protectionism? Aren't we already practicing protectionism by protecting within the city walls the ways that favor the chains and agribusiness at the expense of the rural farm? Would this new deal in hamburgers be truly more expensive than the transformation of Latin America into an overpopulated new Sahel or Sahara, necessitating changed patterns of migration of insects and birds, quick cash crops like cocaine and marijuana, political chaos owing to rural poverty, epidemic tropical diseases, and tremendous emigration pressures northward? Certainly, my hamburger is more cost-efficient than paying to fight wars with our, and other people's, deaths and amputations. What we eat in Pittsburgh is tied in with the Contra scam and the death squads and the missing, and the endless civil wars. What a hamburger costs *actually* is not at all what you pay at the hamburger stand.

This opening of the city's self-enclosed walls exemplified in my hamburger story could be told in other stories — of eating and of air conditioning and electric power, of cars and plastic petrochemicals, of trash paper and scrap metal. Our two major exports are bashed up cars as scrap metal and smashed down cartons as waste paper, sent off to other countries to be turned into new machines and new boxes to be sold back to us. Ivan Illich has told the story of water in his book H_2O and how the incredible fantasy of Clean produces huge waste. Every act of consumption is shadowed by its true cost and its shadow waste. These are not economic rules, or only rules of physical matter like output equals input minus friction — that there is always waste in any production. Waste and burn-off are inescapable shadows of modern transformative material operations. No, these are psychological rules that govern behavior. There is a shadow side to every act no matter how ideal, hopeful, and progressive. The Chinese knew this thousands of years ago: no bright Yang without at the same moment dark Yin.

A City In Service

My keynote this evening has been to underline the dark Yin — the loss in regard to Pittsburgh's older fantasy of itself as an industrial capital technologically productive. I have touched on the psychopathology of cities, their self-enclosed paranoia and deep self-hatred. And I have tried to show by means of the hamburger how the simplest act opens the city out into the world. Now I want to close by tying my point about city open to nature — the ecological city — with a final point about service.

The facts are already visible. This nation is no longer production based. The service sector makes up the larger part of the Gross National Product. We spend more money on services than on things, and of the things we do produce, an enormous part of them are not productive in that they are weapons and capabilities for weapons, which are never used, becoming waste before they are ever consumed. The service sector is not pouring and rolling steel, not making motors, motor oil, or pickles — not making anything. Billions of dollars change hands without any product coming from these hands. Many of these dollars are transacted in Yin's moonlight. We are more and more a nation in service to one another, employing each other in complex relationships: cleaning and washing, teaching and talking, delivering and receiving, guarding, counting, arguing, explaining, entertaining, classifying, passing on messages, decorating and designing, repairing, processing words and pushing papers. In all these activities we consume and waste very few raw materials. We take very little from the old mother. People are what we pay for — materials minimal.

This shift from production to service is parallel with a shift in gender consciousness from one-sided male expansive Yang now being balanced with nurturing female Yin. Or, parallel with the long delayed and forever postponed shift from overweight military budget balanced by environmental protection and human welfare and services.

Although this is going on in fact, the fact has not yet affected our fantasy. We have not developed an *imagination of service*. The word itself still evokes servitude, servile, serf, and the immigrant history of oppression and the even worse history of slavery. The fantasy of the industrial revolution imagined the transformation of raw materials into finished goods to be the great upgrading. Then the downside caught up with this one-sided fantasy: the downside of actual cost in human and animal life-quality, waste disposal, and ecological disaster. The industrial fantasy created a reality we are just beginning to pay for.

The new fantasy — a city in service — is also transformative, also an upgrading. For repairing, teaching, nursing, communicating, guarding, cleaning, designing — these upgrade the quality of life. A good drink, a clean shirt, a safe street, a child taught ABCs, tended and kept from harm. The city in service offers a new way to evaluate what is good for a city and what is a good city. The best city would have the least trash. The good city would have good public services. The good city would have a long memory. The good city would have programs calling on its people's idealism to serve its maintenance.

Service does not replace construction and production. We shall have bridges and steel to carry them across rivers, and we shall go on needing glass and paint and micro-technology and industry. It's not either/or — Yang or Yin. Rather, service enlarges the relation of the City with Nature, transforms its feeling, softens its walls, its paranoia, so that its citizens regard themselves, right in the midst of downtown doing their urban jobs, as serving the upkeep of the planet, in service to the wider world that is civilization and nature both, performing the greatest service possible — maintaining the continuity of this beautiful, this loveable planet.

31

Look Out: Three Occasions of Public Excitation

How mean a thing a mere fact is, except as seen in the light of some comprehensive truth.
— S.T. Coleridge

Vision is the art of seeing the invisible.
— Jonathan Swift

The occasion today and tomorrow invites adventure. We are trying to turn psychology inside out. We are looking for the inside outside. This move attempts to deliteralize the idea of psychology as an examination of human subjective processes inside our minds, our feelings, our behaviors, our relationships, because this idea of psychology leaves the world out there abandoned to sociology, economics, and science, quite disemboweled of soul.

Strange to realize, shameful to admit, that a whole century of psychology has been devoted to this illusion. We psychologists who believe ourselves so smart have located all the invisibles — spirits, demons, complexes, energies, syndromes, archetypes, moods, dreams, feelings and fantasies — only inside us humans. How swollen we must be to contain all these invisibles. What pretension, what anthropocentrism, what imperialism! The most ordinary indigenous person anywhere knows there is an inside out there and that invisibles inhabit things and places and creatures, and cannot be held within our human bodies.

A talk originally presented at the opening of the Archetypal Activism Conference in Santa Barbara, Calif., June 1999, and first published in *Depth Psychology: Meditations in the Field*, eds. D.P. Slattery and L. Corbett (Einsiedeln: Daimon, 2000).

So my companions and I are not breaking new ground so much as returning to very old ground, the ground of the planet, its life, its soul.

For my part I want to mention three writers whose thought gives impetus and direction to what I have to say. First, Norman O. Brown, who offered his method of fragments in *Closing Time* and *Love's Body*. A method I love and also find in Giambattista Vico and Heraclitus, but I have never been able to practice it. Today I shall try, here and there, to break with my own propensity for the rhetoric of narrative.

Second, Robert Jay Lifton, who sets the task: we must awaken from what he calls "psychic numbing" (and which I call an-aesthesia) so, as Lifton says borrowing from Buber, "to imagine the real." We try to imagine through and beyond the real. We call something "real" mainly because we do not recognize that beyond its familiarity, it is also fantasy. The task is to see through to the soul's intentions, and this is an aesthetic move towards essence that feels delightful, beautiful. Lifton repeats the old cry of the teacher from Socrates and the cave to David Miller and the playful, from Krishnamurti to Freud: What else is going on besides what you are blind to and therefore call real? In the gross is the subtle; the gross *is* subtle, *shtula* holds *suksma* in its embrace: *suksma* wraps *shtula* in its evanescent light.

A method from Norman Brown, a direction from Robert Lifton, and, third, a motto from Jean-Paul Sartre: a Frenchman no less: "There is an incommensurability between essences and facts, and . . . whoever begins his researches with facts will never attain to essences."[1]

Furthermore, besides fragments, this inquiry shall try something else I have never ventured before: to focus on immediate actual occasions of public excitation. They are Kosovo, Littleton, and the President's impeachment for perjury.

Kosovo

Saddam Hussein, Khomeini, Quaddaffi, Castro, Ho Chi Minh, North Korea — now Slobodan Milošević. We bombed, we blitzed, we invaded, we mined harbors, we blockaded, embargoed, froze assets. Gunboat diplomacy. Force. And these enemies: *They did not go away!*

The primary mistake of warfare: underestimating the enemy. How does the American mind estimate the enemy? Facts: comparative fire-power, tonnages, numbers of men under arms, vulnerability of command and control, technology. What about estimating the will to win, the stubborn capacity to endure, the importance of honor, and honor above death. What about cultural pride, national ambition? Human networking at subsistence levels versus high-tech networking? What about the sustaining strength of the enemy's history, its myths?

We seem to have no means for taking the measure of the enemy's madness except in terms of our own madness. We define power in our terms, and poverty too. (We shall come back to poverty.) We do not imagine the reality of the other as a *psychic* fact, a *psychic* force, only their material facts and their material force. There is a reasoning of the blood, of the grandfathers and ancestor spirits. There is always a desire to sacrifice life for them. There are spirits in the land living on spilled blood and always asking for more.

But we who have never fully landed, only one or two generations here, or dragged here in chains, do not understand the power of place. Nor can we understand the magma of hatred, the Furies and Titans waiting to rise at the slightest shift in the tectonic plates of ethnic proximities. We euphemize the potential volcanic fires with happy so-lutions: "diversity," "melting pot," "tolerance," "folk culture." What do we know of the passionate ecstasy of revenge? Do-or-die patriotism? The brutal reality of the return of the repressed?

We cannot estimate a culture of death, what strength it harbors. So we can easily deal it out, but not take it in. War without woundings. Not one death may mar our campaign. No wounded. In the victory parade down Fifth Avenue in New York after the Gulf War, veterans in wheelchairs were not allowed to take part, to be witnessed or remembered. How account for the underestimation?

First, demonizing the victim assures us of righteousness. The enemy is already slotted, labeled: Bad, Evil, War Criminal. No further imagining necessary. Second, since our technical style of warfare requires no sense of the physical actuality, we can push the button and pull the lever without emotion. "Hey, no problem." Smart bombs, dumbed people. No emotion means also no imagination. Third, we project rather than imagine. We project onto the enemy our kind of mind. Anyone in his right senses in the USA would at once realize the folly of a one-sided war that wipes out control centers, infrastructure, communications, transportation, power, utilities. Let alone the rising insecurity and disruption of consumption. To suffer all this merely for the idea of a remote, impoverished part of the country populated largely by non-Christians! Of course Milošević will capitulate: we would. We project our mind's values and reasons instead of imagining their mind's values and reasons.

Our estimations are made by the impoverished American imagination of an impoverished American culture. Impoverished? Our notions of poverty are confined to the statistical economics of the poverty line: annual income, minimum wage, number of amenities like cars, fridges, TVs, computers. A poor way of seeing things. Our assessments are impoverished and so we underestimate, we undervalue the power of culture because ours is underdeveloped.

So long as the United States cannot imagine the non-American components of the world's society who do not believe as we do, value as we do, measure as we do, we are imaginatively incompetent, and therefore morally unjustified in policing the world. Old ostrich isolationism may serve the world better than the spread under the flag of righteous nobility of our impoverished fundamentalism of faith and fact.

Littleton

Columbine High. *Nomen est omen:* Columba = dove; columbine, a dove-like plant. The dove of peace and the Holy Spirit. Columbus, our "discoverer," that intrepid missionary who brought the Bible, genocide and extermination to the Caribbean people. Founder of our New World. What do our mentors say: imagine the real. Search for essence. To find the essence, *imagine* the boys — their minds, their desires, their lives, their world.

Instead, we collect the facts and discuss practical measures of prevention. Why did the SWAT team take so long to enter, allowing one student to bleed to death? How did the boys smuggle all that equipment into the school? Smart kids: resourceful, inventive. We track the guns, the ammo: where bought, how, when; track the Internet: how to make pipe bombs; reconstruct the entire incident; collect every bit of shrapnel from the pockmarked walls; lay out the timing minute by minute — map out where each person was, what they saw, heard, did. Interviews, records, photographs, lists . . . follow every lead. Like a thick American biography — all the evidence, no understanding. Like Kenneth Starr's report: know ye the facts, the whole mountain of them, and ye shall know the truth. And blame: the movies, TV, the parents, the gun lobby.

Another kind of facts: facts of atmosphere, of culture, of language, of architecture. In what cosmology did the boys live; what ideology fed their souls, what passion was eating at their hearts? Architecture? William Hamilton in *The New York Times:*

> Designers of the newest American suburbs say they have largely ignored or avoided one volatile segment of the population — teenagers . . . three dozen urban planners, architects, environmental psychologists . . . and experts on adolescent development agreed that community planning and places for teenagers to make their own are missing.[2]

Architecture: that Georgia boy who, soon after Littleton, shot up his school, resided in an exurban brick fortress of a house on an acre-and-a-half lot of a subdivision called Hanover Square (why are they never called Montezuma Heights, Senegal Bend or Bratislava Court?) "Where the lawns are lush and manicured as putting greens."[3] Price range: two hundred thousand to half a million.

Architecture: Lawrence Diller, M.D., reports: The United States produces and uses ninety percent of the world's Ritalin. "Attention Deficit Disorder in adults is now statistically as common as severe clinical depression or drug abuse." "ADD diagnosis and Ritalin remain overwhelmingly a phenomenon of white, suburban, middle- and upper-middle-class children." "The Ritalin explosion . . . a warning to society that we are not meeting the needs of our children."[4]

Dream House in exurbia. The American Dream, the American Home: site of emotional poverty, madness, and a gun case. Children in their private rooms. Columbine High had high density classrooms. Local taxpayers had recently turned down a tax increase that would have lowered the ratio of students to teacher. Imagine the *buildings* of schools: the cafeterias, the food, the corridors, surveillance monitors; materials and design: Modernist Institutionalism — like a government administration block, like a clinic, like a social service center, like the blown-up building in Oklahoma City.

Adolescent protest. Violent rioting of teenagers goes back three hundred years, even in East Coast Ivy League schools. *Litima,* as it is called by the Gisu people of Uganda, is a red force in the soul that teenage boys are meant to express by running wild through the village, and setting fires, doing damage. It belongs to a cosmology, and is watched over by elders. Read Michael Meade: *Litima* is "the source of the desire for initiation and of the aggression necessary to undergo radical change."[5]

Where can they carry on today? Where is the supportive ideology, the larger cause that cries out for truth, envisions beauty and demands justice? Where is Berkeley today? And the riders and marchers in Alabama? Where are Woodstock and the outraged milling crowd of Chicago '68? Tiananmen Square, a dead stop. That calamity echoes far beyond Chinese internal politics. Shoot down the youth. Imprison the youth. Fail the youth. Expel the youth. In Texas (G.W. Bush's state), one in six ninth-graders fail to become sophomores. Cut them loose, drop them out from learning and exploit them to consume.

Search and Destroy. Fail and Expel. For any local school system to show statistics of improvement, simply constrict the sample from all children age 14 to only those in school, then, further, to only those in regular classes. Omit from the facts those in special education and those disabled who are already not in school. Remove the bottom, the top rises, looks better. Improved scores prove the educators' success. And the others? Disappeared from the facts. We have our own *desparacedos* in the United States.

Outsiders. The Littleton boys were outsiders. Some considered the Georgia boy an "outcast." Cast out of what? Outside is where art begins and revolution, and sparks of new consciousness. *Litima* remains, charging the interior soul, but no place for it in the clean well-lighted place.

Litima without social context — the lonely outsider without vision, sullen rage without beauty, despair without solace, inventive intelligence and meticulous planning focused on a pathetic, senseless target.

Senseless? The world took notice. Whether they knew it or not, they died for their unreason — more than our volunteer soldiers are allowed to do for our noble reasons. In the year 1996 of a calendar we call our Lord's, in Japan, Germany, Great Britain, and Canada, *together*, handguns murdered 364 persons — one a day. In the United States, also in 1996, handguns killed 9,390 people — roughly 26 a day. Gun as ultimate hard core fact. Not just access to guns — and why do they want them so? Why are we so afraid of them, and *they* not?

Every year the suicide rate for American teenagers rises; every year the suicide rate for American little children rises. What percent are in prison, on probation, in juvenile court? Left back, in special education? The anxieties, the pressures — and for what? William Bennet would throw the *Book of Virtues* at them. I say read Michael Meade, or Shakespeare.

Shakespeare? In many expensive colleges, you can major in English and graduate without having had to read one piece of Shakespeare. In the state of Arizona, poetry is no longer on the school curriculum, anywhere. Orwell's *1984* world enacted in Phoenix: poetry eliminated. Instead, a computer for every kid from first grade on, courtesy of the generous corporations. And what is poetry, but fact condensed, transformed to essence; imagination seized in the act of creating itself.

Cut the arts budgets, the high school bands, pay more to the coaches; install more technology, more armed guards, demand higher math scores. A culture of poverty.

About math — let me get started! Our national testing stresses math — not articulate speech or foreign language, not history, nor the arts and drama. Drop-out and repeating is due largely to math failures, math resistance. The student body divides between those who can do math and those who can't or won't, and the division is partly racist, genderist. The math requirement fosters a large underclass of school drop-outs, a sociological, psychological, political disaster. An unreflected residue of nineteenth-century worship of science, and a carryover of models of thinking that have no bearing on the actualities of today's life or the poverty of its culture.

Yet, as we sit here, a new national curriculum and test is being devised — aimed to bring U.S. eighth-graders in line with math levels in forty nations. Our eighth-graders placed only twenty-seventh. This won't do, won't do at all! We'll lose our competitive edge, or such is the thinking of the silent majority — read "numbed" for silent — and epitomized in the national math committee headed jointly by the Republican Governor of Wisconsin and the CEO of IBM.

Math is the "bellwether of future achievement in school," says the newspaper report. Math is "the bane of many a student," also says the report. What's in the symptom? That is the question of psychological activism: what's at the essence of this factual paradox that math is so important and math is so resisted? What is the soul of the American eighth-grader saying that is not being said by other kids elsewhere in the world? Is the math resistance a resistance to a math-based culture, whereas elsewhere, perhaps, the eighth-grade soul is less impoverished, better nourished by its culture?

Why so honor math, unquestioning? What kind of thinking does basic math teach? Pure fact, free of value, free of ambiguity, free of psyche, either true or false, right or wrong, easy to test and easy to score, perfectly fitting our fundamentalist literalism. Math, beyond one year of combined basic algebra and geometry, should be an elective like any other foreign language. It has been established — factually — in the State of North Carolina that students who get much music in schools do better in *all* their scores, language and math too. Plato was right. He pushed music. Ancient Greeks played music — even before battle. Manly as guns.

Sean Altman, composer, recommends an "all-out music awareness juggernaut" in the schools. "Any overheard schoolyard conversation," he says, "is evidence that nothing excites kids more than music. Musicians, even more than athletes, are the heroes of youth . . . No student should be able to graduate without having experienced live, in school renditions of the eleven Indispensable Post-Renaissance Compositions,"[6] from the Brandenburg Concerto No. 5 and the Ode to Joy, to Hound Dog, Yesterday, and Free Bird.

Gresham's Law in music. The bad drives out the good. Kids deprived of an education of their musical interests and tastes and talents are left impoverished, with only commercial crapola and psychic numbing.

Impoverished imagination lowers the capacity to discriminate, to tell fantasy from action, reinforcing the Christian notion that there should be *no distinction* between what we imagine in mind and what we do in action, "and I say unto you everyone that looketh on a woman to lust after her hath committed adultery with her already in his heart."[7]

The boys made no distinction in mind between fantasy and action. Again and again the commentators piously declare we will never understand the mystery of this tragedy. No reason for it. They come up with nothing. *Nihil.* (But a kid in Georgia glimpsed something and set off to do the same.) No reason for it, but know what to do about it, say the authorities: act with authority. Parenting as surveillance; watching over becomes watching. Counseling as inquiring. School uniforms. More curfews, more groundings, more pharmaceuticals. No more Doom and Quake on the Internet; interiorize the doom and quake. Cold War brought home. Parental spying on concealing kids.

Rolling Stone reports the facts of kid harassment, freak hair, piercings and tattoos, secret slang, black colors in any form — look out, look out especially for the clever ones, the computer nerds. But doesn't the future of the economy require just these very nerds who prefer to do homework than socialize (the Georgia boy)! Weed out the exception before he kills. "Kids who already felt like outsiders are being made to feel like killers as well."[8]

Is this adult retreat from imagining the real, from the poetics of tragedy, not part and parcel of the impoverished imagination that produced the boys? Denying the possibility of penetration to the essence exposes the culture's nihilism, its *absence of essence.* And the boys in the firelight of their *litima* exposed it, exposed us. They were more sensitive in their desperate way to the culture than the commentators who would explain them.

What did the boys especially target? Their aim, their intention? Jocks, compeers of color. What does this suggest to you? These are the contemporary insiders, for jocks and blacks and Latinos have a style, a culture, a language, a recognizable identity that confirms their *being*. The two boys tried to find theirs in Mafia identification, a subculture, and vicious yes, but one that requires honor, blood-truth, loyalty, initiation — and popular celebrity. The boys of suburban white culture were outside of *being*, searching to be Celebrity, the shortcut to being. Celebrity and celerity — cognates. A woman of Littleton said, "I always wanted this town to be famous for something — and now it is — but then I realized what I was saying." Look out, and into the other. See the void in the imagining heart of the most powerful, wealthy, technically progressed people on earth. Forget family psychology; the boys had families, lived in private houses, good old Fourth-of-July-white-church-green lawn-small-town-USA, Littleton: *nomen est omen.*

Forget psychology of progressive development, of genetic determinism.

Read Brett Easton Ellis's *American Psycho*, the psychology text of our time and our people. Read Phillip Roth's *American Pastoral*, the case study of the good exurban father and the killer exurban daughter.

The boys as avatars of awakening from psychic numbing. In their firepower, the power of fire. Demanding initiation, a call to the culture of no-problem, have-a-nice-day, enjoy, smile. How many more horrors will it take for us to see Columbine as it has become? The dove holds a pipe bomb in its beak? Littleton a space made sacred by dead children. Their deaths as sacrifices to implacable Gods who ask for more from the white nation that occupies this original Indian land. Shiva, too, is a God, and Kali, and there is a God in every disease.

The President's Impeachment for Perjury

To look out is to look into. Activism looks to the facts; *psychological* activism inquires into essences. In the President's case, facts and essence fall apart, that is, when facts are narrowly defined, "I did not have sexual relations with that woman" — clearly denies the facts, contradicts the facts. The facts made perjury of his statement.

As at Littleton, the Republicans collected the facts.

Why stop at the facts?

Essentially, he did not have sexual relations with that woman. They did not join in flesh, consummate their passion. He withheld himself; "unrelated." He may have abandoned his judgment but not his psyche. Sexual relations is a psychic phenomenon, of the soul. It is more than hanky-panky, messing around, making out, heavy petting. Sexual relations has always meant true scoring, a home run. Clinton and Lewinsky didn't get past third base.

Let me bear witness: I know analysts who have played sexually with their patients, patients who have played sexually with their analysts. They kept a barrier, a frame, by not having sexual relations. No coitus. Psychic reservation ritualized in the style of actions.

Those analysts and the President follow a more subtle tradition in keeping with Clinton's old-fashioned Southern style. This style is also common in Ireland, France, and Italy, and probably in many other lands whose habits of desire I am less familiar with. There, mothers may even instruct their daughters: you may mess around genitally in all sorts of methods and procedures without losing virginity. In Ireland a hand-job, a blow-job, even anal penetration did not impugn virginity. These forms of pleasure are not sexual relations, merely genital contact.

In France there is a term for a person who enjoys sex without sexual relations: a *demi-vierge*. Statistical fact: in 1991 a researcher of the Kinsey Institute asked 599 Indiana students whether "they considered oral sex to be sex." 59% of them did not. When this report was published in the prestigious *Journal of the American Medical Association*, its editor, George Lundberg, was fired. Establishment America does not want to know even the facts.

The old definition of rape required penetration: the classic grounds for Catholic dissolution and annulment of marriage depended not upon whether there had been genital contact, but upon coitus. Coitus as consummation, not orgasm. D. H. Lawrence, as obsessively occupied with sexual complexities as anyone writing in the twentieth century, adamantly insisted that only full nude bodies conjoined constituted sexual relations. All else — partial groping, partially unclothed, underwear (thongs), and other come-ons — is merely pornography. Did the President lie — or stick to the essence?

To Barr, Starr, Rogan, and Mr. Hyde (*nomen est omen*), Clinton lied because facts are concrete particulars: sexual means *genital,* relations means *contact.* Genital contact equals sexual relations. *Eo ipso,* perjury. Yet the *lack* of sexual relations is just what Lewinsky whined about.

Fact: the first paragraph of Lewinsky's handwritten document submitted by her lawyer to gain for her immunity says: "Ms. Lewinsky had an intimate and emotional relationship with President Clinton beginning in 1995 . . . Ms. Lewinsky and the President had physically intimate contact. This included oral sex, but excluded intercourse."[9] The damning fact of the damned spot on the blue dress is concrete evidence of the lack of sexual relations. That spot is factual evidence not of Clinton's lying, but of his essential truth.

Starr said, "I am in pursuit of the truth." What truth? Truth as defined by fact. The prosecutors collected the facts as at Littleton: where, when, how, what, how long, how often. Dates, times, positions, body parts. Bits of shrapnel. Their inquiry never penetrated to essentials; thus Starr's inquiry remains moralistic and prurient both. Starr, a *demi-vierge*.

Truth: which truth, whose truth? Of Hermes, of Venus, of Zeus, of Juno? When we swear to tell the truth, the whole truth. and nothing but the truth, the whole truth goes beyond the factual truth. The whole truth is full of holes; like an undersea gelatinous membrane, its edges waver. It deconstructs itself even as it fills itself out with embroideries, avoidances, and factual lies. I touched this, I did that, but I did not have sexual relations — that is the whole truth. Deep inside that bastion of the secular state, the White House, you can find a myth. Remember Virgil's tale of Dido and Aeneas?

Aeneas, son of Venus, warrior king on his way from ruined Troy to found the new city and empire of Rome, paused to dally awhile in Carthage, where he was received by its Queen, Dido, whose first move in her seduction was to take Aeneas's little son into her lap. Venus had transmuted this boy into Cupid, so that the connection between the lovers is via the little boy. What do we say now? Infantile sexuality, polymorphous perverse foreplay, Clinton's immaturity?

The tale of these lovers ends disastrously. After much Virgilian description of her desperate hots for him, Dido and Aeneas meet in a dark cave to consummate their passion. The meeting is all prearranged as a political compromise between Juno and Venus, Juno favoring Dido, Venus Aeneas, who is, after all, her son. So the two humans unite in the grips of their personal passions. Actually, in the grip of their respective inhuman divine protectors. For Dido it means marriage. For Aeneas it is desire in a dark cave. One among others. Venus, goddess of promiscuity.

In each other's arms, but each in his and her myth. Not sharing the same fantasy. What did Lewinsky want from Clinton further down the road? Marriage. Juno can even get at Valley girls. Then, to cut this short (which one should never do with a myth), Aeneas is called by his patron, Jupiter, via Mercury, to continue his task, set sail on his ship of state, found Rome, leaving a disconsolate Queen who, as Shakespeare writes: ". . . stood [Dido] with a willow in her hand, / Upon the wild sea-banks, and waft her love / To come again to Carthage."[10]

Shakespeare took it lightly. Dido didn't. She remains eternally deserted, caught in hell forever, bitter, betrayed. Hope of personal relations through impersonal sex destroyed: "He didn't really love me; just used me," the typical complaint stemming from Juno's vision of Venus. Read the *Aeneid*, Book IV, to compare the details of emotion in the White House with those in Carthage.

This devotion of fact-finding, this faith in fact, that fact leads to truth, that those who do not bear with this truth are liars, smart-asses, perverts, even evil, is the myth that dominates America's righteous activism. The myth of facts cannot contain the psyche's propensities for more inventive modes of understanding. When the plane blew up over Long Island Sound, every bit, large and small, was fished from the sea and assembled in a giant hangar to establish the facts of the disaster; still there remained fantasies of a military missile having struck it, a supposed secret kept from the public and denied by officials. Somewhere there is an undiscovered essence.

Years after, perhaps forever after, the Warren Report stated the facts of the Kennedy assassination, the report confirmed and reconfirmed, yet there remains a host of other fantasies. Facts do not hold the richness of the mind's conjectures. Intelligent complexity is its meat. The myth-making psyche with its inquiring nose, its hankering after the suspect, its delight in the fantastic and beautifully absurd, its affinity with the underworld — no, the psychological mind cannot be laid at rest by facts. What is this American faith in facts? This blindness to essence? Why can't we imagine the real? Whence American literalism?

In other times there was little ability for measurement of men and material. Greeks, Romans, Persians decided political questions — even the decisive battles — by inviting the Gods to display their intentions by oracle, haruspicy, portents, and the motions of birds. Thermopylae, the victories of David, Caesar in Gaul, Agincourt (celebrated in Shakespeare's *Henry V*), Napoleon's defeat at Moscow, the defeat of the Spanish Armada, Grant held back in Virginia, Hitler at Leningrad, all show in various ways that estimation by fact does not assure victory. Even more, these events show that faith in the force of facts can lead to ruin.

What lies at the psychological essence of American activism that so hates jocks and darks that it will blow them, and everyone else, away, so hates the evil criminal of Belgrade that it will take out a civilization's infrastructure, that so hates the President that it will ruthlessly, blindly, and righteously shake the foundation of the Republic?

The canker that distorts our American vision of liberalism, tolerance, and justice is our Biblical literalism. I once heard Joseph Campbell declare, "The Bible, it's simply a bad book." And Campbell knew a thing or two about books, especially books of myth. How could he make such an offensive statement? Especially since that very book, those very Gods are now held up as cures for our societal disorder. Bob Barr of the Judiciary Committee wants the commandments on the wall of the classrooms: prayer in schools, return to faith in the Bible as Fact. Therefore, Clinton's perjury was more than legal misdemeanor. It was a sacrilege! Do we not swear on the Bible?

Joseph Campbell must have meant that the Bible tends to take itself literally and that's why it is "bad." It too often announces itself as fact, historical fact. It suffers amnesia that its tales are just that, tales, extraordinary stories, images of indelible power, truths of many sorts. But somehow, somewhere these marvels collapsed, the imaginative air of fantasy squeezed out of them. No longer stories to be pondered, imagined, but facts to be believed. The spirit gone, only the words remain; the word become fact; literalism the faith; that faith, the American myth.

To put it another way, from the viewpoint of Michael Ventura: "At the end of an epoch: enantiodromia. The virtues turn into vices, vicious."

Though the words retain the former virtuous intention, they become hollowed out, so that the acts coming from the words become vicious. This is not merely classical hypocrisy — far more, far deeper. It is the good intentions themselves that produce bad effects. The better the intentions, the shorter the road to hell.

At a time of enantiodromia the Devil and Christ change places. The truth-seeking Special Prosecutor and Judiciary Committee; the school authorities and good willing community in Littleton; NATO against genocide — all in the name of the good — yield destructive results. Inescapable enantiodromia.

No matter in which way we as Americans bring psychology into the public arena, our acts will be governed by our myths. All things are full of Gods, said Euripides, including our acts, and the God in our acts is the God in our disease of literalism. The Biblical God. Whatever constructive vision we aspire to must be accompanied all along by deconstruction of our own motives, our own subjectivity, our biblical righteousness. For we are each and all, willy-nilly, like it or not, children of the Biblical God. It is the fact of the American essence. If the Bible is fundamental to our kind of consciousness, then we must read it, learn it, know it, and see through its dangerous literalism.

Closing time. No summary, no conclusion. There can be no closure since we are right in the middle of it all. No armistice resolves Kosovo; no reopening of Columbine High ends its devastating witness to our civilization; Starr and Hyde may themselves fade, but the State is ever after cursed by those oily phantoms.

1. J.-P. Sartre, *Sketch for a Theory of the Emotions* (New York: Routledge, 2002), p. 7.
2. *The New York Times* (May 6, 1999).
3. David Firestone in the *New York Herald Tribune* (May 22–23, 1999), p. 3.
4. *Future Survey* 21:3/116 (March 1991).
5. M.J. Meade, *Men and the Water of Life: Initiation and the Tempering of Men* (San Francisco: Harper, 1993), p. 234.
6. S. Altman in *The New York Times* (June 19, 1999), Op-Ed page.
7. *Matthew* 5:28. Rather than imagining facts as images, the literal mind receives images as facts. For instance, another tale from Georgia as reported in The New York Times (October 6, 2005, p. A24): "The family of a 16-year-old honors student who was expelled in 2003 over a journal entry sues the Fulton County School Board to

clear her disciplinary record and win $1 in damages. The suit charges that the First Amendment rights of the girl, Rachel Boim, were violated when a teacher read aloud from her personal journal an account of a dream in which a gunman opened fire on a class she was attending. The next day she was removed from class by a police officer and expelled for making terrorist threats . . . After Ms. Boim's case received national attention, the expulsion was reduced to a suspension, but the school board ruled she would have to repeat the ninth grade."

8. Cary Goldberg in *The New York Times* (May 1, 1999) p. A11.
9. The New Yorker (November 15, 1999), pp. 73–74.
10. W. Shakespeare, *The Merchant of Venice*, Act 5, Scene 1.

Part Four

Responsive Environmentalism

32

Ten Core Ideas

Preamble

I

As we are born into the world, we respond to it. From the first moment when air cools our skin and our eyes meet light, human nature finds itself in and responds to environment. We are never divorced from this animal level of participation. With increasing differentiation and sensitivity the human response becomes more finely attuned to the world, and these responses shape human civilizations, their religious observances, economic practices, political structures, and aesthetic cultures.

II

"Environmentalism" is nothing more, nothing other than this general responsive sensitivity focused upon specific concerns, e.g., air, water, soil, habitat, etc., and their interrelated communal well-being. Whether large scale or small, whatever the specific focus, the urge to action derives from a primal aesthetic response. Disorders in this response find clinical descriptions as autism, alienation, narcissism, denial, egocentricity, and in those endemic syndromes of world-neglect: introspective depression and attention deficit.

Originally written in October 2000 for a study group, The Human Place in Nature, sponsored by the Nathan Cummings Foundation, which met regularly between 1999 and 2000 under the leadership of its president, Charles Halpern. "Ten Core Ideas" presents a digest of contributions emerging from the discussions among participants: Mermer Blakeslee, Jackie Brookner, Fred Buell, Edward Casey, Sandy Gellis, Jeff Golliher, Ned Kaufman, Margot McLean, Paul Mankiewicz, Nina Sandovich, and Mark Walters, among others. Not previously published.

III

A common phoneme, "spon," connects response and spontaneous. From the Latin *spondeo* in various forms we have *sponsus* (spouse, husband), *sponsor* (guarantor), *sponsion* (a formal solemn promise), despond (abandon, resign, give up), and responsibility = able to respond. Responsive means both answering and sympathetic, impressionable. In neurology a response refers to a physical reaction to a specific stimulus or situation. In mechanics responsiveness describes a system that adjusts quickly to suddenly altered external conditions. *Spons*, in Latin usage, means without prompting; of one's own nature or agency. In short, the places and things of the world afford intelligence to which human nature is able to respond spontaneously and responsibly.

IV

Responsive environmentalism aims to rekindle the natural urge that ties humans to habitat. It encourages the primary aesthetic response — the feelings that prompt activism, feelings that lie below the passion of programs and warring partisanship. Because these feelings are given with human nature, we assume the aesthetic response is shared by all protagonists. As these feelings call us to the world, so a responsive environmentalism calls us out from the anesthesia of passive acceptance. An aesthetic response appears in your individual anger at desecration and exploitation, your fear of toxicity and pollution, your delight in well-made structures and open spaces, and your desires to preserve history, culture, and diversity. These responses may be formulated by economics, physical science, moral theology, and social theory, but their common ground lies in the congenital response of an intelligent organism in a shared world.

V

More a practice than a program, responsive environmentalism considers awakening the aesthetic responses of the heart to be the first environmental task. The practice begins simply in noticing our worlds and our reactions. "Enemies" of environment are less developers, profiteers, polluters, and grandiose consumers than our individual apathy and laissez-faire. Each citizen's personal responses are the heart of activism of any kind in any place. The urge to engage, the sense of responsibility arising spontaneously in protest to ugliness, carelessness and waste, and in defense of beauty and value shows that an aesthetic response is also political action.

Ten Core Ideas

1. Environmental Engagement Starts from a Personal Response

Human nature is embedded in a world. The organic health of human beings, their sensory systems and psychic awareness, are in constant reciprocal relationship with a world that acts upon us as much as we act upon it. To be alive is to be a responding, responsive, responsible creature. Even our self-activation and individuality take their start in recognition of where we are and what we are feeling in regard to where we are. Diminished attention to our minute spontaneous responses characterizes the modern condition of anesthetized passive conformity and random aggressive protest. This psychic numbing, or anesthesia, is a major cause of environmental degradation, so that the awakening of primal responsiveness has become the first challenge for environmentalists.

2. Every Environment Is Communal

"Environment" implies a common surrounding that gathers together many disparate parts. "Diversity," "complexity," "bioregion" are current terms stating the fact that places, organisms, and things compose a mutually dependent field. The planet's welfare affects all, inseparably. Just as a catastrophe transcends gender, age, economics, political alignments, genetic, and ethnic differences, so the commonality of environment is essentially democratic. We are all in this together. An environment functions inclusively; all pieces belong. This realization gives a human life a sense of belonging, which may obviate that need for belongings which drives acquisitive consumption.

3. "Place" Replaces "Environment"

The vaguer term "environment" can be more precisely defined as "place." This foundational idea in Western philosophy precedes the later, emptier abstraction, "space."

Places present qualities and are lived qualitatively. They are neither fungible nor fully measurable. Place transcends the usual divides between natural and cultural, urban and wild, sacred and profane. Their interwoven textures embody habitat, climate, geology, history, memory, story and language, jurisdiction, economic use, etc., and also the *spiritus loci* (spirit of the place). Because of this multidimensionality, places intersect and overlay one another. They can be specified as widely as a watershed area, historic battlefield, strip mall, school district, abandoned rail line, rain forest, or as particularly as your back yard. Feelings evoked by places spur political engagement.

4. Aesthetic Judgment Belongs to Environmental Decisions

Since artists and critics of the arts generally represent more differentiated aesthetic sensitivity, they, along with other "experts" (technicians, conservationists, biologists, bankers, lawyers, etc.), belong in environmental decision-making from the start. And, since the sense of beauty and ugliness and the responses to forms, proportions, qualities, materials, etc., are innate to every human's make up, aesthetic judgments will enter into all environmental discussion, even if they are not explicitly acknowledged.

5. Broadened, More Generous Style of Discourse

Proponents of any cause are pressed by the cause to overcome obstacles and resist opposition, often redoubling their energy and losing support for a common goal. Intense advocacy is often equated with advancing the project. Momentum is then carried by experts, technocrats, moneymen, and lobbyists. Originating ideals give way to ideology, resulting in a discourse of personal opinion, propaganda, negative criticism and destructive irony. The grave situations affecting the planet call for gravity in our responses and sincerity in our collaborations. A return to the original ideals rekindles enthusiasm, as the long-term vision of the common good invites that wider participation and broader comprehension which can overcome the rancor of partisan opinion.

6. Programs Derive from Ideas, Ideas from Visions

Ideas can be entertained and visions encouraged, enthusiastically and for themselves, before discarded as impractical. The elevation of implementation above speculation, appreciation, or thought promotes an instrumentalist philosophy and shallow pragmatism, in which thought becomes only a tool for problem-solving, vainly idle unless productive of measurable results.

7. Knowledge Can Be Harnessed by Respect

The scientific method of acquiring environmental knowledge now mainly based on measurement, experiment, and the accumulation of data, can travel hand-in-hand with respect for phenomena. Knowledge is also gained from emotional intimacy, anthropomorphic empathy, aesthetic appreciation and ritual devotion. These other methods of knowing, customary in societies closely attached to their localities and respectful of their spirits, suggest ways to broaden current modes of environmental knowing.

8. Religion and Ethics Shape Environmental Positions

Our notions of "right action," "good" and "bad," our beliefs about justice, about equity, the origins of the world, and the comparative status of human beings among living organisms contribute unavoidably and necessarily to environmental responses. Ethical and religious beliefs determine positions regarding the sanctity of life, the preservation of wilderness, the definition of growth and progress, the relations between technology and nature, and the soul of animals. These beliefs need to become more clearly articulated so as to unburden environmental discourse of hidden agendas and unspoken nihilistic and dogmatic cosmologies.

9. Laws Reflect a Communal Definition of Justice

Since civilization depends on a viable environment, laws and their enforcement intending to maintain civilization will focus on environmental impact. Restitution of tort (injury, wrong) can extend beyond anthropocentric humanism. The rights of non-human species, which so largely depend on the human sense of justice, will affect the formulation of laws. The definition of eminent domain, sacred sites, and of private property will require reconsideration in light of the commonality of environment. Criminal law, too, by drawing upon precedents in international law, prisoner-of-war conventions, and crimes against humanity, can expand its purview and codify environmental crimes. The communal sense of justice leads to the shifting of intent from protection of private goods to the promotion of the common good, where "common good" extends beyond the only or predominantly human.

10. Slowness: A Primary Virtue and Measure of Value

Environmental thinking follows the rhythms of long-term nature and culture. Urgency remains a motivating drive, but does not legitimize immediacy of action. The planet's age is old; compared with that of humans its life span is immensely long. Except for eruptive cataclysms, nature's patterns are largely cyclical and repetitive, and evolutionary change is almost imperceptible. Therefore, slowness becomes a guiding principle in evaluating projects, while contemplation, the arts, longitudinal studies, field and historical research become methods for engaging the earth's disorders and their remedies. Slowness also fosters a deeper, more thorough and loving understanding.

33

Where Is the Environment?

According to dictionary definitions, the word "environment" means "surrounding." It comes from a French word, *virer*, meaning "turns around, rings and circles." All kinds of things turn around in rings and circles, and the moment we think of that, we think about ourselves in the middle of that circle. So the narrow sense of environment is the immediate world of things that are mainly natural — things close at hand. The middle sense of environment is a habitat, an ecosystem, on which anything depends; it's interactive; we're involved with it: things that turn on each other or evolve together, co-evolution, turning around on each other. The widest sense of environment we find in psychology; for example, Jung's sense of the objective psyche or the collective unconscious or Freud's *id*. Theodore Roszak made a beautiful point of saying that the id of Freud and the collective unconscious are actually the physical environment. It's out there. Or you can say it is the Gaia world of Lovelock and Margulis or what David Abram calls the *ruach elohim*, the breath of God, the air, atmosphere, spirit, breath-world. That is the wider sense of what encircles or is around.

But where does the "around" stop? Where does the environment stop? Are there degrees of the environment? Is anything around environment? Is anything in this room, is everything in this room, the environment? And where does it stop physically, geographically? My

---

A talk from notes given at a conference on environment at Esalen Institute, Big Sur, Calif., and expanded for publication in *Cultural and Spiritual Values of Biodiversity*, ed. D.A. Posey (London: International Technology Publications for United Nations Environment Programme, 1999).

breakfast bananas from Ecuador, where do they stop? Are they the environment when I'm sitting with them in the kitchen or I'm eating them? Or does that include Ecuador where they're grown? For instance, the sea sounds outside your bedroom, is that part of the environment? Where do they stop? And is the inorganic also part of the environment? Because we tend to think mainly of the organic world as environment.

Then, another major question: how do all these parts of the environment form a whole? We might call everything in this room the environment, but is it only because it's in this room? What forms the whole of an environment? It could be that it's a matter of a foreground and background, that some things are in the foreground and other things in the background, and they are less environmental because they're in the background. So we take them as less significant in the environment. But then, what puts things in the foreground and some things in the background? In our world today we take certain things as very important in the foreground — the air or noise pollution or light pollution. For other people or other parts of the world or other creatures of the world, these may not be in the foreground at all.

What forms the whole environment? Is it a composition? Is there some kind of formal law that makes for an environment? This would bear on artwork. Is there a composition that goes into making an environment so that we can speak of "an environment?" Must there be a relationship with it? Is it an I-thou relation? Is that important for environment? Or is there environment without any relation: we are just there in it. Or it's just there.

Now the *Gestalt* philosophers would say that there has to be some sort of formal quality that makes for a whole. It would have to be an expressive form or an aesthetic frame. Or there would have to be organic mutuality: the insects depend on the plants and the plants depend on the soil and the soil requires a certain amount of moisture and the insects live in the soil and the roots of the plant so there is an organic mutuality. That is an environment. So you can't disrupt any piece of that. But again, what cuts some things out, or do you include everything in? These are also aesthetic questions because certainly when you're working on a piece of art, you're cutting some things out and not including everything that is there.

Further, could there be an inherent tension that requires certain things to stay together and other things to drop out — an inherent tension like that which holds a drop of water? There are barriers all the way through the world, not just the natural, but there are things that close in on themselves and keep other things out. And that becomes an environment. There is a skin to it, so to speak.

Other questions come up: the relation between parts of the environment. Whatever you're using as the environment, your kitchen or the garden or Gaia, the planet, whatever world you're using — are the parts related internally or externally? This is a philosophical question. If the parts are related internally to each other, they are necessary to each other and they are co-present to each other. You can't have one without the other. If they are externally related, then you have to raise the question of how does this relate to that. So you have to create some kind of force or some kind of modality, some bridge, a third component, that connects things in external relationships.

An internal relationship would be like Yin and Yang. They are necessary to each other: they are co-present or co-terminate or mutually required. That may be what is essential for an environment: the parts are internally related, one to another. So I think "environment" can be expressed not just biologically; it can be expressed philosophically as an internal relationship. And, if an environment is internally related, its parts could be related not just logically but also invisibly, and that is what I'm particularly interested in.

There are problems posed by this word "environment." The power of the word, ringed around or encircled, tends to put a *me* in the middle. And therefore, because of the way we tend to think, I can do what I want and not notice too much how I affect the other components of the environment. That's one problem posed by the word. Another is that the word "environment," ringed around, evokes the archetypal image of the enclosed garden, a *hortus inclusus*, the Catholic image some may remember. Mary was considered an enclosed garden. You see a lot of medieval images of an enclosed garden with a unicorn in it or Mary sitting in a walled garden. Or Eden, paradise, the garden surrounded by a river, the four rivers. This is the idea that the environment is in some way a sanctuary. That archetypal image of the enclosed garden motivates lot of green work by environmental, green people. The restoration of the perfect world, the Garden. When the environment becomes nature and nature becomes touched by that archetypal fantasy of a walled, perfectly closed space, then nature becomes an idealized place.

We return now to the idea that items that make up an environment are related or belong together or fit invisibly. What is the logic of the invisible? I'm trying to get away from the idea that an environment is just simply what's there, what's hanging around and happens to be there and that anything is the environment. For there's some kind of internal necessity that this word is covering. This word is a mask covering something much more than simply the bushes and trees that we call the "environment" or what environmentalists call "the environment."

I want to get at what this word "environment" is doing. What is its power? There may be formal laws that hold. Something invisible is determining the visible. The word "fitting" is one of those words Plato was concerned with — appropriate, fitting. Now perhaps this invisible holding of the environment is more biological or bioregional, i.e., a mutual organic necessity that forms a bioregion. Yellowstone Park, for example, doesn't stop with the geographic borders of Yellowstone Park, as marked on the map, but it's the whole bioregion around it. So when wolves or bison are protected in Yellowstone and then go over the border of the park, they're shot because they're outside of the park, but they're not outside of the bioregion.

Is what holds together a simple location? That is, all these things are in the same perceptual field. They are all in this room, so the simple fact that they're all here is the law that holds them together. Simple location. They're here, present in this place. It seems to me that that's not enough of an idea, just simple location. Because it's meaningless that these phenomena all happen to be in this room at the same time, accidental, a mere collection of stuff. Unless you're mystical and say God put them all here at this place and that's it.

Maybe what holds them all together is a common symbolic meaning under a dominant theme such as the environment of a church where all the things belong because they are held together by the church. Or your kitchen, where they're all held together by the theme of the kitchen — the utensils, the pots, the pans — all the things that belong to the environment.

Perhaps it is time that gives them an internal relationship. Then, the invisible glue is time, simultaneity. They are all here at the same time. It's just chance, but they're all here at the same time and that makes this environment or that environment.

These are not biological ways of thinking. I am attempting to get the word "environment" freed from where it is, trapped in biology and then trapped in nature — in our fantasies of nature. So that we can think more aesthetically. I want to break down the green approach to the environment and get back to the city and all the other kinds of environments that are so crucial.

So what is the invisible logic or force that holds together the discrete items in a surrounding? Let's take a look at the word "invisible." The word has this little prefix "in," which means two very different things. It means on the one hand, *not*. It is not visible — in the same way as *in*articulate, *in*ept, *in*capable, *in*conclusive, or *in*sensitive mean *not* any of those virtues. The other meaning of "in," as a prefix, has to do with direction, motion, or situation: into, innate, inherent, interior, inside, going in. This leads to a lot of confusion. The first meaning of invisible is what is not presented to the senses. At the same time, in our minds, it also means what is therefore inside or interior. If what's not visible is not present to the senses, then you go *in* to find it. The inside is not allowed to be presented. But maybe it is!

There are many things that are not visible. We live under the power of invisibles — all sorts of ideas, gods, laws, principles, rules. Much of what dominates us is present and invisible. Life is governed by invisibles. And I'm suggesting now, to make it a little shorter here, that "environment" is one of these invisibles that has come to replace the very idea of the invisible. It is the presenting of something else in the midst of the visible. I am suggesting that the power of the word "environment" is a substitute for something even more powerful: the invisible. That is why we can't quite define what it is. Environment is not just whatever is around, because what is really always around is something we are unable to seize, the invisible, which many cultures recognize all the time, do dances for, perform rituals for, propitiation and smudges,

paying careful attention, because of this invisible that sustains and supports, or curses if it's not treated right. Yes, this idea of invisibility
invites a more religious and aesthetic, even pagan, approach.

In our modern materialistic culture today, we're using the environment and the foggy notions of it to replace the invisible. So we need
to sophisticate our thinking; we need to make more specific what environment is. For instance, I'm curious to know why our civilized minds
insist that environment equals "nature." Why do we feel when we talk
about the environment that we're talking about natural things — rain,
rivers, leaves, wood, birds. And yet we live in cities! By not realizing
that the environment is not merely nature, but is something invisible
besides, we have something that needs to be teased out or defined in
some other way. We say the gods are in nature, not in the city — the
devil is in the city. The only fantasies we can have then about what
to do about cities is to make them more like the woods or nature and
bring in the parks, green belts, water walls, and so on – as if that were
the way to return goodness to cities. I think it is important to sophisticate our notion of environment beyond identifying it with nature.
Therefore my emphasis upon the invisibility idea as the ground on
which the idealization of nature rests.

We must not fall into the split between city and nature. Let us try
to understand environment as a co-presencing of the invisible and the
visible. I would prefer to drop the word environment and use the word
co-presence. But that isn't satisfactory either. I think what we go to
nature for is this invisible. And we haven't had enough teaching in how
to discover the invisible in the city. We have such condemnation of
the city, such hatred of the city and disgust about the city, that we let
the city go and don't pick up enough of the urban invisible, the radiance of what Plotinus calls "divine enhancement" in the city.

34

Dreaming Outside of Ourselves?

A reply to the question, "What will psychoanalysis be in the coming century?" depends on what we consider psychoanalysis to be, how it is defined. The sure solidity of its definition has been, especially in the past twenty years, seriously eroded. In fact, psychoanalysis can no longer define itself from within, since its own definitions as a science of human nature, as a method of treatment, as a dialectical process of investigation and a theory of human development — have been thoroughly critiqued, refuted, and even held up as cultish shallow mysticism, or worse, fraud.

Since I do not know what "it" essentially is, I cannot speak about what "it" will become. So rather than prediction, I would prefer to address the question of evaluation. What of its various virtues and strengths continue to prove fruitful and are worth maintaining?

Before we get to the fruitful, let's clear away what seems most barren. Let us ruthlessly ask psychoanalysis some questions, interrogate the field itself without denigrating its dedicated practitioners or its pioneering founders. First question: What value has psychoanalysis in this contemporary world of an endangered planet? Would the fish approve, the tropical forests? The undernourished, the jailed who do not deserve to be jailed? Does it bear in any way on the escalating technological networks of information? As a consciousness-raising

Originally published in *Where Id Was: Challenging Normalization in Psychoanalysis*, eds. Anthony Molino and Christina Ware (London/New York: Continuum, 2001).

societal force, has it brought beauty anywhere? As a programme of self-reflection and sublimation has it internalized wasteful consumption; has it sophisticated entertainment, differentiated language, or heightened sensitivity to injustice?

Obviously, my inquisition intends a generalized "No." Psychoanalysis would have to bow its head in shame and admit its failure to address the major issues of our time. But then, maybe its defense rests on a simpler base. Psychoanalysis was never meant to carry responsibility for any of these large-scale dilemmas such as environmental distress and societal injustice. It is "merely" a humanistic science aimed at relieving individual dysfunction by means of investigative insights leading to behavioral changes.

Yet even with this mildest definition of itself, it stands on wobbly legs. Individual dysfunction can be relieved promptly and effectively by pharmaceuticals; while the very idea of "mind" is being radically challenged by evolutionary psychology, biogenetics, and bioengineering. Moreover, the "human" part of its humanistic science is narrowly western, white, and young, and the "science" part mainly an indoctrination of dogma by means of an orthodox systematic hermeneutics. So much for summing up in one paragraph what psychoanalysis has been accused of in the past twenty years.

What then remains? Where lies the residual good? I follow Ernest Jones in believing that Freud's formulation of repression and the unconscious were his most significant conceptual ideas. To me these two ideas recapitulate Plato's "Myth of the Cave" (*Republic*): the human being is ignorant (unconscious) and ignores this ignorance (repression). This Socratic-Platonic intuition of the human condition, translated by Freud into psychoanalytic language, is the main value of what his work brought into modern times from the Classical heritage (not Oedipus, Thanatos, Phallos, Libido, etc.). I would like to believe this value will be carried into the next century and any century thereafter!

This view states that the unconscious is neither a region of the mind, a system of dynamic impulses, nor a reservoir of images. Rather, it is a pragmatic idea that functions to tame the Promethean urges of human *hubris*. It says: you do not know what you know; all your truths are half-truths; all your life and its actions are shadowed by unknowing.

Human life is situated in a profound invisibility that can never be mastered, and you, human being, keep this ignorance out of your awareness by means of repression.

Psychoanalysis acts as a critic of this ignorance, as violator of the innocence that is reinforced by repression. Therefore, its practice is a work of knowing in the midst of feeling the unknown and unknowable, a self-limiting, self-inhibiting ethical discipline, casting doubt on certitude, bringing hesitation to irrelevant desire and reflection to megalomania. Psychoanalysis: a last refuge of the moral reflex in a psychopathic civilization.

Because the discipline of psychoanalytic thinking tries to stay alert to the inevitable presence of the cave, psychoanalysis takes up positions outside the cave. Its thinking is that of the outsider, subverting and deconstructing the pervading innocence and persuasive delusions that inform society in general. It finds itself subversive, in essence revolutionary. In this way, as well as for its ethical concern, psychoanalysis remains in the Jewish tradition from which it originally sprang.

Finally, the dream. How shall we regard it now, a hundred years after Freud's extraordinary book? First, let us review just what Freud's accomplishment was in 1900. His *Traumdeutung* brilliantly solved the problem of the dream as it was then formulated. During the nineteenth century three dominating hypotheses held sway and conflicted with one another. The *Romantic* view regarded the dream as a personal message from the "beyond" with personal significance for the dreamer. The Rationalists denied sense to dream content altogether. Romantics and Rationalists agreed that the dream — because it was nonsensical garbage produced by the mind/brain while resting (Rationalist) or it was poetic mystical inspiration from the deep soul or elsewhere (Romantic) — did not belong to the province of science. The *Materialist* view, in contrast, favored scientific research, but only to prove the organic origin of the dream, its source in physiology. This research aimed to reduce dream events to body activities and sense stimuli.

Freud's genius synthesized the three opposing views. By reasserting the ancient tradition that the dream has an immediate personal meaning for the dreamer, he absorbed the Romantic position. He also recognized the nonsense and irrationality of dream language, yet gave a rational account of the causality of this nonsense in what he called "the dream work." Thus his view was not only Romantic but Rational as well. Then, by means of the sexual theory of the libido, he could integrate the Materialist position that there was an organic basis for the dream. He thus brought together these contrasting strands of the nineteenth century and wove them into a coherent theory of dreams.

A hundred years later, what do we want to hold onto of this "coherent theory of dreams"? Because of what has been so widely refuted and surpassed, we will no longer be captivated by Freud's "science." We will have to find new values in the dream other than revelations of infantile reminiscences and disguised sexuality. While holding onto the dream's importance, we will have to revise why it is important, no longer because it offers intrasubjective information, all about me. And we will hesitate to interpret the dream by lifting repression from it with the selfish, empowering aim of gaining territory and energy so as to consolidate and strengthen the Promethean "me." Let's not forget, Prometheus was a Titan whose human-centred focus offended the Gods, cleaving us from them and disturbing the balance of the cosmos.

At this perilous point in the planet's history, we will have to go further out than even the Romantics, by drawing on archaic ideas of dreaming as a source of imaginal information from a psyche that is not merely mine, attached to my brain and within my skull. If the psyche is more than subjective, but has a collective, objective, transpersonal or archetypal aspect — which philosophical tradition calls the *anima mundi* — then the dream, too, must he referred beyond the person of the dreamer to the soul of the world.

This suggests that our dreams are dreamings of the "other." This other is not merely the other parts of myself ("my unconscious") or the other as the repressed, forgotten, distorted, disguised. Rather, the dream brings in the *fundamental* other, the "not me" of the world and the specifics of how I am with it, in it. The world's soul echoes and moves its imagination in my dream.

The dream still remains "mine." It occurs in my part of the night. But as the night is not made by me, neither is the dream. In actuality, during the dreaming, I am in it, moving among its figures and scenes, held in its drama, which I did not write. I am in it until the moment of awakening, when I reverse the facts and take possession of the night by saying, "I dreamt," asserting that the dream is in me. Yet all night long I was in the dream.

Freud saw that the sickness of the other comes through the *via regia* of the dream. In his day, that sickness used young city women in centers of patriarchal empire (Paris and Vienna) to demonstrate its symptoms. Today, the symptoms are everywhere. The *anima mundi* is sick and the "other" cannot be contained within the consulting room. After one hundred years, severe psychic illness permeates the planet itself.

I am suggesting that we meditate dreams for a wider awareness of the cosmos that impinges upon us through the night window of the soul. To refer the dream to the *anima mundi* implies that the dream be welcomed for its information regarding the state of the soul of the world. The *via regia* would now lead away from a human-centred psychology and into a world-focused cosmology — psychology deconstructing itself as it dissolves into cosmology.

We would still be following Freud's intentions and maintaining the deepest values of his thought because unconsciousness would still be the concern of the work. However, the location of unconsciousness would now be out there rather than in us. We would still aim at lifting repression, though the content of the repressed would be different. For what is repressed today is the *soul* of the world, that the world of nature, of things, of technology and systems is not merely Cartesian dead matter, a barren objective *res extensa*, but also a *res cogitans* — layered with psychic potential once we shift our cosmology. That shift might end psychoanalysis as we now practice it, but it would provide a fresh vision for another century of Freud, his investigative intellect, his radical spirit, his therapeutic concerns for civilization, and his ideal of formulating a universally valid theory of psyche.

35

The Virtues of Caution

Avarice, gluttony, vanity, lascivity, envy, wrath, and sloth — to these classical seven deadly sins, according to Aldous Huxley, we moderns, despite our inventive genius and after so many centuries, have been able to add only one new sin. The sin? Haste, hurry, rush, speed, momentum, acceleration. Our Zeitgeist ruled by the *Geist* of *Zeit*. We live in the economics of hurry, and the planet itself heats up with the energy of our hastening. Time is money, and therefore the old adages have been cast aside: look before you leap; haste maketh waste; a stitch in time saves nine; fools rush in where angels fear to tread; an ounce of prevention is worth a pound of cure.

Haste, the spirit of hurrying time, affects human biology as well. Menarche comes on earlier and earlier; children grow taller faster; athletes break records, hurdling faster, leaping higher, farther. And haste affects our psychiatric diagnostics: who wants to be considered slow, retarded, passive, withdrawn, regressed, or fixated?

Because time is imagined as a racing river, gathering speed as it flows in one direction only, "He who hesitates is lost." Caution can only be imagined as timidity, pessimism, recalcitrant obstinacy, stubborn and stupid, clinging to old ways. Moreover, the images and rhetoric that urge caution and resistance to the headlong rush revive the images and rhetoric of the ancient God of Mediterranean and Renaissance culture,

Speech delivered on the occasion of receiving the Medal of the Presidency of the Italian Republic in Rimini, Italy, October 2001, and first published as "The Psychology of Precaution" in *Il Fuoco nel Cristallo*, vol. 2 (Verucchio: Centro Ricerche Pio Manzù, 2001).

Saturn/Kronos — old, slow, cold, negative, stable, limiting, and mean, an enemy of change.

Thus, when the precautionary principle enters public debate, the sides are drawn on archetypal, even mythical lines. On the one side, optimism, futurism, expansion, positive thinking, a progressive advance that meets obstacles as they arise and overcomes them with redoubled energy. This is the heroic mind, moving single-mindedly forward, rising to every challenge, confident in its own ability, no monster too large, no swamp too dismal, no wall too impenetrable.

As long as time is imagined in accord with the heroic impulse, caution is doomed from the start. It can only be envisioned as blocking, stopping, an impediment in the river, clogging its flow, producing backwaters and stagnant pools. Caution has only the one face given by heroic single-mindedness.

Three other characteristics of our times are hurled along by the same river: the cults of technology, competition, and celebrity. The principle improvements brought by technological change, until the electronic computer age, were labor-saving and space-saving. A technological advance was measurable in the number of working hours saved by machine, and the machine could compact and reduce materials into more manageable and transportable size. But now technological change brings mainly the benefit of speed: more done more quickly. What is saved is time.

Time also curses the joys of discovery. It is no longer enough to experiment, ponder serendipitously, discover. There is a crushing competitive pressure to be first with a formula, a method, a product. The first to publish may get a Nobel award; the first in the market makes the most gain. We are in the age of the short-cut, corporate espionage, and falsified results — because of competition. As in a foot race, only the one coming in first qualifies; the others are "seconds" or simply losers. A culture that promotes winners gets more and more losers. I like to remember a precept I was told of Sikh religion: "Always come second." Precaution as a virtue.

As for the cult of celebrity — the idea that each of us may have our "fifteen minutes of fame," in the words of Andy Warhol — has radically altered the notion of fame. In Roman and Renaissance times, *fama*, or reputation, was imagined to be like an invisible accompanying spirit, one's own genius passed to one by one's ancestors. It was more precious than one's own life, to be served, honored, enhanced by one's actions and to be kept untarnished. Its lasting benefits passed on to one's heirs, descending to future generations with the family crest and name. Now fame has been speeded up and replaced by celebrity the root of which word is akin to *celeritas, celeritatis,* and the English "acceleration."

How else might we consider the principle of precaution rather than only from the mythical premises and images of the hurrying heroic ego? By the way, that heroic ego, whose epitome in Mediterranean mythology was Hercules, went mad after racing through his twelve labors and had to descend to the Underworld of phantoms and the dead, or, in another tale, sit quietly spinning, turning, and turning the self-same wheel, all forward action spent.

It is important to remind ourselves what this principle of precaution more exactly refers to. I will define it by a statement neither from international agreements where it has been incorporated into protocols, nor from policies of the German and Swedish governments where it carries the force of law. Instead my definition comes from a most unlikely source, the Administrator of the Environmental Protection Agency of the current Bush administration, Christie Whitman, who said at the National Academy of Sciences Meetings in Washington, D.C.: "Policymakers need to take a precautionary approach to environmental protection. We must acknowledge that uncertainty is inherent in managing natural resources, recognize it is usually easier to prevent environmental damage than to repair it later, and shift the burden of proof away from those advocating protection toward those proposing an action that may be harmful."[1]

So far so good, but the Whitman statement remains in the realm of means — how best to proceed, or not proceed. What about the ends which the means serve? What is the wider purpose of a project, what is its *telos,* in Aristotle's term, "that for the sake of which" the project has been conceived? If the ends are for competitive advantage, increased profitability, taxation advantages, do not these ends disqualify the means no matter how protective of the environment they must be?

Suppose, however, the ends seem more noble — safer cures, a cooler Earth, cleaner water, species conservation — are then the means justified by these ends?

Moral philosophy holds that long-term ends, no matter how noble, can never justify the short-term means, but that the ends must show their nobility in each moment of the means. The precautionary principle has something to offer here for resolving this dilemma of correlating means and ends. That they correlate only too well in predatory corporate economics is visible the world over: exploitation of mineral resources (ends) correlates with the means of ravaged Earth, oppressed indigenous peoples, destruction of ecological balance, deterioration of culture. But how is it possible to correlate means and ends in a positive way?

By slowing and questioning the most evidently efficient means, precaution invites innovations and experiment. This is an invitation to Hermes with his mercurial mind to try out previously unimagined ways of arriving at the same ends and in accord with those ends. The necessity caused by caution actually becomes the mother of invention.

Finally, as a psychologist I need to offer psychological grounds for caution beyond the reasonable advantages and mythical implications. Three such grounds are particularly noteworthy.

First, the Hippocratic maxim: *primum nihil nocere*. Before all else, above all, first, do no harm, harm nothing. Before any action or plan for action, consider first the downside before the upside. Explore the risks rather than the benefits. Expenditures on research shall focus on worst-case scenarios and fully extend the notion of harm.

The Hippocratic maxim suggests two thoughts, at least. First, intervention in the ways of the world, despite the delusions that heroic goodness brings to its ambitions, always invites a shadow. Yin accompanies Yang, always and everywhere. Weigh the consequences of what might lie in the dark of your helping urge, your bright vision. Second, this maxim implies that the Earth has its own virtues and forces: nature may be acting in ways that lack of caution does not let us see. Hippocratic caution brings with it a background in ancient animism, a respect for the dignity and power of phenomena, beyond human cost benefits and risk assessments, so as to discover *their* values and intentions beyond ours, so that we might work with them, even follow *their* lead, for their sake as well as ours.

The next backdrop to the precautionary principle is Socrates's *daimon*. In several places in the writings of Plato, Socrates is described as holding back from an action because his daemon, spirit, angel, inner voice, invisible twin, this "autonomous psychic factor" (Jung) has been called a "cautionary spirit" by commentators on these passages. Its most remembered appearance occurs in the cell where Socrates awaited his hemlock poison. When asked why he did not escape, he said he had not been urged to by his daimon and, as he explains, the cautionary spirit never tells one what to do: it acts only as a caution. It speaks in a peculiarly non-statistical unscientific manner — anecdotally, superstitiously, symptomatically, with omens and hints and whispers, even by bodily events like sneezes, yawns, and hiccoughs.

A third psychological background to caution is quite simply the endemic background of Westernized societies anywhere: depression. Depression slows all heroic endeavors: the very thought of action is too much! Hence, depression, whether of the psyche or of the economy, is desperately feared in Westernized societies and every possible measure mobilized against it. The pressures we feel, the drugs we take, the expectations we nurture and the dictates of global economic expansion are all anti-depressive measures. Psychiatry could easily say the headlong rush of the river itself is a manic defense against depression.

Precaution finds little value from this perspective. In fact, the furious opposition that the precautionary principle provokes conforms exactly with outbursts of fury from manic patients when interrupted, slowed, or even asked to repeat themselves. To insinuate caution into a manic society means to it only depression, and therefore the precautionary principle must be introduced in manic terms as innovative, progressive, cutting-edge thinking, visionary, and beneficial on a world-wide scale. Which, by the way, it could very well be!

Besides the Hippocratic, Socratic and depressive background to the psychology of caution, there is a fourth: beauty. As noted by Thomas Aquinas, and repeated by James Joyce: beauty arrests motion. Beauty brings us up short. We catch our breath, stand in surprise, or in awe and wonder or even terror, as Rilke said. This momentary suspension in the face of the moment of beauty is true as well for ugliness, for as Plotinus said, "ugliness makes the soul shrink back within itself and turn away."

The gasp, "ahh-h," lies at the root of the word "aesthetic." This aesthetic response whether to the ugly or the beautiful, shows an immediate instinctual awareness regarding the world prior to aesthetic judgment. Beauty comes upon us at a glance, seizes and lets go; as does horror. The aesthetic response is given with the psyche like the inner cautionary daimon that holds one back, like the depressive mood that refuses action.

Beauty, however, prompts action. The naïve aesthetic response leads to aesthetic protest against ugliness on the one hand, and on the other, to aesthetic desire to preserve, protect, and restore the beautiful. Of course, the various attempts to conserve can turn into reactionary conservatism hostile to technological change. But going backwards is not the intention of the aesthetic response, or of precaution. Going backwards results from the identification of beauty with the particular moment of its appearance — a particular style, which then crystallizes into an ideology of beauty, whether naturalism, romanticism, modernism, formalism, nationalism, popularism, vernacularism, or idealism. Each of these holds the aesthetic response captive, chained to dogma and deprived of its naive spontaneity, whereas what the response more freely seeks is a heightened sensitivity and breadth so that the response comes into play ever more frequently and perceptively. In earlier times this was called the gradual improvement of taste.

Here we must distinguish the moment of arrested movement from identification with the arrest itself, as if beauty must stand still. But beauty, like caution, is not meant to stand still. The saying is not "Don't leap" but "Look before you leap." Beauty means only for us to arrest for a moment the senseless insensitive forward thrust, in order to open the senses by inviting the aesthetic response. Then, as the arresting moment flees, the principle of precaution can incorporate into its innovative explorations an aesthetic awareness, insisting that any plan or project does not neglect the demand that beauty makes, or the deleterious effects of ugliness.

Were we to arouse our senses from their psychic numbing, their anesthesia, many of the products and programs, the very river of time itself, hastened on its course by the powers that rule governments, economists, corporations, media, and industries, would slow enough to seep into other channels that have not yet been irrigated and so have never had a chance to bloom.

Anesthesia seems necessary to heroic fortitude. Like a blinkered horse, its eyes only on the prize, it rushes headlong into ugliness—the very world it has constructed. Were our aesthetic responses to awaken, we would not need the admonitions implied by the principle of precaution — not even Hippocratic warnings and Socratic omens. The individual human's aesthetic response, similar to a dog's cringing at a screeching noise or a cat putting its nose into a bowl of flowers, would alter the very course of history and the shape of things we live among.

Our noses too, and our eyes and ears, are political instruments, protesters. An aesthetic response is a political action. Like the daimon of Socrates who indicates only what not to do, we, too, know instinctively, aesthetically when a fish stinks, when the sense of beauty is offended. Standing for these moments — and these moments occur each day, within every airless office building, seated in each crippling chair, inundated by senseless noise, and fattened on industrial food — standing for our responses these aesthetic reverberations of truth in the soul may be the primary civic act of the citizen, the origin of caution and of the precautionary principle itself with its warnings to stop, look, and listen.

1. *Scientific American* (January 2001), p. 18.

36

Soul and Money

Money is a kind of poetry.
— Wallace Stevens (1957)

I

Whatever we say about money in its relation with analytical practice, whatever we say about money at all will be conditioned by the mind-set of our cultural tradition. We speak first of all at an unreflected level, with the voice of collective consciousness, to use Jung's term. In order to gain purchase on the money question in analysis, we have first to see through our collective consciousness, the very deep, old, and imperceptible attitudes that archetypally have already fixed money within a definite framework, especially in regard to soul.

This framework is that of our entire culture, and it is Christian. So we are going to have to look first of all at Christian ideas and images regarding money and soul. I set forth now without benefit of Christian apologetics and exegetics, without recourse to scholarly apparatus, simply as the plain man who opens his Bible in a hotel room and takes the words there within the framework of his collective consciousness. For the words of Jesus in regard to money, whether or not we are directly conscious of them, are still sounding in us as members of this culture. Here are a few of the passages in the Gospels which I want briefly to remind you of before drawing some conclusions.

Panel Talk (slightly expanded here) at the Eighth International Congress of the International Association for Analytical Psychology, San Francisco, 1980, and published in *Soul and Money* (Dallas: Spring Publications, Inc., 1982).

John's Gospel puts the first of these money stories at the beginning of Jesus' ministry (John 2:14):

> And he found in the temple those that sold oxen and sheep and doves, and the changers of money sitting [*kollubistes*, literally "coin clippers"]. And he made a scourge of cords and cast all out of the temple, both the sheep and the oxen; and he poured out the changers' money, and overthrew their tables. And to them that sold the doves he said, Take these things hence; make not my Father's house a house of merchandise [a market].

Mark's (11:17) version has Jesus saying "a den of robbers," specifically referring to both buyers and sellers.

The second incident is more a saying than a story. I refer to Matthew 19, Mark 10, and Luke 8:25 from which last I quote: "For it is easier for a camel to enter in through a needle's eye, than for a rich man to enter into the kingdom of heaven." Is it not curious that in these first two allegories, money is expressed directly in the language of animals? Even the sheep and oxen, so significant in the birth milieu of Jesus, are driven from the temple, and the camel now becomes that animal fatness, that richness which cannot pass the strait and narrow gate where the soul must enter. In these first two images, the exclusion of money is also exclusion of the animal.

If ever the word archetypal meant anything like permanent, ubiquitous, at the roots or made in heaven, then the relation between money and animals is archetypal. The animal is the very *arché* of money. "Pecuniary" derives from cattle; "fee," from *faihi* (Gothic for cattle); "capital" refers back to cattle counted by the head. The Greek coin, *obolos*, refers to the *obelos* or spitted portion of flesh of a sacrificial bull, and the ancient Roman currency, *as*, originally meant a piece of the roast, a hunk of meat.[1] The vow of poverty entails the vow of chastity; money and animal life are driven from the temple together.

The third story concerns taxes that play a special role right from the beginning. Jesus' birth took place in Bethlehem because Joseph and Mary had to proceed there to register for the tax rolls (Luke 2).

The topos "Bethlehem" not only brings Jesus together with David, Jesus and animal together, Joseph and Mary together, the Magi of various races and orientations, but also holds in one image the Emperor's rule of the world by means of taxes and Christ's star pointing beyond the world. In the image of "Bethlehem," as they say, no problem. In Matthew 17 (and Matthew is the Patron Saint of tax collectors, assessors, and bankers), Peter is asked whether Jesus pays his half-shekel or didrachma in taxes. Peter says: Yes. But as it turns out, the tax Jesus pays to the Temple is not common money of this world. It is got by miracle: "go thou to the sea," he tells Simon Peter, ". . . and take up the fish that first cometh up; and when thou hast opened his mouth, thou shalt find a shekel: take that and give unto them for me and thee." Again, by the way, an animal together with money.

The main tax tale is the one told in Matthew 22, Mark 12, and Luke 20. I'll give the passage from Mark: "Master . . . is it lawful to give tribute unto Caesar, or not?" to which Jesus answers, "bring me a penny that I may see it . . . And he saith unto them, whose is this image and superscription? And they said unto him, Caesar's. And Jesus said unto them, render unto Caesar the things that are Caesar's, and unto God the things that are God's."

Here it is money itself which divides into two alternative ways — spiritual and worldly. It is money which is used for the parable of two different and distinct worlds. If money divides the two realms, is it also that third which holds them together? We shall come to this later.

According to the texts, it sounds as if it is clearly better to be without money, even to be in poverty, than to be with money. (This in spite of Joseph of Arimethea and other followers who were wealthy.) For instance, in the tale of the poor widow (Luke 20, Mark 12) who is praised for her meager giving — a lesson Jesus draws out for his disciples as he sits "over against the treasury" in the temple. For instance, poverty becomes mandatory: when the twelve are sent on their mission, two by two, with authority over unclean spirits or *daimones* (Mark 6, Luke 9, Matthew 10), they are expressly instructed not to carry money. Luke 12 brings wealth and soul directly into relation. In a passage about inheritance (the parable of the rich fool) Jesus says, "A man's life consisteth not in the abundance of things which he possesseth" as he tells about a rich man laying up corn for his retirement so as to have his soul's ease, only to have his same soul (psyche) called by God to death that very night. And again, Matthew 26 and Mark 8: "What doth it profit a man to gain the whole world and lose his own soul [psyche]?"

Is not by now the division utterly clear? Money belongs to Caesar's Palace, not God's Temple. The first act of cleansing the temple of money is reaffirmed all along and of course nowhere more bitterly than in the final story, the selling of Jesus by Judas for thirty pieces of silver. (Judas is already attributed with the telltale sign of evil — a money bag or box in the scene of the supper [John 13:29].) Could money be given a more negative cast?

II

We are situated in this collective consciousness. We have to start from this schism between soul and money in the basic text stating the values of our tradition. The schism can lead us into taking up one side or another such as exposed by Dr. Covitz and by Dr. Vasavada.[2] Together with Vasavada, we can deny money in order to do a spiritual kind of soul-work; or together with Covitz, we can affirm money in order to become therapeutically more effective in the world. They each showed the division we already have seen: the more one concentrates on money the more one involves oneself in the world, and the more one neglects money or abjures it, the more one can be removed from the world.

But I wish to make another kind of move by taking a third position, not high road nor low road, neither spirit nor matter. I see money as an archetypal dominant that can be taken spiritually or materially, but which in itself is neither.

Rather, money is a *psychic reality*, and as such gives rise to divisions and oppositions about it, much as other fundamental psychic realities — love and work, death and sexuality, politics and religion — are archetypal dominants which easily fall into opposing spiritual and material interpretations. Moreover, since money is an archetypal psychic reality, it will always be inherently problematic because psychic realities are complex, complicated. Therefore, money problems are inevitable, necessary, irreducible, always present, and potentially — sometimes actually — overwhelming. Money is devilishly divine.

One of Charles Olson's *Maximus* poems sets out this archetypal view most compactly:

> the under part is, though stemmed, uncertain
> is, as sex is, as moneys are, facts!
> facts, to be dealt with, as the sea is . . .[3]

This is an extraordinary statement. "Facts to be dealt with as the sea is." The first of these facts is that money is as deep and broad as the ocean, the primordially unconscious, and makes us so. It always takes us into great depths, where sharks and suckers, hard-shell crabs, tight clams and tidal emotions abound. Its facts have huge horizons, as huge as sex, and just as protean and polymorphous.

Moreover, money is plural: "moneys." Therefore I can never take monies as an equivalent for any single idea: exchange, energy, value, reality, evil, whatever . . . It is many-stemmed; it is uncertain, polymorphous. At one moment the money complex may invite Danae who draws Zeus into her lap as a shower of coins, at another moment the gold may invite Midas. Or, Hermes the thief, patron of merchants, easy commerce. Or it may be old moneybags Saturn who invented coining and hoarding to begin with. As on the original coins the Greeks made, there are different Gods and different animals — owls, bulls, rams, crabs — each time the complex is passed from hand to hand.

Money is as protean as the sea-God himself; try as we might with fixed fees, regular billings, and accounts ledgered and audited, we never can make the stems of money balance. The checkbook will never tally; the budget will never stay within bookkeeping columns. We invent more and more machinery for controlling money, more and more refined gauges for economic prediction, never grasping what Olson tells us: the facts of money are like the facts of the sea. Money is like the id itself, the primordially repressed, the collective unconscious appearing in specific denominations, that is, precise quanta or configurations of value, i.e., images. *Let us define money as that which "possibilizes" the imagination.*

Monies are the riches of Pluto in which Hades' psychic images lie concealed. To find imagination in yourself or a patient, turn to money behaviors and fantasies. You both will soon be in the underworld (the entrance to which requires a piece of money for Charon).

Therapy draws back. Do you know the study done on therapeutic taboos? Analysts were surveyed regarding what they feel they must never do with a patient. It was discovered that touching and holding, shouting and hitting, drinking, sleeping, kissing, nudity, and intercourse were all less prohibited than was "lending money to a patient." Money constituted the ultimate taboo.

For money always takes us into the sea, uncertain, whether it comes as inheritance fights, fantasies about new cars and old houses, marriage battles over spending, ripping off, tax evasion, market speculations, fear of going broke, poverty, charity — whether these complexes appear in dreams, in living rooms, or in public policy. For here in the facts of money is the great ocean, and maybe while trawling that sea floor during an analytical hour we may come up with a crazy crab or a fish with a shekel in its mouth.

Just as animals were spirits or Gods in material forms, so, too, is money, a kind of third thing between only spirit and only the world, flesh, and devil. Hence, to be with money is to be in this third place of soul, psychic reality. And, to keep my relation with the unclean spirits whether the high *daimones* or the low *daimones*, I want some coins in my purse. I need them to pay my way to Hades into the psychic realm. I want to be like what I work on, not unlike and immune. I want the money-changers where I can see them, right in the temple of my pious aspirations. In other words, I try my darndest to keep clear about the Christian tradition I have just exposed because I think it disastrous for psychotherapy and for the culture as a whole.

The cut between Caesar and God in terms of money deprives the soul of world and the world of soul. The soul is deflected onto a spiritual path of denial, and the world is left in the sins of *luxuria*, avarice, and greed. Then the soul is always threatened by money, and the world needs the spiritual mission of redemption from the evil caused by the *Weltbild* that cuts Caesar from God. That money is the place where God and Caesar divide shows that money is a "third thing" like the soul itself, and that in money are both the inherent tendency to split into spirit and matter and the possibility to hold them together.

This equation — "money = psyche" — is what we Jungians have been trying to say when we translate money images in dreams into "psychic energy." "Energy," however, is heroic Promethean language. It transforms the equation into "money = ego," that is, energy available to ego-consciousness. Then, Hermes/Mercurius, Guide of Souls, has to appear as the thief, and in our sense of loss (of money, of energy, of identity) in order for the equation "money = psyche" to return again. (Poverty is simply a way out of ego, but not a hermetic way.) For Hermes the Thief is also Hermes Psychopompos, implying that from the hermetic perspective exactly there, where money is no longer available to ego consciousness, is also where Hermes has stolen it for the sake of soul. In soul work, losing and gaining take on different meanings, a sensibility that Promethean language about "energy" is too active and goal-directed to apprehend.

If money has this archetypal soul value, again like the ancient coins bearing images of Gods and their animals and backed by these powers,[4] money will not, cannot, accept the Christian depreciation. Christianity time and again in its history has had to come to terms with the return of the repressed — from the wealth of the churches and the luxury of its priests, the selling of indulgences, the rise of Capitalism with Protestantism, usury and projections on the Jews, the Christian roots of Marxism, and so on.

One particular shadow of the Christian position appears right in analysis: the old sin of simony or exchanging spiritual and ecclesiastical benefits for money. Are not the elaborate systems analysts have derived for guaranteed payments from their patients for healing or individuation of the Self, and from their trainees for ordination into the analytical profession, modern forms of simony? This sin the Church was far more conscious of than we are today. The Church was anyway more aware of money for "possibilizing" the imagination than we are in psychotherapy. It has always recognized the fantasy power of money preventing the soul from the Church's doctrinal spiritual path.

As long as our belief system inherently depreciates money, it will always threaten the soul with value distortions. Depression, inflation, bad credit, low interest — these psychological metaphors have hardened into unconscious economic jargon. Having "de-based" money from its archetypal foundations in psychic reality, money attempts a new literal and secular foundation for itself as "the bottom line." But this bottom does not hold, because any psychic reality that has been fundamentally depreciated must become symptomatic, "go crazy," in order to assert its fundamental archetypal autonomy.

We live today in fear of this autonomy, called financial anarchy. Anarchy means "without archai"; and of course money, conceived without soul, without an animal life of its own, without Gods, becomes crazy, anarchic, because we forget that like sex, like the sea, it, too, is a religious dominant.

Now I am referring back through the word itself to the Goddess Moneta, the Roman equivalent of Mnemosyne meaning *memoria, imaginatio,* Mother of the Muses. In her temple of Moneta, money was kept; in the word "money," a temple too, Moneta reappears. Money is thus a deposit of mythical fantasies. It is a treasury that mothers and remembers images. Money is imaginative, as I have been saying. Thus, money in the hand awakens imaginal possibilities: to do this, go there, have those. It reveals the Gods which dominate my fantasies — Saturnian tightness, Jupiterian generosity, Martial show, Venusian sensuality. Money provokes my behavior into mythical fantasies, so very different in different people. Why should people agree about money — where to invest it, on what to spend it, which horse to put it on? It is a truly polytheistic phenomenon in everyday life. As such, coined money is a highly cultural phenomenon. It came into history with the Greeks and not before them. It belongs in the constellation of the Muses, necessary to imaginal culture, and hence it does become devilish when imagination is not valued. The ugliness, the power corruption, the purely quantitative nature of money today is not money's fault, but that of its having been severed and then fallen from the Gods from which it came.

Of all the fallen fields of human endeavor, economics must take first place, which therefore locates its high priests on Hell's lowest ring. In no other discipline does the reign of quantity hold such sway. Economics abstracts money into theoretical laws, cleans its animal stench — no longer filthy lucre and the root of all evil but rather a "science" fit to be included among the Nobel awards.

Where astrophysics and microbiology rely on imagination, the disciples of economics seem unable to admit money as an incalculable psychic factor in their formulae of economic forces and projections The "un"-imagination of economics shows up in its obsession with growth, a concept transported from biology implying an innate life force in money. Thus, we ordinary consumers take for granted that the GDP should grow, that gradual inflation is an organic necessity of capitalism, that deflation and depression be held off at all costs. Grow or die is the *mantra*, further establishing the fantasy of the business corporation as a legitimate person with a right to life and a need to expand.

Is it money itself that wants to grow? Is this a subliminal compulsion stemming from its animal history? Is it money itself that invents compound interest, derivatives, options — modes of generating money out of money? What possesses a quiet citizen looking over his or her assets as the books close at the end of the year to want to see larger numbers than the years previous? No matter how much I might have — three hundred thousand, millions more in property, my condo, my land — I want to see the three become four and then five. Reason cannot account for this rage for ever-higher numbers, exceeding all relations with the cost-of-living index, keeping up with inflation and what I'll need for retirement. No matter how much money one owns, it never states itself as enough. No limits — like the seas.

Money has captured the notion of freedom, weakening its spiritual and political import so that freedom has narrowed to mean free-market economics: the free flow of goods and labor, floating exchange rates, elimination of tariff barriers, open markets, and boundless growth trickling down to the parched level of the dirt-poor. This subtle substitution of unrestricted growth for freedom eventually leads to Libertarianism. Freedom devolves into egoistic economic anarchy — social Darwinism and Hobbes. No sooner free, then opposition arises: left wing ideals of societal responsibility with graduated communitarianism. Or the right-wing companion of Libertarian excess: a super-ego God of moral

prohibition whose commandments are evoked to curb predatory capitalism in which competition fosters the daily bread of covetousness,
theft, false witness, and yes, sophisticated kinds of killing.

III

Let me now connect this theme with another at this Congress; training. On occasion candidates have explained to me that one reason
for their wanting to train is that analytical practice offers a noble way
of earning money. So much of the world's work is soulless, they say,
while analysis pays one for staying with soul, without having to open
a head shop, teach guitar, throw pots, or home-grow squash and to-
matoes. One does not have to be economically marginal. The analyst
combines soul and money; analytical money is good, clean money,
and even well paid. Training tempts, evidently, because it resolves the
Christian dilemma of shekel versus soul without having to follow the
spiritual solution of poverty.

The resolution of a pair of opposites, however, only perpetuates their
opposition: the third requires the other two for it to be a third. Only
when we can step altogether out of the dilemma that divides money
(and soul) into spiritual and material oppositions can we see that there
is psyche in money all the time in every way, that it is kind of "poetry,"
that it is wholly and utterly psychological. Consequently, it needs no
redeeming into good, clean and noble money, and no repressing into
the poverty and asceticism of the spirit turned against matter.

In fact, that equation "money = psyche" suggests that there is more
soul to be found where money problems are most extreme, not in poverty but in luxury, miserly greed, covetousness, and the joy of usury,
and that the fear of money and the importance of money in some persons may be more psychologically devastating, and therefore therapeutically rewarding, than sexual fears and impotence. Extraordinary
demons start up when the money complex is touched. And no complex
is kept hidden with more secrecy. Patients more readily reveal what is
concealed by their pants than what is hidden in their pants pockets.
Freudians who see purses as female genital symbols may discover more
by making the reduction in the reverse direction.

Where exactly is the money complex hidden? Most often it hides in the guises of love, where so much soul is anyways hidden. As Tawney showed, Protestantism and capitalism enter the world together. And, after all these centuries, they still hold hands in mutual affection in so many Protestant families where giving, receiving, saving, participating, supporting, spending, willing (inheritance) are the ways one learns about loving. "Spending" for a long time in English had both a genital and a monetary meaning, while the words bond, yield, safe, credit, duty, interest, share, and debt (as *Schuld* or guilt) all bear double meanings of love and money. The double meanings double-bind; to Protestant-capitalist consciousness, renouncing the family's psychological attitudes often becomes refusing money from home which is felt at home as a rebuff of love. The money = psyche equation is a powerful variant of the Eros and Psyche myth where money stands in for love.

But finally, what does money do for the soul: what is its specific function in "possibilizing" the imagination? It makes the imagination possible in the world. Soul needs money to be kept from flying off into the Bardo realm of "only-psychic" reality. Money holds soul in the vale of the world, in the poetry of the concrete, in touch with the sea as facts, those hard and slippery facts, so perduring, annoying, and limiting, and ceaselessly involving one in economic necessity. For economy means originally "house-holding," making soul in the vale of the world, charging and being overcharged, scrimping and splurging, exchanging, bargaining, evaluating, paying off, going in debt, speculating.

Thus fee negotiation, whether in Dr. Vasavada's style or Dr. Covitz's, is a thoroughly psychological activity. Fee payment may take many styles, from dirty dollar bills plunked on the table before the hour begins to gifts and deals and wheedling, or the discreetly passed envelope to the abstract medical model of depersonalized forms, checks, and monthly statements. And the old joke is always true: "When the man says, 'it ain't the money; it's the principle — it's the money.'" It is the money where the real issue lies. Money is an irreducible principle.

Analysis, as the candidates have perceived, indeed lets soul and money meet. The spirituality of the Christian division is suspended: one renders unto the Gods and Caesars in one and the same payment. We pay tribute to the costliness of soul work, that it is rare, precious, most dear. And we pay out the common buck "for professional services rendered," a phrase equally appropriate to the physician, the plumber, and the whore.

That analysts have trouble justifying their outrageous fees (and at the same time feel they never earn enough compared with lawyers and dentists) belongs to the archetypal nature of money as we have been viewing it. The money question can no more be regulated so as to settle into easiness than can sex or the sea. The underpart stems into the many directions of our complexes. That we cannot settle the money issue in analysis shows money to be one main way the mothering imagination keeps our souls fantasizing. So, to conclude with my part of this panel, Soul and Money: yes, soul *and* money: we cannot have either without the other. To find the soul of modern man or woman, begin by searching into those irreducible embarrassing facts of the money complex, that crazy crab scuttling across the floors of silent seas.

1. Cf. William H. Desmonde, *Magic, Myth and Money: The Origin of Money in Religious Ritual* (New York: The Free Press of Glencoe, 1962), pp. 109–19.
2. Dr. Covitz and Dr. Vasaveda present contrasting approaches to charging for professional psychological services.
3. Charles Olson, *The Maximus Poems* (New York: Jargon/Corinth Books, 1960), p. 2.
4. Cf. my "Silver and the White Earth," *Spring 1980*, pp. 35–37, for a discussion of coinage.

37

Welcoming Toast to Soviet Guests

Ladies and gentlemen, most welcome and most honored citizens from the Soviet Union and its Republics, distinguished guests and gracious hosts.

Thank you for allowing me to be here with you this afternoon and to speak my thoughts. This day, June 14th, is a special one in my calendar. On this date in 1946, forty-four years ago, I stepped ashore on the soil of Europe in Bremerhaven, not finally returning to this country — so was I held by the sway of Europe! — until 1978, thirty-two years later. I tell this personal tale only to say that my heart belongs in both continents, and that welcoming Europeans here is a continuing inner process of welcoming into my American soul that part of me that is European.

In keeping with the theme of this meeting, I have put to myself the psychological question: what is the most apocalyptic fantasy, the most frightening idea that I can imagine? I have tried to keep away from those I have already imagined. These I already know — world plague, AIDS, genetic mutations, nuclear winter, Holy Wars of genocide, invasion of aliens, collision of planets, financial collapse, releasing The Four Horsemen, greenhouse climatology, extended pollution, starvation, and a Great New War — these are indeed terrifying. But they are already on the evening news. They are the doom familiar, the already imagined end-of-the-world, and therefore less *psychologically* menacing because they are less unconscious.

These remarks were made at the Second "Facing Apocalypse" Conference, Newport, R.I., June 1990.

So, I have turned inward, away from world catastrophe, the "out there" as place of catastrophe, to myself, a Western man, to my subjectivity, my psyche in search of the apocalyptic fantasy of — not world as such — but *Weltbild*, world view.

The world view that I most cling to, that supports my behavior and reflections and which I most fear losing is the very one I am expressing now: this "I," this subjectivity, this sense of "me" as interlocutor and answerer. My individuality. To lose it means either anonymous mass man, a victim of forces, slavery, psychosis, loss of moral center, a center of will and freedom of choice and action, imprisonment, hence also evil, depression, and paralysis. Not even suicide, since that is an individual's act.

The world view of individualism has become our mythology. It is the source of our psychology of persons, our fascination with personal biography, and our theology of Gods locus in the individual soul, as well as the theology of the salvation of the individual soul, to say nothing of our economics of individual invention and enterprise. We believe thought goes on in individual minds, feeling in our personal hearts, and that our names refer to a reality inside our skins.

For millennia this was not the case. Tribal culture, even high cultures such as the Egyptian, do not, did not, live in an individualistic *Weltbild*. Names reflected the Gods, the plants, animals, and the world out there. Whatever "I" am is what they are.

This sense of the dissolution of the subjective personal into the wider world is a revelation given to C.G. Jung in his very old age and reported by him on the last page of his autobiography, *Memories, Dreams, Reflections*. Allow me to read from it:

> When Lao-tsu says, "All are clear, I alone am clouded," he is expressing old age . . . This is old age, and a limitation. Yet there is so much that fills me: plants, clouds, day and night . . . The more uncertain I have felt about myself, the more there has grown in me a feeling of kinship with all things. In fact it seems to me as if that alienation which so long separated me from the world has become transferred into my own inner world, and has revealed to me an unexpected unfamiliarity with myself.

A welcoming toast after dinner is hardly the moment to make complex philosophical arguments about subjectivity. However, my readings in Russian literature do suggest that such talk is not strange to
you, our guests, even if not usual here at home. Our American style is
entertainment. I shall be helping your digestion by helping you feel
happy, avoiding the serious because it could be unpleasant.

So I'll conclude with this little, and rather apocalyptic fantasy:

Some in the West, in Washington, D.C. especially, believe that the
Wall and Iron Curtain came down because the West "won." Capitalist
individualism beat — like a football game — socialist collectivism.
Another term for capitalist individualism is "consumerism." Consumerism is rather like what the Church might once have called the sins of
gluttony, envy, and curiosity. Western individualism has declined into
consumerism, and the apocalyptic fantasy that most threatens individualism plays itself out in the haunting fear displayed so brutally in
Eastern Europe and the Soviet Republics: empty shelves. My individuality is emptied out, voided, if I cannot affirm my subjective will by
accumulating and consuming.

The idea that consumerism has won the Cold War actually maintains the Wall of that war, because it maintains the curtain between
individualism and collectivity, which I prefer to call *Gemeinschaftsgefühl*
or communal feeling. So long as I go on thinking that individualism is
victorious, I am imagining the individual opposed to and defensively
against collective, communal feeling.

I prefer a different fantasy about the raising of the Curtain and the
fall of the Wall. I prefer to imagine that individualism is no longer
needed as a defense against the collectivity called Soviet Communism.
When the Wall is down, then defensive individualism is also down.
Then Hermes opens the gates to an exchange of a free flow of feeling
in which individualism flows into the community and the individual
becomes communal. We recognize how collective we each are, really,
and nowhere better expressed than in the utter collectivity of our consumerism.

A change takes place on both sides of the old Curtain — not only on
your Eastern side. For now on our side I, this individual, can no longer
regard myself, my *proprium*, as a private possession or my consumption

as my individual expression and right. In fact, the defeat of the former enemy — as the defensive individualism likes to imagine the fall of the Wall — has in fact brought about my own defeat. The apocalypse has happened. The old "I" has been wiped out.

Now Karl Marx can return from the lands to which he was exported, return back home to his main concerns: Western Society; return from his literalized locus in history, positivism, economics, materialism; return to his deepest concern: his *Gemeinschaftsgefühl*, for the "exploited," who have nothing to lose but their chains, the people dulled by the opiates of belief. Let us remember according to Marx: "Criticism of religion is the foundation of all criticism." And today, Western religion manifests as the belief in individualism, the literalism of my personal subjectivity. That is the God who determines my life by giving me the myth that it is *my* life.

Who are the exploited today? It is no longer the proletariat industrial worker, no longer the share-cropper serf. Today the exploited are the very ones exploited by their beliefs, the victims of unconscious religion. It is the religion of individualism, the belief in consumerism that won the victory. I am the exploited, I, the media-information, mass-marketed consumer, believing in the fantasy of my choices, living the religion of individualism. This fantasy succeeds in locking us each away from the actual world, its interdependence, its deep ecology, its communal brother- and sisterhood with the plants, animals and clouds, a vision of communal collective destiny so that individualism can be emptied out, dissolved, apocalypticized, a Dionysian *Lysis*, a loosening of boundaries, the collapse of the final wall: the fantasy wall of separated individualism and its cult of personality.

Ladies and Gentlemen: A Toast!

To the return of Karl Marx to his Western homeland, de-literalized, de-historicized, de-economized, de-constructed — and to a compassionate vision for a just society implied by his work.

38

Farewell to Welfare

Before we get into this hot and tangled topic symbolized into the word "welfare," I do need to offer you a justification for my presence. After all, why a psychologist? Surely the issues of welfare belong to experts of social theory and public policy, to the case workers in the front line, to the economists of cost benefit analysis, and no less, perhaps above all, to the administrators of churches, charities, and foundations.

I do believe that these usual confines of expertise too tightly box our topic, which may be one reason for the heat and the tangle. Hot and tangled issues ask for a wider level of reflection, a step back and a step outside, less data, more questions. And this is where psychology comes in. The tangle may result from the narrow angles of special interests.

To apply a psychotherapeutic method to a public case as if it were a private person requires that we first of all consider the context, the situation in which the mess appears.

Not that reflection means a cool head only, since the issues of welfare call loudly to the heart. This heart, my heart, is the second justification, for my presence as a person now and not only as a professional. For this person, this me, has a passionate concern with the welfare of millions of my fellows, especially children and youth and the future welfare of my nation. Or, better said, youth *is* the future welfare of our nation.

Public lecture given at a civic forum co-sponsored by the Analytical Psychology Society of Western New York, The Western New York Foundation, and twenty other public and private institutions in Buffalo, N.Y., in November 1997, and first published as a booklet by the Analytical Psychology Society of Western New York in 2001.

Another explanation that may justify a psychologist in the presence of your forum: in recent years I have more and more shifted my
psychological practice from the individual psyche in the consulting
room to the wider psyche in the public arena, and its deeper roots in
root ideas. I call my work now a therapy of ideas rather than a therapy
of persons. For I have learned that persons suffer unwittingly from the
influence of impersonal ideas as much as from personal relationships,
memories, fears, and traumas.

Ideas we do not know we have, have us. They hold our minds in
their grip. This means that therapy of people and their problems cannot proceed without therapy of ideas and their problems. This also
means that therapy today goes back long before Freud and Jung, back
to Socrates and Aristotle. Aristotle said, famously, "Man is by nature a
political animal." The human being has a political instinct, is by nature
a citizen. This instinct, too, must be satisfied. If we are not in the political arena in some way or another, we are instinctually deprived. The
consulting room is usually too narrowly personal. Therapy requires
recognition of the political instinct.

Socrates made even clearer the relation between what goes on in
the state of the nation and the state of the soul. Tangles in the mind are
also tangles in the body politic, for Socrates. His idea of justice meant
both the right order within the individual and the right order within
society; both together, inseparable. This implies for you and me that
we cannot put in order the personal welfare of our souls unless we address the welfare of society.

The tangled mind usually tries to untie its binds by pulling on two
ends of the string. Every issue gets caught in this oppositional pull,
for and against. Adversarial debate becomes the one method we apply
to every different kind of tangle, an American knee-jerk response, an
American addictive idea. Liberal or Conservative, right or left, pro-life
or choice — two sides to every question: school vouchers, affirmative
action, global warming, and of course, welfare. If only the other side
would let go of its end, all would be simple and straight. Trying to
straighten things in this oppositional manner only builds more heat
and tightens the knot. We citizens caught by the heat, burn out; our
hands let go in despair. "These problems can never be solved; over-

whelming, too big, too complicated." Yet the very way we approach issues — the logic of either/or and two sides to every question — that is partly responsible for the polarization of our society and the malaise among our citizens.

The idea of welfare does not escape this TV-style of adversarial debate. The first question asked about my talk this evening was boxed into this mind-set: "Are you for or against welfare reform? What side are you on?" At once I felt hot with anger and tangled up trying to answer.

My answer, though, is clear: I am on the side of the problem. As a therapist, I am always on the side of the issue, the problem, and the symptom. We go where it's hot. You can't do anything about anything unless you first side with it, get inside it, and explore its hidden ideas. And this is exactly what I want us to be doing this evening: enter the tangle and sort through some ideas.

To finish off with this personal preamble let me lay out the starting point for what follows. It is the Preamble of the Constitution of the United States. The Preamble declares the intention, the reasons for the Constitution, one of which is: "to promote the general welfare."

Here are the actual words that formulate the original American Dream:

> We, the People of the United States, in order to form a more perfect union, establish justice, insure domestic tranquility, provide for the common defense, promote the general welfare, and secure the blessings of liberty to ourselves and our posterity, do ordain and establish this Constitution for the United States of America.

Depression and the Dream

The first thread I would like to follow is spun of pure gold, or is it fake gold? Hard to tell. But surely, woven all through the welfare problem is the American Dream. The American Dream, that began with im-migrant visions of gold in the streets and even earlier with colonists' visions of a new Jerusalem, supports our most noble ambitions and craven schemes.

Yet our pursuit of happiness is itself pursued by unhappy shadows. Inside, the white picket fence and upholstered home of happiness ap-pliances; outside, a procession throughout our history of half-breeds, slaves, tramps, runaways, urchins, vagrants, hoboes, beggars, cripples, bums, drunks, hustlers, junkies, wetbacks, bag ladies, street people and homeless. Different decades, different outcasts, different names.

Two newer categories have emerged to spoil the golden dream, ap-plying to those mainly outside the white fence. One comes from soci-ology, the "underclass," and we shall come back to it. The other from psychiatry, the "depressed." Let's look at the idea of depression.

Depression has only recently been discovered to be endemic in the American population. Depression is today the major psychopathology afflicting our compatriots, afflicting even those who do not know that they have it — like early stages of AIDS or TB or syphilis. But it can be "discovered" by mental health testing, and treated mainly by patented, that is, expensive, highly profitable drugs.

The diagnosis of depression affects thinking about welfare because one word, "depression," combines both economics and psychology, suggesting that any downward trend in economics points toward dis-ease and any melancholic phase in personal psychology could herald economic disaster. I must keep smiling, up and running, or go broke. Economic growth may not slow down else we citizens may become sad with regrets and remorse. Look forward, not back. So, Prozac and its companions become necessary for maintaining both our individual health and our national welfare.

Yet, depression remains endemic. The superb health of the economy is not accompanied by the health of the people. The two, health and wealth, seem, in fact, to move in different directions — health going down as wealth goes up. One simple statistic: "More children and adolescents in the United States today die from suicide than from cancer, AIDS, birth defects, influenza, heart diseases, and pneumonia *combined*." The United States ranks below Iran and Romania in the percentage of low birth-weight babies. *At least* fifteen million children today are living below the official poverty line. Depressing statistics; statistics of depression. The link between depression and welfare is a correlation, not a causal relation. Depression may result as well from the state of their economics as from the state of their psyches.

We may not assume a rising tide raises all boats. Depression is sinking some.

Besides the pathology of the dejected trooping by outside the picket fence, another pathology syndrome seems to have crept inside: domestic violence. It is not enough well known that you are more likely to be raped, beaten, or killed in the home than out in the street. The private home — that essential image of the American Dream — is in general the most dangerous place to be.

In short, shadows of unhappiness pursue the American Dream despite the golden brilliance of our market economy. And this shadow is projected upon and carried by welfare.

This leads to the idea that by reforming welfare into workfare, bringing into the productive economy the parade of so-called undeserving rejects and misfits whom I listed, both the health and the wealth of the nation would improve. Yet, recent trends show the two, health and wealth, in negative correlation. Not merely do they not go up and down together, but when wealth goes up, health seems to decline. As the GNP grows, Medicare costs also escalate, and even faster than economic growth. And this escalation is not only to be blamed on the abundance of physicians, the complexities of diagnostics, the scams and profits in insurance and health providers, the limitless awards in malpractice suits, the environmental aspects of illness, the aging population, overeating, the high charges for high tech equipment, and profit margins in drugs and hospital supplies.

The psychiatric thread of endemic depression leads deeper in to the body politic than more efficiently managing health care costs. The thread does suggest a cruel conclusion. Could there be an inverse relation between health and wealth in our society? If increased wealth in our society as a whole (standard of living, gross domestic product) runs parallel with less health (rise of endemic depression, cancer risk, sexually transmitted diseases, tuberculosis, dysfunctional families, obesity, learning disabilities, childhood dyspnea), dare we conclude that as our society becomes more wealthy, it also becomes less healthy? And may we surmise that the failing health, especially depression, be indirectly supportive of increasing wealth, actually benefiting the oligarchic economic system?

Perhaps nothing better suits the rulers than that the ruled are depressed, inert, passive, unable to resist, rebel, or revolt, that is, a lamed political instinct, believing their depression is utterly, as contemporary psychiatry would insist, internal, personal, a disorder to be treated with medicines, and not linked to the wider economic system and aesthetic milieu in which it occurs. Unbridled late-stage capitalism euphemistically called "a free-market economy" aims in one direction only. It is single-mindedly obsessed with growth of profit, which throws the shadow of depression into society as downsizing, pink slips, expansion of debt and bankruptcies. Also forced higher productivity. Just one example: in the last ten years workspace of the white-collar office worker has been cut 25%. Confinement in ever-smaller partitions in the vast "open office," as they are happily named, surely must exacerbate feelings of claustrophobia, entrapment, and yes, depression.

Let's now take up another thread.

Laziness

Classical ideas about welfare show a standard division between the deserving and undeserving poor. In the first group are those who are infirm, aged, and temporarily or chronically handicapped ("challenged" is today's term), widows without support, as well as seasonal layoffs whose dire straits are only accidental and contingent. These deserving poor are imagined to be hard workers, honest job seekers, morally straight. They deserve a handout or a leg up.

The undeserving poor, however, supposedly have marginal morals, are substance addicted, often with criminal records, unskilled, uneducated, endlessly promiscuous, crafty, untrustworthy, and in the popular white imagination composed predominantly of a non-white population (which is not borne out by the fact). Above all, they don't really want to work. Instead, they turn welfare into a way of life, cheating with food stamps, moonlighting, dealing, and riding on the backs of honest taxpayers by exploiting the underground economy as well as all social services, public and private, that they learn about through the grapevine.

About food stamps: twenty percent of the households receiving food stamps include a disabled person. Are these recipients morally undeserving or physically unable? Fifty percent of those receiving food stamps are children. Are these recipients lazy, or hungry? Is underperformance in school due to bad habits or bad diet?

In recent years the idea of the undeserving poor has been conceptualized into the "underclass." The psychology of members of this class sharply contrasts with the deserving hardworking poor who are simply down on their luck. Not only does this underclass not want to work; they are stigmatized as fundamentally shiftless. They incorporate the idea of laziness. Moreover, it is argued that welfare promotes this inherent laziness.

Let me explain how this idea of laziness infiltrates our minds. Since poverty persists despite the enormous welfare programs, the War against Poverty of the Johnson administration, and despite the attempts to resolve it as far back as the thirties when Roosevelt called attention to the one third of a nation, ill-fed, ill-clothed, and ill-housed, and despite the charities, their workers and donors, and the kindness of strangers, there must be something fundamentally wrong with the welfare effort itself.

Since the poor are still with us, a stubborn fault must lie in their nature. After all, "poor people have poor ways" — as my unreconstructed grandfather from Mississippi used to say. Are they inherently, incorrigibly unhelpable? This further implies to some minds that welfare agencies may actually be aiding and abetting this inherent laziness. Collusion: the crafty poor are taking us taxpayers for a ride with the help of bleeding-heart social workers.

Ruthlessly, the argument continues: by externalizing the inner drive to be agent of one's own life, to take charge and get going, social agencies reinforce the passivity of the underclass who prefer to sit around or screw around, talk, smoke, drink and hang. Welfare, supposedly, lames the work ethic, depriving its recipients of their bootstrapping initiative, which, in this so-called underclass, is anyway defective and deficient.

The idea of inherent laziness, or passivity, to use the psychological term, echoes one of the classical seven deadly sins, sloth, defined in Catholic philosophy as an "indolent shunning of exertion." That laziness is inherent in the poor, and that's why they are poor, condemns them to a circle in Hell, and to the vicious circle in actuality of circular repetitive degradation. We do not really expect them to break the circle. They can't; too lazy.

We need to recognize here how much contempt for all human nature, and not only the nature of the poor, is insinuated by this idea of laziness. For the idea — an idea shared even by some classical Jungians — makes us believe that stupidity and inertia are more fundamental than enterprise and ambition, that humans basically hate useful activity, that people must be urged (motivated is today's term) to learn and to work, as if desires of enterprise were less natural, less basic than laziness. The fear of downtime, of wasted time, of lazy time in ourselves and the projection of it onto others seems immensely widespread. Think of the English colonials sipping tea and finding the Irish and the Africans lazy; think of southern planters reclining on their verandas seeing laziness in their slaves. A clinching example of the projection we find in Iceland, where anthropologists have reported that Icelanders on the north coast say that those on the south coast are lazy, enjoying the sun and drink, not good workers, unscrupulous, and so forth. Projections of laziness on others, as if embedded in their character, completely omits the degrading conditions to which the others submit — slavery, colonialism, or in the case of welfare, hunger, poverty, ugliness, dirt, and bureaucracy. So when we try to think more clearly about welfare, let's extract from the tangle this thread of inherent laziness.

Cheating

We have looked into laziness, now let's look at cheating. This theme runs through much of our political life today, from local politics, income tax reform, white-collar crime, corporate subsidies, campaign financing, etc. None, however, are more accused of cheating than those on welfare roles. Against them we throw the whole of William Bennet's *Book of Virtues.*

To look into the idea of cheating, I need to intersperse something from another founding document, not ours though one considerably older and larger than ours, the *Mahabharata,* that mammoth collection — eight times longer than the *Odyssey* and *Iliad* of Homer combined — of myths, legends, teachings, moral instructions, and practical counsel for daily conduct. In India they say, "If you do not find it in the *Mahabharata,* you will not find it in the world."

What you can learn from this savvy and outlandish compendium is a great deal about cheating. For instance it presents forty ways of embezzlement. In a section on "proper conduct" — shall we say "politically correct behavior" — you will find these methods described: gifts or bribery; conciliatory obsequious, even servile, charm; maya or deceit, fraud, trickery and magic; overlooking or deliberately neglecting, turning a blind eye.

Cheating operates in a variety of styles. More important than these descriptions, however, is the justification, the morality of cheating, yes the morality of cheating. I quote [Book XII of the *Mahabharata*]:

> The last word of social wisdom is, never trust.
> Might is above right; right proceeds from might.
> When thou findest thyself in a low state, try to lift thyself
> up, resorting to pious as well as to cruel actions.
> Before practicing morality, wait until thou art strong.

The *Mahabharata* gives me the psychological ground for attacking Mr. Bennet and his Virtues. His virtues are for the haves applied to the have-nots. They should just say "no"; should not cheat on welfare. They should tell the truth. Does the Pentagon, the CIA, the

White House, the Party spokespersons, the Justice Department, the Criminal Justice system? The Department of Housing and Urban Development ran one of the greatest scams in our history during the Reagan years, and this was the department directly responsible for improving inner city blight.

The maxims from the *Mahabharata* bear on our theme. They say, in short, that the rulers and the ruled follow different rules. If right follows might, then the haves must obey the rules of virtue — no scams, no bribes, no tax evasions, no cruelness, fraud, deceit, or perjury. But, it is not "proper conduct" to expect from the powerless what is expected of the powerful. In short, if the government and institutions are not open and honest with its disempowered citizens, then we may not expect that these citizens be open and honest with government and institutions. It is for the mighty to be righteous: they must apply their rules to themselves, the rulers, before inflicting them on the ruled as a further mode of disempowering them.

Figures Don't Lie

At least, figures don't lie. If people cheat, we can turn to numbers. All government departments that have to do with welfare from the Government Accounting Office to the Bureau of the Budget rely on figures upon which we base our political positions, and eventually frame laws, like the welfare reform bill.

Now, a most curious thing has happened over the years to the idea of figures. They have become numbers. In English, figure referred to a person seen as a visible form, a usage that expanded to mean figures of speech, figures of imagination, figurative language, and also to figure as to imagine. Only in the middle of the last century with industrial capitalism on the rise was the word appropriated by arithmetic to mean number, and then it was that figure entered our language as a verb meaning to reason or calculate, as when we say, your figures just don't figure.

The process by which economics takes over words needs to be remembered, for it implies the tyrannical colonizing of economics over all other kinds of thought. Just look at the words that once carried

deep psychological value and how they now belong to banks, bro-
kers, and speculators: trust, interest, growth, goods, develop, security,
bond, share, insure, yield, loss, demand, appreciation, industry.

"Welfare" itself went through a radical change. "Welfare," the word
as we know it, is barely fifty years old. Long, long ago, welfare meant
"happiness, good health, or fortune." As well it meant, "Good cheer,
extravagant living, or entertainment." We have come a long way from
this sense of welfare as when we scold those who use food stamps to
buy shrimp and lobster and fresh farm-market produce rather than the
dreary convenience store basics appropriate to the needy. So, to say
"farewell welfare" means both waving it goodbye and also wishing it
good cheer and good fortune.

These amazing changes in the meaning of words — changes which
have made words so much meaner — partly derive from this basic
transformation of figure into number.

Originally, the word figure, from Latin, meant form or shape; the
way something is fashioned; appearance, visibility. Much as we still
say, "that woman has a good figure." *Figura* in Italian means a face card
(Jack, Queen, King); the French *figure* means simply face; in Spanish,
hacer figuras means to make facial grimaces. In short, the figures of welfare are the faces of welfare.

The human face demands an ethical response. It is the most immediate, personal, and salient fact of our existence as human beings.
I take this idea directly from our century's most profound ethical philosopher who died in France just a few years ago, Emmanuel Levinas.
He re-founded philosophy on a moral basis rather than on a logical,
linguistic, or metaphysical one. His, we might say, is an existentialism
of the face which carries echoes of the religious implications of the
face of Jahweh and the face of Jesus. The face of a person presents a
claim; it asks for a response; it requires direct acknowledgement. Facts
alone cannot lead to just decisions; we must *face* the facts, that is, return welfare numbers to actual figures.

Here we meet the great divide between those who make the laws
and construct the budgets, the buildings, and the bureaucracies of welfare and those who climb the stairs, meet the cases, and visit the cells,
one by one, face to face.

The claim of the face still forms our news with the camera right in the face of the mother of a shot child, the survivor of a fire, a flood — all worldly goods gone. This is prime-time news because it is not abstract. And, as the world becomes more and more abstract — witness the computer — and more faceless, as figures dissolve into numbers, and as problems search for numerical solutions only, the frontal fact of persons in their misery and tragedy become more like affronts. We say cheap, sensational, exploitative, intrusive. But these are the facts with faces. And the homeless bag lady, the child who sleeps in a cardboard carton, the disheveled vet, those we turn from looking at, looking into the eyes of — is where the reforms of all abstract figurings of welfare truly must take their start.

In "Circus Animals' Desertion," Yeats writes,

> . . . out of what began?
> Old kettles, old bottles, and a broken can,
> Old iron, old bones, old rags, that raving slut
> Who keeps the till. Now that my ladder's gone,
> I must lie down where all the ladders start,
> In the foul rag-and-bone shop of the heart.

Church and State

As we come towards a close, I want to tug on one huge submerged rope tied to what anchors our nation in the deeps of its dream: the separation of Church and State.

Western history shows that both nobles and clergy helped the poor carry their loads. Of course, both also oppressed the poor and both were responsible for the penurious conditions in European history and its colonizing which so largely influenced our own.

Kings and Queens distributed alms, received petitions, healed by laying on of hands. The clergy provided sanctuaries and built hostels of refuge, made charity their province and took the oath of poverty themselves. At least one moral ideal set the aims for both church and state: charity, mercy, dignity, justice, magnanimity must govern human actions. John Quincy Adams stated this forcefully and clearly in his presidential message to Congress: "The great object of civil government is the improvement of the conditions of those who are parties to the social compact."

As time went on and for all sorts of reasons, especially the reason of reason itself, a hard line, a wall of stone, stood between church and state. To the church fell the lot of the needy. Care and compassion belong to its calling and accord with religious principles whatever the creed or denomination. The principle of separation allowed the state to justify its negligence. The principle of separation promotes a careless state. The indigent are not among the state's concerns unless they disturb domestic tranquility or prevent a more perfect union. Nothing in the Constitution says the state shall *provide* welfare. The verb is promote, not provide.

Separation of Church and State also tends to separate law and conscience, so that the word guilt loses its moral inwardness — becoming only an external legal description sometimes at odds with the larger idea of justice.

This wall, of course, has large holes. The state provides all sorts of services to promote the general welfare. Moreover, direct public relief at public expense has a long American tradition. Schools, hospitals, asylums, fire and police protection, public health, veteran's benefits, transportation, subsidies, prisons. All this, yes. But what about welfare, especially of the so-called "undeserving" and "underclass?" Are they the state's obligation? Yes, if we follow the Preamble. "To promote the general welfare" insures domestic tranquility and establishes justice for a more perfect union, since a house divided cannot stand, whether this division is between races or economic classes.

A strict construction of separation implies that the obligations of charity belong to the church. May the state then tithe its citizens for charitable purposes and redistribute their wealth? Is it not more in keeping with the separation of Church and State to let the rich give to the poor according to conscience and belief rather than to have their gains taken from them by the graduated income tax? Let private charities do the job! This opinion circulated widely during the Reagan era.

Only in 1913, after the gilded age and its robber barons, was the income tax amended to the Constitution. To some, this breached the

wall between church and state, redistributing wealth by law instead of
by will. So today the prospect of a tax reform by means of the simplici-
ties of flat tax and sales tax equitably assessed on all alike adds another
strand to the tangle of welfare. For without the graduated income tax,
would not even less money trickle down from top to bottom?

The noble aim of separation — to assure a tolerant state — has
fostered a shadow side. The state becomes only a secular bureaucratic
necessity, and its workers less servants of the people than functionar-
ies of the system. We forget the state is the instrument of the national
will, the institutionalization of its ideals and the practical manifestation of its heart. We forget the state is founded for the public good, as
the Preamble declares "to promote the general welfare."

Conclusion

I want to leave you with three closing ideas. The first two are cautions,
the last an appeal.

First, beware of taking capitalist free-market economics as a science,
as a progressively developing system, or as equivalent with and necessary to political democracy or our American Dream. The economy
that governs our lives is also a morality, a psychology, and even a
monotheistic belief which converts all values into its one bottom line.
Notice the distaff facts of this economic system: that forty million
people in our nation have incomes below the poverty line and 40%
of these people are children; that only 36% of unemployed workers
in 1993 got insurance while out of work compared with 75% twenty
years earlier; that at least two thirds of married couples' wives generate
earnings so as to keep up and pay the bills.

Bear in mind: one in four Americans falls below the poverty line
in the course of a decade. Why do young and able people fall into
poverty? Their uneducated stupidity? Their messed-up immoral personal psyches? Beer and cigarettes? TV? Something genetic that needs
medication? Or could their economic failure attest to the failure of
economics to guide a life?

Notice, too, the ideas of degradation concealed in economic arguments. For instance, poor single mothers are characterized as outside

the social norm, giving birth to bastards, whereas more and more actual births are to single mothers who are more and more the actual
norm. And it is not teenagers who dominate the field of non-marital
births. Why does our society always point the finger at youth? Only
30% of out-of-wedlock births are by teenage mothers (1995), whereas
35% are mature women over twenty-five years old. What about the
school dropouts even as schools upgrade — sometimes as corporate
gifts — their expensive computer instructional systems? What about
prison building, imprisoned youth, prison honor, while economic statistics show how much safer your streets are? Three strikes and you're
out — we're not talking baseball here; we're talking life!

And keep an eye on the Japanese model — oh, not on the team-
work and quality control that business tells about; but the other side
they don't tell about: business infiltrated by big-time crime. As Professor
Maurice Punch of the Netherlands School of Business writes about the
latest trends in business: "business provides a crimogenic arena: . . . the
virtual corporation [multinational, computerized] in a global economy
spells out rich new opportunities for corporate deviance . . . almost certainly the professions will become more deeply involved in criminal activities as the underworld comes increasingly to rely on the expertise of
lawyers, investment bankers, and computer specialists." Anyone here
able to recall the BCCI scandal; the S & L scam of billions bailed out by
you taxpayers?

Let us not forget: the reform of welfare aims at saving money and
not saving people, especially young people. It uses economic arguments to continue the historical American attack on the unsuccessful, the deviant, the weak — (a paradoxical attack on its own dream
of welcoming the oppressed and favoring the underdog). Their economic plight is blamed on their psychology and morals. We frighten
them with homelessness, or what were once called poorhouses. We
take away their children; we proscribe their sexuality; we cluster them
in ghettos; we dispossess them for debt and oppress them with usury.
And, of course, we put away as many as the jails can hold with nothing
for them when — or if — they come out.

By "we" I mean we, you and I, who participate in and maintain this
psychology of intimidation and injustice in the name of economics.

If we were not in passive accord, our voices would not be silent, our complicity so shameful.

One hundred years ago, Teddy Roosevelt took on the corporations, the monopolies, the trusts. So did the unions. There was dying in the streets, in the sweatshops and the mines. There was protest and rebellion against economic injustice. If the conditions of the 1990s resemble in principle those of the 1890s, then the citizens, you and I, need to shift our focus from self-help psychology — which also means help yourself and the devil take the hindmost — to what in the economic system makes so many of us feel we are helpless.

Second, do not consider welfare to be the true issue. It is more likely another one of the great diversions keeping us from feeling and focusing upon planetary extinction. Like the gender war, like racism, the future cyber-world, like diet and health, like self-help and spiritual growth, welfare keeps us human-centered and human-obsessed; all the while the globe is slowly dying. If the Titanic goes down, rich and poor, men and women, and all the colors of skin go down together. Promoting the general welfare must be re-conceived more widely as a true generality: this planet.

Deep ecology says the planet is the first priority and all human systems — the production and distribution of goods, the consumption of goods — must conform to patterns of the planet and serve its welfare. Social justice must be aligned with planetary justice. For instance, if the poor are raised to a higher standard of living, does this mean consumption increases, hastening ecological disaster as we see in Southeast Asia? Only when the exploitative ideas of unharnessed capitalist economics, coupled with the Neo-Darwinian fad of the selfish gene and soulless genetics, is seen through to its appalling moral psychology can we "promote the general welfare" that will mean the conservation of the planet.

In the last decades this nation has moved from a production economy to one of services. Services are the fastest expanding segment of the economy. We need as well to expand the idea of service. To whom, to what, for what do I serve? What ideals do I serve and what fears divert and demean my service? For services are not merely social services, to other humans for human values. To serve is the vocation to life, the calling to be here in this world on this planet so that it might fare well. Without these thoughts and feelings uppermost in our actions we are actually, daily, bidding farewell to this globe.

I have presented my two cautions. First, welfare reform begins with harnessing and bridling the runaway nightmare called free-market capitalism. Its reform would take the moral, psychological, and economic saddle off the poor, who are all, each and every one, undeserving of that burden. Second, welfare presented as an issue all of its own is a diversion unless reformulated within the context of promoting the general welfare of the planet.

Some advice from an older citizen: If we truly want to promote the welfare of the general, then we old ones especially have a task. It is for us to remember the Preamble's words about securing the blessings for our posterity. It is for us to ensure that the air is clean and the water good and plentiful, that all smaller abuses among individuals and families be reflected within the context of the larger abuses of the society as a whole, this nation, our tribe, of which we are the elders, representing the ancestors. It is for us to ensure that the soils are channeled with loving care, not Love Canals, and that the land our forefathers took away dishonorably from the natives and their Gods at least be honorably conserved, and that the blessings of our culture, its arts and its extraordinary cities, be fostered for posterity.

Grandfather! Grandmother! Come off the golf courses and the cruise ships! Who sold you the idea you "deserve?" Get back into the action conserving the ideals of the Constitution that supported the long life you have enjoyed. We have duties before dying, duties to ideals, to beauty and justice and truth and service. If the poor have been accused of the sin of sloth, then we have the sin of avarice on our backs. Between 1974 and 1994 children living in poverty increased by half, from 14% to 21%. During the same twenty years the percentage of elderly in poverty — though their actual numbers increased — went down from 16% to less than 12%. If the pie is limited as our leaders pretend, then we old ones are stealing from the young.

Let us worry less about security. Let us not become an airbag nation. Insurance-ridden, pension-planned, medicated, anesthetized, with a self-centered, single-issue pressure group called AARP, an association of the retired! Retirement? Let them put us on an ice floe and shove us out to sea on the day we are no longer valuable, but until then we have still much to give back. Have we not the task of elders?

We can aid in the construction of a healthy and just nation by deconstructing its — and our — unhealthy and unjust dependence on economic thinking. For then we could say farewell to welfare as we conceive it, at the same time say "fare ye well," fare forward with well wishes for accomplishing the American Dream, its ideals, its visions, attending to the true needs of its nature, its culture, its people who are first of all neither producers nor consumers, but in service, as we old ones must be. For we stand in for the ancestors. We are the grandfathers and grandmothers of the society. There must be grandiosity in our eyes, in our service to that society in the freedom of an enterprising spirit whose pursuit of happiness shows in each act of generosity, with malice towards none and charity for all.

39

Selling Out to Developers

To the Editor:

May I question your editorial judgment in giving main place to land development in your news and lead articles.

I moved to Thompson, Connecticut, from Dallas, Texas, after residing six years in the "heart" of that developers' paradise. The time there taught me that development panic is partly due to the reporting of it. When economic news is imagined to be the main news, it becomes the main news. To live in a house wondering what you could get for it, to look at your fields thinking of their bankable value, to consider a stone wall a capitalist asset — that is "Dallas."

And maybe it is all right there since the landscape offers little and there is much to build. But here, riches, beauty, and culture are around any bend. Yes, life does imitate TV, particularly "Dallas," but the *Observer Patriot* could be a holdout, part of the resistance movement, resisting the encroaches of so-called development by resisting encroaching developer mentality in its readers.

Panic happens not only when the bottom falls out. Northeast Connecticut knows about that; it's had hard times. Panic happens, too, when you rush for the bandwagon of big bucks. I know about that kind from Dallas.

Could it be that history is repeating itself around here? Long ago Native Americans sold out to the first developers (settlers) whose descendants may be selling with similar shortsightedness.

Letter to the Editor, published in the *Putnam Observer Patriot,* 19 March 1986.

40

Thompson Must Address Questions

To the Editor:

Many older towns and semi-rural communities have begun to resist big developers, whose experts and engineers rarely have a stake in the geography. Moreover, their ideas of progress are out of step with grassroot conservation.

An example of this antiquated, authoritative structure is the Thompson Water Pollution Control Authority. The following questions about the TWPCA and its sewer project must be addressed:

- Can the judgment and competence of the TWPCA be trusted in light of current investigations of appropriation of funds, recent resignations by two members of the committee and by the chairman?

- How wise was the decision to engage an engineering company involved in corruption of officials in Meriden, which resulted in the conviction and imprisonment of at least one of those officials?

- In whose interest is construction of a multimillion-dollar sewer for four of 72 properties declared unable to be rectified to meet current codes? Yet those same four properties have satisfactorily functioning waste-disposal facilities and could be grandfathered into compliance.

Letter to the Editor, published in the *Norwich Bulletin*, 15 April 2000.

- Why does the TWPCA project awarded to the Maguire Group have a significantly larger percent for management than that submitted by Lenard Engineering?

- Why did the TWPCA reject a high-tech, low-cost solution used successfully in other towns? This solution has many advantages over the old deep-dig, ledge-blasting and costly gravity system.

- Why have no caps been set on costs? Voters should know what potential financial burdens they may be assuming.

- Government funding is not guaranteed, so why have the consequences for the mill rate and bond rating not been publicized?

- What effect would more effluents have on the wastewater plant? The river? Eventual breakdowns, and our aquifer?

- Have residents been satisfactorily informed by town authorities of the effects of the expandable, large pipe, deep-dig system on old walls, trees, and house foundations, permanently impacting the character of a unique historic site?

- Why hasn't an independent Environmental Impact Study been done?

Until residents are truly informed about each of these questions and the option of a lower-cost, high-tech, shallow-trench sewer is thoroughly, openly, and democratically discussed, Thompson may best preserve its character and project its future by resisting top-down pressure, delaying hasty expenditures, and voting no on this funding referendum. Then our town can arrive at a more suitable compliance with the Department of Environmental Protection consent order.

41

City, Soul, and Myth

I

Since the first third of my title, City, has been widely and well expanded upon in these days of discussions, my job will pay more attention to Soul and Myth. And, curiously enough, the contemporary use of the word *soul* comes straight out of the city: soul music, soul food, soul brother, and soul sister. Not from the churchyard cemetery, but from the city streets. Less from suburbia and exurbia than from old neighborhoods and night town.

This intimacy between city and soul seems already given, that is, unless cut from each other by predefined ideas of efficient urban planning on the one hand — the city as a kind of technocrat's spaceship immune to fun, funk, and fury — and on the other hand, ideas of soul that keep it exclusively personalized, a chambered interiority quite apart from jostling on the public sidewalk.

The idea of soul that we shall now be pursuing has two sources, neither at all personal nor private. The first comes from John Keats: "consider the world the vale of soul-making, and then you will find the use of the world." The other is more ancient, all the way back to Plato and Renaissance thought: the idea of the *anima mundi* or soul in the world, of the world, inseparable except in abstract thought from one's own personal psyche. Both Keats and Plato imply the soul is all around us, or as the psychologist C.G. Jung wrote: not the psyche

Closing remarks at the "Symposium on Urban Transformation" at the Royal Society of Arts, Rhode Island School of Design, Providence, 7 June 2005.

is in me, but I am in the psyche. In the world of the street my soul is being made.

Street is implied by the very word for city in Greek. *Polis* means throng, crowd, flow, as the populace moves along the streets, the vehicles course along the highways, and currents of goods, ideas, and information circulate through the city gates. *Polis* in its roots connects with *poly* (many), with *plus* (more), *pleroma* (full), with *palude* (marshland, swamp).

If the inherent soul of the city reveals itself in the flow of "polis" — a word more in tune with connotations of "Liverpool" than of "Providence" — then perhaps it becomes clearer why there is such strong desire to straighten out cities, to organize them rationally, to maintain schedules, to plan for crowd control, and create academic departments of urban design. If the city is nominally related to the swamp and threatened with overcrowding and overpopulation, the congestion caused by the city's historic drawing power, then of course planning imagines renewal as opening, widening, clearing, hastening as did Paris with Haussmann, New York by Moses, or Washington, D.C., the enlightenment city par excellence raised upon swamplands. Our projects recapitulate in our projects the earliest myths of city-building, of civilization: Gilgamesh constructing the thick walls of Uruk against the primeval chaos; Marduk, founder of Babylon, overcoming the swamp monster Tiamat. So the bulldozer and drainage culvert flatten and widen and dry out our civilized cities, symbolically overcoming the fetid and rank threat of the uncivilized wild, symbolically homaged with well-spaced plantings of leafy trees.

"Civilized" — isn't that what we aim for with our concern for cities. When we look for inspiration, for regeneration, urban transformation, renewal, for cities of quality — topics addressed by the symposium roundtables — are we aiming to establish a more civilized city? When we ask about the future of the city, of progress, improved urban design, better health and services, have we not been caught up by the myths of progressive march of civilization? And when we move to an air-cooled highrise way above the street, or the exurban subdivision, or retire into the gated, guarded asylum, is not the fear of the swamp monster still lurking in our souls along with visions of the New Jerusalem, the Heavenly City, the City on the Hill?

What is a civilized city? What do we mean by "civilization"? I have turned to my own profession to find a reply, for I have asked myself and my colleagues: is psychoanalysis a work of civilization or of culture? By becoming more civilized — tamed, mannered, adapted, and participatory — do we therefore become more cultured? If civilization requires cohesive structures of architecture, engineering, law, government, education, finance, supply and distribution — in short, bureaucracies of maintenance — to name but a few of the institutions that support civilization and are essential to cities, where does culture figure in, if at all? A city can be imagined, constructed, and can function efficiently, and progressively improve its functioning without theaters and music, think tanks, artists' quarters, red-light districts, stray dogs, and sparrows, without a helter-skelter variety of eateries, street vendors, and pubs, without celebrations and commemorations, even without controversial newspapers and multiple radio stations.

Culture and its ferment may be a desirable accessory, but is it necessary to civilized order and security? Moreover, should places and budgets for culture be provided in urban planning? Such provisions may as well stifle culture as promote it. Culture seems to be beyond rational control of civilization.

I have come to the conclusion that the work of psychoanalysis is one of culture because we have given up the addiction to the progress myth and adaptation to the institutions and conformities that civilization rightly demands. Our work with soul tends to follow the *resistances* to civilization, those symptoms of inadaptability — depression, breakdown, outrage, panic, idiosyncratic peculiarities which have drawn the patient deeper into questions of fate, love, death, purpose, questions of soul that seem so often at odds with the requirements of civilization. "What's madness," asks the poet Theodore Roethke, "but nobility of soul at odds with circumstance?"

II

There is a mythical component within these contrasting impulses of civilization and culture. A look over the shoulder at the model *polis* of the historical imagination with its protective Goddess, Athene, shows the contrasting myths at work.

Athene has been summoned up as "protectress of the civic order" and source of the idea of rational progress.[1] Many of her images present her dressed in defensive armor, shielded, helmeted, weaponed, with a small figure of victory on her shoulder. She guided the city magistrates and the city's generals with grey-eyed sober counseling. She was called a fortress, expressed by the militant defensiveness of a city's spirit, and the renewal of that spirit in victory: compare the team of Liverpool over Chelsea, over Milan! (In fact, and just by the way, the melting pot integration of the disparate populations of the bulging American cities at the turn of the twentieth century was enabled by the whole city's identification with its baseball team and the public democracy of the local stadium.)

Athene also gave intelligence, reflection, wise decision-making to leaders such as Ulysses,[2] and the foresight we now literalize as planning. She gave skills and inventive devices, and wove together irreconcilable factions — weaving of wool was one of those skills and "belonged" to Athene. From Athene's perspective, we might say, the soul of the civilized city was like a fabric, an integrated fabrication laboriously constructed by many minds and many hands.

To keep civic order means keeping youth in line. Athene was patroness of the men's societies called *phratria*[3] — rather like clubs or fraternities or guilds — that wove together young men with civic feeling. As well, she protected the institution of marriage: parents took their daughters to the Athenian acropolis before marriage to bring them under her aegis. Athene's mind, and its civilizing ideals, furthered the progress of an intelligent civic order. Her influence extended to Rome where she became Minerva, one of that city's great triad of ruling dominants. Her complex mind was there given to simpler, practical civilizing skills: Roman roads and arches, Roman laws, schools and teachers, and schools where teachers learn, "normal" schools as we call them. To civilize, Minerva-Athene normalizes.[4]

The term "normal" comes from *norma*, a Latin word meaning a carpenter's square. *Normaliter* means in a straight line, directly; *normalis* means according to the square, and *norma* itself is a technical term for a right angle. The right angle is applicable anywhere, universally identical, like the Roman law of the Empire, like the theorems of plane geometry, like the international style of right-angled architecture of

Corbusier and Richard Meier. Thus, civilizing the unwieldy land has come to mean normalizing with the straight lines of the surveyor, with plats, overriding actual terrain and the existing boundaries of local cultures. These archetypal roots in language and myth don't die; even today our common speech uses "straight" and "square" for a normalized person.

Athene did not rule alone — there were twelve Olympians and others beside. In fact, Athene had particular trouble with Dionysos, Poseidon, and the goddess of sensual pleasure and sexual love, Aphrodite. Dionysos frequently referred to as Lord of Souls, with his dancing crowd of followers, his wine, and his underworld relation to cult mysteries and the natural force of life's vitality was hardly civilized in Athene's sense. No moderation here, no sober prudence or foresight, no defensive strategy or victory; rather, Dionysos was often a victim. His associated animal, the goat, was not allowed on Athene's grounds.

The conflict with the great god of oceans and rivers, Poseidon, lies in the very foundation of the Athenian city. In the beginning, says the myth, both an olive tree and a spring of salt-water appeared miraculously out of the ground. A slim majority of the people, by one vote only, decided for Athene's gift, the olive so necessary for civilization — olive oil for cooking, for lighting, for healing. Yet barely preferable over the wild sea surge, the unpredictable floodings, and the luring deeps. Poseidon and Athene were also conflicted over the gift of the horse: this animal "belonged" to Poseidon, but the controlling bridle was given by Athene.

Control, discipline, order, the marriage, and the household as central to the city. While Athene reinforced the home and gave honor to its handwork, Dionysos calls young women to desert their tasks and run to the hills to dance. And, while Athene was always called "virgin," Aphrodite was promiscuity itself. She was shown almost or altogether naked, with doves and roses, open to temptation, while Athene is clad in stiff armor with a giant shield that warns, "Keep your distance." These three archetypal powers seize our eyes and loins with desirable embodiments of beauty, flood our emotions, and call us out of the city altogether in youthful riot. Their excess inspires beyond civility and urbanity.

Their diverging styles do show a common trait: subversion, interruption, surprise. Is this not exactly how culture affects civilization,
and how the soul of the street often disorders well-made plans? Let
me put the distinction this way: Civilization gets the job done as well
and reasonably as possible. Culture is song; the song that breaks out
in the midst of the job. Civilization looks back to learn and forward
with hope. Culture pops up, sprouts in a petri dish. It infiltrates the
city, subversively, through the back alleys of disrepute. Like a disease it
finds its own carriers. Whether helped or hindered by civilization, culture is essentially autonomous, unpredictable, and largely unlearned.
Culture breaks into civilization and is often assimilated by it. Coun-
terculture, avant-garde, street fashion, pop music, dance, and slang
become appropriated by civilization. From slum wall to modern art
museum in only a few years.

I am trying to insist upon the uncaused, timeless aspects of culture:
that it is marked mainly by surprise. Surprise, which means seized by
the sudden, is a category of its own, not merely something new. Surprise offers more than novelty; the renewal it brings is a freshening,
enlivening, blessing. To confuse novelty with spontaneity keeps us
still within the framework of rational development, as if it were possible to develop a surprise. It seems surprise is genuinely so shocking
and disruptive that it has to be tamed by comparisons with the known
and old. How ready civilization is to disparage cultural surprises with
words like "That's nothing new!" And how often those who would
make culture try so hard to do something "new." But "new" and "old"
are terms belonging to progressive civilization; they are curses when
applied to culture. The soul is neither new nor old, or it is both at
once, utterly fresh as each morning's dream, yet rooted in archaic patterns of eternal myths.

Culture does not so much evolve or decline. It seems rather to appear and disappear. For a while in this city, this *quartier,* this café, this
theater troop or little magazine, architecture team or graduate department, there is a flourishing. Then it goes elsewhere. Its origins are mys-
terious and its endings sometimes explosive, or accidental, or simply
peter out. In this sense culture has more than linguistic affinities with
the occult and the cult. The beginnings of my own field in Vienna and

Zurich, and its later peculiar blooming in Paris show this combination of cult, occult, and culture. Above all, it is a shared phenomenon in which the little groups involved are themselves surprised by their shared love for their common imagining, becoming soul brothers and soul sisters.

Think of the motley few in Elizabethan taverns who gave English its marvelous language, the few who made the German Romantic movement, think of the intellectuals in Vienna before World War I, of Mistra in the late middle ages, Ficino's academy, friends of the heart, in Florence in the fifteenth century that reinspired cultures across Europe, Dada in Zurich, Bloomsbury, Silicon Valley, Black Mountain College, the painters, their critics, their women in Manhattan in the 1950s, the few friends who became the "Invisible College" that began the Royal Society. Think also of four young guys and their girls in a Liverpool garage. Small groups sharing each other's minds, madnesses, and mattresses. The French Revolution began, it is claimed, with a conversation in a Parisian café. Did Liverpool, did Providence recreate themselves so surprisingly owing to a common inspiration within a small group? Did the renewal of these two cities arise from Athenian wise counsel alone, or was something else at work?

Perhaps the general term "culture" is too civilized; perhaps there are only subcultures, countercultures, emerging cultures, lost cultures, and culture clashes. Perhaps the city that can pride itself on its culture will boast less of its symphony orchestra and foreign movie theatres, but rather of the mix of differences—backgrounds, social experiments, distinct neighborhoods, historical remnants—and of a general sense of possibility that here in this city something can begin, something generative, non-conforming, unhampered by the city as such, a place where Aphrodite or Dionysos or Poseidon, or any other of the immortals and the Muses, may alight awhile, and smile.

Please understand that my references to myths, my reliance on myths is for the sake of imagination. These myths were the source of the incredible imaginative powers of the Greeks in every field — the sciences, mathematics, architecture, city-building, warfare, political theory, language, and philosophy, as well as the arts, especially theater.

The Greek mind so filled with myths continues to nourish imagination, for these myths are a primordial source of both Western culture
and Western civilization long ago and still today.

III

The *polis* as plural, and as a mix of differences, bears upon one of the
more pressing concerns of city life today: immigration. How can the
various subcultures be integrated into the dominant civilization? Can
they be integrated unless they are first welcomed? As Jacques Derrida[5]
observed, the question of immigration turns essentially upon hospitality. Immigration asks cities to be hosts.

Already some cities are taking the lead in determining attitudes
toward immigrants by offering justice and protection — classic gifts
of Athene. Even more, some cities are beginning to take the lead in
determining their own destiny by resisting subservience to the nation
state. Fifty-six United States cities have adopted referendums to create
less fearful conditions for migrants from elsewhere; in particular, these
cities have moved *not* to allow their local police to enforce federal
immigration laws. For instance: *Chicago*. Executive Order 89-6 establishes that no city agency shall request information about or otherwise
investigate . . . the citizenship or residency status of any person unless
required by legal process. *Detroit*: Local Resolution (12/02); and Balti-
more City Council Resolution (5/03): Police Departments shall refrain
from enforcement of federal immigration laws. *Los Angeles*, Special Order 40 (11/79, in revision), prohibits the Police Department from ini-
tiating police action with the objective of discovering the immigration
status of a person and from enforcing immigration law. Anchorage;
San Francisco; Portland, Maine; Minneapolis; Albuquerque are among
the fifty-six.

Mary Watkins,[6] who assembled this data, asks whether this is a first
small step toward a post-national consciousness. Do we reconstitute the
city as the core of civilization values prior to the nation-state, reconstituting both *historically* back to the city powers of ancient Greece, and
still under the Roman Empire, through the city-states of Italy until 1860
and Germany until Bismarck? And further than history: are these refer-

endums declaring an independence of the City *archetypally*, attempting to align the current city with the ideal City on the Hill, since these ordinances in effect declare that it is to the city we must turn for justice and dignity and for the guarantees of security from totalitarian centrism.

Again, Derrida: "If we look to the city, rather than the state, it is because we have given up hope that the state might create a new image for the city." And Watkins: "When a nation goes far astray in the practice of humane conduct, then our cities could become more like autonomous zones that can differentiate themselves from national agendas," recovering the ethic of hospitality, realizing the longing for fairness and a welcoming heart. In other words, cities of soul . . . remember the street: soul brother, soul sister.

A city of soul will be invitational, curious, and appreciatively receptive to what moves at the margins, in the marginalized, whether in the *barrios* or *favelas*, or among groups of unacclaimed artists, or activist protestors with radical agendas. The city of soul will allow, maybe even find ways to provide for, the spontaneous uprising of the unfitting. The immigrant is not a barbarian because he speaks a foreign language; rather he and she are importing another culture into a preestablished harmony that harbors tendencies of totalitarian intolerance.

Immigration brings to the city every sort of administrative problem — education, social services, job market, housing. These concerns are already well-known and addressed by competent experts. The further task is one of psychology: the fantasized threat and fear of the alien.

As there is a statistical criminal and a statistical madman in each human psyche, so there is a statistical immigrant, an alienated outsider, if not newly arrived, at least with a fresh eye, an outsider's views upon our all-too-familiar city. This "inner" immigrant sees the faults, the ruthlessness and ugliness, as well as the astounding opportunities of the civilization he or she shares with the hosts. This critical unassimilated observer has much the same perspective as the artist and the critic, the philosopher and the psychological analyst. It is like an eye of culture.

To discover the immigrant component of one's own psyche is a major calling of leadership, and then to use this perspective of the outsider all the while committed to Athene's civic order, and to lead the city by inviting the immigrant component with its unconventional aesthetic perceptions into the deliberations regarding every aspect of the city's plans from traffic routing, street signage, and lighting to school curricula and budget pruning — this is a leadership task.

Little need to remind you here that this city, Providence, was founded by a convicted man who escaped and who considered himself a kind of immigrant among the native land-owning people. Roger Williams exemplifies leadership that sees the faults of his society with the eyes of the culturally oppressed. May I suggest he was a man of soul who stood against the superior civilized colony to his north that had no tolerance for subcultures?

IV

Let us recapitulate. The regeneration of cities must look to the street as well as to the structures rising from it, to culture as well as to civilization, to soul as well as to project. This because ultimately Aristophanes matters more than aqueducts. Ultimately civilization, even when it has the upper hand and enforces the rules it makes, is only the administrative service to culture's productive imagination. Therefore, the valences shift: instead of finding support for culture — artists' grants, public spaces for manifestations, honoring subcultures, proactive participation by leaders in cultural life, and restraining the heavy hand of uniform nationalism in favor of local civic feeling — rather than these praiseworthy integrative attempts of civilization to normalize culture, the city would turn to poets and chefs, radical visionaries, movie-makers and teachers, and nurses, protestors from subcultures, animal proponents, tour guides and fashion designers, curmudgeon traditionalists, nerdy students, and the journeymen who work the streets. They are not merely "the public." Each is a seed of the spontaneous. Each with rebellious critiques and peculiar fantasies that are usually left outside the development of the cities they inhabit. Though outsiders and amateurs to urbanism's civilized discourse and complexities, they are the real insiders, the throng of culture for whom civilization's plans are made. They need to be drawn to the drawing board, invited to think carefully, devise and project, introducing them to the mental work of Athene, for after all, in their own worlds each is a skilled practitioner whether of the saxophone or of the *crêpe suzette*. Culture has the possibility of rising up when a handful of people fall in love with each other's ideas. They become drunk and insane with ideas. Dionysos, Poseidon, Aphrodite enter the agora of discourse. This moves the culture. In this way we harness the outrage, bridle the objections, and possibly generate fresh surprises. Urbanism and these incredible works of artistry — our society's great cities — cannot be left only to the normally sensibly civilized if the soul of the city is our care — for the soul is not altogether civilized.

1. Ann Shearer, *Athene: Image and Energy* (London/NY: Viking Arkana, 1996), pp. 21, 28.

2. W.B. Stanford, "The Favorite of Athene," in *The Ulysses Theme* (Dallas: Spring Publications, 1992).

3. Karl Kerényi, *Athene: Virgin and Mother in Greek Religion* (Dallas: Spring Publications, 1988).

4. James Hillman, "On the Necessity of Abnormal Psychology: Ananke and Athene," in *Mythical Figures*, Uniform Edition of the Writings of James Hillman, vol. 6.1 (Putnam, Conn.: Spring Publications, 2007).

5. Jacques Derrida, *Of Hospitality: Anne Dufourmantelle Invites Jacques Derrida to Respond*, trans. Rachel Bowlby (Stanford, Calif.: Stanford University Press, 2000); *On Cosmopolitanism and Forgiveness*, trans. Mark Dooley and Michael Hughes (New York: Routledge, 2001).

6. Mary Watkins, "Psyche and Cities of Hospitality" (unpublished talk, 2005).

42

Ground Zero: A Reading

I

Two years ago at this time we were approaching the turn of centuries, of ages, and a panicky worry gripped the Western world. Not a visceral panic; one more sophisticated and abstract named Y2K: Year 2000. Would our electronic systems fail because they had not been programmed for these zeros in the date of the new century? Would this unpredicted zero make the data banks disappear and computers no longer carry messages? Would the system somewhere break down and instantly cause gaps and voids unpredictably elsewhere — bank accounts lost, electricity grids, hospitals, emergency services, shipping, railroads, government records, disease control laboratories, military defense, nuclear power — a civilization at risk?

One of my friends was a member of the White House committee focused on Y2K. This seriously thoughtful man was gravely concerned. One random glitch could throw the developed world into confusion, if not disaster.

January 1, 2000, came and went. The transition from the 1900s passed without a misstep. No light went out. A triumph of rational planning and foresight, of technical know-how. The fears had been exaggerated, infused with religious apocalyptic forebodings. The world could proceed on its "metalled ways" (T. S. Eliot), and the

A talk delivered for the benefit of the Meyerhoff Art Education Center for Disabled Children at the Tel Aviv Museum of Art, Milan, 30 November 2001. First published in Luigi Zoja and Donald Williams, eds., *Jungian Reflections on September 11* (Einsiedeln: Daimon Verlag, 2002).

demon Y2K had been defeated like an imaginary dragon, lying pros-
trate at the feet of heroic technical globalism. The stock market, led
upward by faith in high tech, soared.

Looking back two years, we should have snatched some defeat from
the jaws of this victory. Or perhaps the victory was a disguised defeat.
The slaughter of Dragon Y2K blinded us to the reality of our fears of a
catastrophic, world-shattering, apocalyptic moment. For what did not
happen on 1/1/2000 did happen on 9/11/01.

Profound changes in consciousness choose their dates arbitrarily.
Historians who like dates claim that the nineteenth century began in
1798, and ended not at New Year's Eve 1899 but in 1912 when the
Titanic went down, along with revolutionary explosions in art, science, and thought. 9/11/01 has become the date the eon changed.
To come to some psychological understanding of this date, let us go
to the place itself, to what is called Ground Zero, the physical center
of the Zero Moment in the change of consciousness, the place of the
Twin Towers, their burning and their fall. Once standing tall in the
sunlight, gleaming glass and metal, brightly lit at night, overlooking
the river, the harbor, the flatlands and the streets, such a tower was not
the "orrible torre" whose door was nailed shut, imprisoning Ugolino
and his sons in Dante's *Inferno*; rather these towers were extraordinary
architectural splendors in and out of which each day thousands and
thousands of people of sixty nationalities freely passed in commerce
with the world at large. Precisely this, this towering magnificence of
twentieth-century world commerce has fallen, emblematic of falling
civilizations.

T. S. Eliot uses the tower image in "The Wasteland":

> Falling towers
> Jerusalem Athens Alexandria
> Vienna London
> Unreal . . .

I must clarify here what I mean by a "psychological" understanding.
Or, at least state what I do not mean by psychology: not a *psychologiz-
ing* of the *deus ex machina*, Bin Laden, his motives, his family, his pathologies. Nor a parallel diagnosis of Bush, *pater et fils*, and mother, Barbara.

Nor do I intend to dissect the American character — its consumerism, its isolationist blindness and childlike devotion to innocence, and the irresponsible *laissez-faire* that accompanies that innocence. Nor its good-will Christianism, nor its optimistic belief in technological progress as solution to all ills, whether in marriages, hospitals, or on the battlefield. Nor shall I rely on the Jungian notion of "shadow," that is, the mutual projection of evil and the mutual identification with God's will, as well as the globalization through sixty nations of both capitalists and terrorists.

These psychological accounts including the psychology of culture, Islam, and the Christian West, fill the newspapers and are the property of elucidating experts, of which I am not one. Rather, this evening, and very briefly, I would explore with you the basic simple image of the falling towers from an archetypal or mythic perspective to discover, perhaps, what the deepest, a historical imagination of the collective psyche might reveal about what we read in the newspapers.

II

First, the Fall, *la Chute*, as Gilbert Durand discusses it in his masterly work *Les Structures anthropologiques de l'imaginaire*. Durand, formerly at the University of Grenoble, follows the path opened by Bachelard, Corbin, and Jung. A phenomenology of the Fall shows these motifs: first of all, fear, vertigo, loss of orientation. One does not know where to turn, how to pick up life again. There is an overwhelming heaviness, gravity, and ruin, and the fall is marked by an inhibition: a refusal to ascend.

Second, Durand notes that *la Chute* is a phenomenon of feminization, either brought about by female forces (such as Eve who supposedly caused Adam's Fall) or falling into feminine territory (Hercules, Bellerophon, and Icarus into the sea as maternal), or onto earth, physis, matter, and into the body.

A third major set of themes of the Fall is punishment, so that after wild falling through the air — as for instance shown in Christian iconography where people land in the burning pits of hellfire — ripped body parts, pain, terror, ugly flames, smoke, and excrements.

We do not need to look far or fantasize much to witness the enactments of the archetypal imagination taking place at Ground Zero: panicked running, post-traumatic anxieties, the turn to therapy and religion to find orientation, dread of tall buildings, resistance to flying in planes, hunkering down in modest family relations, as well as the drop to bottom of financial markets away from high-tech and financials and toward manufacturers of common daily products. As for the feminization: it appeared immediately in the care and tenderness, and endurance, shown by helpers, mourners, nourishers. Restaurants laid out free meals, schoolchildren gave their little sandwiches, vendors and suppliers opened their storage rooms and freezers. Strangers were invited in and given beds and clothes; the doors of New York, usually locked up tight, opened. New Yorkers paid no attention to money; value was returned to soul.

The feminization goes yet deeper, and perhaps needs to lose that gender description. Not feminine, but rather soul. The soul of the city emerged, the soul that inhabits the streets, the public servants, the common gritty language, the down-to-earth *gravitas* of Mayor Giuliani. Soul emerged from the ruin of the spirit, those exemplars of the top, the big shots, celebrities, executives, professionals, politicians. They seemed empty, posturing, vain — in some cases transformed and brought suddenly down to earth.

The third of Durand's themes, punition, also appeared immediately after the fall. Pompous preachers of the religious right interpreted the catastrophe as God's avenging justice upon America for its sins: abortion, faithlessness, religious diversity, gay marriage and homosexual love, promiscuity and adultery. America had wandered from its Biblical faith and was morally degenerate. On a secular level and without Biblical references, the left-leaning commentators also moralized: America got what was coming to it. It had been greedy and isolated, ignoring the plight of the rest of the world. From the secular and militaristic right came yet a different blame, again moralistic. America had grown soft and comfortable. It had lost its backbone, its muscle. We were too lax with immigrants, too focused on people of color. Our liberal laws handicapped the police and the FBI. The burning towers signified a wake-up call. This was a new Pearl Harbor organized by dark, strange, and evil men — Taliban as Caliban — calling us to re-armament and tightened control of the population, its actions, and its thought. Added to the pain inflicted by the wound at Ground Zero, Americans found many other ways to punish themselves further.

III

Let us return to Ground Zero and amplify further the archetypal image of the Tower. Some of the themes etched so clearly by Durand appear in the traditions of towers. For instance, the tower as anti-feminine, or at least inviolate, self-enclosed. Remember Danae, mother of Perseus locked in a tower; remember your Grimm Brothers' stories — the princess — daughters imprisoned in towers by ruthless father-kings. The tower belongs to Santa Barbara, beheaded by her father. Barbara as patroness of architects is invoked as protectress against fire and sudden disaster. Did those who erected the World Trade Center neglect homage to protective powers, relying only on their genial design and construction?

Already in Egypt the hieroglyph of the tower is "the determinant sign denoting height or the act of rising above the common level in life and society." It is basically "symbolic of ascent," or spiritual pride, arrogance, hubris.[1]

Towers dominated many cities of Italy between 1160 and 1260 — including Milan. The Bologna tower of Asinella reached almost 100 meters. The Feudal period with its hierarchy of relationships, its aspiring theological and architectural structures were a time of tall towers. Later, as part of the rebellion against the *consorterie* of ruling families, the height of towers was brought under civil rule. Many were lowered, their upper reaches decapitated or altogether torn down.

The towers alone do not tell the whole story of the falling. There is also fire, the immediate cause of the fall. Engineers say that had the planes not carried such a huge volume of incendiary fuel, the towers would have stood, and they did withstand the impact. But the steel of their bones melted. Fire brought them down. Again, Eliot's "Wasteland":

To Carthage then I came
Burning burning burning burning
O Lord Thou pluckest me out . . .

Carthage — emblem of an eradicated civilization. How arbitrary the selection of those who were plucked out and escaped.

The earliest philosophical imaginers of fire were Empedocles and especially Heraclitus who asserted its pre-eminence among the elements. For him fire was a cosmic force everywhere, the soul or mind of the cosmos, an ever-living, never-still kind of consciousness that runs through all things. Following this line of thinking, the fire that brought down the towers has soul or mind or conscious intention beyond that of the pilots and the plotters, and an end in view beyond sheer destruction, since in the pre-Socratic view of the elements, there is no fiery apocalypse as the end of the Christian Testament, no *Götterdämmerung*, but an ever-renewing cyclic metamorphoses. The way down is the way up, says Heraclitus. Just as a Pluto/Hades, God of the dead and the underworld is also God of fullness and riches. The Gods are not only diseases they are also, after all, Gods. We are justified, archetypally, mythically, to expect something to come from the fall and the fire.

I mentioned Hades/Pluto, the God who ruled the souls in the Underworld, because astrologers keep an eye on Pluto as an archetypal force of terrible intensity. During the period August 2001 through May 2002, astrologers have calculated that Pluto would confront Saturn three times in direct opposition. This opposition occurs very rarely, and tension between these extremist, planetary Gods is of the extremist sort. Saturn in airy Gemini — the Twins: the two towers, the two planes, the doubled insignia "AA"; Gemini, communicators, commerce, neighbors, quick responses. Pluto in Sagittarius, far-reaching, idealistic, religious. The highest sign of fire. The shadow underground figure of Bin Laden with immense hidden wealth and disguised network takes on Plutonic characterization much as the severe methodical generals and old guard of the American war machine — heavy weaponry, leaden language, long-distant, far-ranging surveillance — become missionaries of Saturn.

Order, immobility, structure like rigid steel opposed to chaos, invisible as anthrax, unpredictable like fire. The depths of Ground Zero smoldered for months and the terror sill lurks in Plutonic tunnels. While Pluto affects the Saturnian Pentagon with "stealth" bombers, secret forces and weapons that see in the dark, so Saturn affects the Plutonian terrorists with privation, cold mountains, and barren ground; outcasts at the edge, enduring. Saturnian bones lie deep in the Plutonic depths of Ground Zero.

Is it not strange that the ground is named "zero"? — Zero, an arabic gift to our Western language and calculations. Zero from *sifr*, originally means naught, a nothing, emptiness without content. *Sifr* also became "cipher," the enigmatic sign that must be decoded. In physics a zero refers to a point from which measurements can proceed, either ascending or descending, neither positive nor negative in itself. And the symbolic round circle in the Hindu mathematics from which the sign came represents beginning and end, both fullness (*purna*) and void (*sunya*) — number beyond number, essentially incalculable, of *immeasurable* possibility. That devastated earth in the depths of "lower" Manhattan is the zero Ground of Possibility, emptied of what was and filled with fantasies.

One final amplification if you will allow: the sixteenth enigma or card of the Tarot depicts a tower half-destroyed by lightning fire that strikes its top. Though the tower image is single, it is associated in occult literature with the two columns of Jachin and Boaz, representing the power of individualized life. Sometimes the Tarot card images pieces of the tower falling away and striking a king and an architect of the tower. The Tarot readings connect this allegory with Scorpio (the astrological home of Pluto) and supposedly allude to the dangerous consequences of overconfidence, or the sin of pride.

IV

At the end now of these notes, I would like us to reflect a moment about that extraordinary tower in the Bible, the Tower of Babel, and its destruction by Jahveh. You know the story very well of course, but should the details have slipped your mind, let us read again the text in Genesis 11.1: "The whole earth was of one language and one speech." Then the people said to one another, "Let us build us a city, and a tower with its top in heaven, and let us make us a name; lest we be scattered abroad upon the face of the whole earth" (11.4).

The Lord saw this and said: "Behold, they are one people, and they all have one language; and this is what they begin to do, and now nothing will be withholden from them (11.6) . . . The sixteenth-century Bolognese Talmud scholar Hananeel ben Jacob Sforno explains that this phrase "nothing shall be withholden from them" means "with such unity they can enthrone idolatry." We might pursue this curious relation between unity and idolatry later in our conversation . . .

The Lord punished the people by "confounding their language that they may not understand one another's speech; and scattered them abroad upon the face of all the earth" (11.8).

A short and simple tale, yet Babel has drawn many imaginative commentaries. For instance, the theme of the tower as anti-feminine: the builders were so intense upon their goal of reaching heaven by their own hands that they would not let a woman in labor interrupt to give birth, and many women perished in the construction. And the intent on which their minds were so set was to wage war with God and destroy heaven. Evidently, heaven is protected not by our climbing upward, not by striving spiritually, but by remaining in the polyglot world of diversity.

The image of a tower touching heaven appears in the myths of many peoples, in Mexico, Assam, Burma, and along the Zambesi, for instance. Frazer collected these tales and reports on them in detail. The Bible, however, teaches a more complex lesson by means of this archetypal mythologem. First, the tale tells that the origin of the many different languages is God-given; second, that the diversity of peoples is also God-given; and third, as one commentary, each people in each land has its own speech, tongue, *angelos*, or message. Multicultural diversity spread through the world also results from the fall of the Tower of Babel.

At the simple level, the story seems to say diversity is a punishment, a curse inflicted on humankind for its hubris, preventing humankind from ever speaking with one voice. But looking more deeply, we can see that the Lord's punishment is actually a correction of the error of unity. When the people are all of one sort and have one language living in one place, something happens: they become afflicted with ascensionism. They believe they can climb right up to heaven and take it for themselves. The idolatry of anthropocentrism; the disease of lit-eralized monotheism. A people or a faith without differences, without division and dissension becomes self-assured and self-righteous. "Cer-titude breeds violence," said our great American jurist, Oliver Wendell Holmes. The people become *Himmelstürmer*.

To correct this vertical ascensionism that is the result of unity, the Lord scatters the people horizontally over the face of the earth. As in Manhattan when the towers fell the streets were filled with a diversity of people from all walks of life. Helpers trucked in from far away — Iowa, Virginia, Canada. The city took to walking, the streets were filled. When the towers came down spirit came down into soul. The city of Wall Street plutocrats was deepening its values, uncovering another measure of riches in the Plutonic ruins.

This brings us to the idea I would like to leave you with this evening. God's destruction of the Tower of Babel is more than a punishment, more than a correction. It is also a solution. It offers an exceptionally valuable insight for understanding the fall of the towers in Manhattan. If, as Genesis eleven says, unity leads to hubris, then we must be wary of all attempts at unification — unified field theory in physics, single explanations of evolution in biochemistry and biotechnology, one true religion and one way to practice it, one interpretation of Holy Texts, one global economic system, one astrophysical explanation of the origins of the cosmos, one definition of democracy or of justice, and above all, one system of measurement by means of numbers for assessing value. "There are many ways to kneel and kiss this earth," said Rumi.

Each attempt at unity arises from ambition and results in inflation. The desire for unity expresses the latent hubris of rational anthropo-centrism, attempting to conquer with the human mind the powers of the invisible world which the Bible calls "Heaven." Unlike the impuls-es of spirit, soul differentiates by clinging to matter. It spreads out like a vague mist in the valleys, the low and lowly places, wrapping itself into this tree, that look in the eyes, a keepsake, a photograph, a line of a poem — much as the people in New York after the fall wrote on walls, brought flowers to firehouses, put pictures of their missing in public places, and mourned together with strangers from different nations and different tongues.

"There are many ways to kneel and kiss the earth." The earth to which civilization now kneels is that ground called Zero, the zero that in itself is nothing and cannot be fathomed and yet, like the soul, magnifies whatever it touches. Its hollow center images that void one feels at end and at beginning. "To make an end," says T. S. Eliot, "is to make a beginning/ The end is where we start from." ("Four Quartets" I, IV.5).

To find a way again after the catastrophe, let us stick with the image of Ground Zero. It symbolizes a wound in the deep tissue of the Western psyche. A wound is a break through the surface, below superficiality. It is an opening of heightened sensitivity, like an eye that looks and an ear that listens differently, less blithely, more acutely, and like a mouth that speaks the language of vulnerability. The wound at Ground Zero has opened into the depths below usual life.

In fact, so deep has the ground been opened that the Hudson River has to be shored up to prevent a gigantic wave of water flooding through the subway tunnels of Manhattan. In these deeps the underworld Gods reign. If we follow Jung's dictum —"the Gods have become diseases" — then the wound of Ground Zero has opened access to very specific archetypal forces: Pluto and Saturn.

How may we approach them so that our human world be taken less by surprise and terror? Difficult. Enigmatic. The ancient world considered Pluto invisible: he had no temples or altars above ground. Saturn was called Lord of Silence, a figure most remote. They do not appear, they do not speak, we cannot go to them directly. But they make themselves known as threatening presentiments behind daily life, as a continuing sense of insecurity. They are the ground of terror. Our vulnerability reflects their presence. So long as we admit the wound in the psyche we remain aware of the darker Gods.

Unfortunately, vulnerability has been psychologized and labeled "insecurity," a symptom to be remedied. The basic vulnerability that maintains an opening to the Gods as felt presences in the world, this necessary vulnerability symbolized by Ground Zero, is being denied by measures of heightened security. But tightened security cannot keep out the Gods nor remedy our susceptibility to them. Fear of them may be the beginning of wisdom as it has long been said, but it may also be the beginning of denial: planning genial structures over the wound and sending beams of light into the night sky. Denial as pointing upward even while bodies are pulled from the wreckage and body parts sorted and counted at the carnage station.

"In a dark time, the eye begins to see," wrote Theodore Roethke in one of his most widely known poems. Ground Zero offers an image of the dark time and an eye that begins to see with fewer hopeful illusions, proud denials, and blithe self-centered ignorance. This place is as active and impressive as it ever was, its activity now in imagination and memory. It remembers both the splendor of the Towers and their fall and the dead composted so thoroughly into its soil. The Zero encompasses all that fullness even in its hollow silence. It is a starting point, engendering both upward and downward. All we need do, and likely the best we can do, is to stay with the image, taking our cue from its emptiness, yet constant in our attention to the arising visions occasioned by the darkness.

1. J.E. Cirlot, *A Dictionary of Symbols* (London: Routledge & Kegan Paul, 1962).

About the Uniform Edition

Spring Publications takes pride in publishing, in conjunction with The Dallas Institute of Humanities and Culture, the uniform edition of the writings of James Hillman — the lasting legacy of an original mind. The pioneering imaginative psychology of James Hillman that soon will span five decades has entered cultural history, affecting lives and minds in a wide range of fields. For the creativity of his thinking, the originator of Archetypal Psychology and author of *A Terrible Love of War*, *The Soul's Code*, and *The Force of Character* has received many honors, including the Medal of the Presidency of the Italian Republic. He has held distinguished lectureships at Yale, Princeton, Chicago, and Syracuse Universities, and his books have been translated into some twenty languages. The American public showed its appreciation of his approach to psychology by placing *The Soul's Code* at the top of the best-seller list of serious works of nonfiction.

The uniform, cloth-edition set of 11 volumes of the writings of James Hillman unites major lectures, occasional writings, scholarly essays, clinical papers and interviews — arranged thematically. Each book cover is embossed with a drawing by the American artist James Lee Byars.